G000129933

GEORGINA CAMPBELL'S ireland

the best
of the
best

the **very** best places to eat, drink and stay

Georgina Campbell Guides

Editor: Georgina Campbell

Epicure Press,
PO Box 6173
Dublin 13
Ireland

website: www.ireland-guide.com
email: info@ireland-guide.com

Front cover photographs: Longueville House Hotel, Co Cork
Park Hotel Kenmare, Co Kerry
Olde Post Inn, Co Cavan

Back cover top, (left - right): Merrion Hotel, Dublin 2
Coyle's Cottage, Co Tyrone
Graiguenamanagh, Co Kilkenny
Rathmullan House, Co Donegal
Sheen Falls Lodge, Co Kerry

Back cover bottom, (left to right): Renvyle, Co Galway
Creagh House, Co Cork
Roly's Bistro, Dublin
Ballynahinch Castle, Co Galway
Connemara Landscape

Design and Artwork by The Design Station, Dublin
Printed and bound in Italy
First published 2006 by Georgina Campbell Guides Ltd.

ISBN: 1-903164-21-4

Georgina Campbell Guides Awards

Hayfield Manor Hotel
Hotel of the Year

Restaurant Patrick Guilbaud
Restaurant of the Year

Mark Anderson
Chef of the Year

Vaughans
Pub of the Year

Richmond House
Féile Bia Award

King Sitric Fish Restaurant
Seafood Restaurant of the Year

The full list of awards is on page 7

How to Use the Guide

Location /Establishment name
- Cities, towns and villages arranged in alphabetical order within counties, with the exception of Dublin, Cork, Belfast, Galway and Limerick which come first in their categories
- Establishments arranged alphabetically within location
- In Dublin city, postal codes are arranged in numerical order. Even numbers are south of the River Liffey, and uneven numbers on the north, with the exception of Dublin 8 which straddles the river. Dublin 1 and 2 are most central; Dublin 1 is north of the Liffey, Dublin 2 is south of it (see map). Within each district, establishments are listed in alphabetical order.

Telephone numbers
- Codes are given for use within the Republic of Ireland / Northern Ireland. To call ROI from outside the jurisdiction, the code is +353, dropping the first digit (zero) from the local code.
- To call Northern Ireland from the Republic, replace the 048 code with 028.

Category(ies) of Establishment

Address/contact details
(please phone/fax/email ahead for additional directions if required)
- includes an email address and website address if available

Rating for outstanding cooking, accommodation or features

☆ - Demi star: restaurant approaching star status

★ - For cooking and service well above average

★★ - Consistent excellence, one of the best restaurants in the land

★★★ - The highest restaurant grade achievable

▥ - Outstanding accommodation of its type

▥▥ - Deluxe hotel

▧ - Pub star: good food and atmosphere

(Féile Bia) - Denotes establishment committed to the Féile Bia Charter

€ - 'Best Budget' denotes moderately priced establishment (max approx €100 pps for accommodation, €35 for 3-course meal without drinks)

◉ - Outstanding location, building or atmosphere

🅔 - Editor's Miscellany; a selection of establishments outside the standard categories that should enhance the discerning travellers experience of Ireland

🅝 - Establishments that are new to this edition of the Guide

🏆 - Previous award winner in earlier editions of our guides

Maps are intended for reference only: Ordnance Survey maps are recommended when travelling; available from Tourist Information Offices.

PRICES & OPENING HOURS
PLEASE NOTE THAT PRICES AND OPENING HOURS ARE GIVEN AS A GUIDELINE ONLY, AND MAY HAVE CHANGED; CHECK BEFORE TRAVELLEING OR WHEN MAKING A RESERVATION.

Prices in the Republic of Ireland are given in Euro and those in Northern Ireland in pounds Sterling.

Thanks and acknowledgements
The publication of this guide would not have been possible without the support and encouragement of a large number of organisations, companies and individuals. Particular thanks must go to the sponsors, of course, an also to the many individuals who have given invaluable assistance: sincere thanks to you all.

Georgina Campbell, Editor.

GEORGINA CAMPBELL'S ireland

Introduction

by Georgina Campbell
Editor

Welcome to the first edition of *Georgina Campbell's Ireland - the Best of the Best.* This book was inspired by growing reader interest in the 'Best of the Best' collection in our comprehensive companion guide, *Georgina Campbell's Ireland - the guide,* the independent traveller's guide to over 1,000 establishments in all price ranges throughout the country: every year we have highlighted the tip-top places - starred restaurants, outstanding accommodation (including deluxe hotels), and a small number of exceptional pubs - within that collection. That was the starting point for this much more selective guide to the very best hospitality that Ireland has to offer and, because it has always been our policy to recommend as wide a range of establishments as possible throughout the country, we introduced some new categories. These allow for the inclusion of less expensive places (Best Budget), some that appeal to the senses - a beautiful setting, a particularly interesting building or, perhaps, great atmosphere (Outstanding Location), and an Editor's Choice to include those which don't necessarily categorise very neatly but, we have found, seem to add an extra dimension to travelling around this lovely country.

As always when researching our guides, we have sought out those places which go the extra mile to ensure a happy experience for their guests - yes, the deluxe hotels favoured by many international travellers are there (and some of them are exceptionally hospitable and surprisingly personal), but we also direct you to smaller and, in many cases, more interesting establishments which make up in character and the warmth of hands-on owner management anything they may lack in luxurious accommodation or smart restaurant appointments. We love places which are quietly located away from busy roads, and we especially want to lead you to those that not only offer good cooking but take extra care in sourcing quality ingredients; for this reason we support the international chefs' association Euro-Toques and the international Slow Food movement, which are both dedicated to defending the integrity of food, and also the Féile Bia food traceability programme, which is a reassurance to consumers that a number of identified key products have been purchased through Quality Assurance schemes (see page 12).

We are privilged to visit many wonderful places when researching this guide, and hope that it will, in turn, lead you to memorable experiences too.

Georgina Campbell.

Awards of Excellence

Annual awards for outstanding establishments and staff

Georgina Campbell Guides
gratefully acknowledges the support of the following sponsors:

Féile Bia Award
Creative Use of
Vegetables Award

Seafood Restaurant
of the Year

Ethnic Restaurant
of the Year

GEORGINA CAMPBELL'S ireland

Georgina Campbell Award

Wineport Lodge
Glasson, Co. Westmeath

A new award this year, specially to congratulate Ray and Jane Byrne on their gorgeous newly extended lakeside lodge - a sumptuous signpost to the future for the very best of Irish hospitality.

See page 207

GEORGINA CAMPBELL'S ireland

Hotel of the Year

Hayfield Manor Hotel
Cork

See page 77

2005 WINNER:

Aghadoe Heights Hotel, Co. Kerry

GEORGINA CAMPBELL'S ireland

Restaurant of the Year

Restaurant Patrick Guilbauld

Dublin

See page 41

2005 WINNER:
Casino House, Co. Cork

GEORGINA CAMPBELL'S ireland

Chef of the Year

Mark Anderson
Cherry Tree Restaurant,
Killaloe, Co Clare

See page 70

2005 WINNER:
Raymond McArdle, Nuremore Hotel, Co. Monaghan

Irish Food Board

Creative Use of Vegetables Award

Renvyle House Hotel
Connemara, Co. Galway

Féile Bia - Certified Farm to Fork

Féile Bia is a year round programme that emphasises the importance of food sourcing in hotels, restaurants, pubs and workplaces throughout the country. Féile Bia is the consumer's reassurance that the fresh beef, lamb, pork, chicken and eggs being served are fully traceable from farm to fork. When you see the Féile Bia plaque or logo displayed, you can be sure of the origin of the food being served. Establishments committed to the programme are identified within the Guide by the use of the Féile Bia logo.

2005 WINNER:

Proby's Bistro, Cork

Irish Food Board

Féile Bia Award

Richmond House
Cappoquin, Co Waterford

See page 200

See page 200

2005 WINNER:
Lacken House, Kilkenny

BIM *Ireland*

Seafood Restaurant of the Year

The King Sitric Fish Restaurant
Howth, Co Dublin

See page 57

2005 WINNER:
Out of the Blue, Co. Kerry

Sharwood's

GEORGINA CAMPBELL'S ireland

Wine Award
of the Year

The French Paradox
Ballsbridge, Dublin

See page 48

2005 WINNER:
Ely Wine Bar & Café, Dublin

GEORGINA CAMPBELL'S ireland

Pub of the Year

Vaughans Anchor Inn
Liscannor, Co Clare

See page 72

2005 WINNER:
The Oarsman Bar & Café, Co. Leitrim

GEORGINA CAMPBELL'S ireland

Business Hotel
of the Year

Conrad Dublin Hotel
Dublin

See page 31

2005 WINNER:
Radisson SAS Hotel, Galway

GEORGINA CAMPBELL'S ireland

Family Hotel of the Year

Kelly's Resort Hotel
Rosslare, Co Wexford

See page 217

2005 WINNER:
Derrynane Hotel, Co. Kerry

Host of the Year
Mrs Vi McDowell
Gray's Guesthouse, Achill, Co Mayo

Atmospheric Restaurant of the Year
Toddies Restaurant
Kinsale, Co Cork

Hideaway of the Year
Stella Maris Hotel
Ballycastle, Co Mayo

GEORGINA CAMPBELL'S ireland

Natural Food Award
Neven Maguire
MacNean Bistro, Blacklion,
Co Cavan

Newcomer of the Year
Aldridge Lodge
Duncannon, Co Wexford

Country House of the Year
Delphi Lodge
Leenane, Co Galway

Guesthouse of the Year
Quay House,
Clifden, Co Galway

Farmhouse of the Year
Glendine House
Arthurstown, Co Wexford

GEORGINA CAMPBELL'S ireland

Irish Breakfast Awards

National Winner
Quay House
Clifden, Co Galway

Hotel
Ardmore House Hotel
Westport, Co Mayo

Country House
The Glen Country House
Kilbrittain, Co Cork

Guesthouse
Quay House
Clifden, Co Galway

B&B
McMenamins
Wexford, Co Wexford

Café
Canal Bank Café
Dublin

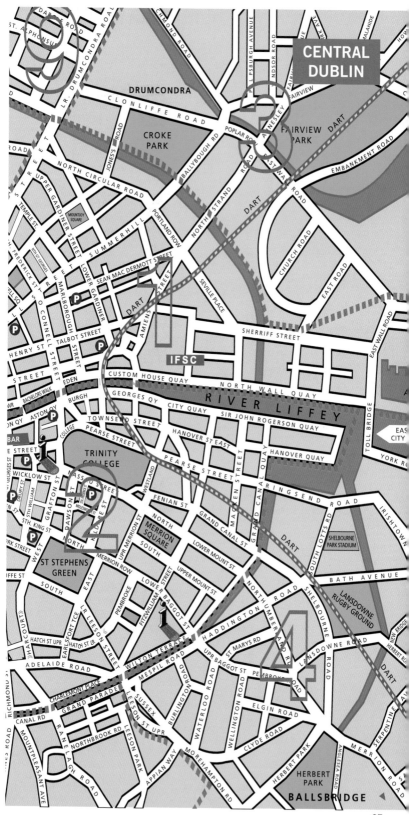

DUBLIN 1

Dublin 1
★ 🏆 RESTAURANT

Chapter One Restaurant

18/19 Parnell Square Dublin 1
Tel: 01 873 2266 Fax: 01 873 2330
Email: info@chapteronerestaurant.com Web: www.chapteronerestaurant.com

téite bia In an arched basement beneath the Irish Writers Museum, one of Ireland's finest restaurants is to be found in the former home of the great John Jameson of whiskey fame. Together with an exceptional team including head chef Garrett Byrne, restaurant manager Declan Maxwell and sommelier Ian Brosnan, the proprietors - chef-patron Ross Lewis and front of house manager Martin Corbett - have earned an enviable reputation here, for outstanding modern Irish cooking and superb service from friendly and well-informed staff. The original granite walls and old brickwork of this fine Georgian house contrast with elegant modern decor to create atmospheric surroundings, and special features include a beautiful carved oyster counter in the reception area, where a champagne menu allows you to choose the perfect bubbly to accompany the noble bivalve. The cooking - classic French lightly tempered by modern influences - showcases specialist Irish produce whenever possible, notably on a magnificent charcuterie trolley, which demonstrates particularly the skills of West Cork producer Fingal Ferguson and is a treat not to be missed, and also an unusual fish plate which is a carefully balanced compilation of five individual fish and seafood dishes, served with melba toast. Other specialities include slow cooked meat - a sweet-flavoured shoulder of spring lamb, for example, with creamed onion and curry spice, roast carrot and garlic, kidney, and boulangère potato - and, of course, a cheese menu offering farmhouse cheeses in peak condition. But many guests will stall at dessert, as an utterly irresistible choice of half a dozen delectable dishes is offered, each with its own dessert wine or champagne... An excellent wine list leans towards the classics and offers many fairly priced treats for the wine buff - and also carefully selected house wines and wines by the glass, including a range of dessert wines. Another special treat is the perfectly timed pre-theatre menu, for which Chapter One is rightly renowned: depart for one of the nearby theatres after your main course, and return for dessert after the performance - perfect timing, every time. Like the lunch menu, early dinner offers outstanding value. Chapter One was our Restaurant of the Year in 2001, and it has been on our Awards shortlist every year since then. *Chapter One also runs the café in the Writers' Museum, (10-5 pm Mon-Sat), and provides banqueting facilities for 60-80 people in the Gallery there. Small conferences. Air conditioning. Parking by arrangement with nearby carpark. Not suitable for children. **Seats 85** (private rooms, 14 & 20). L Tue-Fri, 12.30-2.30, D Tue-Sat, 6-10.45. Set L €28.50. Pre-theatre menu €29.50, 6-6.45; D à la carte (Tasting Menu, for entire parties, €48.50). House wine €20. SC10%. Closed L Sat, all Sun & Mon, 2 weeks Christmas, 2 weeks August. Amex, Diners, MasterCard, Visa, Laser. **Directions:** Top of O'Connell Street, north side of Parnell Square, opposite Garden of Remembrance, beside Hugh Lane Gallery.

Dublin 1
🏨 🏆 HOTEL/RESTAURANT

Clarion Hotel Dublin IFSC

Excise Walk IFSC Dublin 1
Tel: 01 433 8800 Fax: 01 433 8801
Email: info@clarionhotelifsc.com Web: www.clarionhotelifsc.com

téite bia This dashing contemporary hotel on the river side of the International Financial Services Centre was the first in the area to be built specifically for the mature 'city' district and its high standards and central location have proved very popular with leisure guests, as well as business guests and the financial community, especially at weekends. Bright, airy and spacious, the style is refreshingly clean-lined yet comfortable, with lots of gentle neutrals and a somewhat eastern feel that is emphasised by the food philosophy of the hotel - a waft of lemongrass and ginger in the open plan public areas entices guests through to the **Kudos Bar**, where Asian wok cooking is served; the more formal restaurant, **Sinergie**, also features world cuisine, but with more European influences. Uncluttered suites and bedrooms have everything the modern traveller could want, including a high level of security, air conditioning, generous semi-orthopaedic beds and excellent bathrooms with top quality toiletries. There is a sense of thoughtful planning to every aspect of the hotel, and helpful, well-trained staff show a real desire to ensure the comfort of guests. Clarion Hotel Dublin IFSC was our Business Hotel of the Year in 2002.* New bedrooms and a spa are planned at the time of going to press. There's even a 'Sleep Programme' to help you relax before bed! Leisure facilities, in the basement, are excellent and include an 18m pool and large, well-equipped gym. (Open to membership as well as residents' use). While this is not a place for huge conferences, there are various rooms for meetings of anything between 8 and 120 people, theatre style, with state-of-the art facilities. 24 hour room service. Leisure centre (indoor swimming pool, gym). Lift. Children welcome (under 12s free in parents' room, cot available free of charge, baby sitting arranged). No pets. **Rooms 163** (17 suites, 66 executive, 81 no smoking, 9 Disabled). B&B €117.50 pps. Room rate €265, no SC. **Kudos Bar & Restaurant:** Mon-Fri,12-10; **Sinergie Restaurant:** L Mon-Fri 12.30-1.30, D daily, 6-9.30. Set L €11.95; Early D €24.95 (6-7.30); D €19.95-€24.95, also à la carte. House wines, from €19. Sinergie closed L Sat. Kudos no food Sun. [* Comfort Inn, Talbot Street (Tel: 01-874 9202) is in the same group and offers budget accommodation near the IFSC.] Amex, Diners, MasterCard, Visa, Laser. **Directions:** Overlooking the river Liffey in the IFSC.

Dublin 1

HOTEL/RESTAURANT

The Morrison Hotel

Lower Ormond Quay Dublin 1
Tel: 01 887 2400 Fax: 01 874 4039
Email: info@morrisonhotel.ie Web: www.morrisonhotel.ie

Centrally located on the north quays, close to the new Millennium Bridge over the River Liffey, this luxurious contemporary hotel is within walking distance of theatres, the main shopping areas and the financial district. When first opened in 1998 it was a first for Dublin, with striking 'east meets west' interiors created by the internationally renowned designer, John Rocha, and the same team has now overseen a huge development programme with the addition of 48 new bedrooms and extensive conference and meeting facilities - designed around a calm Courtyard Garden, which makes an attractivel venue for receptions, or pre-dinner drinks. Stylish public areas include the cool but comfortable **Café Bar** - just the place for a cappucchino or cocktails - and the former Lobo late night bar is to become a dry spa in 2006, offering holistic and relaxation treatments. Simple, cool bedroom design - the essence of orderly thinking - contrasts pleasingly with the more flamboyant, style of public areas, and there is a welcome emphasis on comfort (Frette linen, Aveda toiletries, air conditioning); all rooms have complimentary broadband, Apple Mac plasma screen with keyboard, wireless mouse and surround sound, iPod docking stations and CD players, safe and mini-bar. Exceptionally friendly and helpful staff make every effort to provide the best possible service for guests, and complimentary room upgrades to studios and suites are given when available. Conference/banqueting (240/140); video conferencing. Children welcome (under 12 free in parents' room, cot available without charge, babysitting arranged). Pets permitted by arrangement. **Rooms 138** (12 suites, 12 studios, 4 family rooms, 5 disabled). Lift. 24 hr room service). B&B €140 pps; ss. No private parking (arrangment with nearby car park). Closed 24-27 Dec. **Halo:** This popular hotel restaurant has moved into a new space next to the riverside entrance, allowing diners at Halo a view over the river and the busy thoroughfare on the quays. The new restaurant lacks the warm opulence of the old Halo setting but, although the décor sends mixed messages (minimalist oriental stools set beside Georgian style claw-footed tables) it is a more relaxed and informal space and, under new head chef Andrew O'Gorman, this change of policy is seen in a more down to earth cooking style .Appealingly hearty dishes with lovely flavour combinations suggest an imaginative but unpretentious chef; breads are all home made, and specialities include monkfish Wellington, traditional short rib beef (served on a big rustic board with crisp potatoes and onion rings), and rice pudding with black cherries,. All day tapas menu includes oysters, various ways, smoked salmon & Guinness bread and Irish cheeses, served with oatmeal biscuits, and there's a new walk-in glass wine cellar, where you can browse and take your pick. The unpretentious, homely quality of the cooking does seem at odds with the décor of this trendy hotel, but the food is delicious, offers good value, and is well worth seeking out. **Seats 120.** Air conditioning. L& D daily, Served all day 12-12 Set L from €25, D from €35, also à la carte; house wine from €25; sc 12.5%. Amex, Diners, MasterCard, Visa, Laser, Switch. **Directions:** Located on the quays near the city centre beside the Millennium Bridge.

Dublin 1
€ CAFÉ

Panem

Ha'penny Bridge House 21 Lower Ormond Quay Dublin 1
Tel: 01 872 8510 Fax: 01 872 8510

Ann Murphy and Raffaele Cavallo's little bakery and café has been delighting discerning Dubliners - and providing a refuge from the traffic along the quays outside - since 1996. Although tiny, it just oozes Italian chic - not surprisingly, perhaps, as Ann's Italian architect husband designed the interior - and it was way ahead of its time in seeing potential north of the Liffey. Italian and French food is prepared on the premises from 3 am each day: melt-in-the-mouth croissants with savoury and sweet fillings, chocolate-filled brioches, traditional and fruit breads, and filled foccacia breads are just a few of the temptations on offer. No cost is spared in sourcing the finest ingredients (Panem bread is baked freshly every day, using organic flour) and special dietary needs are considered too: soups, for example, are usually suitable for vegans and hand-made biscuits - almond & hazelnut perhaps - for coeliacs. They import their own 100% arabica torrisi coffee from Sicily and hot chocolate is a speciality, made with the best Belgian dark chocolate. Simply superb. Open Mon-Sat 9-5.30. Closed Sun & 24 Dec-8 Jan. **No Credit Cards. Directions:** North quays, opposite Millennium Bridge.

DUBLIN 2

Dublin 2
€ RESTAURANT

Avoca Café

11-13 Suffolk St. Dublin 2 **Tel: 01 672 6019** Fax: 01 672 6021
Email: info@avoca.ie Web: www.avoca.ie

téile bia City sister to the famous craftshop and café which have their flagship store in Kilmacanogue, County Wicklow (see entry), this large centrally located shop is a favourite daytime dining venue for discerning Dubliners. The restaurant (which is up rather a lot of stairs, where queues of devotees wait patiently at lunchtime) has low-key style and an emphasis on creative, healthy cooking that is common to all the Avoca establishments. Chic little menus speak volumes - together with careful cooking, meticulously sourced ingredients like Woodstock tuna, Hederman mussels, Gubbeen bacon and Hicks sausages lift dishes such as smoked fish platter, organic bacon panini and bangers & mash out of the ordinary. All this sits happily alongside the home baking for which they are famous - much of which can be bought downstairs in their extensive delicatessen. Licensed. Meals daily, in shop hours. **Seats 100;** Toilets Wheelchair Accessible; Meals daily 10-5 (Sunday 11-5); à la carte. Bookings accepted but not required. SC 10%. Closed 25/26 December, 1 Jan. Amex, Diners, MasterCard, Visa. **Directions:** off Grafton St.

Dublin 2
☆ RESTAURANT

Bang Café

11 Merrion Row Dublin 2 **Tel: 01 676 0898**
Fax: 01 676 0899 Web: www.bangrestaurant.com

téile bia Stylishly minimalist, with natural tones of dark wood and pale beige leather complementing simple white linen and glassware, this smart restaurant is well-located just yards from the Shelbourne Hotel. It is on two levels with a bar in the basement; upstairs, unstressed chefs can be seen at work in one of the open kitchens: an air of calm, relaxed and friendly professionalism prevails. Head chef Lorcan Cribben's menus offer innovative, modern food: a starter of perfectly cooked foie gras served atop a crisp onion bahji with Sauternes jus is typical and well-balanced main course options include a signature dish of bangers & mash (made with Hicks sausages) now also on the menu at the new Clarendon Café Bar; also great fish dishes - using fresh fish from Bantry, in West Cork. Tempting desserts include several fruity finales (Scandinavian iced berries are a speciality) as well as the ever-popular dark chocolate treats, or there's an Irish farmhouse cheese selection. Attention to detail is the keynote throughout and this, seen in carefully sourced food and skilful cooking combined with generous servings and professional service under the management of Kelvin Rynhart, ensures an enjoyable dining experience and value for money (especially at lunch time). **Seats 90.** Private room, 35. Air conditioning. L&D Mon-Sat 12.30-3, 6-10.30 (Thu-Sat to 11). Set L €35, Set D €45. Also à la carte. House wine €20. 12.5% sc on parties of 6+. Closed Sun, bank hols, 1 week Christmas/New Year. Amex, MasterCard, Visa, Laser, Switch. **Directions:** Just off St Stephen's Green.

Dublin 2
Ⓝ Ⓔ RESTAURANT

Bewleys/Café Bar Deli/Mackerel

Bewley's Building Grafton Street Dublin 2 **Tel: 01 672 7719**
Fax: 01 677 4585 Web: www.mackerel.ie

Established in 1840, Bewley's Café had a special place in the affection of Irish people. Bewleys on Grafton Street was always a great meeting place for everyone, whether native Dubliners or visitors to the capital 'up from the country'. It changed hands amid much public debate in 2005 but, despite renovations, it has somehow retained its unique atmosphere together with some outstanding architectural features, notably the Harry Clarke stained glass windows. The popular **Café-Bar-Deli** chain has taken over most of the seating area now, but the coffee shop at the front remains, and also the in-house theatre (phone for details); and, if you go through the coffee shop and up steep stairs to the right, you'll find a new fish restaurant, called simply Mackerel. While far from luxurious, this little restaurant has struck a chord with discerning Dubliners: smart-casual decor - wooden floors, small green marble tables, chandeliers - has youthful appeal and, while there is a printed menu for everything else, the fish dishes are posted on a blackboard menu daily. The range of fish offered is wide, including starters like seafood chowder, pacific oysters, smokies (with natural smoked haddock), tuna carapaccio, and main courses such as organic salmon, grilled whole Dover sole and pan-fried turbot - and the cooking is outstanding. Modern classic is the style and it is achieved with panache; accompanying vegetables have real flavour, classic desserts are delicious (lemon mousses, chocolate pot), and cheeses served in perfect condition on a wooden platter come from Sheridans cheesemongers just across the road. An interesting wine list and good value complete a very attractive package - and the fact that they are open for dinner has transformed the atmosphere of Grafton Street at night. **Seats 46;** Toilets wheelchair accessible; Children welcome but not after 6pm; L daily 12-4, D daily 5-10. * **Cafe Bar Deli** in the same building seats 350 open for food all day 8am-11pm. Closed 25/6 Dec, Bank HolsAmex, Diners, MasterCard, Visa, Laser. **Directions:** Half way down Grafton Street.

Dublin 2
🏛 HOTEL/RESTAURANT

Brooks Hotel

59-62 Drury Street Dublin 2
Tel: 01 670 4000 Fax: 01 670 4455
Email: reservations@brookshotel.ie Web: www.brookshotel.ie

féile bia One of Dublin's most desirable addresses, especially for business guests, the Sinnott family's discreetly luxurious hotel is a gem of a place - an oasis of calm just a couple of minutes walk from Grafton Street. A ground floor bar, lounge and restaurant all link together, making an extensive public area that is quietly impressive on arrival - the style is a pleasing combination of traditional with minimalist touches, using a variety of woods, some marble, wonderful fabrics and modern paintings - and, while a grand piano adds gravitas, there's a welcome emphasis on comfort (especially in the residents' lounge, where spare reading glasses are thoughtfully supplied). All bedrooms have exceptionally good amenities, including a pillow menu (choice of five types) and well-designed bathrooms with power showers as well as full baths (some also have tile screen TV), and many other features. Boardrooms offer state-of-the-art facilities for meetings and small conferences, and there is a 45-seater screening room. Fitness suite & sauna. Children welcome (under 2 free in parents' room; cots available without charge, baby sitting arranged). No pets. **Rooms 98** (1 suite, 2 junior suites, 7 executive, 90 no-smoking, 4 disabled). Lift. Air conditioning throughout. 24 hr room service. B&B €120pps, ss €55. *Special breaks offered - details on application. Arrangement with car park. Open all year. **Francescas:** Pre-dinner drinks are served in a lovely little cocktail bar, Jasmine, and the restaurant has a youthful contemporary look, and a welcoming ambience - an open plan kitchen has well positioned mirrors allowing head chef Patrick McLarnon and his team to be seen at work. Tables are elegantly appointed with classic linen cloths and napkins, and waiting staff, smartly attired in black, look after customers with warmth and professionalism. Patrick sources ingredients with great care (wild salmon, organic chicken, dry aged steak, wild boar sausage), his cooking is imaginative - and there's a strong emphasis on fish and seafood. Speciality dishes attracting special praise on a recent visit included pan-fried Dublin Bay prawns, with smoked bacon, white wine butter sauce and colcannon, and an unusual peat smoked loin of Wexford lamb, with caramelised shallots, tomato fondue and champ, with a rosemary jus - also a delicious lavender scented pannacotta with fresh raspberries. Nice wine selection too. The early dinner offers especially good value, and a very attractive continental buffet breakfast is also served. [*Informal meals also available10 am-11.30 daily.] **Seats 70.** Reservations advised. Children welcome. Air conditioning.Toilets wheelchair accessible. L Daily 10-6, D daily, 6-9.30. Early D € 16.75/20.75 (6-7); also à la carte. Closed to non-residents 24/25th December. Amex, MasterCard, Visa. **Directions:** Near St Stephen's Green, between Grafton and Great St. Georges Streets; opposite Drury Street car park.

Dublin 2

HOTEL/RESTAURANT

The Clarence Hotel

6-8 Wellington Quay Dublin 2
Tel: 01 407 0800 Fax: 01 407 0820
Email: reservations@theclarence.ie Web: www.theclarence.ie

Dating back to 1852, this hotel overlooking the River Liffey on the south quays has long had a special place in the hearts of Irish people - especially the clergy and the many who regarded it as a home from home when 'up from the country' for business or shopping in Dublin - largely because of its convenience to Heuston Station. Since the mid '90s, however, it has achieved cult status through its owners - Bono and The Edge, of U2 - who have completely refurbished the hotel and spared no expense to get the details right, reflecting the hotel's original arts and crafts style whenever possible. Accommodation offers a luxurious combination of contemporary comfort and period style, with up-to-the minute amenities. Public areas include the club-like, oak-panelled **Octagon Bar**, which is a popular Temple Bar meeting place, and The Study, a quieter room with an open fire. Conference/banqueting (60/77); video conferencing on request. Beauty treatments, Therapy @ The Clarence (also available to non-residents). Children welcome (under 12s free in parents' room, cots available without charge). No pets. **Rooms 49** (5 suites, incl 1 penthouse; 44 executive, 6 no smoking, 1 for disabled). Lift. Turndown service. 24 hr room service. Room rate €330; no SC. Several multi-storey carparks within walking distance; valet parking. **The Tea Room:** The restaurant, which has its own entrance on Essex Street, is a high-ceilinged room furnished in the light oak which is a feature throughout the hotel. Pristine white linen, designer cutlery and glasses, high windows softened by the filtered damson tones of pavement awnings, all combine to create an impressive dining room. Table d'hôte lunch and dinner menus are changed daily, and are reasonably priced for an hotel of this calibre, although side dishes are extra in the evening; an à la carte menu is also offered, and a Tasting Menu at €65 per person, which is available for whole tables only. There is no separate reception area for the restaurant so you will be shown to your table before considering choices from a well-balanced selection of five or six dishes on each course, many of them luxurious: tortellini of lobster and crab, with white asparagus and shellfish bisque is a typical starter for example, although specialities include the more homely deep fried bacon and potato cakes with buttered savoy cabbage and caper sauce. A recent visit by the Guide followed major changes in the kitchen and, while some dishes achieved great heights - a perfectly executed main dish of caramelised halibut with crisp potato rösti and a ragôut of wild mushrooms with Alsace bacon was singled out for praise, also a delicious hot lemon soufflé - there was an unevenness to some dishes and, more particularly, to the service, which had not previously been experienced , so perhaps the new team had not fully settled in. A well-chosen, if expensive, wine list includes a selection of very good wines by the glass, and wine service is knowledgeable. * Lighter menus are also available in the hotel - an informal Evening Menu, for example, Afternoon Tea, and The Octagon Bar Menu, offering a light à la carte and a different main course dish every day of the week. **Seats 90.** Toilets wheelchair accessible. L Sun-Fri 12.30-2.30, D daily 6.30-10.30 (Sun to 9.30). Set L €30 (Sun €34.50); Set D €47.50/55/65. A la carte L & D available. House wine from €24.50. SC Discretionary. Octagon Bar Menu,11.30-10pm daily. Closed L Sat; from 24 Dec-27 Dec. Amex, Diners, MasterCard, Visa. **Directions:** Overlooking the River Liffey at Wellington Quay, southside, in Temple Bar.

Dublin 2

🍷 Ⓝ PUB/CAFÉ/BAR

Clarendon Café Bar
Clarendon Street Dublin 2
Tel: 01 679 2909 Fax: 01 670 6900

The Stokes brothers' stylish contemporary café-bar just off Grafton Street is a sister to Bang Café and has a chic exterior with a large glass frontage and some simple little aluminium tables and chairs outside. It's a big place, with bars spread over several storeys, but subtle decor - dark wooden floors, pale walls, chrome bars, comfortable wicker chairs - soft background music, and a warm and friendly welcome create a lovely ambience and there's a very nice buzz about it. And, as in Bang, there's a commitment to interesting food, promised on menus that name suppliers and are not over-extensive yet offer a wide range of tempting dishes: starters might include seafood like smoked haddock and cod fish cakes, or seared scallops with chorizo and roasted red pepper for example, then there are pannini for busy lunch times (and sandwiches made to order), and mains like corn-fed chicken & chive mash with smoked bacon lardons, all scrumptious bangers & mash with a piquant shallot & mustard jus. Great char-grilled steaks are served with classic béarnaise & fries, and there's an accurate description of the cooking, eg 'rare; very red, cool centre' etc, which is a must to avoid confusing orders and make life a lot easier in the kitchen. The wine list is short, but makes up in interest anything it may lack in length - and an exceptional choice is offered by the glass. If this is the way that modern bars are going in Ireland, we're all for it. Open 10-11. Food served: Mon-Sat, 12-8; Sun 12-6. No reservations. Air conditioning. Toilets wheelchair accessible. A la carte. Wines from €15.50. Closed 25 Dec, Good Fri.Amex, MasterCard, Visa, Laser. **Directions:** From St Stephen's Green, walking down Grafton Street - 1st street on left, 100yards.

Dublin 2

🏨 🍽 HOTEL/RESTAURANT

Conrad Hotel Dublin
Earlsfort Terrace Dublin 2
Tel: 01 602 8900 Fax: 01 676 5424
Email: dublininfo@conradhotels.com Web: www.conradhotels.com

BUSINESS HOTEL OF THE YEAR

Situated directly opposite the National Concert Hall and just a stroll away from St Stephen's Green, this fine city centre hotel celebrated its twentieth anniversary in 2005 with the completion of a €15 million refurbishment programme which has seen the entire hotel renovated and upgraded. This is an extremely comfortable place to stay - friendly staff are well-trained and helpful, and many of the pleasantly contemporary guestrooms enjoy views of the piazza below and across the city; nice touches include providing an umbrella in each room - and also a laminated jogging map of the area with one- and three-mile routes outlined. The Conrad has particular appeal for business guests, as all of the bedrooms also double as an efficient office, with ergonomic workstation, broadband, dataports, international powerpoints and at least three direct dial telephones with voice-mail - and the hotel also has extensive state-of-the-art conference and meeting facilities, a fitness centre and underground parking. Public areas include a raised lounge, which makes an ideal meeting place, and the popular **Alfie Byrne's Pub**, which is home to locals and visitors alike and opens on to a sheltered terrace. **Alex** A new head chef, Donnchadh Geraghty, leads the kitchen team at The Conrad's new seafood restaurant. The style is contemporary classic - a bright open plan room, with Elizabeth Cope paintings and low music, has polished tables with crisp white runners, and smart modern place settings - and menus are divided into choices from Land or Sea (Shallow Waters and Deep Sea, listed separately), some of which are available as starters or main courses. Fish choices are extensive - perhaps 15 varieties - balanced by a handful of meat and vegetarian choices. Delicious home-made breads begin your meal, and dishes attracting praise on a recent visit include an imaginative and well-executed millefeuille of smoked and gravad lax salmon, and a beautifully balanced, flavoursome main course of Moroccan spiced monkfish. The dessert menu and wine list could perhaps be improved; (although wine service is knowledgeable) but, overall, dining here should be an enjoyable experience. Conference/banqueting (350/270). Executive boardroom (12). Business centre; secretarial services; video conferencing. Underground carpark (100). Children welcome (under 12s free in parents' room, cots available without charge, baby sitting arranged). **Rooms 192** (9 suites, 7 junior suites, 165 no-smoking, 1 for disabled). Lift. 24 hr room service. Turndown service. Room rate from about €180, SC incl. Open all year. Amex, Diners, MasterCard, Visa, Laser. **Directions:** On the south-eastern corner of St Stehen's Green, opposite the National Concert Hall.

Dublin 2
🏛 HOTEL

The Davenport Hotel

Merrion Square Dublin 2 **Tel: 01 607 3900** Fax: 01 661 5663
Email: davenportres@ocallaghanhotels.ie Web: www.ocallaghenhotels.ie

féile bia On Merrion Square, close to the National Gallery, the Dail (Parliament Buildings) and Trinity College, this striking hotel is fronted by the impressive 1863 facade of the Alfred Jones designed Merrion Hall, which was restored as part of the hotel building project in the early '90s. Inside, the architectural theme is continued in the naming of rooms - Lanyon's Restaurant, for example honours the designer of Queen's University Belfast and Gandon Suite is named after the designer of some of Dublin's finest buildings, including the Custom House. The hotel, which is equally suited to leisure and business guests, has been imaginatively designed to combine interest and comfort, with warm, vibrant colour schemes and a pleasing mixture of old and new in both public areas and accommodation. Bedrooms are furnished to a high standard with orthopaedic beds, air conditioning, voicemail, modem lines, personal safes and turndown service in addition to the more usual amenities - all also have ample desk space, while the suites also have fax and laser printer. The Davenport is known for the warmth and helpfulness of its staff, and makes a very comfortable base within walking distance of shops and galleries; it is the flagship property for a small group of centrally located hotels, including the **Alexander Hotel** (just off Merrion Square) and the **Stephen's Green Hotel** (corner of St Stephen's Green and Harcourt Street). Conference/banqueting (380/400). Business centre. Gym. Children welcome (Under 2s free in parents' room; cots available, baby sitting arranged). No pets. **Rooms 115** (2 suites, 10 junior suites). Lift. 24 hr room service. B&B about € 97.50pps. Open all year. Amex, Diners, MasterCard, Visa. **Directions:** just off Merrion Square.

Dublin 2
€ RESTAURANT

Dunne & Crescenzi

22 South Frederick Street Dublin 2 **Tel: 01 677 3815**
Fax: 01 633 4476 Email: dunneandcrescenzi@hotmail.com

This Italian restaurant and deli very near the Nassau Street entrance to Trinity College delights Dubliners with its unpretentiousness and the simple good food it offers at reasonable prices. It's the perfect place to shop for genuine Italian ingredients - risotto rice, pasta, oils, vinegars, olives, cooked meats, cheeses, wines and much more - and a great example of how less can be more. How good to sit down with a glass of wine (bottles on sale can be opened for a small corkage charge) and, maybe, a plate of antipasti - with wafer-thin Parma ham, perhaps, several salamis, peppers preserved in olive oil, olives and a slice of toasted ciabatta drizzled with extra virgin olive oil... There are even a couple of little tables on the pavement, if you're lucky enough to get them on a sunny day. Indoors or out, expect to queue: this place has a loyal following. *Also at: 11 Seafront Avenue, Sandymount, Dublin 4 (Tel 01 667 3252), and a new more formal restaurant, **Nonna Valentina** (Tel 01 454 9866), opened at 1-2 Portobello Road, Dublin 8 just before going to press. **Seats 60.** Air conditioning. Open Daily 9-11.30. Sun L (12-6). A la carte; wine from about €13. Amex, MasterCard, Visa, Laser. **Directions:** Off Nassau Street, between Kilkenny and Blarney stores.

Dublin 2   # Eden
🅔 RESTAURANT

Meeting House Square Temple Bar Dublin 2
Tel: 01 670 5372 Fax: 01 670 5373
Email: info@eden.ie Web: www.edenrestaurant.ie

A highlight of the Temple Bar area, this spacious two-storey restaurant was designed by Tom de Paor and has its own outdoor terrace on the square - and terrace tables have the best seats for the free movies screened on the square on Saturdays in summer; modern, with lots of greenery and hanging baskets, there's an open kitchen which adds to the buzz and a fresh, contemporary house style is seen quite extensive seasonal menus that make use of organic produce where possible, in updated classics which suit the restaurant well.

Head chef Michael Durkan's menus are clear and to the point: specialities include deliciously simple starter of smokies (smoked haddock with spring onion, crème fraîche and melted cheddar cheese), a fresh-flavoured crab salad, and down to earth dishes like beef & Guinness stew, and belly of pork. Organic beef is a feature - an excellent chargrilled sirloin with red onion, chips and a classic béarnaise sauce, perhaps - and vegetables, which always include a vegetable of the day, are exceptionally varied and imaginative. A three-course pre-theatre menu, offering four choices on each course, is great value at €25. A well-balanced and fairly priced wine list offers several wines by the glass. Great food and atmosphere, efficient service and good value too - Eden continues to fly the flag for Temple Bar. Children welcome, but not after 8pm. **Seats 96** (private room, 14/30; outdoor seating, 40). Air conditioning. L daily,12.30-3 (Sun 12-3). D daily 6-10. Set L €24, Early Bird D €25 (6-7), also à la carte. House wine €22. SC discretionary. Closed bank hols, 25 Dec - 2 Jan. Amex, Diners, MasterCard, Visa, Laser. **Directions:** Next to the Irish Film Theatre, opposite Diceman's Corner.

Dublin 2   # Ely Winebar & Café
🌱 CAFÉ/RESTAURANT/WINE BAR

22 Ely Place Dublin 2
Tel: 01 676 8986 Fax: 01 678 7866
Email: elywine@eircom.net Web: www.elywinebar.ie

Erik and Michelle Robson's unusual wine bar and café is in an imaginatively renovated Georgian townhouse just off St Stephen's Green and, since opening in 1999, they have built on their commitment to offer some of the greatest and most interesting wines from around the world - and earned a well-deserved reputation for a wine list that must surely be the most comprehensive in Ireland. They update their list every year, to offer customers what is best at the time - at the time of going to press they are listing over 500 wines, with 90 available by the glass, thus providing the opportunity to taste wines which would otherwise be completely unaffordable to most people. And this exceptional wine list is backed up by other specialities including a list of premium beers and, on the food side, organic produce, notably pork, beef and lamb from the family farm in County Clare, are a special feature - and not just premium cuts, but also products like home-made sausages and mince, which make all the difference to simple dishes like sausages and mash or beefburgers. Recent refurbishment has created lots more room and greater comfort for adventurous sippers - and the great news is that **'ely chq'** is due to open in the IFSC in 2006, in a 10,000 sq ft grade one listed building built in 1821, and formerly known as Stack A. Here they will have a 350 seater ground floor and basement premises with west facing waterside dining and extensive vaulted basement, providing both wine bar and contemporary dining areas; organic meats and game, plus more extensive seafood choices will be available seven days a week - this is indeed a treat in store. Ely was selected for the Guide's Wine Award of the Year for 2005. **Seats 100.** Open Mon-Sat 12 noon-12.30 am. L 12-3 (1-4 Sat), D 6-10.30 (11 Fri/Sat). Bar open to midnight. Wines from €22. SC 12.5% on groups of 6+. Closed Sun, Christmas week, bank hol Mons.Amex, Diners, MasterCard, Visa, Laser. **Directions:** Junction of Baggot Street/Merrion Street off St Stephens Green.

Dublin 2
🏛 Ⓔ GUESTHOUSE

Harrington Hall
69/70 Harcourt Street Dublin 2
Tel: 01 475 3497 Fax: 01 475 4544
Email: harringtonhall@eircom.net Web: www.harringtonhall.com

Conveniently located close to St Stephen's Green and within comfortable walking distance of the city's premier shopping areas, Trinity College and the National Concert Hall, Henry King's fine family-run guesthouse was once the home of a former Lord Mayor of Dublin and has been sympathetically and elegantly refurbished, retaining many original features. Echoes of Georgian splendour remain in the ornamental ceilings and fireplaces of the well-proportioned ground and first floor rooms, which include a peaceful drawing room with an open peat fire. Beautiful relaxing bedrooms have sound-proofed windows, ceiling fans and lovely marbled bathrooms - and outstanding cooked breakfasts are another special feature. All round this is a welcoming alternative to a city-centre hotel, offering good value, handy to the Luas (tram), and with the huge advantage of free parking behind the building; luggage can be stored for guests arriving before check-in time (2pm). Small conferences (12). Children welcome (under 3s free in parents' room, cot available without charge). Staff are friendly and helpful. Parking (10). **Rooms 28** (2 junior suites, 3 shower only, 6 executive, 2 Family Rooms, all no smoking). Lift. 24 hour room service. B&B €86.50, ss €20. Open all year. Free wireless internet available.Amex, Diners, MasterCard, Visa, Laser. **Directions:** Off southwest corner of St Stephens Green (one-way system approaches from Adelaide Road).

Dublin 2
RESTAURANT

Hô Sen
6 Cope Street Temple Bar Dublin 2 **Tel: 01 671 8181**
Email: timcostigan@hotmail.com Web: www.hosen.ie

ETHNIC RESTAURANT OF THE YEAR

The chefs at Ireland's first authentic Vietnamese restaurant are trained in Vietnam and take pride in bringing their cuisine to this pleasingly simple restaurant in Temple Bar - and in introducing this lighter, clear-flavoured Asian cooking style at prices which are very reasonable by Dublin standards, and especially for Temple Bar, where restaurants are often over-priced- so word spread like wild fire and, from the outset, this has been a busy place. Dimmed lights and candles create an appealing atmosphere from the street and, with comfortably-spaced tables, gentle background jazz and chopsticks supplied as well as western cutlery, the scene is set for an interesting evening. Vietnamese cooking has a reputation for being among the healthiest in the world and, although the familiar Asian styles feature - spring rolls, satays, stir fries and pancake dishes, for example - fresh herb flavours of coriander and lemongrass are dominant, and there is a light touch to both the flavours and the cooking. An extensive menu is shorter than it seems, as it includes many variations on a theme, and dishes are explained quite clearly. Examples attracting praise on a recent visit included an unusual cold shredded beef dish, Bò Tái Chanh, which is a refreshing speciality from Ho Chi Minh city, flavoured with coriander and lime juice, and and Cá Kho Tô, a hotpot made with your choice of fish from the catch of the day, in which a generous amount of fish is cooked in a rich-flavoured 'pork marinade' with mushrooms, ginger root, lemongrass and a mixture of Vietnamese herbs and spices, including chilli. Choosing an appropriate wine might be a little problematic - perhaps beer or tea would be a more suitable choice. Although the presentation isn't fancy, everything is appetising, and service is lovely - pleasant, helpful and efficient. And, as the cooking here is as exciting as the welcome is warm, this place is a little gem. **Seats 120** (private room available seats 25). L Thu-Sun 12.30-2.30 (3 Sun) Value L €10.80; D Tue-Sat 5-11 (10 Sun), Early Bird D €17.50 (5-6.30). Wines from €16.95. Closed Mon. MasterCard, Visa, Laser. **Directions:** In Temple Bar, behind the Central Bank.

Dublin 2
🍷 💶 CAFÉ/RESTAURANT

Kilkenny Restaurant & Café

5-6 Nassau Street Dublin 2 **Tel: 01 677 7075**
Fax: 01 670 7735 Email: info@kilkennyshop.com

téite bia Situated on the first floor of the shop now known simply as Kilkenny, with a clear view into the grounds of Trinity College, the Kilkenny Restaurant is one of the pleasantest places in Dublin to have a casual bite to eat - and the experience lives up to anticipation: ingredients are fresh and additive-free (as are all the products on sale in the shop's Food Hall) and everything has a home-cooked flavour. Salads, quiches, casseroles, home-baked breads and cakes are the specialities of the Kilkenny Restaurant and they are reliably good. They also do an excellent breakfast: fresh orange juice to start and then variations combinations of the traditional fare.[Kilkenny was the Dublin winner of our Irish Breakfast Awards in 2003.] A range of Kilkenny preserves and dressings - all made and labelled on the premises - is available in the shop. Air conditioning. Children welcome. **Seats 190.** Open 8.30-5 (Thu to 7), Sat 9-5, Sun 11-3. Breakfast to 11.15, lunch 11.30-3. A la carte. Licensed. Air conditioning. Closed 25-26 Dec, 1 Jan, Easter Sun. Amex, Diners, MasterCard, Visa. **Directions:** Opposite TCD playing fields.

Dublin 2
★ 🍷 RESTAURANT

L'Ecrivain

109a Lower Baggot Street Dublin 2 **Tel: 01 661 1919**
Fax: 01 661 0617 Email: sallyanne@lecrivain.com Web: www.lecrivain.com

téite bia On two levels - spacious and very dashing - Derry and Sallyanne Clarke's acclaimed city centre restaurant is light and airy, with lots of pale wood and smoky mirrors - and lovely formal table settings which promise seriously good food. Derry's cooking style - classic French with contemporary flair and a strong leaning towards modern Irish cooking - remains consistent, although new ideas are constantly incorporated and the list of specialities keeps growing. Special treats to try might include a wonderful starter of baked rock oysters with York cabbage & crispy cured bacon, with a Guinness sabayon - perhaps followed by a main course of marinated loin of lamb & cutlet, with braised turnip, and caramelised sweetbreads. Thoughtful little touches abound - a fine complimentary amuse-bouche before your first course, for example - and there are some major ones too, like the policy of adding the price of your wine after the 10% service charge has been added to your bill, instead of charging on the total as most other restaurants do: this is an expensive restaurant but a gesture like this endears it to customers who happily dig deep into their pockets for the pleasure of eating here. Seafood, lamb, beef and game, in season, are all well-represented, but menus could also include neglected ingredients like rabbit, which is always appealingly served. Wonderful puddings are presented with panache and might include a hot soufflé or a classic vanilla crème brulée with lemon curd ice cream. Presentation is impressive but not ostentatious and attention to detail - garnishes designed individually to enhance each dish, careful selection of plates, delicious home-made breads and splendid farmhouse cheeses - is excellent. Lunch, as usual in top rank restaurants, offers outstanding value. A fine wine list is augmented by a tempting selection of coffees and digestifs - all this, plus excellent service, adds up to a very caring approach and an exceptional restaurant. **Seats 100.** (private room, 20. outdoor setaing, 25) L Mon-Fri 12.30-2, D Mon-Sat 7-10.30, Set L €45. Set D €70 (Vegetarian Menu about €50). Tasting Menu €110. House wine €30. 10% SC (on food only). Closed L Sat, all Sun, Christmas week, bank hols. Amex, MasterCard, Visa, Laser **Directions:** 10 minutes walk east of St Stephens Green, opposite Bank of Ireland HQ.

L'Gueuleton

Dublin 2

🇪 RESTAURANT

1 Fade Street Dublin 2 **Tel: 01 675 3708**

This no-frills French restaurant took Dublin by storm when it opened in the autumn of 2004, and it has never looked back since - in fact, expansion plans were put into place almost immediately and it has already doubled in size. And the winning format? Simple premises with no-nonsense French bistro decor, and a menu that makes little distinction between courses and offers a combination of less usual dishes (organic parsley soup with frogs legs) and the classic (blanquette of lamb). House specialities include a snail and roquefort pithvier with herb salad and a black pudding and apple tart tatin with blue cheese and Pommery mustard - a fair indication of the thinking behind this unusual kitchen. Add to this great cooking, a well-chosen short (all French) wine list, efficient service and terrific value for money - and you have just the kind of place that Dubliners like best. The only downside is the no reservations policy. **Seats 70.** Open Mon-Sat, L 12.30-3, D 6-10. Closed Sun. A la carte. House wines €18. No reservations. MasterCard, Visa, Laser. **Directions:** At Hogans Bar, off Georges St.

La Maison des Gourmets

Dublin 2

🇪 CAFÉ

15 Castle Market Dublin 2 **Tel: 01 672 7258**

In a pedestrianised area handy to car parks and away from the hustle and bustle of nearby Grafton Street, this French boulangerie has a smart little café on the first floor and also a couple of outdoor tables on the pavement for fine weather. Home-baked bread is the speciality, made to a very high standard by French bakers who work in front of customers throughout the day, creating a wonderful aroma that wafts through the entire premises. The speciality is their award-winning sourdough bread, which is used as the base for a selection of tartines - French open-style sandwiches served warm - on the lunch menu (about €12): baked ham with thyme jus and mushroom cream; duck confit with onion marmalade and gherkins and vegetarian ones like roast aubergine with plum tomato, fresh parmesan & basil pesto are all typical. Add to this a couple of delicious soups (French onion with Emmental croûtons, perhaps), a hot dish like classic beef bourguignon with potato purée, one or two salads - and a simple dessert like strawberries with balsamic reduction and fresh cream - and the result is as tempting a little menu as any discerning luncher could wish for. There is also an extensive choice of infusions, teas, Green Bean coffees and pastries, including many of the French classics. Portions are on the small side, which suits most lunch time appetites, and service can be a little slow; but everything is very appetising, the atmosphere is chic and you can stock up on bread and croissants from the shop as you leave - just don't think in terms of a quick bite. **Seats 28.** Open Mon-Sat, 9-5.30 (L12-4). Set L €18.50; also A la carte. SC discretionary. House wine €19. Closed Sun, bank hols, 4 days Christmas. Amex, Diners, MasterCard, Visa, Laser. **Directions:** Pedestrianised area between Georges Street Arcade and Powerscourt Shopping Centre.

La Stampa

Dublin 2

👁 RESTAURANT/HOTEL

35 Dawson St Dublin 2 **Tel: 01 677 4444** Fax: 01 677 4411
Email: dine@lastampa.ie Web: www.lastama.ie

Reminiscent of a grand French belle époque brasserie, this is one of Ireland's finest dining rooms - high-ceiling, with large mirrors, wooden floor, candelabra, Victorian lamps, plants, flowers and various bits of bric-a-brac, the whole noisily complemented by a constant bustle. It is a fun and lively place, offering international brasserie-style food in delightful surroundings; at the time of going to press Dubliners awaited the promised arrival here of celebrity chef Jean-Christophe Novelli, which suggests gearing up of ambitions in the kitchen. **Seats 230.** L & D daily. **Hotel:** Very attractive rooms have sumptuous fabrics, echoing the ambience of the restaurant and bar below. **Rooms 30.** Room rate about €135. Open all year. Amex, Diners, MasterCard, Visa. **Directions:** Opposite the Mansion House.

Dublin 2
☆ 🌮 RESTAURANT

The Mermaid Café
69-70 Dame Street Dublin 2
Tel: 01 670 8236 Fax: 01 670 8205
Email: info@mermaid.ie Web: www.mermaid.ie

Ben Gorman and Mark Harrell's unusual restaurant on the edge of Temple Bar is not large, but every inch of space is used with style in two dining areas and a wine lounge. They celebrated a decade in business in 2005 and, during that time, they've achieved well-earned recognition for a personal style of hospitality, imaginative French and American-inspired cooking and interesting one-off decor. Innovative, mid-Atlantic, seasonal cooking can be memorable for inspired combinations of flavour, texture and colour - and specialities like New England crab cakes with piquant mayonnaise, the Giant Seafood Casserole (which changes daily depending on availability) and pecan pie are retained by popular demand on daily-changing menus. Vegetables, always used imaginatively, are beautifully integrated into main courses - rump of lamb with cherry tomatoes, capers and minted pea mash is a good example, and there are many more like it on each day's menus. Then delicious desserts, wonderful Irish cheeses (like the deeply flavoured Gabriel and Desmond from West Cork, served with apple chutney) and coffees with crystallised pecan nuts: attention to detail right to the finish. Lunch menus are extremely good value, and Sunday brunch is not to be missed if you are in the area. Wines are imported privately and are exclusive to the restaurant. **Seats 55** (private room, 24). Reservations accepted. Air conditioning. Toilets are not wheelchair accessible. L 12.30-2.30 (Sun to 3.30), D 6.00-11 (Sun to 9). Set L €23.95; Set D €34.95; also à la carte. House wine €19.95. SC discretionary. Closed Christmas, New Year, Good Friday. *Next door, **Gruel** (Tel 01 670 7119), is a quality fast-food cafe (75 seats) under the same management, with a large & loyal following; open Mon-Fri 7.30-9.30; Sat & Sun 10.30-4.30. Amex, MasterCard, Visa, Laser. **Directions:** Next door to Olympia Theatre.

Dublin 2
🏛️🏛️☆ HOTEL/RESTAURANT

Merrion Hotel
Upper Merrion Street Dublin 2
Tel: 01 603 0600 Fax: 01 603 0700
Email: info@merrionhotel.com Web: www.merrionhotel.com

Right in the heart of Georgian Dublin, opposite Government Buildings, this luxurious hotel comprises four meticulously restored Grade 1 listed townhouses built in the 1760s and, behind them, a contemporary garden wing overlooks formal landscaped gardens. Public areas include three interconnecting drawing rooms (one is the cocktail bar with a log fire), with French windows giving access to the gardens; Irish fabrics and antiques reflect the architecture and original interiors with rococo plasterwork ceilings and classically proportioned windows - and the hotel owns one of the most important private collections of 20th-century art. Maintenance is immaculate - refurbishment of soft furnishings, for example, is so skilfully effected that it is completely unnoticeable. Beautifully furnished guest rooms and suites have sumptuous bathrooms (all with separate bath and shower) and all the extras expected in a hotel of this calibre, including broadband. Discreet, thoughtful service is an outstanding feature of the hotel and staff, under the excellent direction of General Manager Peter MacCann, are exceptionally courteous and helpful - likewise, the pamper-factor in the splendid leisure complex, The Tethra Spa - which is romanesque, with classical mosaics - is predictably high. Dining options match standards elsewhere in the hotel: choose between the elegant vaulted Cellar Restaurant (see below) and **Restaurant Patrick Guilbaud** (see separate entry), which is also on site. Conference/banqueting (50). **Rooms 143** (20 suites, 10 junior suites, 80 no smoking, 5 disabled). Children welcome (under 4s free in parents' room, cot available free of charge, baby sitting arranged). Air conditioning. Lift. B&B €155 pps.

Complimentary underground valet parking. Open all year. **Cellar Restaurant:** Warm, friendly staff swiftly seat arriving guests at beautiful classically appointed tables in this elegant vaulted dining-room, and explain well-balanced menus which are changed daily and have a refreshingly straightforward tone. With comfortable furniture and thoughtfully designed lighting and ventilation, this is a very relaxing room - and the philosophy is to source the best ingredients and treat them with respect in a simple style that shows the food to advantage without over-emphasis on display. Merrion fish & chips with mushy peas and tartare sauce somehow seems a most appropriate signature dish in a restaurant where accomplished cooking goes without saying, and delicious flavours, excellent service and great value for the quality of food and surroundings are the priorities. A good wine list also offers value, including wines by the glass. Open all year. Amex, Diners, MasterCard, Visa, Laser.

Dublin 2　　　　　　　　　　　　　　　　　　　　　　　　　# Montys of Kathmandu
E RESTAURANT　　　　　　　　　　　28 Eustace Street Temple Bar Dublin 2 **Tel: 01 670 4911**
Fax: 01 494 4359 Email: montys@eircom.net Web: www.montys.ie

Shiva Gautham's modest-looking restaurant opposite the Irish Film Centre is the only one in Ireland's to specialise in Nepalese cuisine, and the food here can have real character - at agreeably moderate prices. The chefs are all from Nepal and although all the familiar Indian styles are represented- tandoori, curry etc - the emphasis is on Nepalese specialities and varying standard dishes by, for example, using Himalayan spices. The menu is quite extensive and includes a platter of assorted starters which is a good choice for a group of four, allowing time to consider the rest of the menu without rushing; there's also a fair selection of vegetarian dishes, including a traditional Nepali mixed vegetable curry which can be served mild, medium or hot. Friendly staff are happy to offer suggestions, or to choose a well balanced meal for you, including specialities like Kachela (a starter of raw minced lamb with garlic, ginger, herbs and spices which is said to be a favourite amongst the Newars in Kathmandu, served with a shot of whiskey) and Momo - these Nepalese dumplings served with a special chutney require 24 hours notice and are 'the most popular dish in Kathmandu'. But you will also find sound renditions of old favourites here, including Chicken Tika Masala: moist pieces of tender boneless chicken cooked in the tandoori, and served in a creamy masala sauce. This can be a really rewarding restaurant and, in addition to a very adequate wine list and drinks menu, they even have their own beer, 'Shiva', brewed exclusively for the restaurant. Children welcome. **Seats 60** (private room, 30) L Mon-Sat, 12-2.15; Set L €17, D from €20; D daily 6-11.30, (Sun to 11), Tasting Menu about €30-45. L&D à la carte available. SC discretionary. House wine from about €17. Closed L Sun, 25-26 Dec, 1 Jan & Good Fri. Amex, MasterCard, Visa, Laser. **Directions:** Temple Bar - opposite the Irish Film Centre(IFC).

Dublin 2　　　　　　　　　　　　　　　　　　　　　　　　　　　# Number 31
E GUESTHOUSE　　　　　　　　　31 Leeson Close Lr Leeson Street Dublin 2 **Tel: 01 676 5011**
Fax: 01 676 2929 Email: number31@iol.ie Web: number31.ie

Formerly the home of leading architect Sam Stephenson, Noel and Deirdre Comer's hospitable 'oasis of tranquillity and greenery' just off St Stephen's Green makes a relaxing and interesting city centre base, with virtually everything within walking distance in fine weather. Public areas of the house are spacious and very comfortable, and fresh, elegant bedrooms good bathrooms and nice little extras including complimentary bottled water as well as phones, TVs and tea/coffee trays. Breakfasts served at communal tables inside, and in the conservatory are not to be missed - freshly baked breads and delicious preserves, and lovely hot dishes like kippers or mushroom frittata cooked to order... Prices are moderate for central Dublin, and secure parking adds greatly to the attraction of a stay here. Not suitable for children under 10. No pets. Rooms at the back are quieter. **Rooms 20** (all en-suite & no smoking). B&B from about €75, ss €25. Open all year. Amex, MasterCard, Visa. **Directions:** From St. Stephens Green onto Baggot St., turn right on to Pembroke St. and left on to Leeson St.

Dublin 2
★ 🌱 RESTAURANT

One Pico Restaurant

5-6 Molesworth Place Schoolhouse Lane Dublin 2
Tel: 01 676 0300 Fax: 01 676 0411 Web: www.onepico.com

Quietly located in a laneway near St Stephen's Green, just a couple of minutes walk from Grafton Street, Eamonn O'Reilly's One Pico is one of Dublin's most popular fine dining restaurants. The surroundings are elegant, with crisp white linen and fine china and glassware, and the cooking is exceptionally good: sophisticated, technically demanding dishes are invariably executed with confidence and flair. The range of menus offered includes lunch and pre-theatre menus which, as usual in restaurants of this calibre, represent great value, an 8-course Tasting Menu, a vegetarian menu (on request), and an à la carte, with about ten quite luxurious dishes offered on each course, plus optional side dishes which should not be necessary as each main course is individually garnished. There is an occasional small nod to Irish traditions, but this is classical French cooking with a modern twist, albeit based for the most part on the very best local ingredients. Dishes which attracted special praise on a recent visit, for example, included a large plate of bouillabaisse, with roast fish presented on the fish sauce and vegetables and a side bowl of anchovy and potato aoili to accompany, and a confit of pork belly with ham hock fondant, star anise and carrot jus - Eamonn O'Reilly cooks with first class ingredients, turning them into classic dishes with lovely clean flavours, and his own unique style on each dish. To finish, it is difficult to decide between an innovative and delicious cheese menu, or beautifully presented desserts that taste as good as they look - and include refreshing choices like a luscious carpaccio of watermelon and strawberry soup, with tequila lime granite. Service, under the direction of restaurant manager Andrew Scott, is professional and friendly, and sommelier Arnaud Legat provides impressive wine service. This is a fine restaurant and has earned its place among the city's very best. *A sister restaurant is **Bleu Bistro Moderne**. **Seats 75** (private room, 45). Air conditioning. L& D Mon-Sat: L12-3, D 6-11. 2/3 courses Set L €25, Early D €35 (6-7.30); Set D from €35, Tasting Menu €80, also à la carte. House wine €23. SC 10%. Closed Sun, bank hols, 25 Dec-6 Jan. Amex, Diners, MasterCard, Visa, Laser. **Directions:** 2 mins walk off St Stephens Green/Grafton Street near government buildings.

Dublin 2
☆ RESTAURANT/WINE BAR

Pearl Brasserie

20 Merrion Street Upper Dublin 2
Tel: 01 661 3572 Fax: 01 661 3629
Email: info@pearl-brasserie.com Web: www.pearl-brasserie.com

Just a few doors away from The Merrion Hotel, Sebastien Masi and Kirsten Batt's stylish basement restaurant has an open peat fire and colourful blue banquettes picking up tones from an aquarium that runs the length of the bar, where aperitifs and a light bar menu are served. The style is contemporary international, with a classic French base and a pleasing emphasis on clean flavours highlighting the high quality of ingredients. Menus lean towards towards fish and seafood, which Sebastien cooks with accuracy and flair - an unusual starter of freshwater crayfish comes with a saffron mayonnaise and mixed herb and ginger confit salad, for example, and a main course of seared king scallops and caramelised pork belly is served with apple ravioli. Specialities from the land include luscious pan-fried foie gras with toasted brioche with strawberry compôte (and an optional glass of Montbazillac, which is hard to resist) and a more familiar main course of pan-fried fillet beef with fondue of spinach and roquefort croquette potato - and a separate vegetarian menu is also offered. Desserts are a highlight and include particularly good ices, and coffee is served with home made chocolates. Charming, efficient and well informed service complements Sebastien Masi's unusual and beautifully presented meals. The wine list is a good match for the food, favouring France and including a good choice of half bottles. *Separate Wine Bar area serving nibbles & light bar menu. Also available for cocktails and apperitif and digestif drinks. Children welcome. **Seats 80** (private area, 10); Air-conditioning. L Tue-Fri 12-2.30, D daily 6-10.30. 'Value' L €25, D à la carte. House wine €19.50. SC discretionary. Closed bank hols. Amex, MasterCard, Visa, Laser. **Directions:** Opposite Government Building, near Merrion Hotel.

Dublin 2

Peploe's Wine Bistro

E RESTAURANT/WINE BAR

16 St Stephen's Green Dublin 2

Tel: 01 676 3144 Fax: 01 676 3154 Web: www.peploes.com

The brainchild of the aptly-named Barry Canny, this is a restaurant with a difference, as its location, long opening hours, flexible menus all add up to a relaxed place for a rendez-vous at any time - and he has an excellent team in head chef, Sebastien Scheer, and head waiter, Frederic Pelanne. It's in the basement of the Georgian terrace than runs along the north side of St Stephen's Green, making it very handy to both the Grafton Street area and the nearby offices - perfect territory for a laid-back wine bar (an extensive wine list includes a dozen or more champagnes and about thirty wines by the glass). Lunch and dinner menus are both informally arranged by style of dish - breads & savouries, soups, charcuterie, fish & shellfish, pasta, grills, roasts & pies - an approach which has found favour with customers. This is still pretty serious food, all the same - foie gras terrine with brioche, half a grilled lobster with garlic butter, and Italian rabbit stew are typical lunch time examples, and dinner moves up a notch or two in the same style. Service is smart, the atmosphere is great and the cooking has style - all this and a reasonable bill too. **Seats 95.** Reservations required. Air conditioning. Toilets wheelchair accessible. Children welcome. Open noon-11 daily; L 12-4, D 6-10; Set D €45, also à la carte. Closed 25 Dec, Good Fri. Amex, MasterCard, Visa, Laser, Switch.

Dublin 2

The Porterhouse

PUB

16-18 Parliament Street Temple Bar Dublin 2

Tel: 01 679 8847 Fax: 01 670 9605 Email: porterh.indigo.ie

Dublin's first micro-brewery pub opened in 1996 and, although several others have since set up and are doing an excellent job, The Porterhouse was at the cutting edge. Ten different beers are brewed on the premises and beer connoisseurs can sample a special tasting tray selection of plain porter (a classic light stout), oyster stout (brewed with fresh oysters, the logical development of a perfect partnership), Wrasslers 4X (based on a West Cork recipe from the early 1900s, and said to be Michael Collins' favourite tipple), Porter House Red (an Irish Red Ale with traditional flavour), An Brain Blasta (dangerous to know) and the aptly named Temple Brau. But you don't even have to like beer to love The Porterhouse. The whole concept is an innovative move away from the constraints of the traditional Irish pub and yet it stays in tune with its origins - it is emphatically not just another theme pub. The attention to detail which has gone into the decor and design is a constant source of pleasure to visitors and the food, while definitely not gourmet, is a cut above the usual bar food and, like the pub itself, combines elements of tradition with innovation: Carlingford oysters, Irish stew, beef & Guinness casserole are there, along with the likes of homemade burgers and a good range of salads. This is a real Irish pub in the modern idiom and was a respected winner of our Pub of the Year award in 1999. No children after 9pm. **Seats 50.** Open noon - 11.30 daily (Thu-Sat to 12.30). Bar food served 12-9.30 daily (Sun from 12.30). Closed 25 Dec & Good Fri. [*The original Porterhouse is located on Strand Road on the seafront in Bray, Co. Wicklow and, like its sister pub in Temple Bar, it offers bar food daily from 12.30-9.30. Tel/Fax: 01 286 1839. There is also a Porterhouse in London, at Covent Garden.] MasterCard, Visa.

Dublin 2
€ CAFÉ

Queen of Tarts

4 Cork Hill Dame Street Dublin 2 **Tel: 01 670 7499**

Behind Yvonne and Regina Fallon's quaint traditional shopfront near Dublin Castle lies an equally quaint traditional tea room, with warmly welcoming friendly and efficient staff, and wonderful smells wafting across the room as they struggle to make space for new arrivals to the comfortable, lived-in little room. Yvonne and Regina both trained as pastry chefs, but there's nothing 'cheffy' about the good home baking that you'll find here - the emphasis is on wholesomeness and real flavour. Service begins with breakfast (including a vegetarian cooked breakfast) which is served until the lunch/afternoon menu takes over at noon. Home-made scones, buttermilk brown bread, roast chicken & coriander tartlets, warm plum tarts with cream, chocolate fudge cake, orange chocolate pinwheel cookies and much else besides taking their place on a surprisingly extensive menu, which includes some seriously good sandwiches and salads - most people pop in for a snack, but you could just as easily have a 3-course lunch. Inexpensive, consistently excellent food, lovely atmosphere and great service - what more could anyone ask? [*Also at: City Hall, Dame St. Tel 01 672 2925. Open museum hours: Mon-Sat 10-4.30, Sun 2-5.] **Seats 25.** Air conditioning. Toilets wheelchair accessible. Children welcome. Open daily: Mon-Fri 7.30-6 (L12-6); Sat 9-6; Sun 9.30-6. Closed 24 Dec-02 Jan, bank hols. **No Credit Cards. Directions:** Opposite the gates of Dublin Castle.

Dublin 2
★★ RESTAURANT

Restaurant Patrick Guilbaud

21 Upper Merrion Street Dublin 2
Tel: 01 676 4192 Fax: 01 661 0052
Email: restaurantpatrickguilbaud@eircom.net Web: www.restaurantpatrickguilbaud.ie

RESTAURANT OF THE YEAR

For almost a quarter of a century this spacious, elegant restaurant in a Georgian townhouse adjoining the Merrion Hotel has been the leading French restaurant in Ireland. Approached through a fine drawing room, where drinks are served, the restaurant is a bright, airy room, enhanced by an outstanding collection of Irish art, and opens onto a terrace and landscaped gardens which make a delightful setting for drinks and al fresco dining in summer. Head chef Guillaume Lebrun has presided over this fine kitchen since the restaurant opened and is renowned for exceptional modern classic cuisine, based on the best Irish produce in season: his luxurious, wide-ranging menus include a wonderfully creative 9-course Tasting Menu (€130), themed as 'Sea & Land', perhaps, and celebrating traditional Irish themes with Gallic flair; at the other end of the spectrum, a daily table d'hôte lunch menu offers the best value fine dining in Dublin. Contemporary French cooking at its best, combined with the precision and talents of a team of gifted chefs, produces dishes of dexterity, appeal and flavour: a speciality starter of lobster ravioli, for example, is made from Clogherhead lobster coated in a coconut scented lobster cream and served with hand made free range egg pasta, toasted almonds and lightly curry-flavoured olive oil and, later, an assiette of chocolate ends your meal in spectacular fashion, with a plate of no less than five cold and hot chocolate desserts. Consistent excellence is the order of the day: cheeses are supplied by Sheridan's cheesemongers, breads are home-made, and the mostly French wine list includes some great classics, alongside some reasonably-priced offerings. A recent visit by the Guide was an experience to treasure, each dish a masterpiece of beautiful presentation, contrasting textures and harmonious flavours, all matched by faultless service - under the relaxed supervision of Restaurant Manager Stéphane Robin, service is invariably immaculate, and Patrick Guilbaud himself is usually present to greet guests personally. Every capital city has its great restaurant and this is Dublin's gastronomic heaven: Restaurant Patrick Guilbaud continues to set the standard by which all others are judged. Children welcome. **Seats 86** (private room, The Roderic O'Conor Room is available for up to 25 people; outdoor seating, 20). Air conditioning. L Tue-Sat 12.30-2.15, D Tue-Sat 7.30-10.15. Set L €33 or € 45. Vegetarian Menu (Main courses from €28). 9-course Tasting Menu €130. L&D à la carte available. House wine from €32. SC discretionary. Closed Sun & Mon, bank hols, Christmas week. Amex, Diners, MasterCard, Visa, Laser. **Directions:** Opposite Government Buildings.

Dublin 2

Shanahan's on the Green

Ⓔ RESTAURANT   119 St. Stephen's Green Dublin 2 **Tel: 01 407 0939** Fax: 01 407 0940
Email: sales@shanahans.ie Web: www.shanahans.ie

This opulent restaurant was Dublin's first dedicated American style steakhouse - although, as they would be quick to reassure you, their wide-ranging menu also offers plenty of other meats, poultry and seafood. However, the big attraction for many of the hungry diners who head for Shanahan's is their certified Irish Angus beef, which is seasoned and cooked in a special broiler, 1600-1800°F, to sear the outside and keep the inside tender and juicy. Steaks range from a 'petit filet' at a mere 8 oz/225g right up to The Shanahan Steak (24 oz/700g), which is a sight to gladden the heart of many a traditionally-minded Irishman - and, more surprisingly perhaps, many of his trendier young friends too. Strange to think that steak was passé such a short time ago. There is much else to enjoy, of course, including a dramatic signature dish of onion strings with blue cheese dressing. The wine list includes many special bottles - with, naturally, a strong presence from the best of Californian producers. Not suitable for children. **Seats 100.** Reservations required. Air conditioning. L Fri only (except for groups), 12.30-2. D daily, 6-10.30. Set L €45; otherwise à la carte. (SC discretionary, but 15% on parties of 6+). Closed Christmas period. Amex, Diners, MasterCard, Visa, Laser **Directions:** West side St Stephen's Green.

Dublin 2

Thornton's Restaurant

★ ★ 🏵 RESTAURANT   128 St Stephen's Green Dublin 2
Tel: 01 478 7008 Fax: 01 478 7009
Email: thorntonsrestaurant@eircom.net Web: www.thorntonsrestaurant.com

Seriously good cooking is to be found at Kevin and Muriel Thornton's famous restaurant, which is on the top floor of the Fitzwilliam Hotel, overlooking St Stephen's Green. You can take a lift up through the hotel, but it is best approached from its own entrance on the Green: mounting the wide staircase, deep-carpeted in dark blue, conveys a sense of occasion. Once inside, the decor is simple and elegant: pale walls washed with colour reflected from heavy primrose silk curtains highlight a series of subtle oil paintings, and understated linen-clad tables leave you in no doubt that the food is to be the star here: A welcoming team of waiting staff set a tone of friendly professionalism from the outset, offering an aperitif at the neat reception area, or the maître d' - Kevin's brother, Garret Thornton - may show you straight to your table to consider a menu which, literally, bears the hand of the master on the cover. Kevin Thornton offers creative cooking of the highest class: he has a perfectionist's eye for detail with a palate to match, and uses only the very best seasonal ingredients. Menus offered include a concise lunch menu, a vegetarian menu and a table d'hôte dinner menu, in addition to a shortish à la carte offering about eight luxurious choices on each course - Kevin Thornton has a name for generosity with truffles and he will not disappoint: a vegetarian first course of warm white asparagus is served with truffle hollandaise and green asparagus bavarois for example, and among the seafood dishes you will find a luxurious signature dish of sautéed prawns with prawn bisque, and truffle sabayon. Other signature dishes include braised suckling pig, and trotter served with glazed turnip and a light poitin sauce - and variations on these creations appear throughout an 8-course Surprise Menu (€125) which is just that - there is nothing written and the menu created for each table is unique. Although beautifully presented, this is not show-off food - the cooking is never less than sublime and the emphasis is always on flavour. Service is impeccable, from the moment breads are offered to the final presentation of assorted petits fours accompanying coffees and teas. Sommelier Julie Martin joined the team in 2005 and, at the time of the Guide's most recent visit, planned revisions to the extensive wine list, including an increase in the number of house wines offered. Thornton's offers good value at all levels - and at lunch it is exceptional. Reservations required. Children welcome. Air conditioning. **Seats 80** (private area, 30). L Tue-Sat, 12-1.45; D Tue-Sat, 7-10.30. Set L €30/40. Set D €65; Set D €65, Surprise Menu €125, A la carte also offered. House wine from €28. SC discretionary. Closed Sun & Mon, 1 week over Christmas. Amex, Diners, MasterCard, Visa, Laser. **Directions:** On St Stephen's Green.

Dublin 2
ⓃⒺ RESTAURANT

Town Bar & Grill
21 Kildare Street Dublin 2
Tel: 01 662 4724/4800 Fax: 01 662 3857
Email: reservations@townbarandgrill.com Web: www.townbarandgrill.com

Warmly professional staff and a delicate hand with the decor - warm floor tiles, gentle lighting and smart but not overly-formal white-clothed tables with promising wine glasses - create a welcoming tone on arrival at Ronan Ryan and Temple Garnier's L-shaped basement restaurant under Mitchell's wine merchants. Although the name of the restaurant is meaningful (many would define 'town' as within walking distance of the nearby Dawson Street car park) it may not prepare some first-time diners for the strongly New York/Italian theme on both menu and wine list. Starters include a really excellent antipasti plate and dishes rarely seen elsewhere, such as grilled fresh sardines, while classics like osso bucco Milanese with a pea and saffron risotto and gremolata may be among main courses which will also offer several interesting fish dishes and, in season, game such as crown of pheasant - served with confit leg, soft polenta and glazed shallots, perhaps. Moreish desserts may include classics like strawberry Pavlova or refreshing red wine poached pears with yoghurt and ice cream - the combinations are sometimes unusual, and tastes superb. Confident, accurate cooking, zesty flavours and simple presentation on plain white plates - all this is impressive, and interested, well-informed staff ensure a memorable meal. Prices are fair for the high quality of food and service offered, with lunch and pre-theatre menus offering very good value. There is also - perhaps uniquely in a city centre restaurant of this calibre - a special children's menu, offering healthy low-salt and low-sugar 'real' food such as char-grilled chicken breast bruschetta with buffalo mozzarella & tomato salsa, and home-made fish fingers with oven roasted chips. Full marks. **Seats 90.** Open Mon-Sat: L 12.15-5.30; pre-theatre menu € 29.95 6-7.15 (excl Sat); à la carte D 5.45-11. Sun open 5-10. Closed 24-27th Dec. Amex, Diners, MasterCard, Visa, Laser. **Directions:** Opposite side door of Shelbourne, under Mitchell's wine shop.

Dublin 2
Ⓔⓞ RESTAURANT

Unicorn Restaurant
12B Merrion Court off Merrion Row Dublin 2 **Tel: 01 676 2182**
Fax: 01 662 4194 Web: www.unicornrestaurant.com

In a lovely, secluded location just off a busy street near St. Stephen's Green, this informal and perennially fashionable restaurant is famous for its antipasto bar, piano bar and exceptionally friendly staff. It's particularly charming in summer, as the doors open out onto a terrace which is used for al fresco dining in fine weather - and the Number Five piano bar, which extends to two floors, is also a great attraction for after-dinner relaxation with live music (Weds-Sat 9pm-3am). Aside from their wonderful display of antipasto, an extensive menu based on Irish ingredients (suppliers are listed) is offered, including signature dishes such as risotto funghi porcini (which is not available on Monday), and involtini 'saltimbocca style' - pockets of veal stuffed with Parma ham, mozzarella and sage, braised in white wine and lemon sauce; good regional and modern Italian food, efficient service and great atmosphere all partially explain The Unicorn's enduring success - another element is the constant quest for further improvement. There is always something new going on - the 'Unicorn Foodstore' round the corner, on Merrion Row, is a relatively recent addition to the enterprise, for example, also the Unicorn Antipasto/Tapas Bar - and they have now decided to extend the food service by introducing a bar menu in the piano bar, which is a fair indication of the popularity of this buzzing restaurant. Many of the Italian wines listed are exclusive to The Unicorn: uniquely, in Ireland, they stock the full collection of Angelo Gaja wines and also the Pio Cesare range. Not suitable for children after 9pm. **Seats 85** (private room 20; outdoor 40). Reservations required. Air conditioning. Open Mon-Sat, L12.30-4.30, D 6-11 (Fri/Sat to 11.30). A la carte. House wine €23.50. SC discretionary. Closed Sun, bank hols, 25 Dec-2 Jan. Amex, Diners, MasterCard, Visa, Laser, Switch. **Directions:** Just off Stephen's Green, towards Baggot St.

Dublin 2
🏨 HOTEL/RESTAURANT

The Westbury Hotel

Grafton Street Dublin 2 **Tel: 01 679 1122** Fax: 01 679 7078
Email: westbury@jurysdoyle.com Web: www.jurysdoyle.com

féile bia Possibly the most conveniently situated of all the central Dublin hotels, the Westbury is a very small stone's throw from the city's premier shopping street and has all the benefits of luxury hotels - notably free valet parking - to offset any practical disadvantages of the location. Unashamedly sumptuous, the hotel's public areas drip with chandeliers and have accessories to match - like the grand piano on The Terrace, a popular first floor meeting place for afternoon tea, and frequently used for fashion shows. Accommodation is similarly luxurious, with bedrooms that include penthouse suites and a high proportion of suites, junior suites and executive rooms. With conference facilities to match its quality of accommodation and service, the hotel is understandably popular with business guests, but it also makes a luxurious base for a leisure break in the city. Laundry/dry cleaning. Mini-gym. Conference/banqueting (220/200). Business centre. Secretarial services. ISDN lines. Children welcome (Under 12s free in parents' room; cots available). No pets. **Rooms 205** (3 suites, 4 junior suites, 24 executive rooms, 160 no-smoking, 2 for disabled). Lifts. B&B from €218 pps. Car park. Open all year. **Restaurant:** After a drink in one of the hotel's bars - the first floor Terrace bar and the Sandbank Bistro, an informal seafood restaurant and bar accessible from the back of the building - the **Russell Room** offers classic dining, with some global cuisine and modern Irish influences. **Seats 100** (private room, 14). Air conditioning. SC 15%. L daily, 12.30-2.30; D daily 6.30-10.30 (Sun to 9). Set L from about €28, D à la carte. House wine about €25. Amex, Diners, MasterCard, Visa, Laser, Switch. **Directions:** City centre, off Grafton Street; near Trinty College & Stephens Green.

Dublin 2
🏨 HOTEL/RESTAURANT

The Westin Dublin

College Green Dublin 2 **Tel: 01 645 1000** Fax: 01 645 1401
Email: sandra.bethke@westin.com Web: www.westin.com

féile bia Two Victorian landmark buildings provided the starting point for this impressive hotel, and part of the former Allied Irish Bank bank was glassed over to create a dramatic lounging area, The Atrium, which has a huge palm tree feature and bedroom windows giving onto it like a courtyard (effective, if strangely airless). The magnificent Banking Hall now makes a stunning conference and banqueting room, and the adjacent Teller Room is an unusual circular boardroom - while the vaults have found a new lease of life as **The Mint**, a bar with its own access from College Street. It's an intriguing building, especially for those who remember its former commercial life, and it has many special features including the business traveller's 'Westin Guest Office', designed to combine the efficiency and technology of a modern office with the comfort of a luxurious bedroom, and the so-called 'Heavenly Bed' designed by Westin and 'worlds apart from any other bed'. A split-level penthouse suite has views over Trinity College (and a private exercise area). Very limited parking (some valet parking available, if arranged at the time of booking accommodation). Fitness room. **Rooms 164** (13 suites, 5 junior suites, 19 for disabled). Lift. Room rate from about €230 (max 2 guests). **The Exchange:** An elegant, spacious room in 1930s style, the restaurant continues the banking theme and, with a welcome emphasis on comfort, it simply oozes luxury. Everything about it, from the classily understated decor in tones of cream and brown to the generous-sized, well-spaced tables and large carver chairs says expensive but worth it. And, in the Guide's experience, that promise generally follows through onto the plate in well-executed menus - a fairly contemporary style, and confident, unfussy cooking endear this restaurant to visitors and discerning Dublin diners alike. Westin Smart Dining options (moderate in calories and fat) and vegetarian options are highlighted on menus. Friendly service from knowledgeable young waiting staff. The Westin Sunday Brunch has live jazz and is quite an institution, and the pre-theatre dinner menu offers very good value. **Seats 75.** Breakfast daily 6.30-10, L Mon-Fri 12-2.30, D daily 6.30-10 (Fri, Sat, Sun to 10.30). Sun Brunch 12-4.30, €40; live music (jazz). Restaurant closed L Sat. Hotel open all year Amex, Diners, MasterCard, Visa, Laser. **Directions:** On Westmoreland Street, opposite Trinity College

DUBLIN 3

Dublin 3
🏵 RESTAURANT

Kinara Restaurant

318 Clontarf Road Dublin 3 **Tel: 01 833 6759** Fax: 01 833 6651
Email: info@kinara.ie Web: www.kinara.ie

This smart two-storey restaurant specialising in authentic Pakistani and Northern Indian cuisine enjoys a scenic location overlooking Bull Island. Fine views - especially from the first floor dining room - are a feature at lunch time or on fine summer evenings, and there's a cosy upstairs bar with Indian cookbooks to inspire guests waiting for a table or relaxing after dinner. A warm welcome from the dashing Sudanese doorman, Muhammad, ensures a good start, and the restaurant has a very pleasant ambience, with soft lighting, antiques, interesting paintings, the gentlest of background music and streamlined table settings. The menu begins with an introduction to the cuisine, explaining the four fundamental flavours known collectively as 'pisawa masala' - tomato, garlic, ginger and onions - and their uses. Each dish is clearly described, including starters like kakeragh (local crab claws with garlic, yoghurt, spices and a tandoori masala sauce) and main courses such as the luxurious Sumandari Badsha (lobster tails with cashew nuts, pineapple, chilli and spices). There is a declared commitment to local produce - notably organic beef, lamb and chicken - and a section of the menu devoted to organic and 'lighter fare' main courses (typically Loki Mushroom, a vegetarian dish of courgettes and mushrooms in a light spicy yoghurt sauce). The kitchen team have over 80 years experience between them and the quality of both food and cooking is exemplary: dishes have distinct character and depth of flavour, and everything is appetisingly presented with regard for colour, texture and temperature - and fine food is backed up by attentive, professional service and fair prices. Care and attention marks every aspect of this comfortable and attractive restaurant, earning it a loyal following. [Kinara was the Guide's Ethnic Restaurant of the Year in 2004.] **Seats 70** (private room 20). Air conditioning. Children welcome. L Thu, Fri & Sun, 12.30-3; D daily, 6-11.00. Set L €14.95; early D €19.95 (Mon-Thu, 6-7.30pm); also à la carte L&D. House wine about €17.25. Closed 25-26 Dec, 1 Jan. Amex, MasterCard, Visa, Laser. **Directions:** 1.5 miles north of city centre on coast road to Howth (opposite wooden bridge).

DUBLIN 4

Dublin 4
🏵 GUESTHOUSE

Aberdeen Lodge

53 Park Avenue Ballsbridge Dublin 4
Tel: 01 283 8155 Fax: 01 283 7877
Email: aberdeen@iol.ie Web: www.halpinsprivatehotels.com

Centrally located (close to the Sydney Parade DART station) yet away from the heavy traffic of nearby Merrion Road, this handsome period house in a pleasant leafy street offers all the advantages of an hotel at guesthouse prices. Elegantly furnished executive bedrooms and four-poster suites offer air conditioning and all the little comforts expected by the discerning traveller, including a drawing room with comfortable chairs and plenty to read, and a secluded garden where guests can relax in fine weather. Staff are extremely pleasant and helpful (tea and biscuits offered on arrival), housekeeping is immaculate - and, although there is no restaurant, a Drawing Room menu offers a light menu (with wine list), and you can also look forward to a particularly good breakfast of fresh and stewed fruits, home-made preserves, freshly-baked breads and muffins, big jugs of juice and hot dishes cooked to order - including delicious scrambled eggs and smoked salmon, kippers and buttermilk pancakes with maple syrup, as well as numerous variations on the traditional Irish breakfast. Guests may join residents for breakfast - a useful service for early morning meetings - and the spa at the nearby sister property, Merrion Hall, is available for guests' use. [Aberdeen Lodge was the Dublin winner of our Irish Breakfast Awards in 2004.] Boardroom, business and fitness facilities for business guests - and mature secluded gardens. Small conferences/banqueting (50/40). Children welcome. No pets. **Rooms 17** (2 suites, 6 executive rooms, 10 no-smoking).24 hour room service. B&B €75 pps, ss €35. Residents' meals available: D (Drawing Room Menu) about €19 + all-day menu. House wines from €30. Open all year. Amex, Diners, MasterCard, Visa. **Directions:** Minutes from the city centre by DART or by car, take the Merrion Road towards Sydney Parade DART station and then first left into Park Avenue.

Dublin 4

⊞⊞⊞ HOTEL/RESTAURANT

Berkeley Court Hotel

Lansdowne Rd Ballsbridge Dublin 4
Tel: 01 665 3200 Fax: 01 661 7238
Email: berkeleycourt@jurysdoyle.com Web: www.jurysdoyle.com

téile bia Set in its own grounds, yet convenient to the city centre, this luxurious hotel has long been a haunt of the rich and famous when in Dublin. The tone is set by an impressively spacious chandeliered foyer, which has groups of seating areas arranged around it, with bars, restaurants and private conference rooms leading off. The hotel is renowned for its high standards of service and accommodation. **Berkeley Room:** A fine hotel restaurant with very professional staff and some reliable specialities - seafood dishes are especially good and they are renowned for their roast beef. **Seats 60.** Air conditioning. L Sun-Fri, 12.30-2.15; D Mon-Sat, 6.30-9.15. A la carte. Toilet wheelchair accessible. Restaurant closed L Sat, D Sun. On-site facilities include health & beauty treatments, a barber shop and giftshop/newsagent. Conference/banqueting (400/380) Video conferencing, business centre, secretarial services, ISDN lines. **Rooms 187** (1 penthouse suite, 6 luxury suites, 24 executive rooms, 35 no-smoking, 4 for disabled). Lift. Car Park. B&B about €190 pps, ss15%. Open all year. Amex. Diners, MasterCard, Visa, Laser, Switch. **Directions:** Near Lansdowne Road rugby stadium; approx 13km from Airport.

Dublin 4

€ RESTAURANT

Canal Bank Café

146 Upper Leeson Street Dublin 4 **Tel: 01 664 2135**
Fax: 01 664 2719 Email: info@tribeca.ie Web: www.tribeca.ie

BEST CAFÉ BREAKFAST

Trevor Browne and Gerard Foote's well-known almost-canalside restaurant is a rather sleek modern reinterpretation of Dish, their original arty-simple restaurant in Temple Bar. The format is designed to meet the current demand for quality informal food or 'everyday dining', but the original philosophy still applies and only the best ingredients are used - organic beef and lamb, free-range chicken and a wide variety of fresh fish daily. The menu is user-friendly, divided mainly by types of dish - starters like crispy fried calamari with lemon mayonnaise, big salads (Caesar, niçoise) and, for those who need a real feed, steaks various ways and specialities like Brooklyn meatloaf with spinach, onion gravy & mashed potatoes. There's a good sprinkling of vegetarian dishes - and they also do terrific breakfasts, offering some classic county house specialities like Ger's famous eggs Benedict or Florentine as well as the traditional combinations. A carefully selected, compact wine list includes a good choice of house wines - and a range of brunch cocktails too. Children welcome. **Seats 70.** Air conditioning. Open 8am-11pm daily (Sun from 11 am, Sun D 6-11). A la carte. House wine €20.95. SC 10% on parties of 6+. Closed 24-28 Dec & Good Fri. Amex, Diners, MasterCard, Visa, Laser **Directions:** Near Burlington Hotel.

Dublin 4

🍴 € CAFÉ

Expresso Bar Café

1 St Mary's Road Ballsbridge Dublin 4
Tel: 01 660 0585 Fax: 01 660 0585

Great flavour-packed food, good value and efficient service attracts a loyal following to Ann-Marie Nohl's clean-lined informal restaurant, which is renowned for carefully sourced ingredients that make a flavour statement on the plate. An all-morning breakfast menu offers many of the classics, often with a twist: thus a simple poached egg on toast comes with crispy bacon and relish, porridge is a class act topped with toasted almonds and honey, and French toast comes with bacon, or winter berries and syrup. Lunch and dinner menus tend to favour an international style, but the same high standards apply: whether it's a Dublin Bay Prawn pil pil with chili, coriander, char-grilled lime and crusty bread, or panfried cornfed chicken breast stuffed with goats cheese sundried tomato and Mediterranean vegetables & red pepper coulis, or just a vegetarian pasta, it's the quality of the ingredients and cooking that make the food here special. An informative and well-chosen wine list offers a fair choice by the glass. Weekend brunch is a must. **Also at:** Custom House Square, **IFSC**, Dublin 1 (01 672 1812) and **The Gables**, Foxrock, Dublin 18 (01 289 2174). Not suitable for children after 8pm. Air conditioning. **Seats 60.** Open Mon-Sat, 7.30am-9.30pm (B'fst 7.30-11.30, L12-5, D 5-9.30), Sun brunch 10-5. Closed D Sun, D Mon, 25 Dec, 1 Jan, Good Friday. MasterCard, Visa, Laser. **Directions:** Opposite Hibernian Hotel, off Baggot Street.

Dublin 4

🏨 HOTEL/RESTAURANT

Four Seasons Hotel

Simmonscourt Road Ballsbridge Dublin 4
Tel: 01 665 4000 Fax: 01 665 4099
Email: reservations.dublin@fourseasons.com Web: www.fourseasons.com/dublin

féile bia Set in its own gardens on a section of the Royal Dublin Society's 42-acre show grounds, this luxurious hotel enjoys a magnificent site, allowing a sense of spaciousness while also being convenient to the city centre - the scale is generous throughout and there are views of the Wicklow Mountains or Dublin Bay from many of the sumptuous suites and guest rooms. A foyer in the grand tradition is flanked by two bars - the traditional wood-panelled Lobby Bar and the newer Ice, which is deliciously contemporary. Accommodation is predictably luxurious and, with a full range of up-to-the-minute amenities, the air-conditioned rooms are designed to appeal equally to leisure and business guests. A choice of pillows (down and non-allergenic foam) is provided as standard, the large marble bathrooms have separate bath and shower, and many other desirable features - and there's great emphasis on service, with twice daily housekeeping service, overnight laundry and dry cleaning, one hour pressing and complimentary overnight shoe shine: everything, in short, that the immaculate traveller requires. But the Spa in the lower level of the hotel is perhaps its most outstanding feature, offering every treatment imaginable - and a naturally lit 14m lap pool and adjacent jacuzzi pool, overlooking an outdoor sunken garden. Outstanding conference and meeting facilities make the hotel ideal for corporate events, business meetings and parties in groups of anything up to 500. **Rooms 259** (67 suites, 21 no-smoking, 7 disabled). Room rate €275 (max. 2 guests). No SC. Open all year. **Seasons Restaurant:** This spacious, classically-appointed restaurant overlooks a leafy courtyard and no expense has been spared on the traditional 'grand hotel' decor - the style is a matter of debate (the ultra modern **Ice Bar** more recently added has attracted high praise from Dubliners), but nobody denies that this is an extremely comfortable restaurant - and, more importantly, that the service is exceptional. Executive Head Chef Terry White's contemporary international menus have their base in classical French cooking and offer a wide-ranging choice of luxurious dishes, with a considerate guide to dishes suitable for vegetarians, 'healthier fare' and dishes containing nuts. The standard of cooking is high and, while it may not rival the city's top independent restaurants as a cutting edge dining experience, this is a fine hotel restaurant with outstanding service, and a good pricing policy ensuring value for money in luxurious surroundings. Sommelier Simon Keegan's excellent wine list includes some very good wines by the glass. *Informal menus are also available at varying times in The Café (daily), and in Ice Bar (Tue-Sat); Afternoon Tea, served daily in the Lobby Lounge, includes an extensive menu of classic teas and infusions. Air conditioning. **Seats 70** (private room, 12). Breakfast 7-11 daily, L 12.30-2.30 daily, D 6.30-9.30 daily. Set L from €24; Set D €72; à la carte also available D). House wine from €28. SC - 15%. Amex, Diners, MasterCard, Visa. **Directions:** Located on the RDS Grounds on corner of Merrion and Simmonscourt Roads.

Dublin 4
👁 RESTAURANT/WINE BAR

The French Paradox

53 Shelbourne Road Ballsbridge Dublin 4
Tel: 01 660 4068 Fax: 01 663 1026
Email: chapeauwines@eircom.net

WINE AWARD

On a busy road near the RDS, this inspired and stylish operation has brought an extra dimension (and a whiff of the south of France) to the concept of wine and food in Dublin. French Paradox combines a wine shop, a large and atmospheric ground floor wine bar (where weekly wine tastings are held) and a room on the first floor, which gains atmosphere from the irresistible charcuterie on display close beside the tables. The main emphasis is on the wide range of wines available by the glass - perhaps 65 wines, kept in perfect condition once open using a wine sommelier, with inert gas. Pierre and Tanya Chapeau are renowned for their directly imported wines - an small illustration of their skillful selection is seen in the results of a recent blind tasting of over 200 Vins de Pays, in which four French Paradox wines were selected for the top 20, and two of them made it into the top six. Food is, in theory, secondary here but, although the choice is deliberately limited (a small à la carte offers a concise range of dishes, as single or shared charcuterie plates), the quality is exceptional and everyone just loves it - sitting outside on a sunny summer day, enjoying a plate of charcuterie with any one of the dozens of wines available by the glass, you could be lunching in the south of France. Classic desserts - chocolate terrine, crème brulée - and excellent coffees to finish. Wines offered change regularly (the list is always growing), and food can be purchased from the deli-counter to take home. Not suitable for children after 7pm. **Seats 25.** Air conditioning. Toilets wheelchair accessible. L&D Mon-Thu, 12-3 & 5-9.30; open all day Fri & Sat, 12-9.30. Set L €19.50; Set D €29. A la carte. House wines (4) change monthly. Closed Sun. Amex, Diners, MasterCard, Visa, Laser. **Directions:** Opposite Ballsbridge Post Office.

Dublin 4
 👁 RESTAURANT

The Lobster Pot

9 Ballsbridge Terrace Ballsbridge Dublin 4
Tel: 01 660 9170 Fax: 01 668 0025 Web: www.thelobsterpot.ie

On the first floor of a redbrick Ballsbridge terrace, conspicuously located near the Herbert Park Hotel - and just a few minutes walk from all the major Ballsbridge hotels - this long-established restaurant has lost none of its charm or quality over the years. The whole team - owner Tommy Crean, restaurant manager (and sommelier) John Rigby and head chef Don McGuinness - have been working here together since 1980 and the system is running very sweetly. How good it is to see old favourites like dressed Kilmore Quay crab, home-made chicken liver paté and fresh prawn bisque on the menu, along with fresh prawns mornay and many other old friends, including kidneys turbigo and game in season. The menu is a treat to read but there's also a daily fish tray display for specials - dishes are explained and diners are encouraged to choose their own combinations. All this and wonderfully old-fashioned service too, including advice from John Rigby on the best wine to match your meal. If only there were more places like this - long may it last. L Mon-Fri, 12.30-2, D Mon-Sat, 6.30-10.30. House wine €22.50. SC 12.5%. Closed L Sat, all Sun, 24 Dec-4 Jan, bank hols. Amex, Diners, MasterCard, Visa, Laser. **Directions:** In the heart of Ballsbridge adjacent to the US embassy.

Dublin 4

🍷 RESTAURANT

O'Connells Restaurant

Bewleys Hotel Merrion Road Dublin 4
Tel: 01 647 3304 Fax: 01 647 3398
Email: info@oconnellsballsbridge.com Web: www.oconnellsballsbridge.com

Located in a large semi-basement under Bewley's Hotel, this remarkable restaurant strives to provide quality ingredient driven modern Irish cooking - simple food, with natural flavours, often emphasised by cooking in a special wood-fired oven. It has dark wood-panelled walls and floor to ceiling windows overlooking a courtyard used for al fresco dining in summer - arriving by the courtyard steps rather than through the hotel helps the ambience considerably. The restaurant is run by Tom O'Connell, a brother of Darina Allen, of Ballymaloe Cookery School, and of Rory O'Connell, previously of Ballymaloe House, who visits regularly and works closely with the kitchen team. More recently Rosemary Kearney, author of 'Healthy Gluten Free Eating', has joined the team as a consultant, and the goal is for O'Connell's to become Ireland's most coeliac-friendly restaurant. Menus are a hymn to quality ingredients, stating that pork, beef, eggs and catering supplies are sourced using Bord Bia's Quality Assurance Schemes, and also naming a number of individual artisan producers and suppliers, often in dishes that have become house specialities - typically, a starter salad is made with Fingal Ferguson's Gubbeen smoked bacon, from Schull in Co. Cork, and Ashe's Black Pudding, from Annascaul, Co. Kerry servied with sautéed potatoe, Bramley Apple and Mustard Sauce. Specially aged beef comes from the Co. Wexford and organic pork is from Tipperary; Irish farmhouse cheese, matured on the premises, is served with home-made biscuits and excellent classic desserts range from deliciously homely sugar crust apple tart served with lightly whipped cream to a light summery strawberry délice or (genuinely) home-made ice creams. A highly informative wine list, which includes an extensive selection of by-the-glass and 24 house wines, reflects the same philosophy and gives details of vintage, region, grape, grower/shipper, merchant, taster's notes, suggested food partnership, bottle size (including some magnums) and price - invariably moderate for the quality offered - for every wine on the list; even the house water, Tipperary, (served by the carafe at Ireland's lowest price, €1.50 per litre) gets 'the treatment' (region, taster's notes...) Service can seem to be under pressure, even the cooking occasionally uneven, but this remains an unique restaurant, offering meals based on the very highest quality ingredients at quite reasonable prices. **Seats 170** (summer courtyard 60). Air conditioning. Buffet L daily 12.30-2.30 (Sun to 3). D daily 6-10 (Sun to 9.30). Early D from €19.75 (6-7pm). Set D 19.75/27.50. Also à la carte D available. SC discretionary (10% on parties of 6+).House wines from €19.85. Closed eve 24- eve 27 Dec. Mineral water complimentary with full evening menu. O'Connells have started serving an all day menu at value for money prices. Amex, Diners, MasterCard, Visa, Laser. **Directions:** Off Merrion Road at Simmonscourt Road, opposite the Four Seasons Hotel.

Dublin 4

🅔 GUESTHOUSE

Pembroke Townhouse

90 Pembroke Road Ballsbridge Dublin 4
Tel: 01 660 0277 Fax: 01 660 0291
Email: info@pembroketownhouse.ie Web: www.pembroketownhouse.ie

Conveniently located close to the RDS and Lansdowne Road, this fine guesthouse has all the amenities usually expected of an hotel. There's a drawing room and study for residents' use and comfortably furnished, individually designed rooms have a safe and facilities for business guests (wi-fi is available in all areas), as well as direct dial phone, cable television, tea/coffee facilities and trouser press (but no tea / coffee making facilities). Breakfast is the only meal served, but it offers full buffet and less usual dishes like sautéed lambs liver served on a bed of sautéed onions and topped with bacon, as well as the traditional cooked breakfast. When arriving by car, it is best to go the carpark at the back, as you can then take a lift with your luggage (avoiding heavy traffic and steep steps to the front door). Wine licence. Private parking at rear. **Rooms 48** (4 shower only, 2 disabled, 24 no smoking). Lift. Limited room service. B&B €75 pps, ss €20. *High Speed WI FI Internet access is now available in all areas of the Pembroke TownhouseAmex, Diners, MasterCard, Visa, Laser. **Directions:** Pembroke Road leads onto Baggot St. On the right hand side going towards town.

Dublin 4
HOTELRESTAURANT

Radisson SAS St Helen's Hotel

Stillorgan Road Dublin 4
Tel: 01 218 6000 Fax: 01 218 6030
Email: reservations.dublin@radissonsas.com Web: www.dublin.radissonsas.com

Set in formal gardens just south of Dublin's city centre, with views across Dublin Bay to Howth Head, the fine 18th century house at the heart of this impressive new hotel was once a private residence. Careful restoration and imaginative modernisation have created interesting public areas, including the Orangerie Bar and a pillared ballroom with minstrels' gallery and grand piano. Bedrooms, in a modern four-storey block adjoining the main building, all have garden views (some of the best rooms also have balconies) and air conditioning, and are well-equipped for business guests. Rooms are comfortably furnished to a high standard in contemporary style, although some are less spacious than might be expected in a recent development. Conference/banqueting (350/220); also St Helen's Pavilion (600/800) in summer. Fitness centre; beauty salon. Garden; snooker. Ample parking. Children welcome (cots available without charge, baby sitting arranged). **Rooms 151** (25 suites, 70 no-smoking, 8 for disabled). Room rate from €155 (max. 3 guests). Open all year. **Talavera:** In four interconnecting rooms in the lower ground floor, this informal Italian restaurant is decorated in warm Mediterranean colours and, with smart wooden tables dressed with slips, modern cutlery, fresh flowers and Bristol blue water glasses, it is atmospheric when candle-lit at night. A well-balanced menu offers a balanced choice of dishes inspired by tradition and tailored to the modern palate. Head chef Giancarlo Anselmi specialises in authentic dishes from Tuscany and Basilicata, and an exceptionally fine antipasti buffet sets the tone for a very pleasing dining experience, where skilful cooking is matched by a good atmosphere and caring service from friendly, efficient staff, under the supervision of Restaurant Manager Silvano Bastaniello. Risotto - so popular, yet rarely cooked correctly - is a speciality; a rather exotic version with asparagus & truffle scent is a signature dish, as is branzino in Brodetto, an 'Italian Bouillabaisse' of sea bass in a fish and vegetable broth. The wine list offers a strong selection of regional Italian bottles to match the food. *Lighter menus are also offered all day in the Orangerie Bar and Ballroom Lounge. **Seats 110.** Air conditioning, toilets wheelchair accessible. D daily 6.30-10.30. Set menus from €35; also a la carte; Early Bird Menu €25 Sun-Thu 5.30-7. Amex, Diners, MasterCard, Visa, Laser. **Directions:** Just 3 miles south from the city centre, on N11.

Dublin 4
GUESTHOUSE

Raglan Lodge

10 Raglan Road Ballsbridge Dublin 4
Tel: 01 660 6697 Fax: 01 660 6781

Helen Moran's elegant mid-19th century residence is peacefully situated near the US embassy, on a road where the poet Patrick Kavanagh once lived, an association immortalised in the ballad On Raglan Road . It is good area for a base in Dublin, as it is quiet, reasonably priced, and has private parking, yet it is convenient to the city centre and has a range of good restaurants nearby. Well-proportioned, high-ceilinged reception rooms are reminiscent of more leisurely times and the en-suite bedrooms are exceptionally comfortable. Raglan Lodge is renowned for the high level of comfort and service provided, and particularly for outstanding breakfasts: a white-clothed sideboard displays freshly squeezed orange juice, fresh fruits and compôtes, home-made muesli and cereals, creamy porridge, yoghurt and cheeses, then a choice of kippers, scrambled eggs with smoked salmon or a fine traditional breakfast delivered piping hot under silver dome covers - a great start to the day. Raglan Lodge was the Dublin winner of our Irish

Breakfast awards in 2001. Theatre reservations can be arranged. Children welcome (under 10s free in parents' room, cot available without charge). No pets. Garden. **Rooms 7** (All en-suite, 3 shower only, 2 no-smoking). B&B €60-80 pps, ss 10%. Closed 18 Dec-7 Jan Amex, Diners, MasterCard, Visa. **Directions:** Heading south from city centre take a right at the US embassy onto Eglington Rd, then left at roundabout on to Raglan Road.

Dublin 4
☆ RESTAURANT

Roly's Bistro

7 Ballsbridge Terrace Ballsbridge Dublin 4
Tel: 01 668 2611 Fax: 01 660 8535
Email: ireland@rolysbistro.ie Web: www.rolysbistro.ie

féile bia This bustling Ballsbridge bistro has been a smash hit since the day it opened. Chef-patron Colin O'Daly (one of Ireland's most highly regarded chefs) and head chef Paul Cartwright present imaginative, reasonably priced seasonal menus at lunch and an early dinner, and also an evening à la carte menu. A lively interpretation of classical French cooking gives more than a passing nod to Irish traditions, world cuisines and contemporary styles, and carefully sourced ingredients are the sound foundation for cooking that never disappoints. Dublin Bay Prawns are always in demand (and may be served Neuberg, a speciality that comes with a tian of mixed long grain and wild rice), and an upbeat version of traditional Kerry lamb pie is another favourite. Service is efficient but discreet, cooking is invariably excellent, everyone loves the buzz, and Rolys has always given great value for money - they were the first to offer a good range of wines at an accessible price, for example, and famously ran a whole selection at £10; now they offer a Euro version which doesn't have quite the same ring to it but it's a good deal all the same. Offering quality with good value has been the philosophy of the restaurant from the outset; it continues to fulfil this promise well and the set menus - lunch, pre-theatre and the table d'hôte - all offer particularly good value. **Seats 200.** Air conditioning. L daily 12-3, D daily 6-10 Set L €19.95; Early D €21.95 (Mon-Thu, 6-6.45); L&D also à la carte. SC10%. Closed 25-27 Dec inc. Amex, Diners, MasterCard, Visa, Laser. **Directions:** Heart of Ballsbridge, across the road from the American Embassy.

DUBLIN 6

Dublin 6
☆ RESTAURANT

Mint

47 Ranelagh Village Dublin 6
Tel: 01 497 8655 Fax: 01 282 7018

This striking, glass-fronted restaurant in Ranelagh village is stylish and minimalist, with a view of the busy street, and classy, understated decor décor in a combination of materials that lends an air of spaciousness to a small area. Friendly, professional staff quickly bring you to your stylish, simply-appointed table - there is no room for a reception area, which is a small downside, but all the niceties are observed and a tasty little amuse-bouche from the chef quickly settles new arrivals in. Head Chef Oliver Dunne is one of the most exciting younger chefs in Ireland today and, in menus that are ambitious yet simply stated, he offers dishes which are quite luxurious and sometimes others in which inexpensive everyday ingredients have been used to create something wonderful, which takes great skill. A terrine of foie gras and smoked duck, with sauce gribiche and toasted brioche, was singled out for special praise on a recent visit - also main courses of perfectly cooked rack of lamb neck, with aubergine crushed potatoes, and aubergine & cumin purée, red pepper purée and red pepper jus and a sweetly flavoursome fillet of monkfish with peas à la française, smoked bacon lardons and a dashing vermouth cappuccino. Desserts - which often tend to favour fruit - include inspired combinations such as a crème brulée of tea-soaked Agen prunes with an apple shot: magic! A cheeseboard is also offered - but, surprisingly, restricted to French cheeses; this is a pity considering the range of wonderful Irish artisan cheeses to choose from, even though 'modern French cuisine' is the declared house style. With pleasing surroundings and faultless food and service (and a well matched, interesting wine list), Mint has earned a following, and it may take several days to get a reservation, even during the week. As in other leading restaurants, set lunch and early dinners are very good value. Childen welcome, but not suitable after 8pm. **Seats 45.** Reservations advised. L Tue-Sun, 12-3; D Tue-Sun, 6-10. Set 1-3 course L €15-25; Early D €27 (6-6.45); D also à la carte. Wines from €19. Closed Mon, bank holidays. Amex, MasterCard, Visa, Laser. **Directions:** Centre of Ranelagh.

DUBLIN 8

Dublin 8
E RESTAURANT

Locks Restaurant
1 Windsor Terrace Portobello Dublin 8
Tel: 01 454 3391 Fax: 01 453 8352

féile bia In an old building with a lovely canal-side setting, Claire Douglas's two-storey restaurant celebrated its 25th anniversay in 2005 and is decorated in a warm and elegant style with soft lighting, open fires and a soothing atmosphere. There's a timelessness about it which is extremely refreshing - the tone is set by a lovely Jeremy Williams menu cover - and head chef, Alan Kinsella is putting real heart into the cooking. He offers an ambitious range of menus including a Table d'Hôte and an extensive (and pricey) à la carte dinner menu, a set lunch (which is a real snip) and also a Tasting Menu on some Wednesday evenings - you can opt to have anything from five to eight courses, and it is invariably booked out. The stated policy is to use quality Irish ingredients, in a cooking style that is predominantly contemporary French/Irish, although other influences do creep in - in a speciality starter, for example, a stylish dish of loin of rabbit with chorizo mousse, rillette and spring roll, served with with a fig compôte & rosemary jus. Some dishes are very luxurious, typically a signature main course of stuffed boneless squab pigeon, which is graced by the inclusion opf both foie gras and truffle, and served with a wilted lettuce and pea velouté. Desserts tend towards the sophisticated - a pyramid of white chocolate & coffee mousse, with Earl Grey anglaise froth and pistachio ice cream, perhaps Accomplished cooking, caring service and a warm ambience make this a lovely restaurant, and the dining experience should be memorable. The wine list favouring France, notably Bordeaux, includes a choice of about ten half bottles and is fairly priced for the quality. Children welcome. **Seats 55** (private room, 24). L Mon-Fri,12.30-2; D Mon-Sat, 6.30-10. Set L €28.95, Set D 3-5 course €48.95; 5-8 course Tasting Menu, €59. L&D à la carte also available. Early Bird D €38.95 (6.30-7.15). House wine from €28.00. SC 12.5%. Closed L Sat, all Sun, bank hols, Christmas week. Amex, Diners, MasterCard, Visa, Laser **Directions:** Half way between Portobello and Harold's Cross Bridges.

Dublin 8
E RESTAURANT/ATMOSPHERIC PUB

The Lord Edward
23 Christchurch Place Dublin 8
Tel: 01 454 2420 Fax: 01 454 2420
Email: ledward@indigo.ie Web: www.lordedward.ie

Dublin's oldest seafood restaurant/bar spans three floors of a tall, narrow building overlooking Christchurch Cathedral. Traditional in a decidedly old-fashioned way, The Lord Edward provides a complete contrast to the current wave of trendy restaurants that has taken over Dublin recently, which is just the way a lot of people like it. If you enjoy seafood and like old-fashioned cooking with plenty of butter and cream (as nature intended) and without too many concessions to the contemporary style of presentation either, then this could be the place for you. While certainly caught in a time warp, the range of fish and seafood dishes offered is second to none (sole is offered in no less than nine classic dishes, for example), and the fish cookery is excellent, with simplest choices almost invariably the best. There are a few non-seafood options - traditional dishes like Irish stew, perhaps, or corned beef and cabbage - and desserts also favour the classics. This place is a one-off - long may it last. Bar food is also available Mon-Fri, 12-2.30. Children welcome. **Seats 40.** L Mon-Fri, 12-2.15, Set L €17.20/25. D Mon-Sat 6-10.15. 5 course D €35; also à la carte. House wine from €15. Reservations required. Closed Sun, 24 Dec-2 Jan, bank hols. Amex, Diners, MasterCard, Visa, Laser. **Directions:** Opposite Christchurch Cathedral.

DUBLIN 9

Dublin 9
Ⓔ CAFÉ/WINE BAR

Andersons Food Hall & Café

3 The Rise Glasnevin Dublin 9 **Tel: 01 837 8394**
Fax: 01 797 9004 Email: info@andersons.ie Web: www.andersons.ie

Previously a butchers shop, and still with its original 1930s' tiled floor, high ceiling and façade, Noel Delaney and Patricia van der Velde's wonderful delicatessen, wine shop and continental style café is quietly situated on a side road, so the unexpected sight of jaunty aluminium chairs and tables outside - and a glimpse of many wine bottles lining the walls behind the elegant shopfront - should gladden the hearts of first-time visitors sweeping around the corner from Griffith Avenue. Oak fittings have been used throughout, including the wine displays, and the chic little marble-topped tables used for lighter bites suit the old shop well - in the extension behind it, there are larger tables and space for groups to eat in comfort. Now, where cuts of meat were once displayed, there's a wonderful selection of charcuterie and cheese from Ireland and the continent: an Irish Plate offers a selection of ham, pastrami, Irish stout cured beef and Irish farmhouse cheeses, for example, while The Iberian Selection comprises Serrano ham, chorizo salamis, Mediterranean vegetables, olives and Manchego sheep's milk cheese - all served with speciality breads - and a Children's Selection educates the younger palate with the likes of hot panini with smoked turkey and Emmenthal cheese. A short blackboard menu of hot dishes and specials (penne pasta with tomato, spicy meat & aubergine for example), plus a daily soup, a range of salads, gourmet sandwiches, wraps, hot paninis, pastries and classic café desserts (and luscious ice creams from Murphys of Dingle) complement the charcuterie and cheese which have the gravitas to balance the collection of wines lining the walls - and, in addition to the wine list, which changes regularly, you can choose any bottle to have with your food at a very modest corkage charge. There's also an extensive drinks menu, offering speciality coffees and teas, and some unusual beverages, like Lorina French lemonade. **Seats 43** (outside seating 18). No reservations. Children welcome, Toilets wheelchair accessible. Open daily: Mon-Wed, 9am-7pm; Thu-Sat, 9am-8.30pm, Sun 10am-7pm (last food orders half an hour before closing). 14 House Wines (€15.95-€22.95) & 160 wines available from the wine shop at €6 corkage. Closed 4 days over Christmas, Jan 1, Good Friday. MasterCard, Visa, Laser. **Directions:** Off Griffith Avenue, near junction with Mobhi Road.

COUNTY DUBLIN

Dun Laoghaire

⊕ RESTAURANT

Cavistons Seafood Restaurant

59 Glasthule Road Dun Laoghaire Co Dublin **Tel: 01 280 9245**
Fax: 01 284 4054 Email: info@cavistons.com Web: www.cavistons.com

Caviston's of Sandycove has long been a mecca for lovers of good food - here you will find everything that is wonderful, from organic vegetables to farmhouse cheeses, cooked meats to specialist oils and other exotic items. But it was always for fish and shellfish that Cavistons were especially renowned - even providing a collection of well-thumbed recipe books for on-the-spot reference. At their little restaurant next door, they serve an imaginative range of healthy seafood dishes influenced by various traditions and all washed down by a glass or two from a very tempting little wine list. Cavistons food is simple, colourful, perfectly cooked - it speaks volumes for how good seafood can be. Start with Cavistons smoked salmon plate, perhaps, or tasty panfried crab and sweetcorn cakes with red pepper mayonnaise, then follow with seared king scallops with a saffron and basil sauce - or a more traditional panfried haddock fillet with tartare sauce. Gorgeous desserts include timeless favourites like chocolate brownies with chocolate sauce & cream, or you can finish with a selection of Cavistons cheeses (they sell a great range in the shop). Don't expect bargain basement prices though - this may be a small lunch time restaurant, but the prime ingredients are costly - and it's a class act. Children welcome. **Seats 28.** L 12-3. A la carte. SC discretionary. Closed Sun, Mon & Christmas/New Year. Amex, Diners, MasterCard, Visa, Laser. **Directions:** Between Dun Laoghaire and Dalkey, 5 mins. walk from Glasthule DART station.

Dun Laoghaire
🍺 ATMOSPHERIC PUB/CAFÉ

The Purty Kitchen

3-5 Old Dunleary Road Dun Laoghaire Co Dublin
Tel: 01 284 3576 Fax: 01 284 3576
Email: info@purtykitchen.com Web: www.purtykitchen.com

Established in 1728 - making it the second oldest pub in Dublin (after The Brazen Head) and the oldest in Dun Laoghaire - this attractive old place has seen some changes of late, but its essential character remains, with dark wooden floors, good lighting, large mirrors and a good buzz. It's well set up for enjoyment of the bar food for which it has earned a fine reputation, with shiny dark wooden tables (a candle on each) and inviting menus which still have old favourites like the famous Purty Seafood Chowder and Purty Seafood Platter, but also good steaks and more creative seafood dishes, presented attractively on different shaped plates. Although the cooking has been a little inconsistent recently (the menu is perhaps too long, and there are blackboard specials too), it is always an enjoyable bar food experience and, at its best, this is lovely fresh food with a home cooked flavour. A list of House Favourites also includes some dishes that have stood the test of time, such as a traditional breakfast, home-made beef burgers and seafood quiche, all at reasonable prices. A garden terrace is a great alternative to the bar in summer, and there is a Food & Wine Emporium specialising in artisan Irish foods. Live music (Tue & Fri). Bar food 12 noon-9.30pm daily. Veg menu also available. Toilets wheelchairr accessible. House wine from €15 (€4.50 per glass). Live music Tue and Fri evenings. Closed 25 Dec, Good Friday Amex, Diners, MasterCard, Visa, Laser. **Directions:** On left approaching Dun Laoghaire from Dublin by the coast road.

Dun Laoghaire
Ⓔ RESTAURANT

Rasam

18-19 Glasthule Road Dun Laoghaire Co Dublin **Tel: 01 230 0600**
Fax: 01 230 1000 Email: info@rasam.ie Web: www.rasam.ie

Above The Eagle pub in Glasthule, this is an appealing dining space, impressively decorated in dark teak, with traditional Balinese furnishings and generous, well-spaced tables. Rasam offers something different from other Indian restaurants, as the cuisine is lighter and more varied - the menu is laid out like a wine list with the name of the dish and a brief (but clear) description underneath and the name of the region it comes from opposite, alongside the (surprisingly reasonable) price. You might begin with a modestly priced Tamatar Shorba, a chilled Indian tomato soup, from Hyderabad, or Jhinga Ajwaini (jumbo prawns with lemon juice and carom seeds, grilled in the tandoor, served with tomato coulis), while main courses might include a relatively simple Kori Gassi, from Coorg (chicken simmered in a spicy masala of brown onions and tomatoes, with a special blend of coorgi masala) and a large selection dish of lamb, fish and chicken, Mansahari Thali, which is very good value. Many special ingredients are used in the cooking here, including rare herbs and spices unique to the restaurant, all ground freshly each day; everything is made on the premises, including the poppodums. For a great Indian dining experience, Rasam has earned a place at the top of the league. The wine list is thoughtfully selected for compatibility with Indian food. Children welcome. **Seats 75.** Reservations required. D daily, 5-11 (Sun 4.30-10.30). Closed 25-26 Dec, Good Fri. **Directions:** Over The Eagle pub.

Dun Laoghaire
⊚ RESTAURANT

Roly @ The Pavilion

8 The Pavilion Dun Laoghaire Co Dublin
Tel: 01 2360 286 Fax: 01 2360 288

Roly Saul's purpose-built restaurant just across from the Royal St George Yacht Club is full of light, with gleaming contemporary decor balanced by some traditional gilded mirrors and light and dark leather upholstery (ageing to a deep burgundy); different levels and a mixture of banquettes and high-back chairs are used to break the area up and give it interest and semi-private areas. It's a favourite haunt of many from the area (and beyond) who appreciate both the hospitality and the work of a youthful kitchen team, who relish the challenge of creating international cuisine. True to his philosophy of offering an accessible wine list and real value, Roly has managed to keep the (French) house wines (and many other good bottles) at fair prices. The set lunch menu is especially good value. Outside eating area. Air conditioning. Not Suitable for children under 7 after 7 pm. **Seats 100.** L&D daily. Closed 25-27 Dec, Good Fri. Amex, MasterCard, Visa, Laser. **Directions:** Opposite Railway Station.

Howth
⊚ RESTAURANT

Aqua Restaurant

1 West Pier Howth Co Dublin **Tel: 01 8320 690** / 1850 34 64 64
Fax: 01 8320 687 Email: dine@aqua.ie Web: www.aqua.ie

Previously a yacht club, this is now a fine contemporary restaurant with plenty of window tables to take advantage of sea views westwards, towards Malahide, and take in the island of Ireland's Eye to the north. Behind a glass screen, head chef Brian Daly and his team provide entertainment as well as zesty cooking of colourful food that is cooked with panache and thoughtfully, but quite simply, presented - a refreshing change from the overworked presentation in many restaurants at the moment. What was once a snooker room is now a characterful bar with a unique blend of original features and modern additions - with an open fire and comfortable seating, it has retained a cosy, clubby atmosphere and is a lovely place to relax before or after your meal . Brian Daly's style of cooking is strong, simple and modern; seafood is the natural choice her and menus vary daily depending on the catch, but dry aged steak - with grilled peppers, roasted baby potatoes, balsamic vinegar and extra virgin olive oil, perhaps - is also a speciality. Menus offer a pleasing repertoire of broadly Cal-Ital origin - crostini of Serrano ham with rocket, asparagus & extra virgin oil, char-grilled breast of chicken with roasted corn salsa, red pepper coulis, herb oil - although changes could be introduced more often with benefit, to give new choices to a loyal local clientèle. The waterside location, well-sourced ingredients, skilful cooking and solicitous service all make dining at Aqua a pleasure; à la carte menus are pricey but well-balanced set menus for early dinner, lunch and the popular jazz lunch on Sunday all offer very good value. **Seats 100.** D Tue-Sun 5.30-10.30, Sun 6-9.30; L Sun 12.30-4 (Bar L Tue-Sat, 1-3). Early D €29.95 (5.30-7), Set Sun L €29.95. Also à la carte. House wine €21.95, SC discretionary. Closed Mon, 25/26/27 Dec, Good Fri. Amex, MasterCard, Visa, Laser. **Directions:** Left along pier after Howth DART Station.

Howth

N € RESTAURANT

Cibo

Main Street Howth Co Dublin **Tel:** 01 839 6344

Developed from a successful meals-to-go business on the Howth harbour front, Brian Hearne's
all day restaurant achieved instant popularity with
discerning diners of all ages when it moved up to
larger premises in the centre of the village, to
become a fully-fledged restaurant. Informal easy-
going dining out is the aim, with the emphasis on
high quality ingredients, simple meals - and value
for money. Gourmet pizzas are a speciality, also
delicious salads, charcuterie, hot dishes of the
day and classic desserts - menus are not exten-
sive, but the high quality of ingredients wins the day every time. Breads are not made on the
premises, but are impeccably sourced - from the Guilbaud bakery, no less. No reservations are
accepted, but customers waiting for a table in the evening are directed across the road to the smart
contemporary bar **Bá Mizu** at the **Baily Hotel** (www.baily.com), and will be called when a table is
available. Concise, well-chosen wine list. MasterCard, Visa. **Directions:** In the centre of Howth village,
opposite the Baily Hotel.

Howth # King Sitric Fish Restaurant & Accommodation

☆ 🍷 👁 RESTAURANT WITH ROOMS

East Pier Howth Co Dublin
Tel: 01 832 5235 Fax: 01 839 2442
Email: info@kingsitric.ie Web: www.kingsitric.ie

SEAFOOD RESTAURANT OF THE YEAR

Named after an 11th century Norse King of Dublin who
had close links with Howth and was a cousin of the
legendary Brian Boru, Aidan and Joan MacManus' striking
harbourside establishment is one of Dublin's longest established
fine dining restaurants. The bright and airy first floor restaurant
takes full advantage of the sea and harbour views, which are especially enjoyable on summer evenings and at lunch time and, from
this East Pier site, chef-patron Aidan MacManus can keep an eye
on his lobster pots in Balscadden Bay on one side and the fishing
boats coming into harbour on the other. Aidan is well known for his
dedication to quality produce, and informative notes on menu
covers state the restaurant's commitment to local producers, some
of whom are named - and gives a listing of Irish fish in six
languages. Specialities worth travelling for include a luscious red
velvet crab bisque, crab mayonnaise, and calmar frites with tartare
or tomato sauce; less well known seafood, such as locally fished
razor shell clams in garlic butter, often shares the menu with classics like sole meunière and Dublin
lawyer (lobster with whiskey sauce) - and, in winter, lovers of game also wend their way here for treats
on both lunch and dinner menus. Farmhouse cheeses and lovely desserts are always worth leaving
room for - the house dessert, meringue Sitric, may even be seen by some as a challenge. And Aidan
MacManus oversees one of the country's finest wine lists, with special strengths in Chablis, Burgundy
and Alsace. A special feature of the King Sitric is a temperature controlled wine cellar on the ground
floor, where tastings are held. It is cleverly incorporated into the reception area, with only a glass door
between them, so diners can enjoy the ambience while having an aperitif. The house wine, Pinot Blanc
Cuvée Les Amours Hugel (a special reserve for the King Sitric) is outstanding for both quality and
value, and a perfect match for his delicious fish cooking. Although this is a fine dining restaurant,
Aidan and Joan MacManus work hard to keep prices accessible - lunch is especially good value, also
their Special Value Menu (D Mon-Thu, no time restriction). The King Sitric received the Guide's Wine
List of the Year Award in 2001 and the restaurant operates a Food & Wine Club off-season. Banqueting
(65). **Seats 65** (private room, 30). Air conditioning. L Mon-Fri,12.30-2.15; D Mon-Sat, 6.30-10. Set
L from €29. 'Value' D €30 (Mon-Thu all year, no time restrictions); 4-course Set D €55; also à la
carte; house wine from €23; SC discretionary (12.5% parties 8+). Closed L Sat, all Sun, bank hols.
Accommodation: There are eight lovely rooms, all with sea views and individually designed bathrooms.
Rooms 8 (2 superior, all no-smoking). B&B from €72.50 pps, ss €32.50. Amex, MasterCard, Visa,
Laser, Switch. **Directions:** Far end of the harbour front, facing the east pier.

Malahide
☆ RESTAURANT

Bon Appetit

9 St James Terrace Malahide Co Dublin
Tel: 01 8450 314 Fax: 01 8450 314
Email: info@bonappetit.ie Web: www.bonappetit.ie

féile bia In the basement of a Georgian terrace near the marina, Patsy McGuirk's highly-regarded restaurant is warmly decorated, with a welcome emphasis on comfort and an interesting collection of local watercolours. Patsy McGuirk is a fine chef in the classic French tradition, occasionally tempered by Mediterranean and modern Irish influences, and years of dedication in the kitchen have produced a long list of specialities. Fish cookery probably tops the bill, and seafood, mostly from nearby Howth, is very tempting: fresh prawn bisque with cognac is a favourite, and a long-established house speciality is Sole Creation McGuirk (whole boned black sole, filled with turbot and prawns, in a mustard cream sauce), a dish so gloriously old-fashioned that it's now come full circle - alternatively, classical sole on the bone is presented whole at the table, then re-presented bone-free and neatly reassembled. Delicious roast crispy duckling Grand Marnier on a potato & herb stuffing is another speciality, also ostrich - medallions, perhaps, served on red cabbage champ with onion marmalade and port wine jus - and steaks, and lamb from Wicklow or Kilkenny, are perennial favourites too. It's worth leaving room for pretty desserts, usually including some with fruit: fresh sweet pineapple boat with a home-made sorbet is typical, or there's cheese - Stilton, perhaps, or smoked Gubbeen, served traditionally with celery grapes and biscuits - and petits fours with your coffee. A fine wine list has its heart in France; there are helpful tasting notes and a special selection of a dozen or so Wines of the Month, as well as about ten fairly priced house wines. While not inexpensive, prices have held steady at the Bon Appetit, and the set lunch menu is particularly good value. Restaurants like this, in the classic tradition, are increasingly precious these days: long may it remain to restore us. Not suitable for children after 9pm. Booking essential, especially for dinner. Small weddings catered for. **Seats 60** (private room, 24). Air conditioning. L Mon-Fri.12.30-2, D Mon-Sat 7-10; Set L €25, Set D €48, also à la carte; house wine from €22; SC discretionary. Closed Sun, bank hols & several days at Christmas & a week before Easter. Amex, Diners, MasterCard, Visa, Laser. **Directions:** Coming from Dublin go through the lights and turn left into St James's Terrace at Malahide Garda Station.

Malahide Area
🏛 COUNTRY HOUSE

Belcamp Hutchinson

Carrs Lane Malahide Road Balgriffin Dublin 17
Tel: 01 846 0843 Fax: 01 848 5703
Email: belcamphutchinson@eircom.net Web: www.belcamphutchinson.com

Dating back to 1786, this impressive house just outside Malahide takes its name from the original owner, Francis Hely-Hutchinson, 3rd Earl of Donoughmore. It is set in large grounds, with interesting gardens, giving it a very away-from-it-all country atmosphere - yet Belcamp Hutchinson is only about half an hour from Dublin city centre (off peak) and 15 minutes to the airport. The present owners, Doreen Gleeson and Karl Waldburg, have renovated the house sensitively: high ceilinged, graciously proportioned rooms have retained many of their original features and are furnished and decorated in keeping with their age. Bedrooms are very comfortable, with thoughtfully appointed bathrooms and views over the gardens and countryside. Although its convenient location makes this an ideal place to stay on arrival or when leaving Ireland, a one-night stay won't do justice to this lovely and hospitable place. No dinner is served, but the restaurants (and good shopping) of Malahide are nearby. Walled garden; maze. Golf, equestrian, walking, garden visits, tennis and sailing are all nearby. Not suitable for children under 10. Pets welcome. **Rooms 6** (all with full bath & overbath shower). B&B €70 pps, no ss. Closed 20 Dec-1 Feb. MasterCard, Visa, Laser, **Directions:** From city centre, take Malahide Road; past Campions pub, 1st lane on left (sign on right pointing up lane).

Portmarnock
🏛☆ HOTEL/RESTAURANT

Portmarnock Hotel & Golf Links

Strand Road Portmarnock Co Dublin
Tel: 01 846 0611 Fax: 01 846 1876
Email: sales@portmarnock.com Web: www.portmarnock.com

Originally owned by the Jameson family of whiskey fame, Portmarnock Hotel and Golf Links enjoys a wonderful beachside position overlooking the islands of Lambay and Ireland's Eye. Very close to the airport, and only eleven miles from Dublin city centre, the hotel seems to offer the best of every world - the peace and convenience of the location and a magnificent 18 hole Bernhard Langer-designed links course. Public areas, including an impressive foyer, are bright and spacious, with elegant modern decor and a relaxed atmosphere.

The Jameson Bar, in the old house, has character and there's also an informal **Links Bar and Restaurant** next to the golf shop (12-10 daily). Accommodation is imaginatively designed so that all rooms have sea or golf course views, and all - including some in the original house which are furnished with antiques, two with four-posters and executive rooms with balconies or bay windows - are furnished to a high standard of comfort, with excellent bathrooms. Conference/banqueting (350/250) Business centre. Golf (18). Oceana, health & beauty: gym, sauna, steam rooms & a wide range of treatments. Children welcome (under 4 free in parents' room, cots available without charge, baby sitting arranged). No pets. Garden. **Rooms 98** (14 executive, 61 no-smoking, 32 ground floor, 3 disabled). Lift. 24 hour room service. B&B €157.50 pps, ss about €75. Open all year. **Osborne Restaurant:** Named after the artist Walter Osborne, who painted many of his most famous pictures in the area including the view from the Jameson house, the restaurant is in a semi-basement overlooking gardens at the side of the hotel - and first-time visitors may not find it easily, so inquire at reception. The room is very formal in a traditional style, with rather many busy patterns for contemporary tastes, but beautifully appointed tables and very professional, mostly French, staff who anticipate every requirement from the moment of arrival. Head chef Mark Doe's menus are constructed with the international traveller in mind, offering about eight dishes on each course and using the best quality ingredients available - especially seafood from the nearby fishing port of Howth including, typically, a baked parcel of scallops, served as a starter with pea purée and herb velouté. Perfect cooking and balance of flavours over a wide range of dishes demonstrates the presence of an outstanding talent in the kitchen - highlights on a recent visit included a memorable salad of char-grilled aubergine & rocket served with a chilled goats cheese & pine nut terrine and smoked yellow pepper oil - for this alone a visit would be worthwhile, especially if you are vegetarian. Tempting desserts from pastry chef Eric Groyet may include refreshing fruits, as in a speciality of warm polenta & lemon cake grilled peaches, mascarpone cheese & pistachio biscotti. Outstanding cooking and very professional service make this an exceptional dining experience, although presentation is notable for its formality - regimented removal of cloches remains the norm, for example. An extensive wine list matches the food and service and, considering the high quality offered, an evening at The Osborne Restaurant is good value for money. Air conditioning. **Seats 80** (private room, 20). D only Tue-Sat, 7-10. Set D from €47, Tasting Menu from €50-60. A la carte available; house wine from €19.85; SC discretionary. Closed Sun, Mon. Links Brasserie open 12-10 daily Amex, MasterCard, Visa, Laser. **Directions:** On the coast in Portmarnock.

Skerries
🅔 RESTAURANT/GUESTHOUSE

Red Bank House & Restaurant

5-7 Church Street Skerries Co Dublin
Tel: 01 849 1005 Fax: 01 849 1598
Email: sales@redbank.ie Web: www.redbank.ie

féile bia Golfing breaks are a speciality at Terry McCoy's renowned restaurant with accommodation in the characterful fishing port of Skerries. The restaurant is in a converted banking premises, which adds to the atmosphere (even the old vault has its uses - as a wine cellar) and Terry is an avid supporter of local produce, with fresh seafood from Skerries harbour (including local razor fish) providing the backbone of his menu. Menus, written in Terry's inimitable style, are a joy to read and a statement at the end reads: "All items on the menu are sourced from Irish producers and suppliers. There are too many items for us to list all ingredients after each dish but you can take my word for it, we use local Irish because it's the freshest & so the best." Just so - a few places taking pride in 'organics' that have come half way round the world before arriving on the plate could learn a lot from Terry. Dishes conceived and cooked with generosity have names of local relevance - grilled goat's cheese St. Patrick, for example, is a reminder that the saint once lived on Church Island off Skerries - plainly cooked food is also provided on request, and dishes suitable for vegetarians are marked on the menu. The dessert trolley is legendary - a large space should be left if pudding is to be part of your meal. An informative, fairly priced wine list includes a wide selection of house wines, and a good choice of half bottles. - and the early dinner and Sunday lunch menus offer great value. **Seats 60** (private room,10). D Mon-Sat, 6.30-9.45; L Sun only, 12.30-4.30. Early D €30 (Mon-Fri, 6.30-7.30); Set D €36/40, Gourmet Menu €45. A la carte also available. 4 house wines €20; no sc. Children welcome. Closed D Sun. Restaurant only closed 24-27 Dec. **Accommodation:** 18 fine, comfortably furnished guest rooms have all the amenities normally expected of an hotel. While in the area, allow time to visit Skerries Mills (working windmills (Tel: 01 849 5208)) and the beautifully located Ardgillan Castle and Victorian Gardens (Tel: 01 849 2212) nearby, where there are tea rooms. Facilities for private parties (50). Gourmet Golf breaks - up to 40 golf courses within 20 minutes drive. Children under 4 free in parents' room (cots available free of charge). Pets permitted in certain areas. **Rooms 18** (all superior & no-smoking). B&B €60 pps, ss €15 (DB&B rate is good value at €90 pps). Accommodation open all year. Amex, Diners, MasterCard, Visa, Laser. **Directions:** Opposite AIB Bank in Skerries.

Skerries

€ BAR/RESTAURANT

Stoop Your Head

Harbour Road Skerries Co Dublin **Tel: 01 849 1144**

After a quiet off season drink a few doors along at Joe May's, there can be no greater pleasure in north Dublin than to slip into 'Stoops' for some of Andy Davies' mainly seafood cooking. 'Fresh, simple and wholesome' is how he describes his food, and who could want any more than that? If it's busy you may have to wait at the little bar - where you can opt to eat if you like, or have a look at the menu while waiting for a table (they seem to turn over fairly fast). The surroundings are simple - chunky wooden tables, closely packed - and the menu is not elaborate but there is plenty to choose from, and there are blackboard specials every day too; what could be more delightful than starters of dressed crab, or moules marinière - or perhaps a classic fresh prawn Marie Rose? Prawns are landed in Skerries and a speciality - and like crab claws, are offered as starters or main courses, in irresistible garlic butter. You don't have to eat seafood here - there are other choices like Asian chicken salad, or pasta dishes or even fillet steak medallions - but it would be a pity to miss it. Super fresh and deliciously simple, it's a treat. **Seats 30** (outdoor seating, 20). No reservations. Children welcome. L & D daily: L 12-3, D 5.30-10 (Sun D 4-8). House wine €16. Closed 25 Dec & Good Fri. Visa. **Directions:** On the harbour front in Skerries.

Stillorgan

🌸 RESTAURANT

China-Sichuan Restaurant

4 Lower Kilmacud Road Stillorgan Co Dublin **Tel: 01 288 4817**
Fax: 01 288 0882 Email: Web:

The Hui family's unique restaurant just across the road from the Stillorgan Shopping Centre runs in co-operation with the cultural exchange programme of the State-run China Sichuan Catering Service Company, which supplies chefs and special spices direct from Sichuan province. Since 1986 their refusal to 'bland-down' the style to suit local tastes has earned the restaurant widespread recognition for authenticity, and it was the Guide's Ethnic Restaurant of the Year in 2005. Strong flavours are a characteristic of Sichuan cuisine, and spicy and chilli-hot dishes are identified here on menus - 'Bon Bon Chicken' for example, is a dish of cold chicken shreds in a hot and spicy sauce - but spicing can be varied to suit individual tastes. Garlic dishes are also very typical of the house -and a speciality well worth seeking out is smoked duckling in Sichuan style: seasoned duck is smoked over bay leaves, camphor wood and black Chinese tea leaves, then served hot with plum sauce as a dip; count your blessings when enjoying this dish, as it is not widely available, even in London. While set menus are relatively limited (especially at lunch time), the à la carte offers plenty to tempt the most jaded palate including a wide range of seafood dishes and a particularly strong vegetarian section. * China Sichuan is planning to relocate to new premises in the late autumn of 2006. Children welcome. **Seats 60.** Reservations required. Air conditioning. Toilets wheelchair accessible. L Mon-Fri 12.30-2, L Sun 1-2.30. D daily 6-10.30 (6-11 Sun). Set L about €16 (Sun €17), Set D about €36; à la carte available; house wine €20; SC10%. Closed L Sat, 25-27 Dec & Good Fri. Amex, MasterCard, Visa, Laser. **Directions:** 5 miles south from city, through Stillorgan main road, turn right from Lower Kilmacud Road (200 yards from Stillorgan shopping centre).

Swords
 HOTEL

Roganstown Golf & Country Club Hotel

Swords Co Dublin **Tel: 01 8433118** Fax: 8433303
Email: info@roganstown.com Web: www.roganstown.com

Built around the original Roganstown House and situated conveniently for all the many golf courses in the area and only a few minutes' drive from Dublin Airport, this recently opened hotel enjoys a country setting and is the only golf hotel in the area also offering gym / leisure facilities and beauty therapies - a great amenity for local residents as well as an appealing base for golfers or those using the airport. The Christy O'Connor Junior designed course ('a masterpiece of skill and tactical design') is a major attraction, but the restaurant, **McLoughlins**, is also attracting favourable attention - add a high level of comfort and something of a country house ambience and it's easy to see why this new hotel is already making a mark. Business and conference facilities available. **Rooms 52.** B&B from €85 pps. Midweek specials offered. Open all year. Amex, Diners, MasterCard, Visa, Laser. **Directions:** 5 minutes drive from Swords village.

COUNTY CARLOW

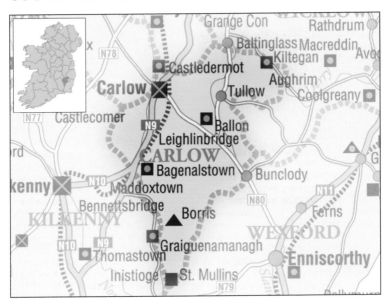

Bagenalstown

🏛 COUNTRY HOUSE

Kilgraney House

Borris Road Bagenalstown Co Carlow
Tel: 059 977 5283 Fax: 059 977 5595
Email: info@kilgraneyhouse.com Web: www.kilgraneyhouse.com

In a lovely site overlooking the Barrow Valley, Bryan Leech and Martin Marley's charming late Georgian house - which (encouragingly) takes its name from the Irish 'cill greíne', meaning 'sunny hill or wood' - is set in extensive wooded grounds that feature, amongst many other delights, a croquet lawn and fine cut-stone outbuildings. It is a serene and restful place with beautiful walks, and Altamont gardens nearby; Bryan and Martin have a great love of gardens - a recent project has been the development of their monastic herb gardens, and the kitchen garden provides plenty of good things for Bryan to transform into delicious dinners, in creative contemporary cooking that makes full use of local and artisan produce, including Lavistown cheese from nearby Kilkenny. A speciality is their own home-smoked duck (with noodle salad and soy & mirin dressing, perhaps), and Bryan also makes a very beautiful dish of wild Slaney salmon wrapped in nori and wasabi, with sauce vierge, and your breakfast next morning will include other local foods. But it is for the sheer sense of style pervading the house that it is most famous - Bryan and Martin's enjoyment in its restoration and furnishing is abundantly clear: elegant, yes, but with a great sense of fun too. Dinner can be shared with other guests at a communal table, or served at separate tables; a short, informative wine list is chosen with care - and non-residents are welcome by reservation. An aroma spa has recently been opened at Kilgraney, offering a range of therapies and massages, for both men and women, including pregnancy treatments. Self-catering accommodation is also available, in two courtyard suites, the gate lodge and a recently restored cottage. Herbal treatment room (massage & aromatherapy). Small conferences. Not suitable for children under 12. **Rooms 8** (2 suites, 3 shower only, all no smoking). No dogs. B&B €70, ss about €10. D (non-residents welcome by reservation), 8 pm. Set 6-course D, €45. (Vegetarian meals or other special dietary requirements on request.) Wines from €20. Closed Sun-Thu off-season (Feb-Jun & Sep-Oct), closed Dec-Feb. Helipad. Amex, MasterCard, Visa, Laser. **Directions:** Just off the R705, halfway between Bagenalstown and Borris.

Bagenalstown
🍷 COUNTRY HOUSE

Lorum Old Rectory

Kilgraney Bagenalstown Co Carlow **Tel: 059 977 5282**
Fax: 059 977 5455 Email: info@lorum.com Web: www.lorum.com

Bobbie Smith's mid Victorian cut stone granite rectory was built for the Rev. William Smyth-King in 1864, and it now makes a warm and welcoming family home. Elegant and homely, there's a library as well as a lovely drawing room where guests can gather around the fire and relax; spacious accommodation includes one particularly impressive guest room with a four-poster- and all rooms are very comfortable, with big beds, phones and tea/coffee trays. But it is Bobbie Smith's easy hospitality that keeps bringing guests back: Bobbie, who is a member of the international chefs' association, Euro-Toques, is committed to using local produce and suppliers whenever possible and is renowned for delicious home cooking using mainly organic and home grown ingredients; rack of local lamb is a speciality, cooked with a honey, mustard & rosemary glaze, and residents have dinner at a long mahogany table, where wonderful breakfasts are also served. This relaxed place was the guide's Pet Friendly Establishment for 2000 and guests are still welcome to bring their own dogs, by arrangement. This area make as an ideal base for exploring the lush south-east of Ireland, and is close to many places of interest, including medieval Kilkenny, Altamont Gardens, New Ross (where river cruises are available, and you can see the famine ship Dunbrody), Kildare's National Stud and Japanese Gardens. Also close by is Gowran Park racecourse and activities such as golf and a riding school (offering both outdoor and indoor tuition). Dinner must be booked by 3 pm; a concise, well priced wine list with tasting notes is offered. Private parties/small conferences (10). Cycling. Own parking. Garden. Children welcome (under 5s free in parents' room). **Rooms** 5 (all en-suite). B&B €60-75 pps, ss €20. Dinner for residents by arrangement(8pm) € 40. Closed Dec/Jan/Feb. Amex, MasterCard, Visa, Laser. **Directions:** Midway between Borris & Bagenalstown on the R705.

Ballon
€ COUNTRY HOUSE

Sherwood Park House

Kilbride Ballon Co Carlow **Tel: 059 915 9117** Fax: 059 915 9355
Email: info@sherwoodparkhouse.ie Web: www.sherwoodparkhouse.ie

féile bia Built around 1700 by a Mr Arthur Baillie, this delightful Georgian farmhouse has sweeping views over the countryside and is next to the famous Altamont Gardens. Patrick and Maureen Owens, who have welcomed guests here since 1991, accurately describe it as "an accessible country retreat for anyone who enjoys candlelit dinners, brass and canopy beds, and the relaxing experience of eating out while staying in". Spacious accommodation is furnished in period style and thoughtful in the details that count - and Maureen takes pride in offering guests real home cooking based on the best of local produce, including "best locally produced Carlow beef and lamb, from Ballon Meats" and fish from Kilmore Quay. There's a lovely garden, Altamont Gardens are on the doorstep (just 5 minutes away on foot) and it's a good area for walking - and fishing the Slaney. Dinner is served at 8pm and is mainly for residents, although non-residents are welcome when there is room - and guests are welcome to bring their own wine and any other drinks.(Please give advance notice if you would like dinner.) Golf nearby. Private parties (max 16). Children welcome (no cot available). Pets permitted by arrangement. Garden. D €35 (BYO wine); non-residents welcome by reservation. **Rooms** 4 (all en-suite & no smoking). B&B €45/50pps, ss €15. Amex, MasterCard, Visa. **Directions:** Signed from the junction of the N80 and N81.

Borris

The Step House

€ GUESTHOUSE   66 Main Street Borris Co Carlow **Tel: 059 977 3209** Fax: 059 977 3395
Email: cait@thestephouse.com Web: www.thestephouse.com

Stylishly decorated and furnished in period style, with antiques throughout, James and Cait Coady's attractive old house has well-proportioned reception rooms including a fine dining room (used for breakfast) and a matching drawing room that overlooks the back garden. Comfortable, elegant bedrooms include one with a four-poster and all are furnished to a high standard with smart shower rooms, TV and tea/coffee facilities. The renovation and upgrading of this fine old house has been accomplished beautifully, including the conversion of the whole of the lower ground floor to make a magnificent kitchen of character, and a relaxed living room area with direct access to the garden - and a sunny decking area beside the dining room allows guests to enjoy breakfast outdoors on fine mornings. *At the time of going to press, The Coadys (who also own the bar next door - and one of Ireland's finest classic pubs, **Tynans Bridge Bar**, in Kilkenny city) are developing a hotel, which is due for completion some time in 2006; meanwhile, The Step House will continue as before and guest accommodation is also available in a number of self-catering houses and apartments, which are available for short term letting, or B&B. NB: there are several flights of stairs, including steps up to the front door. Not suitable for children under 10. Pets permitted. Fishing, walking, garden. Own secure parking (6). **Rooms 5** (all no-smoking & shower only). B&B €45pps, ss10. Closed 20 Dec-20 Mar. MasterCard, Visa, Laser. **Directions:** From main Carlow-Kilkenny road, take turning to Bagenalstown. 8 miles to Borris.

Carlow

Barrowville Townhouse

🍸 € GUESTHOUSE   Kilkenny Road Carlow Co Carlow **Tel: 059 914 3324** Fax: 059 914 1953
Email: barrowtownhouse@eircom.net Web: www.barrowvillehouse.com

Former hoteliers Marie and Randal Dempsey have run this exceptionally comfortable and well-managed guesthouse just a few minutes walk from the town centre since 1989. It is fine period house, set in lovely gardens (where guests are welcome to relax) and there is also a particularly pleasant and comfortable residents' drawing room, with an open fire, grand piano and plenty to read. The house is immaculately maintained and bedrooms - which inevitably vary in size and character due to the age of the building - are comfortable and stylishly furnished with a mixture of antiques and fitted furniture, as well as direct dial phones, tea/coffee trays (for which there is a small charge, if used) and television. Good housekeeping and thoughtfully designed, well-finished bathrooms contribute greatly to a generally high standard of comfort. Marie Dempsey is renowned for her excellent breakfasts (buffet or traditional Irish, cooked to order) served in a handsome conservatory (complete with a large vine) overlooking the peaceful back garden. Barrowville was our Guesthouse of the Year for 2000. Turndown service available. Garden. Private parking (11). Not suitable for children under 15. No pets. **Rooms 7** (2 shower only, all no-smoking). B&B €47.50pps, ss €12.50. Open all year. Amex, MasterCard, Visa. **Directions:** South side of Carlow town on the N9.

Carlow

 CAFÉ/PUB

Lennon's Café Bar

121 Tullow Street Carlow Co Carlow **Tel: 059 913 1575**

téile bia Sinéad Byrne runs this stylish modern café-bar with her husband, Liam, and their deliciously healthy, reasonably priced food is a hit with both locals and visitors to the town. In a manner reminiscent of that great Kerry speciality, the pub that gradually develops into a restaurant at the back without actually having a dedicated restaurant area, the design of the bar - which has a striking metal spiral staircase at the back - helps the atmosphere to shift into café gear as you move through it. Simple, uncluttered tables and speedy service of jugs of iced water bode well for menus that include a host of wholesome dishes ranging from full-flavoured soups and home-baked bread to hot specials like steak & kidney pie with champ, or cod & mussel bake. Consideration is shown to special dietary requirements - vegetarians are highlighted, gluten free bread is available for coeliacs - and everything is really wholesome and freshly made to order from top quality ingredients, with some local sources named on the menu. Home-made desserts might include more-ish hazelnut meringue roulade with raspberry sauce, perhaps, or hot apple crumble. Winner of our Happy Heart Eat Out Award 2003. Breakfast 10-11; L Mon-Fri,12-3, Sat 12-4. Now opening dinner Wed-Sat 5-9 a la carte menu Toilets wheelchair accessible.Closed 25 Dec, Good Fri. **Directions:** At Junction of Tullow Street & Potato Market.

St Mullins

€ ◉ B&B

Mulvarra House

St Mullins Co Carlow **Tel: 051 424936** Fax: 051 424969
Email: info@mulvarra.com Web: www.mulvarra.com

Harold and Noreen Ardill's friendly modern house is in a stunning location overlooking the River Barrow above the ancient and picturesque little harbour of St Mullins and, although it may seem unremarkable from the road, this relaxing place is full of surprises. Comfortably furnished bedrooms have balconies to take full advantage of views of the romantic Barrow Valley, for example, and, not only is there the luxury of (limited) room service, but even a range of treatments (massage, mud wraps, refresher facials) to help guests unwind from the stresses of everyday life and make the most of this magical place. Noreen - a keen self-taught cook - prepares dinners for residents to enjoy in the dining room which also overlooks the river: quality produce, much of it local, is used in home-made soups, salmon mousse, fresh Barrow salmon, baked ham and Baileys bread & butter pudding, all of which are favourites, although menus are varied to suit guests' preferences. Genuinely hospitable and reasonably priced, this is a tranquil place where the hosts want their guests to relax and make the most of every moment. Special breaks available (eg 2 nights B&B, 1 D & 2 treatments, from €165 pps). Walking; fishing; treatments/mini spa (must be pre-booked). Pets permitted by arrangement. Garden. Children welcome (under 2s free in parents' room; cot available without charge; baby sitting arranged). Room service (limited hours). **Rooms 5** (all en-suite, shower-only & no-smoking; full bath in shared bathroom available to any guest). B&B €34, ss €6. Residents D nightly, €30 (7.30pm, by reservation). House wine €20. Closed Mid Dec-Mid Jan. MasterCard, Visa, Laser. **Directions:** 4.5 miles from Graiguenamanagh; take R702 from Borris, turn right in Glynn; signposted from Glynn.

COUNTY CAVAN

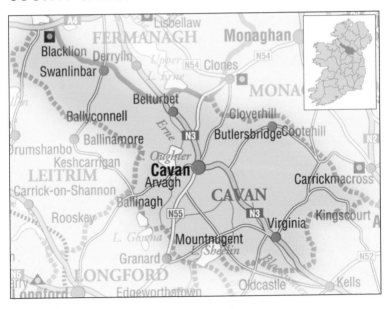

Blacklion

★ ☙ RESTAURANT WITH ROOMS

NATURAL FOOD AWARD

MacNean House & Bistro

Main Street Blacklion Co Cavan
Tel: 071 985 3404 Fax: 071 985 3404

féile bia Some of the best cooking in Ireland is to be found at Neven Maguire's family restaurant in this little border town, and a meal here is definitely worth a special journey. Despite his popularity as a TV chef, author of best-selling cookbooks and celebrity supporter of food events all over Ireland, Neven shows no sign of being distracted from the restaurant and his cooking is better than ever: exact, perfectly judged food, that makes the most of meticulously sourced ingredients from the local and artisan producers he so strongly advocates, is an experience to treasure. Menus, which are admirably simply worded, include a wonderful 10-course Tasting Menu, (with fish and vegetarian variations available), as well as a Sunday lunch which draws admirers from all over the country. The restaurant is not large but it has recently been refurbished, with elegant high-backed chairs, immaculate linen and restrained creamy white crockery, and will have a small bar for the 2006 season, all creating the right ambience for full enjoyment of Neven's exquisite food. Specialities are too numerous to mention, but main dishes are interspersed with all the treats that are part of the dining experience in the grandest restaurants - meals begin with an absolutely gorgeous assortment of warm yeast breads and dipping oil, and there will also be pre-starters, pre-desserts and superb petits fours. To give just one typical dish: caramelised pork belly is a speciality, and might be served with with foie gras, celeriac remoulade and apple sorbet - an inspired dish, marrying a Cinderella cut of meat with the richness of foie gras, and the lightly spiced apple sorbet is a stroke of genius. Desserts have always been a particular passion for Neven and it's a must to leave a little room for one of his skilfully crafted confections - the grand finale is just that in this case and, here again, an extra selection of Chef's Specials is offered, as well as the regular dessert menu. This is outstanding cooking, served with charm by family members - and it is exceptionally good value too, especially for Sunday lunch which combines elements of the traditional meal with more typical choices from other menus. A concise wine list leans towards France and includes eight house wines. Moderately priced accommodation is also offered (to be upgraded for 2006). **Seats 40.** D Thu-Sun (Tue-Sun in high season) 6.30-9.30pm (Sat 2 sittings: 6.30 & 9.30;

Sun to 8); L Sun only, 1-3.30, €27. D €55; vegetarian menu €35; also à la carte. House Wine from €17. Service discretionary. **Accommodation: Rooms 5** (all en-suite), €40 pps. Direct-dial phone, tea/coffee tray & TV in rooms. Children welcome; cot available free of charge. Pets allowed by arrangement. Establishment closed 2 weeks Christmas, 1 week Oct. MasterCard, Visa, Laser. **Directions:** On N17, main Belfast-Sligo road.

Cloverhill
 RESTAURANT WITH ROOMS

The Olde Post Inn
Cloverhill Co Cavan
Tel: 047 55555 Fax: 047 55111
Email: gearoidlynch@eircom.net Web: www.theoldepostinn.com

 Gearoid and Tara Lynch's restaurant is in an old stone building in a neatly landscaped garden which served as a post office until 1974 and, since then, has made an attractive and popular inn. Gearoid is a talented young chef and, with Tara managing front of house with efficiency and charm, they make a good team and, since taking over here in 2002, have earned a reputation for fine food and genuine hospitality that draws guests from well beyond the region. There's a pleasant rural atmosphere about the place, which has a proper bar to enjoy your pre/post-prandial drinks and an old-world style throughout, with bare walls, dark beams and simple wooden furniture - but, comfortably rustic as it may seem, that is far from the case in the kitchen, and elegantly-appointed tables with crisp white linen and gleaming glasses are a hint of the treats to come. Gearoid's route to Cloverhill has included time in some fine establishments - at least one of which lives on here, in a house speciality: 'Le Coq Hardi' chicken breast (stuffed with potato, apple, bacon & herbs, wrapped in bacon and served with an Irish whiskey sauce). A committed Euro-Toques chef, Gearoid sources ingredients with great care and his respect for regional and seasonal foods shows in many ways, notably in adaptations of traditional themes such as a delicious speciality starter of warm bacon and cabbage terrine with a baby leek cream sauce. This is a happy ship and the talent and dedication of a good kitchen team can produce some excellent cooking - made all the more enjoyable by the friendly, helpful service provided by local staff. The Olde Post Inn was the our Newcomer of the Year in 2004. Ample parking. **Seats 80** (private room 25); toilets wheelchair accessible. D Tue-Sat, 6.30-9.30 (Sun to 8.30), L Sun only, 12.30-3. Set D €48; also à la carte. Set Sun L €25. Closed Mon. Accommodation: There are six en-suite rooms at the inn; while not especially luxurious, they are comfortable and have been recently redecorated; most have full baths. Children welcome, under 4s free in parents' room. No pets. **Rooms 6** (2 shower only), B&B about €40 pps. Closed 24-26 Dec. Amex, MasterCard, Visa, Laser. **Directions:** 6 miles north of Cavan town: take N54 at Butlersbridge, 2 miles on right in Cloverhill village.

COUNTY CLARE

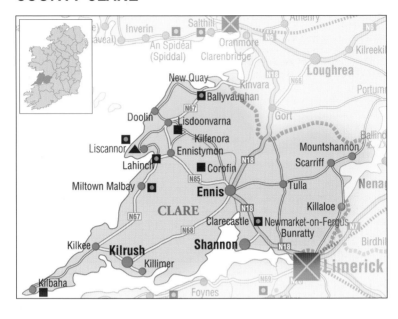

Ballyvaughan
🏛️👁️ COUNTRY HOUSE/RESTAURANT

Gregans Castle Hotel
Ballyvaughan Co Clare
Tel: 065 707 7005 Fax: 065 707 7111
Email: stay@gregans.ie Web: www.gregans.ie

Gregans Castle has a long and interesting history, going back to a tower house, or small castle, which was built by the O'Loughlen clan (the region's principal tribe) between the 10th and 17th centuries and is still intact. The present house dates from the late 18th century and has been added to many times; it was opened as a country house hotel in 1976 by Peter and Moira Haden who (true to the traditions of the house) continued to develop and improve it, together with their son Simon, who is now Managing Director. The exterior is grey and stark, in keeping with the lunar landscape of the surrounding Burren - the contrast between first impressions and the warmth, comfort and hospitality to be found within is one of the great joys of arriving at Gregans Castle. Peace and quiet are the dominant themes: spacious rooms are furnished to a very high standard, with excellent bathrooms and lovely countryside views - and deliberately left without the worldly interference of television. Yet this luxurious hotel is not too formal or at all intimidating; non-residents are welcome to drop in for lunch or afternoon tea in the Corkscrew Bar - named after a nearby hill road which, incidentally, provides the most scenic approach to Ballyvaughan. In fine weather guests can sit out beside the Celtic Cross rose garden and watch patches of sun and shade chasing across the hills. In the morning, allow time to enjoy an excellent breakfast. Children welcome (no concessions, but cot available, €15). No pets. All day room service. **Rooms 21** (3 suites, 3 junior suites) B&B €105 pps; ss €73. No service charge. **The Dining Room:** The restaurant is decorated in a rich country house style and elegantly furnished in keeping with the rest of the house. Most tables have lovely views over the Burren (where there can be very special light effects as the sun sets over Galway Bay on summer evenings) and dinner is often accompanied by a pianist or, more unusually, a hammer dulcimer. A commitment to using local and organic produce, when available, is stated on the menu - all fish is caught locally around Galway Bay, and Burren lamb and beef come from local butchers. Head chef Adrian O'Farrell's wide-ranging menus reflect this philosophy in fresh, colourful dishes that bend traditional values and contemporary style - in a starter of home cured gravadlax, for example, that is served with a caper & rocket salad, sesame tuile and lime coriander dressing, or a main course of slow braised shank of Burren lamb, with Pommes Anna, brunoise of garden vegetables and rosemary glaze. There is always a fine selection of local cheeses, with home-made biscuits - and organic produce is also a feature at breakfast (organic eggs from Hans & Ute Krewer in the East Burren, for example). The wine list is an interesting read and includes an impressive selection of organic and biodynamic wines, leading off with the Spanish house wines. Dinner is a treat at Gregans Castle, but they also offer an attractive short à la carte lunch menu (served in The Corkscrew Bar) and delicious Afternoon Teas too. **Seats 50** (Private Room, 32). Young children welcome before 7pm. D daily, 7-8.30; À la Carte. House wines from €24. Service charge discretionary. Short à la carte lunch is available in the Corkscrew Bar, 12-2.30 daily. Afternoon Tea, 3-5 daily. Hotel closed 1 Nov - late Mar. Amex, MasterCard, Visa, Laser. **Directions:** On N67, 3.25 miles south of Ballyvaughan.

Ballyvaughan
 GUESTHOUSE

Rusheen Lodge

Knocknagrough Ballyvaughan Co Clare
Tel: 065 707 7092 Fax: 065 707 7092
Email: rusheen@iol.ie Web: www.rusheenlodge.com

John and Rita McGann swapped houses with their daughter Karen, who now runs Rusheen Lodge to the high standards for which it is well known, and they live next door so there's no shortage of experienced hands nearby for very busy times - and, as it was John McGann's father, Jacko McGann, who discovered the Aillwee Cave, an immense network of caverns and waterfalls under the Burren which is now a major attraction in the area, the McGanns understand better than most the popularity of Ballyvaughan as a visitor destination. Fresh flowers in both the house and garden create a riot of colour in contrast to the overall green-greyness of the surrounding Burren, suggesting an oasis in a wilderness - which is just what Rusheen Lodge aims to provide. A 3-room executive suite introduced in 2002 has proved popular and all of the generously proportioned, well-appointed bedrooms have phones, tea/coffee trays, TV, trouser press and good bathrooms; all this, plus spacious public rooms, good food and warm hospitality make Rusheen Lodge a particularly pleasant place to stay. While evening meals are not provided, the pubs and restaurants of Ballyvaughan are only a few minutes' walk and breakfast - whether traditional Irish or continental - is a major feature of a stay. Children welcome (under 3s free in parents' room, cot available without charge, baby sitting arranged). No pets. Garden. **Rooms 9** (2 suites, 1 executive room, all no-smoking). B&B €45pps, ss€20. Closed mid Nov-mid Feb. MasterCard, Visa, Laser. **Directions:** 0.75 km from Ballyvaughan village on the N67, Lisdoonvarna road.

Carron
 CAFÉ

Burren Perfumery Tea Rooms

Carron Co Clare **Tel: 065 708 9102** Fax: 065 708 9200
Email: burrenperfumery@eircom.net Web: www.burrenperfumery.com

When touring Clare you will be pleased to find this charming spot - the perfumery is beautifully laid out, with a herb garden (where many native plants are grown - and later used in the organic herbal teas), pleasing old buildings and lovely biodynamic scents. The little tea rooms open onto a courtyard, opposite the perfumery shop - and beside the distillation room, where essential oils are extracted in a traditional still. Although small and simple, the tea rooms are pretty, with floral waxed tablecloths, fresh flowers and cups and saucers all creating a happy mismatch of pastels - and what they do is of high quality, made freshly on the premises, and uses local organic produce. At lunch time there might be summer minestrone & herbs soup with brown bread, or salad plates - a home-made organic goat's cheese & spinach quiche served with mixed salad - or, from a range traditional home baking, you could just have a home-made scone with butter and Maureen's jam. All kinds of teas and tisanes are offered, also natural juices - and coffee is served in individual cafetières. **Tea Rooms: Seats 20,** open daily 9-5pm, Apr-Sep; open weekend only in winter. [Perfumery open daily 9am-5pm all year (except Christmas); high season (Jun-Sep) open to 7pm.] MasterCard, Visa, Laser. **Directions:** In the Burren, east of Gort - off R480 & N67.

Cherry Tree Restaurant

Killaloe
☆ ● RESTAURANT

Lakeside Ballina Killaloe Co Clare
Tel: 061 375 688 Fax: 061 375 689 Web: www.cherrytreerestaurant.ie

CHEF OF THE YEAR AWARD

téile bia Harry McKeogh's impressive modern restaurant is a favourite weekend destination for discerning Limerick residents, who enjoy the lovely waterside location and consistently excellent contemporary cooking. The setting is charming, with just a stretch of grass between the restaurant and the River Shannon, and the high-ceilinged room with well-spaced, classically appointed tables makes a fine restaurant. As you arrive, Chef de Cuisine Mark Anderson and his team are at work in the kitchen, which is reassuringly on view, and Harry or one of his staff will show you to a small reception area nearby or straight to your table, where menus, iced water and delicious home-baked breads will quickly follow. Carefully sourced ingredients have always been the star here, providing a sound basis for a wide range of dishes - many of them admirably simple. Mark Anderson is a talented and dedicated chef, who changes menus monthly and is clearly committed to using the best of local ingredients, many of them organic; menu notes state the philosophy and credit suppliers. Simply worded menus offer a wide, often luxurious, choice of dishes - perhaps eight on each course on the à la carte, which is peppered with ingredients like truffles, foie gras and lobster; but simpler foods are just as good - the Cherry Tree's great salads are legendary, and an outstanding ingredient that has inspired more than one speciality dish is their superb beef; the Cherry Tree received the Guide's Irish Beef Award in 2001, and beef dishes here remain a treat, especially perfectly cooked steaks served with classical accompaniments including béarnaise sauce. Dishes attracting special praise on a recent visit included a tian of crab with smoked salmon and grapefruit, which comes with a smear of guacomole and (a touch of brilliance) a morsel of deep-fried avocado - such attention to detail is typical of Mark Anderson's style - and excellent puddings, including a superb chocolate soufflé with a tiny chocolate brownie and a scoop of berry ice cream with a dash of balsamic vinegar added: simply delicious. There's a fine Irish farmhouse cheese plate too, and an interesting, carefully chosen wine list offers lots of treats, including half a dozen dessert wines, and is augmented by a good choice of aperitifs and digestifs. Set menus - especially Sunday lunch - offer outstanding value. **Seats 60** (private room, 10). Toilets wheelchair accessible. Children welcome. D 6-10 Tue-Sat. Set D €39; also à la carte. House wines €18. Sun L 12.30-3, €24/29 2/3 course, Closed Mon; 24-26 Dec; last week Jan, 1st week Feb. Amex, MasterCard, Visa, Laser. **Directions:** At Molly's Pub in Ballina turn down towards the Lakeside Hotel, the Cherry Tree Restaurant is just before the hotel, on the left.

Barrtra Seafood Restaurant

Lahinch
🐟 ● RESTAURANT

Lahinch Co Clare **Tel: 065 708 1280**
Email: barrtra@hotmail.com Web: www.barrtra.com

téile bia Views of Liscannor Bay from Paul and Theresa O'Brien's traditional, white-washed cottage on the cliffs just outside Lahinch can be magic on a fine evening - and pleasingly simple decor and large windows allow them to take centre stage. Local seafood is the other star attraction - Barrtra was our Seafood Restaurant of the Year in 2002 - and Theresa's excellent, unfussy cooking makes the most of a wide range of fish, while also offering a choice for those with other preferences. Several menus are offered in high season, starting with their famous 5 O'clock Menu which is a real snip - giving value has always been a priority here and local seafood is all offered at customer-kindly prices; lobster is a speciality, when available, and is very reasonably priced - on the dinner menu it only attracts a €10 supplement. Otherwise expect dishes like richly flavoured chowders, glorious crab salads with home-made mayonnaise and bread, and perfectly cooked fish with excellent sauces; exact timing and perfect judgement of flavourings enhances while always allowing the fish to be "itself". Vegetarian dishes are highlighted on menus, and vegetables generally, are another strong point, a deliciously flavoursome combination that will include beautiful Clare potatoes is served on a platter. Paul manages front of house with easy hospitality, and is responsible for an interesting and keenly priced wine list, which includes a wide choice of house wines and half bottles. Children welcome before 7pm. **Seats 32.** D Daily 5-10, L & D Sun 1-9. Early D (3-course) 5-6.30, €24; Set 6-course D €37; also à la carte. House wines from €18. s.c. discretionary. Closed Mon (except Jul-Aug) & Jan-Feb. Phone to check opening hours off season. MasterCard, Visa, Laser. **Directions:** 3.5 miles south of Lahinch N67.

Moy House

Lahinch

🏛️ 🍷 👁 COUNTRY HOUSE

Lahinch Co Clare **Tel: 065 708 2800** Fax: 065 708 2500
Email: moyhouse@eircom.net Web: www.moyhouse.com

This stunning house just outside Lahinch was our Country House of the Year in 2003. It's on a wooded 15 acre site on the river Moy and enjoys a commanding position overlooking Lahinch Bay, with clear coastal views. It is one of Ireland's most appealing (and luxurious) country houses and, although it appears to be quite a small, low building as you approach, its hillside position allows for a lower floor on the sea side - a side entrance below has direct access to the dining room and lower bedrooms (useful for anyone who might have difficulty with the narrow spiral staircase which joins the two floors internally). A large, elegant drawing room on the entrance level has an open fire and honesty bar, where guests are free to enjoy aperitifs before going down to dine, or to relax after dinner. Decor, in rich country house tones, uses rugs and beautiful heavy fabrics to great advantage and bedrooms, which all have sea views, are wonderfully spacious and luxuriously appointed, and lovely bathrooms have underfloor heating. Residents' dinner and breakfast are served at separate tables in a dining room which is elegant, yet also cosy in wild weather. A 4-course dinner menu is offered, with several well-balanced choices on each course - steamed mussels with a creamy white wine sauce, and rosemary & garlic rack of Burren lamb, with peppermint chutney are typical. There's a short but interesting wine list and, all round, this lovely house offers a unique experience. Children welcome (cot available; baby sitting arranged). **Rooms 9** (3 shower only) B&B €119.50 pps, ss €35.50. D 7-9 (reservations required), €45. House wine €21. Closed 23-28 Dec & all Jan. Amex, MasterCard, Visa, Laser. **Directions:** On the sea side of the Miltown Malbay road outside Lahinch.

Vaughan Lodge

Lahinch

Ⓝ 🏛️ COUNTRY HOUSE/RESTAURANT

Ennistymon Road Lahinch Co Clare
Tel: 065 708 1111 Fax: 065 708 1011
Email: info@vaughanlodge.ie Web: www.vaughanlodge.ie

Open shortly before we went to press, Michael and Maria Vaughan's new hotel offers peace and relaxation within easy walking distance of the town centre, and has been purpose-built to high specifications, mainly with the comfort of golfers in mind - you don't have to be a golfer to enjoy staying here, but it must help. Michael Vaughan brings considerable experience in the hospitality industry to this new venture, and it shows in pleasing contemporary design, quality materials and great sense of space in large, clean-lined bedrooms and public areas - including a clubby bar with leather easy chairs and sofas which golfers, in particular, are sure to enjoy; the ambience throughout is of a comfortable gentleman's club, and it is most noticeable in the bar. A drying room is for golfers' or walkers' wet clothing. All this, and excellent food too, in a restaurant that has proved as much a hit with non-residents as with resident guests. **Rooms 22** (4 executive); B&B €130 pps, ss €55. All day room service. Lift. Ample parking space. **Restaurant:** As the intention from the outset was to operate the restaurant for the public as well as residents, it is large in comparison with the rest of the building and situated just off the foyer at the front of the building, giving it a separate identity. Polished tables with linen runners, gleaming glassware and stylish cutlery set the tone, and Philippe Farineau (previously head chef at Hayfield Manor Hotel, in Cork) presents predictably sublime menus listing a wide range of equally desirable dishes based on local products, and all coeliac friendly (no flour); although devised as a 5-course menu, guests may opt for less courses - pleasing the customer is a high priority here, and you might simply share a bowl of the house speciality, bouillabaisse, if you choose. The restaurant was only recently open at the time of the Guide's visit, yet there was an atmosphere of calm professionalism, with excellent service backing up the series of treats coming from the kitchen. There was not a wrong note in a meal that included highlights of seared scallops set on a parsnip mousseline - the mildness of the parsnip perfect with the delicate scallops - and a superb main course of rack of Burren lamb, with broad beans, lemon fondant potatoes, mint pesto and lamb jus, a dish which illustrated the strengths of this kitchen well, with accompaniments carefully tuned to an (excellent) main ingredient. Unusually, Philippe Farineau devises dishes with vegetables having an important role - every dish is garnished individually and, in this case, how delicious to have broad beans with lamb. Gorgeous desserts may include fresh fig carpaccio glazed with champagne sabayon, with a blueberry & crème fraîche ice cream: not fussy, simply packed with flavour. A wine list grouped by price offers a good choice of house wines including half bottles. Good value is offered throughout, but an early dinner menu is particularly reasonable. **Seats 70.** D daily 6.30-9.30 (early D €27, set D €38) House wine €17. No SC. Closed Jan & Feb. Amex, MasterCard, Visa, Laser. **Directions:** On N85 just at the edge of Lahinch on the left.

Liscannor

⭐ PUB/RESTAURANT

Vaughans Anchor Inn

Main Street Liscannor Co Clare **Tel: 065 708 1548**
Fax: 065 708 6977 Web: www.vaughansanchorinn.com

PUB OF THE YEAR

The Vaughan family's traditional bar has great character, with open fires and lots of memorabilia - and it's just the place for some seriously good seafood at fair prices, either in the bar or in a newer restaurant area at the back. Although famed locally for their seafood platters (and they are delicious - and great value) there's much more to the menu than that: Denis Vaughan cooks everything to order and patience is quite reasonably requested on this score, as it gets very busy and everything really is fresh - they offer about twenty varieties of fish, and the menu may even be changed in mid-stream because there's something new coming up off the boats. However, you don't have to eat seafood to eat well here - vegetarian options are offered and they do excellent steaks too. Cooking combines old-fashioned generosity with some contemporary twists: succulent fresh salmon, for example, may be a good thick darne, grilled and served on a bed of just-cooked fennel, with a delicious creamy samphire sauce, while perfectly seared scallops may come on a brilliant bed of crisp-fried smoked haddock & scallion mash with a frothy white wine sauce. It's understandably very popular and they don't take bookings so, get there early - lunch time might be worth a gamble but, if you want to have a reasonably quiet dinner without a long wait, get there before seven o'clock. Good bread, good service - and great value. Children welcome. **Seats 76.** Food served 12-9.30 daily. Toilets wheelchair accessible. Accommodation also available. Closed 25 Dec. (Open Good Fri for food, but bar closed.) MasterCard, Visa, Laser. **Directions:** 2.5 miles from Lahinch on Cliffs of Moher route.

Lisdoonvarna

 HOTEL/RESTAURANT

Sheedy's Country House Hotel

Lisdoonvarna Co Clare
Tel: 065 707 4026 Fax: 065 707 4555
Email: info@sheedys.com Web: www.sheedys.com

John and Martina Sheedy run one of the west of Ireland's best loved small hotels - it offers some of the most luxurious accommodation and the best food in the area, yet it still has the warm ambience and friendly hands-on management, which make a hotel special. The sunny foyer has a comfortable seating area - and an open fire for chillier days - and all the bedrooms are spacious and individually designed to a high standard with generous beds, quality materials and elegant, quietly soothing colours; comfort is the priority, so bathrooms have power showers as well as full baths and there are bathrobes, luxury toiletries and CD music systems,

in addition to the usual room facilities. Fine food and warm hospitality remain constant qualities however - and an original feature has already enhanced the exterior in a way that is as practical as it is pleasing to the eye: the gardens in front of the hotel have been developed to include a rose garden, and also a potager (formal vegetable and herb garden), which supplies leeks, Swiss chard, beetroot and cabbage to the kitchen: magic! Not suitable for children, except babies (cot available free of charge). No pets. **Rooms 11** (3 junior suites, 1 for disabled, all no smoking). B&B €70 pps, ss €20.
Restaurant: A combination of John Sheedy's fine cooking and Martina's warmth and efficiency front of house make Sheedy's a must-visit destination for discerning visitors to the area. A stylishly subdued olive-grey, curtainless dining room with plain candle-lit tables provides an unusual setting for carefully-presented meals that showcase local products, especially seafood; amuse-bouches sent out from the kitchen while you are choosing your dinner (delicious little bites likes parsnip crisps, semi dried tomatoes and black olives in spiced oil) sharpen the anticipation of delights to come. And everything on John's well-balanced menus just seems so appetising: tender and perfectly cooked fresh Atlantic prawns in crisp spring roll pastry, with a dense lightly spiced tomato & chilli jam on the side make a wonderful house starter, for example, and main courses will include local meats - a perfectly pink, deeply flavoured rump of Burren lamb, with a wild mushrooms sauce, for example. Vegetarian dishes are equally appealing - risotto of asparagus and wild mushrooms is typical, served with parmesan cheese and basil pesto. Finish with a gorgeous dessert such as lemon posset with fresh fruit - rhubarb, perhaps, or raspberries - and crisp shortbread. A carefully selected wine list complements the cooking and prices are very fair for the quality provided. The same high standards apply at breakfast, where scrambled eggs with smoked salmon from the nearby Burren Smokehouse is a particular hit (Sheedy's was the Munster winner of our Irish Breakfast Awards in 2004). Not suitable for children. **Seats 27.** D daily, 7-8.45. A la carte. House wine €19.50. SC discretionary. MasterCard, Visa, Laser. **Directions:** 200 metres from square of town on road to Sulphur Wells.

Miltown Malbay

🏛 ♨ GUESTHOUSE/RESTAURANT

The Admiralty Lodge

Spanish Point Miltown Malbay Co Clare
Tel: 065 708 5007 Fax: 065 708 5030
Email: info@admiralty.ie Web: www.admiralty.ie

Golfers - and, indeed, anyone who seeks peace - will love this luxurious guesthouse and restaurant just minutes away from Spanish Point Links Course, and very convenient to Doonbeg and Lahinch. A sweeping entrance leads to the smartly maintained building - there's an old 1830s lodge in there somewhere, with various extensions in different finishes creating the rather pleasing impression of a cluster of buildings - and, once inside, a large reception area with matt cream marble floors, mahogany desk, deep purple chaise longue and two huge elephant feet plants set the tone, and a spacious air of luxury takes over. Smart, comfortable and restful public areas continue in the same vein and large, airy bedrooms have a similar sense of style and generosity, with king size four-posters and sumptuous marbled bathrooms with bath and power shower, flat screen TV and stereo. Children welcome (under 8s free in parents' room). No pets. Garden, walking. Golf nearby. Banqueting (70). **Rooms 12** (2 no smoking, 2 ground floor, 2 disabled). Air conditioning. Room service (all day). Turndown service. B&B €115pps, ss €50. Open all year. **Piano Room:** The restaurant is a long room decorated in warm tones with beautiful Waterford crystal chandeliers, a grand piano, and French doors leading to a large garden. Immaculate table settings set the tone for cooking by head chef Nadine Le Gallo, previously of Ballylickey Manor in Co Cork, who joined the team in 2005. Her menus are quite simple in style, although the execution is sophisticated: a crab starter, for example is served in three variations - a rillette of crab and beetroot emulsion, a jelly of crab & green asparagus, and crab claws in aromatic stock, Japanese style. Quite hearty main courses include a choice of sirloin or fillet steaks - meeting the requirements of hungry golfers, perhaps - and another intriguing trio may appear among the dessert, this time a trio of crème brulées, flavoured with herbs. An Irish cheese selection includes some less known cheeses, such as Wicklow Blue, Dingle Peninsula and Baylough. An informative wine list, includes a couple of dessert wines and some half bottles. Early dinner and lunch menus offer particularly good value. **Seats 55.** Reservations required. Air conditioning. Toilets wheelchair accessible. Pianist weekends or nightly in summer. D Tue-Sun 6-10 (Sun 9.30, Mon residents only); Lounge Menu L daily, 12-3 (except Sun). Early D €30 (6-7), Set D €39. House wine €24. SC discretionary. Restaurant closed Sun L; also on Mon night (except for residents). Closed Mid week Jan/Feb. Heli-pad . MasterCard, Visa, Laser.

Newmarket-on-Fergus

Dromoland Castle Hotel

🏛🏛★ 🍴 ◉ HOTEL/RESTAURANT

Newmarket-on-Fergus Co Clare **Tel: 061 368144**
Fax: 061 363355 Email: sales@dromoland.ie Web: www.dromoland.ie

féile bía The ancestral home of the O'Briens, barons of Inchiquin and direct descendants of Brian Boru, High King of Ireland, this is one of the few Irish estates tracing its history back to Gaelic royal families, and it is now one of Ireland's grandest hotels, and one of the best-loved. Today's visitor will be keenly aware of this sense of history yet find it a relaxing hotel, where the grandeur of the surroundings - the castle itself, its lakes and parkland and magnificent furnishings - enhances the pleasure for guests, without over-powering. It is an enchanting place, where wide corridors lined with oak panelling are hung with ancient portraits and scented with the haunting aroma of wood smoke, and it has all the crystal chandeliers and massive antiques to be expected in a real Irish castle. Guest rooms and suites vary in size and appointments, but are generally spacious, have all been refurbished recently and have luxurious bathrooms. The Brian Boru International Centre can accommodate almost any type of gathering, including exhibitions, conferences and banquets. Conference/banqueting (250/300); business centre; secretarial services on request. Leisure centre (indoor pool, spa, beauty salon, hairdressing); golf (18); fishing, tennis, cycling, walking. Snooker, pool table. Gift shop, boutique. No pets. Children welcome; under 12's free in parents' room (cot available free of charge, baby sitting arranged). **Rooms 100** (6 suites, 21 junior suites, 44 executive, all no smoking, 2 disabled). Lift. 24 hr room service. Room rate €446 (max 2 guests), SC inc. Breaks offered. Open all year.

Earl of Thomond Restaurant: Dining here is a treat by any standards - it is a magnificent room, with crystal, gilding and rich fabrics, and has a lovely view over the lake and golf course. And outstanding food and service match the surroundings, and then some - beginning with an aperitif in the Library Bar, overlooking the eighth green, before moving through to beautifully presented tables and gentle background music provided by a traditional Irish harpist. David McCann, who has been doing a superb job as executive head chef since 1994, presents a table d'hôte menu, a vegetarian menu, and an à la carte offering a wonderful selection of luxurious dishes. The table d'hôte is more down-to-earth - a little less glamorous than the carte but with the same quality of ingredients and cooking. Although the style is basically classic French (with some of the current international influences) some dishes highlight local ingredients and are more Irish in tone: starters like galette of aubergine & St Tola goats cheese with shallot, garlic, celeriac & chilli relish, for example, and seared Galway Bay smoked salmon with creamed leeks & lentils, baby caper & shallot dressing - or a main course assiette of Irish pork with courgette & peach risotto. The cooking is invariably superb, all the little niceties of a very special meal are observed and service, under the direction of restaurant manager Tony Frisby, is excellent. Delicious desserts include a number of updated classics, there's an excellent range of Irish farmhouse cheeses, and a good Sunday lunch menu offers a wide choice of interesting dishes - often including a special Dromoland version of Irish Stew. The wine list - about 250 wines, predominantly French - is under constant review. (House wines from about €25). The breakfast menu includes a number of specialities - buttermilk pancakes with lemon & maple syrup, Limerick ham with mushrooms, poached eggs, toast & cheddar cheese - as well as a well-laden buffet, and the traditional Irish cooked breakfast. A 15% service charge is added to all prices. **Seats 84** (private room 24). D daily, 6-10, L Sun only 12.30-1.30; Set Sun L €40; Set D €65; à la carte D also available.* The Gallery Menu offers a lighter choice of less formal dishes throughout the day (11-7), including Afternoon Tea. *Beside the castle, the **Dromoland Golf and Country Club** incorporates an 18-hole parkland course, a gym, a Health Clinic offering specialist treatments, also the **Green Room Bar** and **Fig Tree Restaurant**, which provide informal alternatives to facilities in the castle, including excellent food (9am-9.30pm). Open all year. Helipad. Amex, Diners, MasterCard, Visa, Laser. **Directions:** 17 miles from Limerick, 8 miles from Shannon. Take N18 to Dromoland interchange; exit & follow signage.

CORK CITY

Cork City
☆ RESTAURANT WITH ROOMS

Café Paradiso

16 Lancaster Quay Western Road Cork Co Cork
Tel: 021 4277 939 Fax: 021 427 4973
Email: info@cafeparadiso.ie Web: www.cafeparadiso.ie

Devotees travel from all over Ireland - and beyond - to eat at Denis Cotter and Bridget Healy's ground-breaking vegetarian restaurant, where they produce such exciting mainstream cooking that even the most committed of carnivores admit to relishing every mouthful. House specialities that people cross the country for include delicious deep-fried courgette flowers with a fresh goats cheese & pinenut stuffing, olive & caper aoili and basil courgettes, which is a brilliant example of the cooking style at this colourful little restaurant. It's a lively place with a busy atmosphere and the staff, under the direction of Bridget Healy, are not only friendly and helpful but obviously enthusiastic about their work. Seasonal menus based on the best organic produce available are topped up by daily specials, which might include a modish dish like lime-grilled haloumi, with harissa sauce on a warm salad of couscous, cherry tomatoes, green beans & chickpeas & chermoula. Irresistible desserts too - gorgeous subtly updated classics like strawberry & vanilla mascarpone tartlet with passionfruit syrup, or dark chocolate silk cake with caramel sauce and espresso ice cream - and a well-priced global wine list features an exceptional choice in New Zealand wines (from Bridget's home country) and a number of organic wines, often included in a tempting blackboard list of wines by the glass. The cooking is never less than stunning - and significantly, in this era of "cheffy" food and big egos, the creator of this wonderful food describes himself simply as "owner cook"; many of Denis Cotter's creations are featured in his acclaimed books: Café Paradiso Cookbook and Café Paradiso Seasons. Café Paradiso may be small, but it packs a mighty punch.***Paradiso Rooms**, offering accommodation over the restaurant, opened just as we were going to press. Initially they are available for dinner guests only, at a room rate of €160. **Seats 45** (outdoor seating, 6). Toilets wheelchair accessible. L Tue-Sat, 12-3, D Tue-Sat 6.30-10.30. A la carte. House wines from €20. Service discretionary. Closed Sun, Mon, Christmas week. Amex, MasterCard, Visa, Laser. **Directions:** On Western Road, opposite Jurys Hotel.

Cork City
Ⓝ ◉ HOTEL

Clarion Hotel Cork

Lapps Quay Cork Co Cork **Tel: 021 422 4900** Fax: 021 422 4901
Email: info@clarionhotelcorkcity.com Web: www.clarionhotelcorkcity.com

féile bia Those who like ultra-modern hotels and enjoy the buzz of the city centre will love the new Clarion. In a briliant central location with a wide terrace and boardwalk along the River Lee, this striking modern hotel embodies many of the best features of other recently built Clarion hotels and has excellent amenities including state-of-the-art conference facilities, spa, swimming pool, and gym. The entrance foyer is highly dramatic, with a atrium soaring right up the a glass roof, and rooms off galleries which overlook the foyer, and well-appointed accommodation includes riverside suites and a penthouse suite. A choice of dining is offered the well-appointed **Sinergie** restaurant offers an international menu, good cooking and attentive service, while the **Kudos** bar provides an informal alternative and serves Asian food to 10pm (weekends to 8pm). **Rooms 191.** Amex, Diners, MasterCard, Visa, Laser. **Directions:** Corner of Clontarf St. and Lapps Quay. Diagonally across from City Hall.

Crawford Gallery Café

Cork City
 RESTAURANT

Emmet Place Cork Co Cork **Tel: 021 427 4415** Fax: 021 465 2021
Email: crawford1info@eircom.net Web: www.ballymaloe.ie

This fine 1724 building with a large modern extension houses an excellent collection of 18th- and 19th-century landscapes. And this is also home to the Crawford Gallery Café, one of Cork city's favourite informal eating places, which is managed by Isaac Allen, grandson of Myrtle and the late Ivan Allen, founders of Ballymaloe House - and, by a remarkable coincidence, also a descendant of Arthur Hill, architect of a previous extension to the gallery, completed in 1884. Menus in this striking blue and white room reflect the Ballymaloe philosophy that food is precious and should be handled carefully, so Ivan Allen's freshly prepared dishes are made from natural local ingredients, and he also offers Ballymaloe breads and many of the other dishes familiar to Ballymaloe fans. Except for a few specialities too popular to take off (such as their spinach & mushroom pancakes), the menu changes weekly but the style - a balanced mixture of timeless country house fare and contemporary international dishes featuring carefully sourced meats, fish from Ballycotton and the freshest of seasonal vegetables - remains reassuringly constant. Substantial dishes, such as classic sirloin steak and chips, with béarnaise sauce - or a big vegetarian option like Mediterranean bean stew with coriander & basmati rice - are great for a real meal, and the home-made pickles, relishes, chutneys and preserves are delicious details. And, for a lighter bite, the home baking is outstanding. A short well-balanced wine list offers some half bottles. Conference/banqueting: available for private parties, corporate entertaining, lectures etc in evenings; details on application. **Seats 60.** No reservations. Toilets wheelchair accessible. Open Mon-Sat, 10am-3pm, L 12.30-2.30. Set L €20; also à la carte. House wine €17.50. Service discretionary. Closed Sun, 24 Dec-7 Jan, bank hols. Amex, MasterCard, Visa, Laser. **Directions:** City centre, next to Opera House.

Farmgate Café

Cork City
 CAFÉ

English Market Cork Co Cork **Tel: 021 427 8134**
Fax: 021 427 8134 Email: knh@eircom.net

A sister restaurant to the Farmgate Country Store and Restaurant in Midleton, Kay Harte's Farmgate Café shares the same commitment to serving fresh, local food - and, as it is located in the gallery above the English Market, where ingredients are purchased daily, it doesn't come much fresher or more local than this. The atmosphere is lively and busy, with constant movement (especially in the self-service area) as people come and go from the market below giving a great sense of being at the heart of things. With its classic black and white tiles, simple wooden furniture and interesting art work there's a combination of style and a comfortably down to earth atmosphere which suits the wholesome food they serve and, having highlighted the freshness of local ingredients for some time in dishes that were a mixture of modern and traditional, Kay Harte and her team have now decided to concentrate on the regional aspect of the food they buy in the market, and have introduced less well known foods such as corned mutton to their menus alongside famous old Cork ones with a special market connection like tripe & drisheen and corned beef & champ with green cabbage. Menus depend on what is available in the English Market each day, including "oysters to your table from the fish stall" and other fish - used, for example, in a chowder that market regulars keep coming back for. And, however simple, everything is perfectly cooked, with careful matching of vegetables and judicious use of fresh herbs and seasonings: a delicious mushroom & Crozier Blue tart with thyme, for example, is perfectly balanced to allow the mushroom flavour to come through; chargrilled chicken comes with a delicate lemon thyme sauce and a delicious mixture of leeks, courgettes and rosemary flavoured roast potatoes, while traditionalists will love the classic Irish lamb stew, with its succulent chunks of lean lamb and perfectly cooked root vegetables. All this and delicious home-baked cakes and breads too, whether as a bite to accompany a coffee, or to finish off a meal, a wonderfully home-made seasonal sweet such as a classic raspberry sponge is always a treat. This is an interesting and lively place to enjoy good food - and it's great value for money. **Seats 110.** Meals Mon-Sat, from 8.30am - 5pm: B'fast 8.30-10.30, L 12-4. Licensed. Closed Sun, bank hols, Dec 25-3 Jan. Diners, MasterCard, Visa, Laser. **Directions:** English Market - off Oliver Plunkett Street and Grand Parade.

Cork City
☆ RESTAURANT WITH ROOMS

Flemings Restaurant

Silver Grange House Tivoli Cork Co Cork
Tel: 021 482 1621 Fax: 021 482 1800 Email: flemingsrestaurant@iolfree.ie

Clearly signed off the main Cork-Dublin road, this large Georgian family house is home to Michael and Eileen Fleming's excellent restaurant with rooms. On a hillside overlooking the river, the house is set in large grounds, including a kitchen garden which provides fruit, vegetables and herbs for the restaurant during the summer. It is a big property to maintain and the entrance can seem a little run down, but this is quickly forgotten when you enter the light, airy double dining room, which is decorated in an elegant low-key style that highlights its fine proportions, while well-appointed linen-clad tables provide a fine setting for Michael Fleming's classical and modern French cooking. Seasonal table d'hôte and à la carte menus offer a wonderful choice of classics, occasionally influenced by current international trends but, even where local ingredients feature strongly, the main thrust of the cooking style is classical French - as in a superb speciality starter of pan fried foie gras de canard with Timoleague black pudding & glazed apple, or a home-made summer tomato consommé. Less usual choices might include roast fillet of rabbit, with herb gnocchi and a Marsala dressing - and there are also favourite ingredients served with a twist - roast best end of lamb with lamb shank in pastry, for example, which is served with a rosemary sauce, and monkfish, wrapped in Parma ham and served on root vegetables, with a champagne & pepper coulis. Vegetables are imaginative in selection and presentation, while desserts may include a deep apple pie served with home made ice cream - and a selection of cheese is served traditionally, with biscuits and fruits. Michael's cooking is invariably excellent, presentation elegant, and service both attentive and knowledgeable. A great antidote to the sameness of modern multicultural restaurants - a visit to a classic restaurant like this is a treat to treasure. Good wine list - and good value all round. Banqueting (80). **Seats 80** (private room 30; outside seating, 30). Children over 5 welcome. L&D daily, 12.30-2.20, 6.30-10; reservations not necessary. Set L €28.50, Set D €38; also à la carte. House wine €22. SC discretionary. **Accommodation:** There are four spacious en-suite rooms, comfortably furnished in a style appropriate to the age of the house (B&B €55 pps, ss €30). Closed 24-26 Dec. Amex, MasterCard, Visa, Laser. **Directions:** 3 km from city centre.

Cork City
🏛🏛 HOTEL/RESTAURANT

Hayfield Manor Hotel

Perrott Avenue College Road Cork Co Cork
Tel: 021 484 5900 Fax: 021 431 6839
Email: enquiries@hayfieldmanor.ie Web: www.hayfieldmanor.ie

HOTEL OF THE YEAR

féile bia Set in two acres of gardens near University College Cork, the city's premier hotel provides every comfort and a remarkable level of privacy and seclusion, just a mile from the city centre. Although quite new, it has the feel of a large period house, and is managed with warmth and discreet efficiency. Public areas include a choice of restaurants, both excellent of their type - the formal Manor Room, which overlooks gardens at the back, and the newer smart-casual Perrotts - and a redesigned bar that skilfully links the contrasting traditional and contemporary styles of the interior. On-site amenities include a leisure centre with indoor pool and beauty treatments. Spacious suites and guest rooms vary in decor, are beautifully furnished with antiques and have generous marbled bathrooms, many with separate bath and shower. **Rooms 88.** Lift. **Manor Room:** Since the refurbishment of Hayfield's Bar - a judicious blend of traditional and contemporary, resulting in the cosy atmosphere of a traditional bar, with chic modern touches - this has become an appealing place for an aperitif before dining in this elegantly-appointed, fine dining restaurant, which overlooks the walled garden at the back of the hotel and has a quiet, serene atmosphere. James Rendall, who has been Head Chef since 2004, makes good use of local produce, and continues the tradition of classical cuisine with an occasional contemporary twist for which this restaurant is well known. Quality Irish ingredients, including many artisan products, take centre stage in accomplished cooking which, together with caring service, should ensure a pleasing and relaxing meal. **Perrotts:** In a new conservatory area at the front of the hotel, this smart and relaxing contemporary restaurant offers an informal alternative to dining in the Manor Room. Open for lunch and dinner daily, it has a bright and airy atmosphere and plenty of greenery, and quickly became established as a favoured destination with discerning Corkonians who enjoy the ambience and stylish bistro cooking, which offers dishes ranging from updated classics (chicken liver parfait with toasted pecan bread & pear chutney; duck cassoulet), to international lunchtime favourites like Perrotts home made burger with bacon and Emmenthal cheese, spicy guacomole and tomato relish dip, and hand cut chips. Stylish surroudings, varied menus, accomplished cooking and helpful, attentive service make for a very enjoyable dining experience. **The Manor Room: Seats 90.** L daily, 12-2.30, D daily, 7-10. Set L €35. Set D €45/65; à la carte L & D also available. House wine from €31.75. SC in restaurant of 10% on parties of 8+. **Perrotts Restaurant**, 12-2.30 & 6-10.30 daily. Amex, Diners, MasterCard, Visa, Laser. **Directions:** Opposite University College Cork - signed off College Road.

Cork City   # Idaho.Café

♨ € CAFÉ   19 Caroline Street Cork Co Cork **Tel: 021 427 6376**

téile bia This friendly and exceptionally well-located little café hits the spot for discerning shoppers, who appreciate Mairead Jacob's wholesome food - this is good home cooking based on the best of ingredients. The day begins with breakfast, and a very good breakfast it is too: everything from lovely hot porridge with brown sugar and cream to warm Danish pastries, muffins, or Belgian waffles with organic maple syrup and the option of crispy bacon; all the little niceties are observed, including hand-sliced bread for your toast, and freshly-baked scones with good marmalade and real butter - and hot drinks include delicious hot chocolate and really great coffee (good and strong, with refills offered). Maybe crispy bacon & melted Cheddar croissants appeal, or a bacon & sausage bap might be your thing - either way you can choose from this menu up to noon, when they ease into lunch, with tasty little numbers like a house special of gratinated potato gnocchi with smoky bacon & sage or, equally typical of the treats in store, crispy duck, spring onion and Irish brie quesadillas or sheperdess's pie (using organic beef). But best of all perhaps, as baking is a speciality, are the 'Sweet Fix' temptations which are just ideal for that quick morning coffee or afternoon tea break - the coeliac friendly 'orange almond' cake has developed a following, and there's a wide of range hot and cold drinks, including 'Hippy' specialist teas. Dishes which are vegetarian, or can be adapted for vegetarians, are highlighted on the menu at this great little place. Great service, and great value too: full marks. **Seats 30.** Toilets not wheelchair accessible. Children welcome. Open Mon-Sat, 8.30-4.30; B'fst 8.30-12, L 12-4.30. House wine from €16.50 or from 2.95 a glass, specialist beers from about €3.75. Closed Sun, Bank Holidays, 24-26 Dec. **No Credit Cards. Directions:** Directly behind Brown Thomas, Cork

---

Cork City   # Isaacs Restaurant

☆ ♨ RESTAURANT   48 MacCurtain Street Cork Co Cork **Tel: 021 450 3805**
            Fax: 021 455 1348 Email: isaacs@iol.ie

téile bia In 1992 Michael and Catherine Ryan, together with partner/head chef Canice Sharkey, opened this large, atmospheric modern restaurant in an 18th-century warehouse and it immediately struck a chord with people tired of having to choose between fine dining and fast food, and became a trend-setter in the modern Irish food movement. The combination of international influences and reassuring Irish traditions was ahead of its time, and it quickly gained a following of people who enjoyed both the informal atmosphere, and the freshness of approach in Canice Sharkey's kitchen: a homely mushroom soup might sit easily on the menu alongside tempura of tiger prawns, scallions & aubergine with soy dipping sauce, and a traditional seafood chowder could be garnished with garlic croûtons. In a quiet, low-key way, this restaurant has played a leading role in the culinary revolution that has overtaken Ireland over the last decade or two. Their original blend of Irish and international themes, together with a policy of providing great food and good value in an informal, relaxed ambience has attracted endless imitations. But the idea behind this restaurant was no gimmick and the Isaacs team have retained the restaurant's original style and - most importantly - its policy of delivering quality at a fair price. Ingredients are carefully sourced, the cooking is consistently accomplished and menus are freshened by occasional inspired introductions (a plate of tapas, for example, which is offered as a starter in the evening, but also makes a lovely light lunch was introduced relatively recently and has become a firm favourite).

A list of about seven special changes twice daily, and most dishes are available with little oil and no dairy produce, on request. The service is terrific too, and a visit here is always great fun. The wine list - which is considerately arranged by style ('dry, light and fresh', 'full bodied' etc) follows a similar philosophy, offering a good combination of classics and more unusual bottles, at accessible prices, and Isaacs coffee is organic and Fair Trade. **Seats 120.** L Mon-Sat 12.30-2.30, D daily 6-10 (Sun to 9.30). Short à la carte and daily blackboard specials; vegetarian dishes highlighted. House wine from €17. Service discretionary. Closed - L Sun, Christmas week, L Bank Holidays. Amex, Diners, MasterCard, Visa, Laser. **Directions:** 5 minutes from Patrick Street; opposite Gresham Metropole Hotel.

Cork City
E RESTAURANT

Ivory Tower

The Exchange Builldings Princes Street Cork Co Cork
Tel: 021 4274665

téte bia Seamus O'Connell, one of Ireland's most original culinary talents, runs this unusual restaurant upstairs in an early Victorian commercial building - and has recently been introduced to a wider audience through his television series, Soul Food. Very best quality ingredients (all local and organic or wild, including game in season), creative menus and excellent details like delicious home-baked breads and imaginative presentation are the hallmarks of The Ivory Tower - and vegetarian dishes interesting enough to tempt hardened carnivores are always a feature. Menus start off with a "surprise taster" to set the mood and examples from a summer menu that show the level of creativity include a signature starter of Roquefort soufflé baked in a globe artichoke & served with truffle beurre blanc, which might be followed by a little granita or sorbet (watermelon & blood orange, perhaps) then, from a choice of about nine dishes, perhaps wild sea trout hot smoked to order over oak, with whiskey & scallion sauce. Desserts are equally unconventional, so why not finish with another speciality - aphrodisiac of tropical fruits? A shortish wine list includes a number of rare treats, including some organic and biodynamic wines.] Not suitable for children under 5. **Seats 35.** D Thu-Sun, 6.30-9.30. 5-course D about €50; Surprise Menu about €75. House wine from about €18. SC discretionary. Closed Mon-Wed. Amex, MasterCard, Visa, Laser. **Directions:** Corner of Princes/Oliver Plunkett street.

Cork City
☆RESTAURANT

Jacobs On The Mall

30A South Mall Cork Co Cork **Tel: 021 425 1530** Fax: 021 425 1531
Email: info@jacobsonthemall.com Web: www.jacobsonthemall.com

téte bia Its location in the former Turkish baths creates a highly unusual and atmospheric contemporary dining space for what many would regard as Cork's leading restaurant. Head Chefs Mercy Fenton and Annette Flanagan do a consistently excellent job: modern European cooking is the promise and, with close attention to sourcing the best ingredients allied to outstanding cooking skills, the results are commendably simple and always pleasing in terms of balance and flavour. Details like home-made breads are excellent, and fresh local and organic produce makes its mark in the simplest of dishes, like delicious mixed leaf salads. Reflecting the availability of local produce, lunch and dinner menus change daily and are sensibly brief - offering a choice of about half a dozen dishes on each course, notably seafood and vegetables in season: a simple meal of organic mixed leaf salad with apple, Cashel blue cheese, sultanas & sunflower seeds followed by grilled sole with crushed olive potatoes, green beans & red pepper tapenade could be memorable, for example. Creativity with deliciously wholesome and colourful ingredients, accurate cooking, stylish presentation and efficient yet relaxed service all add up to an outstanding dining experience. Finish on a high note - with a delectable date and butterscotch pudding, with vanilla ice cream, perhaps, or farmhouse cheeses, which are always so good in Cork, served here with fruit and home-made oatcakes. An interesting and fairly priced wine list includes some organic wines and a good choice of half bottles.* Major developments are expected soon, as Jacobs is developing a building at the back of the restaurant. Children welcome. Special diets willingly accommodated with advance notice. **Seats 130** (Private room, 22, with own bar). Air conditioning. Toilets wheelchair accessible. L Mon-Sat 12.30-2.30, D Mon 6.30-10pm. A la carte. House wines from €19; s.c.10% (excl L). Closed Sun, 25 Dec, L on bank hols. Amex, Diners, MasterCard, Visa, Laser, Switch. **Directions:** Beside Bank of Ireland, at the Grand Parade end of the South Mall.

Cork City   # Jacques
☆ RESTAURANT   Phoenix Street Cork Co Cork **Tel: 021 427 7387** Fax: 021 427 0634
Email: jacquesrestaurant@eircom.net Web: www.jacquesrestaurant.ie

An integral part of Cork life since 1982, sisters Eithne and Jacqueline Barry's delightful restaurant has changed with the years, evolving from quite a traditional place to the smart contemporary space that it is today. But, while the surroundings may go through periodic re-makes, the fundamentals of warm hospitality and great food never waiver and that is the reason why many would cite Jacques as their favourite Cork restaurant - and it is hard to envisage a visit to the city without a meal here. There is always a personal welcome and, together with Eileen Carey, who has been in the kitchen with Jacque Barry since 1986, this team has always a put high value on the provenance and quality of the food that provides the basic building blocks for their delicious meals. Menus are based on carefully sourced ingredients from a network of suppliers built up over many years and this care, together with skill and judgement in the kitchen, shows particularly in having the confidence to keep things simple and allow the food to speak for itself. You could start your meal in delectably civilised fashion with a half bottle of Manzanilla, served with nuts and olives, while considering choices from menus that are refreshingly short, which allows this skilled team to concentrate on the delicious cooking that is their forte. Moreish starters like warm salad of chicken, crispy bacon, nuts & rustic potatoes, with tomato vinaigrette are also available as a main course, and there are numerous wonderful speciality dishes including, perhaps, smoked haddock, crab & spinach cannelloni and traditional roast duck, with potato and apricot stuffing & buttered greens. Ultra fresh fish, simply cooked on or off the bone, is a highlight - and the producers and suppliers who mean so much to this magic restaurant are listed on the back of the menu. Delicious desserts could include rhubarb and custard tart or, if you have a savoury tooth, you might choose Cashel Blue cheese with prune & apple jelly and a walnut biscuit. An interesting, informative wine list matches the food, includes some organic wines, a wine of the month and a god choice of half bottles. Consistently good cooking in stylish, relaxed surroundings and genuinely hospitable service are among the things that makes Jacques special - and it's excellent value too, especially the lunch and early dinner menus. **Seats 60.** Air conditioning. An interesting, fairly priced wine list includes some organic wines and about ten half bottles. L Mon-Sat, 12-3; Set L €15.90; D Mon-Sat 6-10. Early D 6-7, €19.90. Also à la carte. House wine €19. No SC. Closed Sunday, Bank Hols, 23 Dec - 2 Jan Amex, MasterCard, Visa, Laser. **Directions:** City centre, near G.P.O.

Cork City   # Kingsley Hotel
🏨 🏆 HOTEL/RESTAURANT   Victoria Cross Cork Co Cork **Tel: 021 480 0500**
Fax: 021 480 0526 Web: www.kingsleyhotel.com

féile bia Conveniently situated in an attractive location alongside the River Lee, just minutes from both Cork airport and the city centre, this modern hotel has been built and furnished to a high standard and is especially appealing to business visitors, for whom it quickly becomes a home from home. A large, comfortably furnished foyer has a luxurious feel to it - both it and an informal restaurant area a few steps up from it (and overlooking the weir), make good meeting places. This feeling is noticeable throughout the hotel, from the moment guests are greeted on arrival, and accommodation is personally decorated and well-planned to make a good base away from home. Spacious rooms offer traditional comfort and are designed with care: air conditioning, work station with ISDN and modem, interactive TV with message facilities, safes, trouser press with ironing board and same day laundry *Developments due for completion in 2006 will add a further 75 rooms, plus short-stay apartments, spa, a private dining & conference suite, and an underground carpark. Conference/banqueting (9/80); secretarial services; video conferencing, on request; 24 hour room service. Leisure centre (recently refurbished & gym equipment renewed), swimming pool; treatment rooms, beauty salon. Children welcome (under 12s free in parents' room; cot available without charge, baby sitting arranged). Garden. Riverside walks. Pets permitted by arrangement. Parking. **Rooms 69** (all no-smoking; 4 suites, 12 executive rooms, 2 for disabled). Lift. B&B €90 pps, ss €60. Open all year. **Otters at the Kinsgley:** This attractive restaurant appeals to non-residents as well as hotel guests. A warm welcome, promptly presented menus and wine list, simple classy table settings and friendly, staff all help both to impress and relax guests. Although international in style, menus at both lunch and dinner are based on local produce and offer plenty of choice without being overlong: a typical lunch menu might include starters like fresh salmon tossed in chive mayonnaise, and a vegetarian main course of malfatti pasta stuffed with spinach & ricotta cheese, with tomato & basil sauce and cheddar cheese or a spicy dish of chicken breast marinated in coriander, paprika, lemon, garlic and natural yoghurt. Roasted loin of Kerry lamb is a speciality, typically served with pan-fried green beans, baby potatoes & rosemary jus. Service is professional and, as elsewhere in the hotel, outstandingly friendly and helpful. **Seats 100** (private room 60). L & D daily: L 12.30-2.30, (Sun L 12-3), D 6-10. Set L €25; set D from €21; D also à la carte. House wine from €17. SC discretionary. *Lounge and bar food also available through the day. Open all year. Amex, Diners, MasterCard, Visa, Laser. **Directions:** On main N22 Killarney road by Victoria Cross.

Cork City
GUESTHOUSE

Lancaster Lodge

Lancaster Quay Western Road Cork Co Cork
Tel: 021 425 1125 Fax: 021 425 1126
Email: info@lancasterlodge.com Web: www.lancasterlodge.com

This modern purpose-built guesthouse has plenty of parking in its own well-maintained grounds and, together with prompt, friendly and efficient reception, creates an excellent first impression. It was built with vision, to offer hotel quality accommodation, with personal supervision, at a moderate price - and recent visits by the Guide have found everything in tiptop order, with many thoughtful little touches that make a stay here a real pleasure - bottled water on each floor, newspapers in the breakfast room and pleasing surroundings throughout, including original art works. Spacious guest rooms are furnished to a high standard (with free broadband, safes, 12 channel TV, trouser press, tea/coffee facilities and room service as well as the more usual facilities) and the bathrooms, two of which have jacuzzi baths, are well-designed. Excellent breakfasts are served in an attractive contemporary dining room - a bright and airy space, with light oak floors, high quality modern furnishings and art pieces on the walls. A tempting buffet display offers all manner of juices, fresh and dried fruits, yoghurts and so on, while hot dishes - including dishes like pancakes and wild salmon & scrambled eggs as well as the traditional Irish Breakfast and its many variations - are cooked to order. Lancaster Lodge was Highly Commended in our 2005 Irish Breakfast Awards. Children welcome (under 5s free in parents' room, cot available, baby sitting arranged). Free secure parking. 24 hour reception. **Rooms 39** (2 executive rooms, 5 shower only, 2 for disabled). Lift. B&B from €60 pps. ss €27 Closed 23-26 Dec. Amex, Diners, MasterCard, Visa, Laser. **Directions:** On Western Road, opposite Café Paradiso.

Cork City
RESTAURANT

Les Gourmandises Restaurant

17 Cook Street Cork Co Cork
Tel: 021 425 1959 Web: www.lesgourmandises.ie

Just off South Mall, this simple little restaurant feels like an outpost of France - the menu in the window will draw you in and you'll be glad you noticed it. It's run by Patrick and Soizic Kiely - both previously at Restaurant Patrick Guilbaud but, although that says a lot about the key standards, this is an utterly down to earth place far more reminiscent of family-run restaurants in France. The long, narrow room is bright and functional but, although the décor remains rather spare, there can be quite a buzz as the restaurant fills up. Staff - who are mainly French - are pleasant and helpful, swiftly bringing simple menus in the French style, and a lovely wine list. The nearby English market supplies many of the ingredients and a tasting plate of starters is a great idea to get things going (including sample portions of classic dishes like terrine of braised ham, foie gras and roasted sweetbread and tian of crab with roasted cherry tomato & tapenade, perhaps); typical dishes on a lunch menu may include a classic boeuf bourguignon with smoked bacon, mushrooms & pomme purée - which is marinated and very slowly braised, producing superb flavour and melting texture. To finish, there's a good French & Irish cheese selection, a dessert tasting plate and some seasonal dishes - a vanilla & blackcurrant vacherin (with toasted almonds, swiss meringue & blackcurrant sauce), perhaps - as well as the timeless classic like caramelised lemon tart. Presentation is beautiful and the details are excellent - good bread, lovely coffee. A compact, informative list of about 20 wines gives a well-balanced selection from throughout the country and includes several half bottles; excellent house wines are available by the glass. The early dinner menu is more limited, but offers the same high standards at a very reasonable price. Terrific food and good value: a great all-round dining experience. Children over 6 welcome. **Seats 30.** L Fri only (also all of the week before Christmas), 12-2. D Tue-Sat, 6-10. Early D, 2/3 course: €27.50/31.50. Also à la carte. House wine €22. Closed Sun, Mon; Mar, Sep. MasterCard, Visa, Laser, Switch. **Directions:** City centre - access to Cook Street from South Mall.

Cork City
☆ RESTAURANT

Lovetts Restaurant & Brasserie
Churchyard Lane off Well Road Douglas Cork Co Cork
Tel: 021 429 4909 Email: lovetts@utvinternet.com

Home to both the restaurant and the Lovett family since 1977, this fine restaurant is in a late Georgian house situated in mature grounds. Management is now in the capable hands of Niamh Lovett and her business partner and head chef is Marie Harding, a talented and creative cook committed to serious cooking, using the best of fresh, free range and local products. Just reading through Marie's list of suppliers is enough to whet the appetite: smoked salmon and eel from Cresswells of Ummera, Co Cork; mussels and oysters (in season) from Kellys of Clarenbridge; crab from Shellfish de la Mer, and most other fish from Denis Good, both in Castletownbere; Mrs Lombard of Minane Bridge supplies free range chickens, while ducks are from Barry's of Fort Farm, Ballyhooly and mushrooms from Fran & Jim Fraser. Better still, while the menus - which include a separate vegetarian menu and are based on daily availability - are a mouth-watering read, the cooking matches the quality of ingredients, making for an outstanding dining experience. Menus are not over-extensive, yet offer plenty of choice; many dishes highlight the artisan produce that is so highly valued - starters include a West Cork smoked fish platter (a selection of salmon, trout, eel and smoked trout mousse), for example - and daily fish dishes, given on a blackboard menu, may include a speciality such as grilled witch sole with a herb butter & breadcrumb crust. Desserts are delicious (loganberry bakewell tart, with cream, perhaps) and, of course, there's a fine Irish farmhouse cheese plate. The Brasserie operates at the same time as the restaurant, and offers a more informal menu. There's a fully licensed bar (the extensive wine list is Niamh's father Dermod Lovett's particular passion) and private dining is available in the 'Wine Geese' Room. **Seats 35.** (Private room 6-24). Toilet is not wheelchair accessible. D à la carte; Vegetarian Menu €25. House wines from €18.75. 10% SC on parties of 5+, otherwise discretionary. D Tue-Sat, 6.30-9.30. Closed Sun, Mon, 24-31 Dec, 1st week in Aug, Bank Holidays. Amex, Diners, MasterCard, Visa, Laser. **Directions:** Close to south Cork city: from Douglas Road take turning to Mahon and Blackrock and go through a roundabout. Take the fourth turn on the left, Wells Road; Lovetts is off it in Churchyard Lane.

Cork City
🏨 HOTEL/RESTAURANT

Maryborough House Hotel
Maryborough Hill Douglas Cork Co Cork
Tel: 021 436 5555 Fax: 021 436 5662
Email: info@maryborough.ie Web: www.maryborough.com

This hotel, which is quietly situated on the south of the city and very convenient to Cork airport and the Jack Lynch tunnel, has a fine country house at its heart and is set in its own gardens. The main entrance is via the original flight of steps up to the old front door and as a conventional reception area would intrude on the beautifully proportioned entrance hall, guests are welcomed at a discreetly positioned desk just inside the front door. The original house has many fine features and is furnished in period style with antiques; spacious public areas now extend from it, right across to the new accommodation wing through the Garden Room, a spacious contemporary lounge furnished with smart leather sofas. The new section of the hotel - which is modern and blends comfortably with the trees and gardens surrounding it - includes excellent leisure facilities, the main bar and restaurant, and guest accommodation. Guest rooms and suites are exceptionally attractive in terms of design - simple, modern, bright, utilising Irish crafts: rooms are generously-sized, with a pleasantly leafy outlook and good amenities; bathrooms have environmentally friendly toiletries, small baths and towels, and suggestions on saving water by avoiding unnecessary laundry - they are, however, well-finished and well-lit, with plenty of marbled shelf space. Conference/banqueting (500/300). Leisure centre (swimming pool); beauty salon. [*A new spa development is underway at the time of going to press.] Children welcome (under 2 free in parents room, cots available without charge, baby sitting arranged). No pets. **Rooms 79** (2 suites, 3 junior suites, 10 executive rooms, 20 no-smoking, 4 for disabled). Lift. 24 hour room service. B&B €85, ss €25. Closed 24-26 Dec. **Zings:** Creative use of lighting separates areas within this design-led dining area without physical divisions - and the tables are considerably spot lit (ideal for lone diners who wish to read). Gerry Allen, who has been head chef since the hotel opened in 1997 and has earned a local following, offers European cuisine with Mediterranean flavours on quite extensive menus: an example that sums up the style neatly is pan-fried fillet of seabass on a risotto of fresh basil and lemon with oven roast red peppers and a citrus tomato oil. Although international influences dominate, local produce is used - pretty desserts that are worth leaving room for include a commendable number of choices using seasonal fruits, for example, and local farmhouse cheeses are also a strong option, served with tomato & apple chutney, grapes and water biscuits. An unusually wide selection of house wines is offered, all moderately priced. Not suitable for children after 7pm. **Seats 120.** Air conditioning. L daily 12.30-2.30, D 6.30-9.30. Set L €25, D à la carte. House wines from €20. SC discretionary. Amex, Diners, MasterCard, Visa, Laser. **Directions:** Near Douglas village & adjacent to Douglas Golf Club; signed from roundabout where Rochestown Road meets Carrigaline Road.

Cork City
🍸 RESTAURANT

Proby's Bistro

Proby's Quay Crosses Green Cork Co Cork
Tel: 021 431 6531 Fax: 021 497 5882
Email: info@probysbistro.com Web: www.probysbistro.com

féite bia Handier to the city centre than it first appears, this is a pleasant spot for a bite to eat during the day (tables outside for fine weather) as well as in the evening, when menus are more likely to include less usual dishes, such as a main course house speciality of duck confit with custard apple jus, rustic potatoes and sautéed red & green cabbage. Although the style - established before the current wave and competently executed - is global cuisine, with an emphasis on things Mediterranean, plenty of local produce is used: West Cork black pudding is a favourite in starters, for example (the style varies, but it may come in a puff pastry parcel, with mozzarella cheese, and a cider & mustard cream sauce) and fish from Ballycotton, typically baked fillets with a tapenade crust, served with red pepper oil, scallion mash and sugar snap peas. Fast lunch (€7.95 for a gourmet sandwich with a choice of soup, fried or salad) and early dinner menus offer especially good value. A compact, well-chosen wine list offers about 40 wines, including a pair of appealing French house wines, plus quite an extensive menu of aperitifs, beers and after dinner drinks. An extended, covered terrace was due for completion at the time of going to press. Private parties/banqueting (120). Speciality Seafood Night on Wednesday, Set D €25. Children welcome. **Seats 120** (private room 40; outdoor seating, 20). Air conditioning. Open 6 days: Mon-Fri, 10 am-10pm (L 12-5, D 6-10); Sat D only, 6-10. Early D €21 (6-7.30), otherwise à la carte; SC discretionary (except 10% on parties of 8+). House wine €18.50. Closed Sun, Mon bank hols, 24-27 Dec. Amex, MasterCard, Visa, Laser. **Directions:** Adjacent to St. Finbarre's Cathedral and Beamish & Crawford brewery.

COUNTY CORK

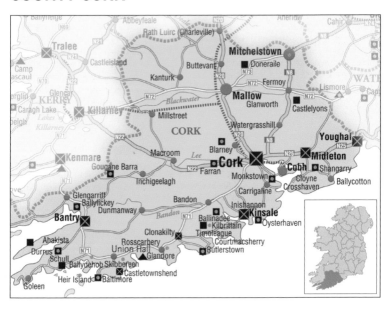

Ahakista

🍽 € FARMHOUSE

Hillcrest House

Ahakista Durrus Bantry Co Cork **Tel:** 027 67045
Email: hillcrestfarm@ahakista.com Web: www.ahakista.com

Hospitality comes first at this working farm overlooking Dunmanus Bay, where Agnes Hegarty's guests - including walkers, who revel in the 55 mile "Sheep's Head Way" - are welcomed with a cup of tea and home-baked scones on arrival. It is a traditional farmhouse with some recent additions, and makes a comfortable base for exploring the area, or a traditional family holiday - there's a swing and a donkey on the farm, rooms are big enough for an extra child's bed and it's only five minutes' walk to the beach. There's a sitting room for guests, with television and an open fire, and bedrooms - either recently refurbished or in a new extension - have power showers or bath, very comfortable beds, electric blankets, hair dryers, tea/coffee making facilities and clock radios. Two new rooms are on the ground-floor, with direct access to a sheltered patio, and parking close by. Fine cooked-to-order breakfasts will set you up for the day, and moderately priced evening meals are available if required - although there are plenty of good restaurants nearby, also pub with traditional Irish music. Hillcrest House was our Farmhouse of the Year in 2001. **Rooms 4** (3 en-suite & no-smoking, 3 shower only) B&B €32-34 pps (cot available without charge.) Evening meals by arrangement (7 pm; about €22); light meals also available. *Self-catering cottage and farmhouse also available, all year - details on the website. Closed 1 Nov - 1 Mar. MasterCard, Visa, Laser. **Directions:** 3 km from Bantry, takeN71 and turn off for Durrus, then Ahakista - 0.25km to Hillcrest.

Ballydehob

👁 RESTAURANT

Annie's Restaurant

Main Street Ballydehob Co Cork **Tel: 028 37292**

Anne and Dano Barry have been running their famous restaurant since 1983 - and, for many, a visit to West Cork is unthinkable without a meal here. Extending into the building next door a while ago allowed them to upgrade the whole restaurant so all facilities, including disabled toilets, are on the ground floor - but it's still the same Annie's, just a bit bigger. Annie is a great host, welcoming everybody personally, handing out menus - and then sending guests over to Levis' famous old pub across the road for an aperitif. Then she comes over, takes orders and returns to collect people when their meals are ready - there has never been room for waiting around until tables are ready, so this famous arrangement works extremely well. As to the food at Annie's, there's great emphasis on local ingredients and everything is freshly made on the day: fish is delivered every night; meat comes from the local butcher (who kills his own meat); their famous roast boned duck is from nearby Skeaganore Farm; their west Cork farmhouse cheeses include one of Ireland's most renowned cheeses, Gubbeen, which is made by Annie's sister-in-law Giana Ferguson; smoked foods come from Sally Barnes and the Gubbeen Smokehouse, where nephew Fingal Ferguson smokes bacon and cheese; and all the breads, ice creams and desserts for the restaurant are made on the premises. And Dano's cooking is simple and wholesome, the nearest to really good home cooking you could ever hope to find in a restaurant. Dano cooks fish like a dream and there is nowhere else like Annie's. Prices are very fair - the 4-course dinner menu is priced by choice of main courses and there's a carefully chosen wine list, with the majority of bottles under €30; annual tasting sessions decide on the six wines selected as House Wines for the year - interesting choices, and all great value at about €19. Wine list features interesting half dozen house selection. Not suitable for children after 9 pm. Toilets wheelchair accessible. Air conditioning. **Seats 45.** D Tue-Sat 6.30-10, Set D €42/44 (priced by choice of main course), à la carte also offered. House wines €19. SC Discretionary. Closed Sun, Mon, & November. MasterCard, Visa, Laser, Switch. **Directions:** Street-side, midway through village.

Ballylickey

🏨 HOTEL/RESTAURANT

Seaview House Hotel

Ballylickey Bantry Co Cork **Tel: 027 50462** Fax: 027 51555
Email: info@seaviewhousehotel.com Web: www.seaviewhousehotel.com

féile bia A warm welcome and personal supervision are the hallmarks of Kathleen O'Sullivan's restful country house hotel close to Ballylickey Bridge. Public rooms, which are spacious and well-proportioned, include a graciously decorated drawing room and a cocktail bar, both overlooking lovely gardens at the front of the house, and with outdoor seating for fine weather, also a cosy library and television room. Rooms vary, as is the way with old houses, and the most luxurious accommodation is in junior suites in a new wing; but many rooms have sea views, all are generously sized and individually decorated, and most have good bathrooms. Family furniture and antiques enhance the hotel, and standards of maintenance and housekeeping are consistently outstanding. Children welcome (cot available, baby sitting arranged). Pets permitted in some areas by arrangement. **Rooms 25** (6 junior suites, 2 family rooms, 5 ground floor rooms, 1 shower only, 2 disabled, all no smoking). No lift. B&B about €95 pps, ss about €25. **Restaurant:** Overlooking the garden, with views over Bantry Bay, the restaurant is elegant and well-appointed with antiques, fresh flowers and plenty of privacy. Set five-course dinner menus change daily and offer a wide choice on all courses; the style is country house cooking, with the emphasis firmly on local produce, especially seafood, in dishes like simple fresh Bantry Bay crab salad with Marie Rose sauce, chicken & celery consommé, baked fillet of lemon sole with tartare sauce or (an all time favourite) roast rack of lamb with rosemary. Choose from classic desserts - strawberry meringue roulade, crème brulée - or local cheeses to finish. Tea or coffee and petits fours may be served out of doors on fine summer evenings. A carefully selected, very informative, wine list offers an extensive range of well chosen house wines, a generous choice of half bottles - and many treats. Service, as elsewhere in the hotel, is caring and professional. **Seats 50.** Children welcome. Toilets wheelchair accessible. D 7-9 daily, L Sun 12.45-1.30; Set D about €40. House wines from €18. 10% sc. Hotel closed mid Nov-mid Mar. Amex, MasterCard, Visa, Laser. **Directions:** 10 mins drive from Bantry, on N71 to Glengarriff.

Baltimore

🍺 🐟 BAR/B&B

Bushe's Bar

The Square Baltimore Co Cork
Tel: 028 20125 Fax: 028 20596
Email: tom@bushesbar.com Web: www.bushesbar.com

Everyone, especially visiting and local sailors, feels at home in this famous old bar. It's choc-a-bloc with genuine maritime artefacts such as charts, tide tables, ships' clocks, compasses, lanterns, pennants et al - but it's the Bushe family's hospitality that makes it really special. Since Richard and Eileen took on the bar in 1973 it's been "home from home" for regular visitors to Baltimore, for whom a late morning call is de rigeur (in order to collect the ordered newspapers that are rolled up and stacked in the bar window each day). Now, it's in the safe hands of the next generation - Tom, Aidan and Marion Bushe - so all is humming nicely. Simple, homely bar food starts early in the day with tea and coffee from 9.30, moving on to Marion's home-made soups and a range of sandwiches including home-cooked meats (ham, roast beef, corned beef), salmon, smoked mackerel or - the most popular by far - open crab sandwiches, served with home-baked brown bread. And all under €9. This is a terrific pub, at any time of year, and was a very worthy recipient of our Pub of the Year Award in 2000. Children not allowed after 10pm. Bar food served 9.30am-8.30pm daily (12.30-8.30 Sun). Bar closed 25 Dec & Good Fri. **Accommodation:** Over the bar, there are three big, comfortable bedrooms, all with a double and single bed, bath & shower, TV and a kitchenette with all that is needed to make your own continental breakfast. There are also showers provided for the use of sailors and fishermen. No pets. **Rooms 3.** B&B €27.50 pps, single rate €35. Amex, MasterCard, Visa, Laser. **Directions:** In the middle of Baltimore, on the square overlooking the harbour.

Baltimore Area

 👁 RESTAURANT/ACCOMMODATION

Island Cottage

Heir Island Skibbereen Co Cork **Tel: 028 38102**
Fax: 028 38102 Web: www.islandcottage.com

Just a short ferry ride from the mainland yet light years away from the "real" world, this place is unique. Hardly a likely location for a restaurant run by two people who have trained and worked in some of Europe's most prestigious establishments - but, since 1990, that is exactly what John Desmond and Ellmary Fenton have been doing at Island Cottage. Everything about it is different from other restaurants, including the booking policy: a basic advance booking for at least six people must be in place before other smaller groups of 2 to 4 can be accepted - not later than 3pm on the day; changes to group numbers require 24 hours notice and a booking deposit of about €15 per head is required to reserve a table (you post a cheque or postal order). The no-choice 5-course menu (about €40) depends on the availability of the fresh local, organic (where possible) and wild island ingredients of that day, which might include wild salmon, shrimp and crab. A typical menu might be: marinated wild salmon on a bed of mayonnaise, with homemade brown bread; roast duck leg (made using hand-reared ducks "of exceptional quality" from Ballydehob) with béarnaise sauce & roast potatoes with rosemary; green salad with a little Gubbeen cheese; hot lemon soufflé; filer coffee. Off season cookery courses offered; also cottages for rent - details from the restaurant. **Seats 24** (max table size 10; be prepared to share a table). Set Menu - no choice, no exceptions D €40. Wed-Sun, 8.15-11.45 pm; one sitting served at group pace. Wine from €20. Off-season: groups of 16-24 by arrangement. Closed Mon & Tue, and mid Sep-mid May (please phone to check off season opening days/times). No credit cards. *Off season cookery courses available. **No Credit Cards. Directions:** From Skibbereen, on Ballydehob road, turn left at Church Cross, signposted Hare Island and Cunnamore. Narrow winding road, past school, church,

Minihan's Bar. Continue to end of road, Cunnamore car park. Ferry (blue boat) departs Cunnamore pier at 7.55 returns at 11.55 (journey: 4 minutes.) For ferry, contact John Moore / Richard Pyburn Tel: 086 809 2447.

Blarney
€ GUESTHOUSE

Ashlee Lodge

Blarney Co Cork
Tel: 021 438 5346 Fax: 021 438 5726
Email: info@ashleelodge.com Web:www.ashleelodge.com

Anne and John O'Leary's luxurious purpose-built guesthouse is just a couple of miles outside Blarney and within very easy striking distance of Cork city. (A bus from the city will drop you outside their door.) Everything is immaculate, from the impressive reception area with highly polished floor to exceptionally well-appointed bedrooms which have king size beds and all the latest technology. The O'Learys are exceptionally helpful hosts and are willing to assist guest in every way possible - notably with local knowledge of the many golf courses nearby; they arrange tee times, provide transport to and from golf courses and generally act as facilitators. They take pride in giving a good breakfast too - an impressive buffet offers everything you could wish for. Hot tub. Garden; fishing nearby. Golf breaks. **Rooms 10** (4 suites, 5 executive). B&B from about €40. Open all year.

Butlerstown
☆ 🎁 ◉ RESTAURANT WITH ROOMS

Otto's Creative Catering - O.C.C.

Dunworley Butlerstown Bandon Co Cork
Tel: 023 40461
Email: ottokunze@eircom.net Web: www.ottoscreativecatering.com

Very close to the spot where they originally started the famous Dunworley Cottage restaurant many years ago, Hilde and Otto Kunze have created a dream of a place here, with the help of their talented son who lives nearby and is a creative and practical woodworker. The house is unusual and only reveals its true personality once you are inside; words cannot do it justice, so you must go and see it for yourself. Deeply committed to the organic philosophy, Otto and Hilde are members of both Euro-Toques and the Slow Food movement - and their vegetable gardens provide a beautiful and satisfying view from the vine-clad dining room, where meals of wonderful simplicity cooked by Otto are presented by Hilde. Take time to marvel at the sheer originality and ingenuity of their home over a drink (brought with you, if you like - no corkage is charged - or chosen from a short list of biodynamically produced wines) in the sitting room, while also pondering a unique dinner menu that offers several choices on each course. Their own organic farm supplies many of the ingredients for the kitchen, and a comprehensive list of producers and suppliers is presented with the menu. Typically your meal may start with a vegetarian salad platter, with organic leaves and several dips or, perhaps, a plate of Anthony Cresswell's smoked organic salmon. Freshly baked breads and butter will be left temptingly close by on the table - try to resist as there are still marvellous soups (based on whatever vegetable is especially prolific at the time, or perhaps Otto's wonderful beef consommé), before you even reach the main courses. Here Otto moves up another gear and, as well as classics - wild salmon caught off the Seven Heads, panfried and served with, perhaps, a lobster cream, or organic T-bone steak well hung in local butcher Dan Moloney's cold room, panfried and served with its own gravy, mushrooms, onions and garlic butter - there are unusual choices like braised ox tongue with a rich red wine gravy and a vegetarian dish such as white organic asparagus with mustard greens and a freshly whisked sauce béarnaise. A magnificent selection of vegetables, with potatoes and rice, accompanies the main course and everything is presented with originality and palpable pleasure. Then there are desserts - apfelstrudel with vanilla ice cream, perhaps, or rhubarb fool with real vanilla custard. Or, if your visit is well-timed, there might be freshly picked top fruit, warm from the trees in the growing tunnels - cherries, plums, apricots, white peaches... This wonderful food needs no embellishment, it is outstanding value for the quality given - and it clearly gives Otto and Hilde great satisfaction to see their guests' appreciation. This place is a must for any food lover travelling in west Cork. *O.C.C. received our Natural Food Award in 2002, presented jointly by the Guide and Euro-Toques. Organic farm. **Seats 30** (max table size 14). D Wed-Sat, 7.30-9. €50, by reservation (24 hours notice if possible); L Sun only, 1.30-3 pm; Set Sun L €35. Organic house wine from €20, or BYO (no corkage). Closed Mon, Tue, mid Jan-March. **Accommodation:** The bedrooms (four) share the fresh originality of the rest of the house and are furnished in a simple Scandinavian style which, like the cleverly designed shower rooms, is intensely practical. And, of course, you will wake up in a most beautiful place - and have more of that superb food to look forward to, at a break-fast that counts home-made sausages and home-produced rashers among its gems. Children welcome (under 4 free in parents' room, cot available without charge.) Pets by arrangement. Walking, fishing. Garden. *Wheelchair access to dining room + toilet only. **Rooms 4.** B&B €60 pps, ss €20. MasterCard, Visa, Laser. **Directions:** Bandon to Timoleague to Dunworley.

Castletownshend B&B

Bow Hall

Main Street Castletownshend Co Cork
Tel: 028 36114 Email: dvickbowhall@eircom.net

Castletownshend is one of west Cork's prettiest villages and this very comfortable 17th century house on the hill is a wonderful place to stay if you enjoy a civilised atmosphere and old-fashioned comforts. With a pleasant outlook over beautiful well-tended gardens to the sea, excellent home-cooking and a warm welcome by enthusiastic hosts, Dick and Barbara Vickery (who 'retired' here from Minnesota 25 years ago), a visit to this lovely home is a memorable experience. The house is full of interest - books, photographs, paintings - but its most outstanding feature is perhaps the food, which is not only imaginative but much of it is home-grown too. Dinner for residents is by reservation only, when available, and is cooked by Barbara; however this treat would be a truly seasonal meal for a special occasion, based on their own produce fresh from the garden - potatoes, courgettes, swiss chard, salads, fresh herbs and fruit - picked just before serving, and cooked with other local specialities such as fresh crab or salmon. Breakfasts are also a highlight, with freshly squeezed orange juice, Barb's 'just out of the oven scones', home-baked breads and muffins, home-made sausages, bramble jelly and other home-made preserves, pancakes, home-made sausage patties with rhubarb sauce, and eggs Florentine among the many delights. On nights when she is not cooking, Barbara directs guests to good restaurants nearby. Non-smoking house. Children welcome (under 2 free in parents' bedroom, cot available without charge; children's play-ground nearby). Garden. Walking. Newsagent, tennis & fishing in village. No pets. **Rooms 3** (1 en-suite, 2 with private bath or shower rooms, all no smoking), B&B €50, ss €5; min 2 night stay preferred. Advance bookings essential, especially in winter. Residents D 8 pm, by reservation; €35 (no wine licence). Closed Christmas week. **No Credit Cards. Directions:** 5 miles from Skibbereen, on main street. Down the hill on the right hand side.

Castletownshend RESTAURANT/ATMOSPHERIC PUB

Mary Ann's Bar & Restaurant

Castletownshend Skibbereen Co Cork
Tel: 028 36146 Fax: 028 36920
Email: maryanns@eircom.net Web: www.maryannsbarrestaurant.com

Mention Castletownshend and the chances are that the next words will be 'Mary Ann's', as this welcoming landmark has been the source of happy memories for many a visitor to this picturesque west Cork village over the years. (For those who have come up the hill with a real sailor's appetite from the little quay, the sight of its gleaming bar seen through the open door is one to treasure.) The pub is as old as it looks, going back to 1846, and has been in the energetic and hospitable ownership of Fergus and Patricia O'Mahony since 1988 - but any refurbishments at Mary Ann's have left its original character intact. The O'Mahonys have built up a great reputation for food at the bar and in the restaurant, which is split between an upstairs dining room and The Vine Room at the back, which can be used for private parties; alongside it there is a garden which has been fitted with retractable awning over the tables, allowing for all-weather dining. Seafood is the star, of course, and comes in many guises, usually along with some of the lovely home-baked brown bread which is one of the house specialities. Another is the Platter of Castlehaven Bay Shellfish and Seafood - a sight to behold, and usually including langoustine, crab meat, crab claws, and both fresh and smoked salmon. Much of the menu depends on the catch of the day, although there are also good steaks and roasts, served with delicious local potatoes and seasonal vegetables. Desserts are good too, but local West Cork cheeses are an excellent option. The O'Mahonys also have an art gallery on the first floor, and it is proving a great success. Restaurant **Seats 32** (private room 40). Toilets wheelchair accessible. Children welcome. D daily in summer, 6-9; L 12-2.30. A la carte. House wine from €16.95. SC discretionary. *Bar food 12-2.30 & 6-9 daily. Closed Mon Nov - Mar, 25 Dec, Good Fri & 3 weeks Jan. MasterCard, Visa. **Directions:** Five miles from Skibbereen, on lower main street.

Clonakilty
 CAFÉ

Harts Coffee Shop

8 Ashe Street Clonakilty Co Cork **Tel: 023 35583**

féile bia Good home cooking is the attraction at Aileen Hart's friendly coffee shop in the town centre. A nifty little menu offers all kinds of healthy meals - ranging from a breakfast ciabatta with bacon, eggs & cheese, through warm baguettes (peppered steak strips, perhaps, with lettuce and mayo), sandwiches toasted and cool - all served with side salad & home-made vinaigrette dressing - to specials such as a west Cork salmon plate with home-made brown bread or an Irish cheese plate with a choice of crackers or bread. A Specials board suggests additions to the regular menu - soups (vegetables, perhaps, or pea & mint) based on home-made stocks, which are also used in traditional stews (beef & Beamish, perhaps), available in regular or large portions. But best of all, perhaps, is the choice of home-baked scones just like your granny used to make, served with home-made jam, and tarts - everything from a vegetarian quiche to an old-fashioned apple tart served with cream - and cakes ranging from healthy carrot cake to gooey orange chocolate drizzle cake. Simple, wholesome, home-made: just lovely! Great selection of drinks too, including freshly squeezed juices, teas and Green bean coffees. Wine licence. **Seats 30.** Children welcome. Open Mon-Sat, 10-5. Closed Sun & bank hols. **No Credit Cards. Directions:** Clonakilty town centre.

Clonakilty
 HOTEL/RESTAURANT

The Lodge & Spa at Inchydoney Island

Inchydoney Island Clonakilty Co Cork
Tel: 023 33143 Fax: 023 21164
Email: reservations@inchydoneyisland.com Web: www.inchydoneyisland.com

This hotel enjoys great views over the two 'Blue Flag' beaches at Inchydoney, which bring crowds to the area in summer, so many guests will prefer this as an off-season destination. The building is architecturally uninspired, but it has mellowed as landscaping of the large carpark on the seaward matures - and once inside the hotel (as opposed to the adjacent Dunes Pub), that pampered feeling soon takes over. Dramatic artworks in the spacious foyer are impressive, and other public areas include a large, comfortably furnished first-floor residents' lounge and library, with a piano and extensive sea views, and a soothing atmosphere. Most of the generously sized bedrooms have sea views and all are furnished and decorated in an uncluttered contemporary style, with air conditioning, safe and all the more usual amenities. Exceptional health and leisure facilities include a superb Thalassotherapy Spa, which offers a range of special treatments and makes Inchydoney a particularly attractive venue off-season, when this a very relaxing place. Special breaks are a major attraction - fishing, equestrian, golf, therapies, or simply an off-season weekend away - and its romantic location ensures its popularity for weddings. Conferences/banqueting (250). Self-catering apartments available (with full use of hotel facilities). Thalassotherapy spa (24 treatment rooms); beauty salon; swimming pool; walking; snooker; pool table. Children welcome (under 4 free in parents' room, cots available, baby sitting arranged). **Rooms 67** (3 suites, 1 junior suite,10 no smoking). Lift. B&B €155, ss about €55. SC10%. Open all year except Christmas. **Gulfstream Restaurant:** Located on the first floor, with panoramic sea views from the (rather few) window tables, this elegant restaurant offers fine dining in a broadly Mediterranean style. Fresh local produce, organic where possible, features on seasonal menus that always include imaginative vegetarian options - and willingly caters for any other special dietary requirements. Lighter dishes for spa guests are also offered, with nutritional information outlined. **Seats 70** (private room 250). Non-residents welcome by reservation. Children welcome. Toilets wheelchair accessible. Air conditioning.

D 6.30-9.45; Set D €49, also à la carte. House wine €20. SC10%. [*Informal/ bar meals also available 12-9 daily.] Amex, MasterCard, Visa, Laser. **Directions:** N71 from Cork to Clonakilty, then causeway to Inchydoney.

Doreraile

 **N** HISTORIC HOUSE

Creagh House

Main Street Doneraile Co Cork
Tel: 022 24433 Fax: 022 24715
Email: creaghhouse@eircom.net Web: www.creaghhouse.ie

While it may be a cliché to describe a house as 'amazing' that is, occasionally, the only word that seems to apply. Michael O'Sullivan and Laura O'Mahony left a perfectly normal home to take on this Regency townhouse in need of renovation in 2000; since then, they have been giving it enormous amounts of TLC on an ongoing basis so that it may, one day, reach its full potential glory. A listed building, with notable historical and literary connections, stately reception rooms and huge bedrooms, its principal rooms are among the largest from this period outside Dublin, and have beautiful restored plasterwork. Yet it is a relaxed family home and place of work (Michael and Laura both have offices in restored outbuildings), and this hospitable couple clearly thrive on the challenge of the restoration process. Accommodation is wonderful, in vast rooms with huge antique furniture, crisp linen on comfortable beds, little extras (bowls of fruit, bottled water, tea/coffee/hot chocolate making facilities), and bathrooms to match - bath and separate shower, and big, soft towels. All modern partitions have been removed to restore the original scale, and 19th century furniture is used throughout, with 18th and 19th century prints and modern paintings. Anyone interested in architecture and/or history is in for a treat when staying here and Doneraile is well-placed for exploring a wide area - Cork, Cashel, Lismore and Killarney are all within an hour's drive. Garden lovers will be fascinated by the 2-acre walled garden behind Creagh House, which is under restoration ("black topsoil four feet deep!") and the house is beside Doneraile Court, which has 600 acres of estate parkland, free to the public. Creagh House is still a work in progress - but what a work! Golf nearby. Children welcome (under 3s free in parents room, cot available free of charge). Pets permitted in some areas by arrangement. Garden. **Rooms 3** (all en suite, with separate bath and shower, all no smoking). Residents' supper (2-course dinner, €20) available with 24 hours notice. B&B €80 pps, no ss. Closed Oct - Mar Amex, MasterCard, Visa. **Directions:** Take N20 (Limerick road) from Mallow - 8 miles.

Durrus

☆ **T** RESTAURANT WITH ROOMS

Blairs Cove House

Durrus Bantry Co Cork **Tel:** 027 61127
Fax: 027 61487 Email: blairscove@eircom.net Web: www.blairscove.ie

Philippe and Sabine de Mey's beautiful property enjoys a stunning waterside location at the head of Dunmanus Bay. Although additions over the years have enlarged the restaurant considerably - including an elegant conservatory overlooking a courtyard garden - the original room at this remarkable restaurant is lofty, stone-walled and black-beamed. However, while characterful, any tendency to rusticity is immediately offset by the choice of a magnificent chandelier as a central feature, gilt-framed family portraits on the walls, generous use of candles - and the superb insouciance of using their famous grand piano to display an irresistible array of desserts. They have things down to a fine art at Blairs Cove - and what a formula: an enormous central buffet displays the legendary hors d'oeuvre selection, a speciality that is unrivalled in Ireland. Main course specialities of local seafood or the best of meat (rib eye of beef, perhaps) and poultry are char-grilled at a special wood-fired grill right in the restaurant and, in addition to those desserts on the piano, full justice is done to the ever-growing choice of local farmhouse cheese for which West Cork is rightly renowned. An extensive wine list favouring France a little offers a balanced selection in a wide price range, including a good choice of house wines and half bottles. The food is terrific, service friendly and efficient and, as a tribute to its memorable ambience, Blairs Cove was selected as our Atmospheric Restaurant of the Year in 2003. **Seats 85.** Reservations required. D 7.30-

9.30 Tue-Sat. Set D €53; house wine €18, SC discretionary. Closed Sun, Mon & Nov-Mar. **Accommodation:** Three small apartments, offered for self-catering or B&B, are furnished in very different but equally dashing styles and there is also a cottage in the grounds. Children welcome, cot available. B&B €105 pps, ss €30; no SC. MasterCard, Visa. **Directions:** 1.5 miles outside Durrus on Mizen Head Road, blue gate on right hand side.

Durrus
☆ **€** CAFÉ

Good Things Café

Ahakista Road Durrus Co Cork **Tel: 027 61426** Fax: 027 61426

Great ingredients-led contemporary cooking is the magnet that draws those in the know to Carmel Somers' simple little café-restaurant just outside Durrus village. Well-placed to make the most of fine west Cork produce, she also sells some specialist foods from Ireland and abroad and a few books including the great little guide to Local Producers of Good Food in Cork, produced by Myrtle Allen and Cullen Allen for the Cork Free Choice Consumer Group, which details many of the artisan producers who supply Good Things Café. The daytime café menu offers a concise list including great salads (mixed leaves with fresh beetroot, fresh broad beans, cherry tomatoes, smoked salmon, quails eggs among the goodies), West Cork fish soup (available, like most dishes on the daytime menu, as a starter or main course), West Cork Ploughmans (a trio of local cheeses served with an onion cassis compôte), Durrus cheese, spinach & nutmeg pizza (a thin-based, crisp pizza with a delicious gourmet topping)...then there are irresistible desserts to choose from a display (raspberries and cream, St Emilion chocolate cups...) Dinner brings a more formal menu, with a choice of four on each course, and will feature some of the daytime treats along with main courses like turbot with dill sauce with wilted spinach and local spuds, or beef fillet with pesto, on a bed of wilted spinach, chard, courgette & beetroot. Service is prompt and attentive from the moment a choice of breads and iced water is brought to your table to the arrival of home-made chocolate truffles with your coffee. Ingredients are invariably superb and, at its best, a meal here can be memorable; this place is a one-off and it is well worth planning a stop when travelling in West Cork, especially during the day, when the bright atmosphere and white café furniture seems more appropriate. An interesting, well-priced wine list includes seven well-chosen house wines, and a good choice of half bottles. *Cookery classes also available; details from the restaurant. Wheelchair Accessible. Ample parking. Children welcome. **Seats 40** (plus 10 outdoor in fine weather). In summer, open all day (10.30-5) Wed-Mon (daily in Aug & during Bantry Music Festival), L 12.30-3; also D Thu-Mon (7-8.30). A la carte. House wine €18. Closed Tue and Sep-Easter. Reservations advised for dinner; a call to check times is wise, especially off-season. MasterCard, Visa, Laser. **Directions:** From Durrus village, take Ahakista/Kilcrohane Rd.

Farran
🏛 COUNTRY HOUSE

Farran House

Farran Co Cork **Tel: 021 7331215** Fax: 021 7331450
Email: info@farranhouse.com Web: www.farranhouse.com

Set in 12 acres of mature beech woodland and rhododendron gardens in the rolling hills of the Lee valley, Patricia Wiese and John Kehely's impressive house was built in the mid-18th century, although its present elegant Italianate style only dates back to 1863. It is beautifully situated with views over the mediaeval castle and abbey of Kilcrea and its location west of Cork city makes this a good base for exploring Cork and Kerry. Since 1993 Patricia and John have painstakingly restored the house to its former glory and, although there are some contemporary touches as well as antiques, none of its original character has been lost - there's a fine drawing room for guests' use (complete with grand piano) and a billiard room with full size table. Despite its considerable size, there are just four bedrooms - all exceptionally spacious and decorated with style; dinner is offered on most nights, by prior arrangement, and a speciality is home-produced lamb, bred and raised at Farran House; when dinner is unavailable, guests are directed to an interesting old pub nearby where good food is served. The house is available all year for private rental by groups and this is, perhaps, its most attractive use. Golf nearby (six 18 hole courses within 20 km). Children welcome (under 10s free in parents' room, cot available without charge). No pets. Garden. **Rooms 4** (all en-suite, 2 with separate bath & shower; all no smoking); B&B from €80 pps, ss €30 (advance bookings only - 10% discount on 3 night stays; off-season rates reduced); residents D €40 (24 hours notice; not available Sun or Mon, but Thady Inn nearby does good meals). Self-catering coach house (4-6 people, from €500 pw); house also available for self-catering (groups of 8-9, from about €3,500 pw). Closed 1 Nov-31 Mar. MasterCard, Visa, Laser. **Directions:** Just off N22 between Macroom & Cork.

Fermoy Area   # Ballyvolane House

🏛 COUNTRY HOUSE   Castlelyons Fermoy Co Cork **Tel: 025 36349**   Fax: 025 36781
Email: info@ballyvolanehouse.ie   Web: www.ballyvolanehouse.ie

The Greene family's gracious mansion is surrounded by its own farmland, magnificent wooded grounds, a trout lake and formal terraced gardens, all carefully managed and well maintained - garden lovers will find a stay here especially rewarding; an information leaflet detailing the garden and walks is available to guests, also one on other walks in the locality. The Italianate style of the present house - including a remarkable pillared hall with a baby grand piano and open fire - dates from the mid 19th century when modifications were made to the original house of 1728. Jeremy and the late Merrie Green first welcomed guests to their home in 1983, and is now run by their son Justin and his wife Jenny; Justin has management experience in top hotels and they are an extremely hospitable couple, committed to ensuring that the standards of hospitality, comfort and food for which this lovely house is renowned will be maintained. And it is a very lovely house, elegantly furnished and extremely comfortable, with big log fires, and roomy bedrooms furnished with family antiques and looking out over beautiful grounds. Ballyvolane has private salmon fishing on 8km of the great River Blackwater, with a wide variety of spring and summer beats, so it is logical that delicious food should be another high point at Ballyvolane, where memorable modern Irish dinners are served in style around a long mahogany table (where breakfast is also served). There is much of interest in the area making this an excellent base for a peaceful and very relaxing break. Exciting plans are afoot at Ballyvolane at the time of going to press - five extra bedrooms are to be built in the form of Mongolian Yurts, in the walled garden, a development which is expected to be unobtrusive, so that the homely house party atmosphere of the main house can be retained. A self-catering cottage is also available. French is spoken. Banqueting. Children welcome, but not suitable for under 12s after 7pm (cot available, free of charge, baby sitting arranged). Pets permitted in some areas. Garden; fishing; walking, cycling. **Rooms 6** (1 shower only). B&B €75 pps ss €30. Residents D €47.50 at 8pm, book by 10am; menu changes daily. Wine list, from €23. Closed 24-31 Dec. Amex, Diners, MasterCard, Visa, Laser, Switch. **Directions:** Turn right off main Dublin-Cork road N8 just south of Rathcormac (signed Midleton), following house signs on to R628.

Glandore   # Hayes' Bar

🛡 PUB   The Square Glandore Co Cork **Tel: 028 33214**   Email: dchayes@tinet.ie

Hayes Bar overlooks the harbour, has outdoor tables - and Ada Hayes' famous bar food. The soup reminds you of the kind your granny used to make and the sandwiches are stupendous. Everything that goes to make Hayes' special - including the wines and crockery collected on Declan and Ada's frequent trips abroad (which also affect the menu, inspiring favourites like Croque Monsieur) - has to be seen to be believed. Just order a simple cup of coffee and see what you get for a couple of euro. Wine is Declan's particular passion and Hayes' offers some unexpected treats, by the glass as well as the bottle, at refreshingly reasonable prices. Great reading too, including a lot of background on the wines in stock - and you can now see some of Declan's paintings exhibited, from June to August. By any standards, Hayes' is an outstanding bar. Meals 12-5, Jun-Aug; weekends only off-season. Closed weekdays Sep-May except Christmas & Easter. **No Credit Cards. Directions:** The Square, Glandore.

Gougane Barra
E 👁 HOTEL/RESTAURANT

Gougane Barra Hotel

Gougane Barra Co Cork **Tel: 026 47069** Fax: 026 47226
Email: gouganebarrahotel@eircom.net Web: www.gouganebarra.com

féile bia In one of the most peaceful and beautiful locations in Ireland, this delightfully old-fashioned family-run hotel is set in a Forest Park overlooking Gougane Barra Lake (famous for its monastic settlements). The Lucey family has run the hotel since 1937, offering simple, comfortable accommodation as a restful base for walking holidays - rooms are comfortable but not over-modernised, all looking out on to the lake or mountain, and there are quiet public rooms where guests like to read. None of this has altered very much over the years, and that's just the way people like it, but 2005 brought a gentle change of direction as Neil Lucey and his wife Katy have taken over management of the hotel from Neil's parents. Their energy is bringing a fresh approach though walking holidays will remain an important part of the business, but there's now a new cultural edge too as Neil has opened a little theatre in the hotel and will host a production each summer. And, while the spirit of the place will thankfully remain unchanged, small but significant improvements are seen in details like replacing paper napkins with linen ones in the dining room, and laying more emphasis on the bar, where visitors are encouraged to drop in for informal meals. Katy's delicious bar menus include specialities like a moreish warm chicken salad, the superb house chowder which Katy brought from her father's kitchen in Lahinch, where her parents ran Mr Eamon's famous restaurant for many years - and her lovely rich walnut and treacle bread. More formal meals, including breakfast are served in the lakeside dining room. This is a magical place - as ever, the monks chose well. No weddings or other functions are accepted. Shop. Garden, walking. No pets. **Rooms 26** (all en-suite & no smoking, 6 shower only). B&B €65 pps, No SS. No smoking establishment. Closed Oct - Apr. MasterCard, Visa, Laser. **Directions:** Situated in Gougane Barra National Forest; well signposted.

Kilbrittain
☆ 🍷 RESTAURANT/ACCOMMODATION

Casino House

Coolmain Bay Kilbrittain Co Cork
Tel: 023 49944 Fax: 023 49945 Email: chouse@eircom.net

féile bia Kerrin and Michael Relja's delightful restaurant is just a few miles west of Kinsale and it is well worth the effort of getting here, as it is one of the best in an area which takes great pride in the excellence of its food. It's a lovely old house and it has an unusually cool continental style in the decor, but Kerrin's hospitality is warm - and Michael's food is consistently excellent, in wide-ranging seasonal menus based on the finest local ingredients: Ummera smoked organic salmon, fresh seafood from nearby fishing ports (don't miss his wonderful speciality lobster risotto) and Ballydehob duck all feature - a starter dish of four variations of duck is another speciality. Tempting vegetarian dishes are often listed ahead of the other main courses - spaghetti with basil oil, lamb's lettuce & feta cheese is typical - and nightly specials will include extra seafood dishes, all with individual vegetable garnishes and deliciously simple seasonal side vegetables. Variations on classic desserts are delicious (a delectable rhubarb & shortbread tartlet, with white chocolate & hazelnut crème and almond ice cream, for example) and local cheeses are always tempting in this area... An al fresco early summer dinner, or Sunday lunch, can be an especially memorable experience. Casino House was our Restaurant of the Year in 2005. ***Casino Cottage:** sleeps two €85 per night (or €155 for 2 nights), everything provided except breakfast - which can be supplied if needed. Longer stays discounted; weekly & winter rates available. **Seats 35** (private room 22; outdoor dining 16). D Thu-Tue, 7-9, L Sun only,1-2.30; all à la carte; house wine from €20.50; no sc. Closed Wed, and 1 Jan-17 Mar. MasterCard, Visa, Laser. **Directions:** On R600 between Kinsale and Timoleague.

Kilbrittain

The Glen Country House

🏛 COUNTRY HOUSE

The Glen Kilbrittain Co Cork **Tel: 023 49862** Fax: 023 49862
Email: info@glencountryhouse.com Web: www.glencountryhouse.com

BREAKFAST AWARD - COUNTRY HOUSE

Although classified (correctly) as a farmhouse, Guy and Diana Scott's home is an elegant period house and they have recently renovated it to a high standard for guests. It is quietly located in a beautiful area, and the four large double bedrooms have lovely views across Courtmacsherry Bay. There's even a family suite (consisting of a double room and children's room, with interconnecting bathroom) and guests have the use of a comfortable sitting room, and a dining room where delicious breakfasts are served - a buffet with fresh and poached seasonal fruits, freshly squeezed orange juice, organic muesli and organic yoghurt, and a menu of hot dishes including free range eggs from their own hens. It's a relaxed place, where dogs are welcome to join the two house spaniels (guests' horses are welcome too!) and, although there are no dinners, evening meals and baby sitting are offered for children, allowing parents to go out to one of the excellent local restaurants - Casino House and Otto's at Dunworley are both nearby. Strictly no smoking in bedrooms. Lots to do nearby - beautiful beaches, walking, golf - and a table tennis room has recently been added in a converted outhouse. Children welcome (under 4s free in parents' room, cot available without charge, baby sitting arranged). Garden. Pets permitted outdoors. **Rooms, 5** (all en-suite & no smoking, 4 shower only). B&B €60 pps, ss €15. Closed Nov-Easter. MasterCard, Visa, Laser, Switch. **Directions:** Signposted off the R600, midway between Kinsale and Clonakilty.

Kinsale

Blindgate House

🅔 GUESTHOUSE

Blindgate Kinsale Co Cork **Tel: 021 477 7858** Fax: 021 477 7868
Email: info@blindgatehouse.com Web: www.blindgatehouse.com

Maeve Coakley's purpose-built guesthouse is set in its own gardens high up over the town and, with spacious rooms, uncluttered lines and a generally modern, bright and airy atmosphere, Blindgate makes a refreshing contrast to the more traditional styles that prevail locally. All bedrooms are carefully furnished with elegant modern simplicity, have full en-suite bathrooms and good facilities including fax/modem sockets as well as phones, satellite TV, tea/coffee trays and trouser press. Maeve is an hospitable host - and well-known in Kinsale for her skills in the kitchen, so breakfast here is a high priority: there's a buffet displaying all sorts of good things including organic muesli, fresh fruits and juices, farmhouse cheese and yoghurts, as well as a menu of hot dishes featuring, of course, the full Irish Breakfast alongside catch of the day and other specialities - so make sure you allow time to enjoy this treat to the full. Children over 7 welcome (under 12s free in parents' room, baby sitting arranged). No pets. Garden. **Rooms 11** (all en-suite & no smoking); room service (limited hours). B&B €72.50 pps, no ss. Closed late Dec-mid Mar. Amex, MasterCard, Visa, Laser, Switch. **Directions:** From Fishy Fishy Café: Take left up the hill, keeping left after St Multose Church. Blindgate House is after St Joseph's Primary School, on the left.

Kinsale

Fishy Fishy Café @ The Gourmet Store

🍴 CAFÉ

Guardwell Kinsale Co Cork **Tel: 021 477 4453**

This delightful fish shop, delicatessen and restaurant is a mecca for gourmets in and around Kinsale and was our Seafood Restaurant of the Year in 2001. There's an agreeably continental air and, although all sorts of other delicacies are on offer, seafood is the serious business here - and, as well as the range of dishes offered on the menu and a specials board, you can ask to have any of the fresh fish on display cooked to your liking. Not that you'd feel the need to stray beyond the menu, in fact, as it makes up in interest and quality anything it might lack in length - and you can have anything you like from seafood chowder or smoked salmon sandwich to grilled whole prawns with lemon garlic & sweet chilli sauce or fresh lobster, crayfish or crab. Vegetarian dishes available on request. [At the time of going to press, Fishy Fishy is on the move to larger premises on O'Connell Street, in Kinsale town.] Not suitable for children under 7. Wheelchair accessible. No reservations. **Seats 36.** L daily 12-3.45 (Mon-Sat only, Oct-Mar); à la carte; house wines from about €18. Closed Sun from Oct to Mar; Christmas week. **No Credit Cards. Directions:** Opposite St Multose church, next to Garda station.

Kinsale

RESTAURANT

Le Bistro

Main Street Kinsale Co Cork **Tel: 021 477 7117** Fax: 021 477 7117
Email: eat@lebistrokinsale.com Web: www.lebistrokinsale.com

When the lease ran out at Jean-Marc Tsai and Jacqui St John-Jones' popular Kinsale restaurant Chow House recently, they decided on a slight change of course and, shortly before the Guide went to press, moved to this new town centre premises (embellished by murals by local artist Sheila Kern) where Jean-Marc is now moving more towards his previously well known continental mode again. In this lively and attractive 'Paris bistro style' restaurant, he offers a unique mélange of classic French and Asian food in the evening, and French bistro style for lunch; Jean-Marc is one of Ireland's great chefs and all who remember the fine dining experience at Chez Jean-Marc, or his superb Asian food at the Chow House will be delighted with this new venture: Vietnamese spring rolls, baked sea bass, 'trou normand' (apple sorbet with calvados), it's all here, on daily-changing menus. Jean-Marc is always in the kitchen and Jacqui is always out at the front, otherwise they are closed. The wine list changes every three months, and offers organic and chemical-free wines - also imported French beers. Off season, Asian nights (Vietnamese, Chinese and Thai) are held on Sundays, for local residents. Gorgeous food, great service, good value - and an enjoyable ambience: this place has it all. **Seats 50.** Children welcome, but not after 8pm. D Daily 6.30 - 10 (Sun 6-10). House Wine from € 18.50. Closed Feb and Tue Oct-Jun. MasterCard, Visa, Laser. **Directions:** In the centre of Kinsale, corner of Market St.

Kinsale

🏨 ACCOMMODATION

Perryville House

Long Quay Kinsale Co Cork
Tel: 021 477 2731 Fax: 021 477 2298
Email: sales@perryville.iol.ie Web: www.perryvillehouse.com

One of the prettiest houses in Kinsale, Laura Corcoran's characterful house on the harbour front has been renovated to an exceptionally high standard and provides excellent accommodation only 15 minutes from the Old Head of Kinsale golf links. Gracious public rooms are beautifully furnished, as if for a private home. Spacious, individually decorated bedrooms vary in size and outlook (ones at the front are most appealing, but the back is quieter) and all have extra large beds and thoughtful extras such as fresh flowers, complimentary mineral water, quality toiletries, robes and slippers. The suites have exceptionally luxurious bathrooms, although all are well-appointed and some have recently been refurbished. No evening meals are served but there's a choice of fine restaurants just outside the door, and Laura also arranges for guests to make special out of town visits, to Otto Kunze's famous organic restaurant at Dunworley, for example, or to Casino House, at Kilbrittain (see entries). Breakfasts include home-baked breads and local cheeses; morning coffee and afternoon tea are available to residents in the drawing room and there is a wine licence. No smoking establishment. Own parking. Not suitable for children. No pets. **Rooms 25** (5 junior suites,8 superior, all no-smoking). B&B from €100 pps, No SC. Closed Nov-1Apr. *Wireless internet throughout the house Amex, MasterCard, Visa, Laser. **Directions:** Central location, on right as you enter Kinsale from Cork, overlooking marina.

Kinsale
🏛 GUESTHOUSE

The Old Bank House

11 Pearse Street Kinsale Co Cork
Tel: 021 477 4075 Fax: 021 477 4296
Email: oldbank@indigo.ie Web: www.oldbankhousekinsale.com

téile bia Marie and Michael Riese's townhouse in the centre of Kinsale has earned a great reputation for quality of both accommodation and service - it has an elegant residents' sitting room and comfortable country house-style guest rooms and suites, all furnished and decorated to the same impeccable standard, with antiques and lovely bathrooms. And breakfast is a treat - an extensive menu is served in a dining room that is set up impressively, like a restaurant, and continental breakfast is available in bedrooms by request. Limited room service is also available for coffee, tea, wine, mineral water etc (which may also be served in the sitting room). For golfers, tee-off times, hire of clubs, transport to course, and golf tuition can all be arranged, and there is a golf storage room. Under 3s free in parents' room; cot €25. Golf-friendly: tee-off times, hire of clubs, transport to course, golf tuition can all be arranged; golf storage room. **Rooms 17** (1 suite, 3 junior suites, all no smoking). Lift. Room service (limited hours).

B&B about €170 per room (max 2 guests). Closed 23-26 Dec. Amex, MasterCard, Visa, Laser, Switch.
Directions: On right hand side at start of Kinsale, next to the Post Office.

Kinsale
☆ RESTAURANT

Toddies Restaurant

Kinsale Brewery The Glen Kinsale Co Cork **Tel: 021 477 7769**
Email: toddies@eircom.net Web: www.toddieskinsale.com

ATMOSPHERIC RESTAURANT OF THE YEAR

The address may give the impression that Pearse and Mary O'Sullivan's recently relocated restaurant is 'out of town' but if you walk down Pearse Street (away from the harbour) and turn right at the T junction, you'll see their sign across the road, outside a fine limestone archway. It's a big change from their discreet restaurant above the harbour, to this bustling down town restaurant and bar above the Kinsale Brewery - with whom there is a strong working relationship as they pump their Kinsale lager, wheat beer and stout directly up to Toddies bar. From the courtyard, exterior stairs lead up to the restaurant, pausing at the large and stylish al fresco dining area provided by two terraces before arrival at the bar and a smart split-level dining room. It's an exciting enterprise, and word quickly spread to a growing fan club who love not only Pearse's fine modern Irish cooking, but also the inside-or-out table arrangements, great service by Mary and her bubbly staff, and the whole atmosphere of the place. Seafood is, of course, the star - home-made ravioli of lobster with a cherry tomato sauce & shaved parmesan is one of many speciality dishes that had already established Toddies as a leading restaurant in the area - but Pearse's high regard for local meats (and west Cork cheeses), ensures a balanced choice. **Seats 50** (outdoor dining,30). Children welcome. L 12.30-3.30, D 6.30-10.30 (L&D every day Jun - Oct). L & D A la carte.(Starters about €6-16; main courses about €22-30). House wine from €19.50. SC discretionary. Closed 10 Jan-10 Feb. *guests can eat at the bar or in the restaurant Amex, MasterCard, Visa, Laser. **Directions:** Drive to the end of Pearse St., take right turn, Toddies is second on the left through limestone arch and into courtyard.

Kinsale Area
🏛 COUNTRY HOUSE

Glebe Country House

Ballinadee nr Kinsale Bandon Co Cork
Tel: 021 477 8294 Fax: 021 477 8456
Email: glebehse@indigo.ie Web: http://indigo.ie/~glebehse/

Set in two acres of beautiful, well-tended gardens (including a productive kitchen garden), this charming old rectory near Kinsale has a lovely wisteria at the front door and it is a place full of interest. The building dates back to 1690 (Church records provide interesting details: it was built for £250; repairs and alterations followed at various dates, and the present house was completed in 1857 at a cost of £1,160). More recently, under the hospitable ownership of Gill Good, this classically proportioned house has been providing a restful retreat for guests since 1989, and everybody loves it for its genuine country house feeling and relaxing atmosphere. Spacious reception rooms have the feeling of a large family home, and generous, stylishly decorated bedrooms have good bathrooms, phones and tea/coffee making facilities. The Rose Room, on the ground floor, has French doors to the garden. A 4-course candle-lit dinner for residents, much of it supplied by the garden, is served at a communal table (please book by noon). Although unlicensed, guests are encouraged to bring their own wine. Breakfasts are also delicious, and this can be a hard place to drag yourself away from in the morning although there are many things to do nearby, including golf, and it is well placed for exploring the area. An indoor heated swimming pool is under construction in the garden at the time of going to press. Two self-catering apartments are also available. The whole house may be rented by parties by arrangement and several self-catering apartments are also available. Children welcome (under 10s free in parents' room, cots available without charge, baby sitting arranged.) Pets permitted. **Rooms 4** (2 shower only, all no-smoking), B&B €50 pps, ss €15. Residents' D Mon-Sat, €35, at 8pm (please book by noon). No D on Sun. BYO wine. Closed Christmas. *Indoor heated swimming pool to be completed for the 2006 season. Diners, MasterCard, Visa, Laser. **Directions:** Take N71 west from Cork to Innishannon Bridge, follow signs for Ballinadee (6 miles). After village sign, first on right.

Mallow
☆🏛 🍴 RESTAURANT/COUNTRY HOUSE

Longueville House

Mallow Co Cork
Tel: 022 47156 Fax: 022 47459
Email: info@longuevillehouse.ie Web: www.longuevillehouse.ie

When Michael and Jane O'Callaghan opened Longueville House to guests in 1967, it was one of the first Irish country houses to do so. Its history is wonderfully romantic, "the history of Ireland in miniature", and it is a story with a happy ending: having lost their lands in the Cromwellian Confiscation (1652-57), the O'Callaghans took up ownership again some 300 years later. The present house, a particularly elegant Georgian mansion of pleasingly human proportions, dates from 1720, (with wings added in 1800 and the lovely Turner conservatory - which has been completely renovated - in 1862), overlooks the ruins of their original home, Dromineen Castle. Very much a family enterprise, Longueville is now run by Michael and Jane's son William O'Callaghan, who is the chef, and his wife Aisling, who manages front of house. The location, overlooking the famous River Blackwater, is lovely. The river, farm and garden supply fresh salmon in season, the famous Longueville lamb, and all the fruit and vegetables. In years when the weather is kind, the estate's crowning glory is their own house wine, a light refreshing white, "Coisreal Longueville" - wine has always been Michael O'Callaghan's great love, and he has recently started using their abundant apple supply to make apple brandy too. Public rooms include a bar and drawing room, both elegantly furnished with beautiful fabrics and family antiques, and accommodation is equally sumptuous; although - as is usual with old houses - bedrooms vary according to their position, they are generally spacious, superbly comfortable and stylishly decorated to the highest standards. Dining here is always a treat (see below) and breakfast is also very special, offering a wonderful array of local and home-cooked foods, both from the buffet and cooked to order; Longueville was the National Winner of our Irish Breakfast Awards in 2003, and it's worth dropping in even if you can't stay overnight - what a way to break a journey! As well as being one of the finest leisure destinations in the country, the large cellar/basement area of the house has been developed as a conference centre, with back-up services available. The house is also available for small residential weddings throughout the year. Conference/banqueting (50/110). Children welcome (under 2s free in parents' room, cot available). No pets. **Rooms 20.** (4 suites, 2 junior suites, 1 superior room, 3 family rooms; all no-smoking). B&B €100pps, ss €45. Closed early Jan-mid Mar. Shooting weekends available in winter; telephone for details). **Presidents Restaurant:** Named after the family collection of specially commissioned portraits of all Ireland's past presidents (which made for a seriously masculine collection until Ireland's first woman president, Mary Robinson, broke the pattern) this is the main dining room and opens into the beautifully renovated Turner conservatory, which makes a wonderfully romantic setting in candlelight; there is a smaller room alongside the main restaurant, and also the Chinese Room, which is suitable for private parties. William O'Callaghan is an accomplished chef, and home- and locally-produced food is at the heart of all his cooking. An 8-course Menu Gourmand is offered for complete parties, and there are daily dishes (which will include a vegetarian choice) in addition to well-balanced dinner menus. Home-produced and local ingredients star, in starters like house smoked salmon, or salad of crab with dry cured Longueville ham and, perhaps, an intriguing speciality dish, trio of Longueville lamb with pakchoi & mint sauce, or home reared pork loin - dishes which sound simple enough on the menu but, in the hands of this creative chef, can be complex on the plate. Home produce influences the dessert menu too, as in a croustade of caramelised apple with Longueville apple brandy ice cream, for example, and it is hard to resist the local farmhouse cheeses. Delicious home-made chocolates and petits fours come with the coffee and service, under Aisling O'Callaghan's direction, is excellent. A fine wine list includes many wines imported directly by Michael O'Callaghan. Children welcome. **Seats 80** (private room 12). D daily, 6-9; early D €35 (6.15-7 Sun-Thu), Set D €55, Menu Gourmand €75; light meals 12.30-5.0 daily. House wine €29, sc discretionary (% added to parties of 8+). CLosed 7 Jan - 16 Mar. MasterCard, Visa, Laser. **Directions:** 3 miles west of Mallow via N72 to Killarney.

Midleton

Farmgate

€ RESTAURANT

The Coolbawn Midleton Co Cork **Tel: 021 463 2771**
Fax: 021 463 2771 Email: farmgaterestaurant@eircom.net

 This unique shop and restaurant has been drawing people to Midleton in growing numbers since 1985 and it's a great credit to sisters Maróg O'Brien and Kay Harte. Kay now runs the younger version at the English Market in Cork, while Maróg looks after Midleton. The shop at the front is full of wonderful local seasonal produce - organic fruit and vegetables, cheeses, honey - and their own super home baking, while the evocatively decorated, comfortable restaurant at the back, with its old pine furniture and modern sculpture, is regularly transformed from bustling daytime café to sophisticated evening restaurant (on Friday and Saturday) complete with string quartet. A tempting display of fresh home bakes is the first thing to catch your eye on entering and, as would be expected from the fresh produce on sale in the shop, wholesome vegetables and salads are always irresistible in the restaurant too. Maróg O'Brien is a founder and stall holder of the hugely successful Midleton Farmers Market, which is held on Saturday mornings, and is committed to handling only produce in season. Mon-Sat - L 12-4, D 6.30 - 9.45. Closed Sun, Bank Hols, 24 Dec-3 Jan. MasterCard, Visa, Laser. **Directions:** Town centre.

Midleton

🏭🌱 COUNTRY HOUSE

Glenview House

Midleton Co Cork **Tel: 021 463 1680** Fax: 021 463 4680
Email: info@glenviewmidleton.com Web: www.glenviewmidleton.com

When Ken & Beth Sherrard acquired their lovely Georgian house near Midleton in 1963 it was virtually derelict. Two years later, Ken bought the entire contents of the Dublin Georgian buildings infamously demolished to make way for the new ESB offices - and today this well-tended, comfortable and elegantly furnished house is the richer for that act of courage. Now, with a welcoming fire in the hall and classically-proportioned reception rooms on either side, it's hard to imagine it any other way. Except for one ground floor room adapted for wheelchair users and with its own entrance), bedrooms in the main house are on the first floor, all spacious and comfortably furnished with en-suite bathrooms (one has an antique bath with a highly original - and practical - shower arrangement built in), hair dryers and tea/coffee-making facilities. There is also some delightful self-catering accommodation in converted outbuildings - with the agreeable arrangement of dinner in the main house as an option. Deliciously homely dinners (asparagus soup, roast fillet of beef with new potatoes, spinach and French beans, lemon syllabub or meringues) are cooked by Beth and served at a large mahogany table, set up as for a family dinner party - and second helpings are offered, just like home. An excellent breakfast next morning follows a similar pattern: a bowl of newly-laid eggs (complete with feather) adorns the table; a choice of fresh fruits and juices may include halved galia melon, filled with other fruits; a fine rendition of the traditional Irish breakfast follows - and saffron coloured scrambled eggs can make for a memorable start to the day. There is a real sense of hospitality in this lovely house and the Sherrards are keen to introduce guests to the many things there are to do in the area: the heritage sites at Cobh and Midleton are nearby, also Fota Wildlife Park, Arboretum & Golf, wonderful walks and much else besides. Glenview has a lovely natural garden and woodland walks. Terrace, croquet, lawn tennis, forest walks, cycling. Children welcome (discounts offered, baby sitting arranged). No pets. **Rooms 7** (4 in main house, 3 in converted coach house, 2 suites (coach house), 4 shower-only, 2 fully wheelchair accessible, all no smoking). B&B €70pps, no ss. Residents D 8 pm, €40 (book by noon). Good, very reasonably priced wine list, from €14. Self-catering available (incl a fully wheelchair accessible apartment). Open all year. *Picnic lunch available on request € 10 Amex, MasterCard, Visa, Laser.
Directions: Drive into Midleton (do not take the by-pass). When you come to the AIB bank, take the L35 (R626) Fermoy road. Continue towards Fermoy for 2.5 miles until reaching a forestry area; look for a sign for Leamara, Watergrasshill and Glenview House. Turn left and immediately right, following signage for Glenview House. Exactly 3 miles from Midleton.

Midleton Area

⭐🏭🌱 COUNTRY HOUSE/RESTAURANT

Ballymaloe House

Shanagarry Midleton Co Cork
Tel: 021 465 2531 Fax: 021 465 2021
Email: res@ballymaloe.ie Web: www.ballymaloe.com

féile bia Ireland's most famous country house hotel, Ballymaloe was one of the first country houses to open its doors to guests when Myrtle and her husband, the late Ivan Allen, opened The Yeats Room restaurant in 1964. Accommodation followed in 1967 and since then a unique network of family enterprises has developed around Ballymaloe House - including not only the farmlands and gardens that supply so much of the kitchen produce, but also a craft and kitchenware shop, a company producing chutneys and sauce, the Crawford Gallery Café in Cork city, and Darina Allen's internationally acclaimed cookery school. Yet, despite the fame, Ballymaloe is still most remarkable for its unspoilt charm: Myrtle - now rightly receiving international recognition for a lifetime's work "recapturing forgotten flavours, and preserving those that may soon die"- is ably assisted by her children, and now their families too. The house, modestly described in its Blue Book (Irish Country House & Restaurants Association) entry as "a large family farmhouse", is indeed at the centre of the family's 400 acre farm, but with over thirty bedrooms it is a very large house indeed, and one with a gracious nature. The intensely restorative atmosphere of Ballymaloe is remarkable, and there are few greater pleasures than a fine Ballymaloe dinner followed by a good night's sleep in one of their thoughtfully furnished (but not over decorated) country bedrooms - including, incidentally, Ireland's most ancient hotel room which is in the Gate House: a tiny one up (twin bedroom, with little iron beds) and one down (full bathroom and entrance foyer), in the original medieval wall of the old house: delightful and highly romantic! Ground floor courtyard rooms are suitable for wheelchairs. Conferences/banqueting (25/50). Children welcome (cot available; baby sitting arranged). Pets allowed by arrangement. Outdoor swimming pool, tennis, walking, golf (9 hole). Gardens. Shop. **Rooms 33** (4 ground floor, 1 disabled, 2 shower only, all no smoking). B&B €125pps, ss€15. SC discretionary. Room service (limited hours). No lift. Self-catering accommodation also available (details from Hazel Allen). **Restaurant:** The restaurant is in a series of domestic-sized dining rooms and guests are called to their tables from the conservatory or drawing room, where aperitifs are served. A food philosophy centred on using only the highest quality ingredients is central to everything done at Ballymaloe, where much of the produce comes from their own farm and gardens. The rest, including seafood from Ballycotton and Kenmare, comes from leading local producers. Jason Fahey has been head chef at Ballymaloe since 2004 and continues the house tradition of presenting simple, uncomplicated food in the 'good country cooking' style, which allows the exceptional quality of the ingredients to speak for themselves. This is seen particularly at Sunday lunchtime when - apart from the huge range of dishes offered, which would obviously be beyond the home cook - the homely roasts and delicious vegetables are as near to home cooking you are ever likely to find in a restaurant, and what a joy that is. Then things move up a number of notches in the evening, when daily 7-course dinner menus (with vegetarian dishes given a leaf symbol) offer more sophisticated dishes - but there is still a refreshing homeliness to the tone which, despite very professional cooking and service, is perhaps more like a dinner party than a smart restaurant experience. Ballymaloe brown bread, crudités with garlic mayonnaise, a tart of locally smoked fish with tomato & chive beurre blanc, superb roast lamb with rosemary & garlic and chateau potatoes, Irish farmhouse cheeses with home-made biscuits and a dessert trolley that include rhubarb compôte and vanilla ice cream are typical of dishes that invariably delight - and, as if a 7-course dinner isn't enough, second helpings of the main course are offered too. The teamwork at Ballymaloe is outstanding and a meal here is a treat of the highest order. Finish with coffee or tea and home-made petits fours, served in the drawing room - and perhaps a drink from the small bar before retiring contentedly to bed. Children welcome at lunchtime, but the restaurant is not suitable for children under 7 after 7pm. (Children's high tea is served at 5.30.) Buffet meals only on Sundays. **Seats 110.** L daily 1-1.15, D daily 7-9.15 (Sun 7.30-8); Set D €62, Set L €38. House wine from €22. Service discretionary. Reservations essential. House closed 23-26 Dec, 12-20 Jan. Helipad. * Self Catering Accommodation also available Amex, Diners, MasterCard, Visa, Laser. **Directions:** Situated between Cloyne & Shanagarry.

Monkstown

 PUB/RESTAURANT/ACCOMMODATION

The Bosun

The Pier Monkstown Co Cork
Tel: 021 484 2172 Fax: 021 484 2008
Email: info@thebosun.ie Web: www.thebosun.ie

Nicky and Patricia Moynihan's waterside establishment close to the both the car ferry across to Cobh and the Ringaskiddy ferries (France and Wales), has grown a lot over the years, with the restaurant and accommodation becoming increasingly important. Bar food is still taken seriously, however; seafood takes pride of place and afternoon/evening bar menus include everything from chowder or garlic mussels through to real Dingle Bay scampi and chips, although serious main courses for carnivores such as beef with brandy & peppercorn sauce and beef & Guinness casserole are also available. Next to the bar, a well-appointed restaurant provides a more formal setting for wide-ranging table d'hôte and à la carte menus - and also Sunday lunch, which is especially popular. Again seafood is the speciality, ranging from popular starters such as crab claws or oysters worked into imaginative dishes, and main courses that include steaks and local duckling as well as seafood every which way, from grilled sole on the bone to medallions of marinated monkfish or a cold seafood platter. There's always a choice for vegetarians and vegetables are generous and carefully cooked. Finish with home-made ices, perhaps, or a selection of Irish farmhouse cheeses. Not suitable for children after 7pm. Restaurant **Seats 80** (max table size 12). Private room 25/30. Air conditioning. Toilets wheelchair accessible. D daily 6.30-9, L Sun 12-2.30, Set D €42, Set Sun L €27.50; à la carte also available; house wine €21, sc discretionary. Bar food available daily 12-9.30). Closed 24-26 Dec, Good Fri. **Accommodation:** Bedrooms are quite simple but have everything required (phone, TV, tea/coffee trays); those at the front have harbour views but are shower only, while those at the back are quieter and have the advantage of a full bathroom. Fota Island Golf Course is only 12 minutes away, also Fota House and Wildlife Centre. **Rooms 15** (9 shower only). Lift. B&B €55 pps, ss €7. Children welcome (under 5s free in parents' room, cot available without charge). No pets. Closed 24-26 Dec, Good Friday Amex, Diners, MasterCard, Visa, Laser. **Directions:** On sea front.

Rosscarbery
🍴 RESTAURANT

O'Callaghan-Walshe

The Square Rosscarbery Co Cork
Tel: 023 48125 Fax: 023 48125 Email: funfish@indigo.ie

This unique restaurant on the square of a charming village (well off the busy main West Cork road) has a previous commercial history that's almost tangible - exposed stone walls, old fishing nets and glass floats, mismatched furniture, shelves of wine bottles and candlelight all contribute to its unique atmosphere - which is well-matched by proprietor-host Sean Kearney's larger-than-life personality. Then there's the exceptional freshness and quality of the seafood - steaks theoretically share the billing, but West Cork seafood 'bought off the boats at auction' steals the scene. Martina O'Donovan's menus change daily but specialities to look out for include the famous Rosscarbery Pacific oysters and, also a superb West Cork Seafood Platter, char-grilled prime fish such as turbot, and grilled whole lobster. Ultrafreshness, simplicity - and a huge dose of personality - add up to make this place a delight. O'Callagan Walsh was the our Atmospheric Restaurant of the Year in 2004. An interesting wine list includes a good choice of half bottles. Not suitable for children after 7 pm. **Seats 40.** D Tue-Sun 6.30-9.15. Set D €45, also a à la carte, house wine €19.70, sc discretionary. Open weekends only in winter (a phone call to check is advised). MasterCard, Visa, Laser. **Directions:** Main square.

Schull Area
🏛 COUNTRY HOUSE

Rock Cottage

Barnatonicane Schull Co Cork **Tel: 028 35538**
Fax: 028 35538 Email: rockcottage@eircom.net Web: www.rockcottage.ie

Garden-lovers, especially, will thrill to the surroundings of Barbara Klotzer's beautiful slate-clad Georgian hunting lodge near Schull, which is on a south-facing slope away from the sea, which is nearby at Dunmanus Bay. A fascinating combination of well-tended lawns and riotous flower beds, the rocky outcrop which inspired its name - and even great estate trees in the 17 acres of parkland (complete with peacefully grazing sheep) that have survived from an earlier period of its history create a unique setting. The main house has style and comfort, with welcoming open fires and bright bedrooms which - although not especially large - have been thoughtfully furnished to allow little seating areas as well as the usual amenities such as tea/coffee making facilities, and recently refurbished en-suite power showers. There's a sheltered courtyard behind the house and also some appealing self-catering accommodation, in converted stables. And Barbara is an accomplished chef - so you can look forward to a dinner based on the best of local produce, with starters like fresh crab salad or warm Ardsallagh goats cheese, main courses of Rock Cottage's own rack of lamb, monkfish kebab, or even lobster or seafood platters (prices for these options on request), beautiful vegetables and classic desserts like home-baked vanilla cheesecake or strawberry fool. Extensive breakfast choices include a Healthy Breakfast and a Fish Breakfast as well as traditional Irish and continental combinations - just make your choice before 8pm the night before. Barbara also offers laundry facilities - very useful when touring around, (€9 per load for washing and drying). Not suitable for children under 10. No pets. garden. walking. **Rooms 3** (2 with en-suite showers, 1 with private bathroom, all no smoking). B&B from €65 pps, ss €25. Breakfast, 8.30-9.30 (order by 8pm the night before). Residents D Mon-Sat, €40, at 7.30; house wine €18. No D on Sun. Open all year. MasterCard, Visa, Laser. **Directions:** From Schull, 6 miles, at Toormore, turn into R591 after 1.5 miles. Sign on left.

Youghal

Aherne's Seafood Restaurant & Accommodation

RESTAURANT WITH ROOMS   163 North Main Street Youghal Co Cork **Tel: 024 92424**
Fax: 024 93633 Email: ahernes@eircom.net Web: www.ahernes.com

The FitzGibbon family's warm hospitality and ultra-fresh seafood straight from the fishing boats in Youghal harbour are the secrets of success at Aherne's, which is now in its third-generation of family ownership - John FitzGibbon supervises the front of house, and his brother David reigns over a busy kitchen. Deliciously straightforward bar food includes oysters, the house chowder, and smoked salmon (all served with the renowned moist dark brown yeast bread), while restaurant meals are naturally more ambitious; seafood is still the undisputed star of the show, but evening menus in the restaurant include some token meat dishes - rack of lamb with a rosemary jus or mint sauce, char-grilled fillet steak with mushrooms and shallot jus or pepper sauce - and David is not afraid of simplicity when it is merited. Specialities like prawns cooked in garlic butter or fresh crab salad can make memorable starters, for example, and who could resist a main course hot of buttered Youghal Bay lobster? These are, in a sense, simple dishes yet they have plenty of glamour too. It is well worth planning a journey around a bar meal at Aherne's - or better still, if time permits, a relaxed evening meal followed by a an overnight stay. A wine list strong on classic French regions offers a good selection of half bottles and half a dozen champagnes. **Seats 55** (private room, 20). Toilets wheelchair accessible. D 6.30-9.30 daily; set D €35; also à la carte; house wine €22, sc discretionary. *Bar food daily, 12-10. **Accommodation:** The stylish rooms at Aherne's are generously sized and individually decorated to a high standard; all are furnished with antiques and have full bathrooms. Housekeeping is exemplary, as elsewhere at Aherne's, and excellent breakfasts are served in a warm and elegantly furnished residents' dining room. Studio apartments more recently added are equipped to give the option of self-catering if required. Conference room (25). Safe & fax available at reception. Children under 5 free in parents' room (cot available without charge, baby sitting arranged). No pets. **Rooms 13** (5 junior suites, 1 for disabled). B&B €100 pps, ss €20. Wheelchair access. Closed 23-29 Dec. Amex, MasterCard, Visa. **Directions:** on N25, main route from Cork-Waterford.

Youghal

Ballymakeigh House

FARMHOUSE   Killeagh Youghal Co Cork **Tel: 024 95184** Fax: 024 95370
Email: ballymakeigh@eircom.net Web: www.ballymakeighhouse.com

Winner of our Farmhouse of the Year Award in 1999, Ballymakeigh House provides a high standard of comfort, food and hospitality in one of the most outstanding establishments of its type in Ireland. Set at the heart of an east Cork dairy farm, this attractive old house is immaculately maintained and run by Margaret Browne, who is a Euro-Toques chef and author of a successful cookery book. The house is warm and homely with plenty of space for guests, who are welcome to use the garden and visit the farmyard. The individually decorated bedrooms are full of character and equally comfortable, and Margaret's hospitality is matched only by her energetic pursuit of excellence - ongoing improvements and developments are a constant characteristic of Ballymakeigh. Margaret Browne has a national reputation for her cooking; an impressive dinner menu is offered every night, and non-residents are very welcome in the restaurant. Garden, walking. Off-season value breaks, special interest breaks. Self-catering accommodation is also available nearby, in a restored Victorian house. Children welcome (under 3 free in parents' room, cot available, baby sitting arranged). Pets allowed in some areas by arrangement. **Rooms 5** (all en-suite & no smoking, 3 shower only). B&B €60 pps, ss €10. D daily, 7-8, residents only; Set D €44; house wine from €20; SC discretionary. House closed Nov 1-Mar1. MasterCard, Visa. **Directions:** Off N25 between Youghal & Killeagh (signed at Old Thatch pub).

COUNTY DONEGAL

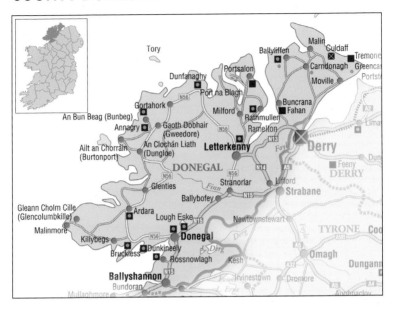

Annagry

🅢🅟 RESTAURANT WITH ROOMS

Danny Minnie's Restaurant

Annagry Co Donegal

Tel: 074 954 8201 Web: www.dannyminnies.com

The O'Donnell family has run Danny Minnie's since 1962, and a visit is always a special treat. There's nothing about the exterior as seen from the road to prepare first-time visitors for the atmosphere of this remarkable restaurant: hidden behind a frontage of overgrown creepers a surprise awaits when, after a warm welcome from Terri O'Donnell, guests are suddenly surrounded by antiques and elegantly appointed candle-lit tables. The menu is presented in both Irish and English, and Brian O'Donnell's cooking is a good match for the surroundings - fine, with imaginative saucing, but not at all pompous. On the wide-ranging à la carte menu, seafood stars in the main courses - lobster and other shellfish, availability permitting - and there is also a strong selection of meats including Donegal mountain lamb, typically served with honey, garlic and rosemary gravy, and Donegal beef, served various ways including classic Beef Wellington. Vegetables are a strength and gorgeous desserts, such as lemon and lime pannacotta with a refreshing rhubarb and strawberry compôte, can be relied on to create an appropriately delicious finale. And, under Terri's direction, friendly and attentive waitresses provide lovely service. There's nowhere quite like Danny Minnie's, winner of the Guide's Atmospheric Restaurant of the Year in 2000. Not suitable for children after 9pm. Reservations required. **Seats 80.** Air conditioning. D daily in summer, 6-10. Set D €40; also à la carte; house wine from €25; no sc. (Phone ahead to check opening hours, especially off peak season) Closed 25/26 Dec, Good Fri & early week off season. [Accommodation is also offered in eight non-smoking rooms, five of them en-suite and one suitable for disabled guests]. MasterCard, Visa, Laser. **Directions:** R259 off N56 - follow Airport signs.

Ardara

👁 € B&B

The Green Gate

Ardvally Ardara Co Donegal
Tel: 074 95 4 1546 Web: www.thegreengate-ireland.com

Paul Chatenoud's amazing little B&B is a one-off. Above Adara, up a steep and twisting boreen (follow his unique signing system) that will reward you with a stunning view on arrival, Paul offers simple but comfortable accommodation in his unspoilt traditional cottage and converted outbuildings. It's a far cry from the Parisian bookshop he once ran, but this romantic little place is magic. In the morning (or whenever you wake up - he will be working around his lovely garden and is happy to stop at any time it suits his guests), he cooks up breakfast while you take in the laid-back homeliness of the cosy cottage sitting room. If the morning is fine he may serve breakfast in the garden (just where is that beautiful music coming from?) while he regales you with stories of famous people who have fallen in love with The Green Gate. Be glad you found it, because he's probably right - it may well be "the most beautiful place anywhere in Ireland"; just leave the Merc at home - and come with an open mind. Children welcome (cot available and baby sitting arranged), but some parents may feel it is rather remote for young children. Pets permitted by arrangement. **Rooms 4** (all with en-suite bathrooms, bath only). B&B €35pps, ss €10. Open all year. **No Credit Cards. Directions:** One mile from Ardara on the hill.

Ballyliffin

Ⓝ 👁 HOTEL

Ballyliffin Lodge and Spa

Shore Road Ballyliffin Co Donegal **Tel: 074 937 8200**
Email: info@ballyliffinlodge.com Web: www.ballyliffinlodge.com

This impressive new hotel in Ballyliffin village is an especially welcome newcomer to the area - with the beautiful view, and the space and comfort it offers. Public areas include a traditional bar, and spacious guest rooms are finished to a high standard with many extras, including safes. General Manager Cecil Doherty, who is also a joint-proprietor of the hotel, has considered every detail including excellent on-site leisure facilities with swimming pool and spa treatments. Head chef Kwangi Chan is well known in Ireland for his accomplished modern European cuisine, and the hotel's Holly Tree Restaurant attracted favourable attention from the outset. Discounts are available for hotel guests at Ballyliffin GC, and short breaks are offered. The hotel also accepts wedding parties. **Rooms 40** (all no smoking). Lift. Restaurant: D daily. Bar meals also available. Open all year except 25 Dec & Good Fri. **Restaurant:** Children welcome. **Seats 60**, reservations required, toilets accessible for wheelchairs, vegetarian menu available. Food served all day. L Sun (10-4) D Sun (6-9) House Wine € 16. Closed 25 Dec, Good Friday. Residents can get a discount on local golf. Helipad Amex, Diners, MasterCard, Visa, Laser, Switch. **Directions:** In Ballyliffin village (signed).

Bruckless

👁 FARMHOUSE

Bruckless House

Bruckless Co Donegal **Tel: 074 973 7071** Fax: 074 973 7070
Email: bruc@iol.ie Web: www.iol.ie/~bruc/bruckless.html

EC Cliff and Joan Evans' lovely 18th-century house and Connemara pony stud farm is set in 18 acres of woodland and gardens overlooking Bruckless Bay - an ideal place for people who enjoy quiet countryside and pursuits like walking, horse-riding and fishing. The gardens are not too formal but beautifully designed, extensive and well-maintained - they really enhance a visit here, as does the waterside location: guests have direct access to the foreshore at the bottom of the garden. Family furniture collected through a Hong

Kong connection adds an unexpected dimension to elegant reception rooms that have views over the front lawns towards the sea, and the generous, comfortably furnished bedrooms. Accommodation include two single rooms and there is a shared bathroom - although the house is large, the guest bedrooms are close together, so they are ideal for a family or a group travelling together. Enjoyed home-produced eggs at breakfast, which is the only meal served - guests are directed to local restaurants in the evening. Self-catering accommodation is also available all year, in a two-bedroomed gatelodge. Garden, equestrian, walking, fishing. **Rooms 4** (2 en-suite, all no-smoking) B&B €60pps, no ss. Weekly rates also offered. *A two-bedroom Gate Lodge, sleeping four, is available for self-catering. Closed 1 Oct-31 Mar. Amex, MasterCard, Visa. **Directions:** On N56, 12 miles west of Donegal .

Bunbeg
👁 HOTEL

Ostan Gweedore

Bunbeg Co Donegal **Tel: 074 953 1177** Fax: 074 953 1726
Email: reservations@ostangweedore.com Web: www.ostangweedore.com

Although its blocky 1970s' architectural style may not be to today's taste, Ostan Gweedore was built to make the most of the location - and this it does exceptionally well. Spacious public areas, including the aptly named Ocean Restaurant and the Library Bar ("the most westerly reading room on the Atlantic seaboard") have superb views over the shoreline and Mount Errigal - as does the Sundowner Wine & Tapas Bar, which offers a wide range of wines by the glass and a menu of small tapas-style dishes to nibble while you watch the sun sinking in the west. The hotel takes pride in the restaurant - extensive menus offer a wide range of dishes based mainly on local produce, especially seafood and Donegal mountain lamb - and it has a strong local following. Most of the bedrooms have panoramic sea views, and although some may seem a little dated, they are all are comfortable. It's a very relaxing place for people of all ages and in high season it is especially ideal for families, with its wonderful beach and outdoor activities, including tennis, pitch & putt and day visits to nearby islands Tory, Gola and Arranmore. If you enjoy fresh air and exercise, ask at reception for the booklet Walks in the Bunbeg Area, which was specially commissioned by the hotel and details a variety of planned walks and cycle paths in the locality. Wet days are looked after too, with excellent indoor leisure facilities including a 19-metre swimming pool, Jacuzzi and gym, supervised by qualified staff, and a new health and beauty spa which offers all the current pamper treatments. This romantic setting is predictably popular for weddings; (conferences/banqueting 250/300). Leisure centre; spa. Fishing and golf (9 hole) available locally. Children welcome Under 5s free in parents' room (cot available without charge, baby sitting arranged). * Donegal Airport, Carrickfin is nearby. **Rooms 36** (3 suites). Ocean Restaurant: D daily, 7-9, à la carte; Sundowner Tapas bar: 7-9.30 daily. B&B €85 pps, ss €20. Closed Nov-Feb. Amex, Diners, MasterCard, Visa, Laser. **Directions:** From Letterkenny, take coast road past hospital.

Donegal
🏛 HISTORIC HOUSE

Saint Ernan's House Hotel

Donegal Co Donegal **Tel: 074 972 1065** Fax: 074 972 2098
Email: res@sainternans.com Web: www.sainternans.com

Set on its own wooded island, connected to the mainland by a causeway built after the famine by tenants as a gesture of thanks to a caring landlord, Brian and Carmel O'Dowd's lovely Victorian country house hotel on the edge of Donegal Town is remarkable for its sense of utter tranquillity. This atmosphere is due, in part, to its unique location - and also, one imagines, to the kindly ghosts who seem to reside here, especially the spirit of John Hamilton, that young landlord who built the house in 1826. That other-worldliness remains there is an almost tangible sense of serenity about the place that makes it the perfect retreat from the stresses of modern life. The spacious public rooms have log fires and antique furniture - plenty of space for guests read, or simply to relax in front of the fire - and the individually decorated bedrooms echo that restfulness; as in all old houses, they vary in size and position but most also have lovely views and all are furnished to a high standard with antiques, and have good amenities including (surprisingly perhaps) television. Many guests would see no need to leave the island during their stay, but there is much to do and see in the area: the craft shops of Donegal Town almost on the doorstep, for example. The dining experience at Saint Ernans follows the same philosophy of quiet relaxation and is only for resident guests; simple country house-style dinner menus offer two or three choices on each course and are based on local produce, with vegetarian dishes on request. Residents Only. **Seats 16** D 7-8 daily, Set D €42-52 (semi-à la carte, priced by course); house wine €25. Closed mid Oct-Easter. MasterCard, Visa, Laser. **Directions:** 1.5 mile south of Donegal Town.

Dunfanaghy
 RESTAURANT WITH ROOMS

The Mill Restaurant

Figart Dunfanaghy Letterkenny Co Donegal
Tel: 074 913 6985 Fax: 074 913 6985
Email: themillrestaurant@oceanfree.net Web: www.themillrestaurant.com

Beautifully located on the shore of the New Lake, which is a special area of conservation, the mill was the home of Susan Alcorn's grandfather and, as they are a family of accomplished painters, the walls are hung with wonderful water colours. Susan and her husband Derek, who is the chef, have earned a dedicated following here, as the location is superb, the welcome warm and the cooking both imaginative and assured - and they offer very good value. The dining room is on two levels, with plenty of windows framing the views, fresh flowers on the tables, soft lighting and some well-placed antiques - a room of character and atmosphere. Menus are based firmly on the best ingredients, local where possible, and change every 4-6 weeks. While based on the classics, the house style is quite contemporary: soups are often unusual (purée of pea, apple & curry, for example), while roast rack of lamb with dauphinoise potatoes & and apricot & mint sauce develops a classic combination. Seafood is well-represented, of course, and a speciality upside down fish pie is anything but humble, with its filling of lobster, crab claws and john dory in a brandy cream sauce. Delicious desserts might include a seasonal fruit crumble tart with custard & ginger ice cream, or there's a good Irish cheese plate. (Lovely breakfasts too.) Children welcome. **Seats 50.** Air conditioning. D Tue-Sun 7-9pm, Set D €38; house wine €17; sc discretionary. Closed Mon, mid Dec-mid Mar. Accommodation is offered in six individually decorated rooms. The decor is simple but stylish, with good new beds and some antique pieces, and there's also a lovely little sitting room off the dining room, with comfy big chairs and sofas to relax in. Children welcome (cot available without charge). No pets. Garden. Walking; cycling. **Rooms 6** (all en-suite & no-smoking, 2 shower only). B&B €43 pps, ss €14.50. Establishment closed Jan-Mar 17. Amex, MasterCard, Visa, Laser. **Directions:** N56 from Letterkenny through Dunfanaghy. 1/2 mile outside Dunfanaghy on Falcarragh road on right hand side at the lake.

Dunkineely
 HOTEL/RESTAURANT

Castle Murray House Hotel

St. John's Point Dunkineely Co Donegal
Tel: 074 973 7022 Fax: 074 973 7330
Email: info@castlemurray.com Web: www.castlemurray.com

Martin and Marguerite Howley's beautifully located clifftop hotel has wonderful sea and coastal views over the ruined castle after which it is named. It is a comfortable and relaxing place to stay, with a little bar, a residents' sitting room and a large verandah that can be covered with an awning in a good summer, so meals may be served outside. Bedrooms have a mixture of modern and older pieces that give each room its own character, and are gradually being refurbished; most have sea views and all are quite large with a double and single bed, good bathrooms (most with full bath) and facilities including digital TV as well as phone and tea/coffee trays. A sun area on the sheltered flat roof at the back of the building has direct access from some bedrooms. Lovely breakfasts are served in the restaurant. Banqueting (70). Children welcome (under 5s free in parents' room, cots available, baby sitting arranged). Pets permitted by arrangement. Garden. Walking. Off-season value breaks. **Rooms 10** (some shower only, all no smoking). B&B €70pps, ss €25. **Restaurant:** The restaurant is on the seaward corner of the hotel and maximises the impact of the dramatic view, including the castle (which is floodlit at night), and an open fire makes for real warmth in this dramatic location, even in winter. Remy Dupuis, who has been head chef since 1994, works alongside Marguerite Howley and there is a consistent house style, with a strong emphasis on local produce. Multi-choice menus (basically 3-course, plus options of soup and sorbet), are sensibly priced according to the choice of main course and there is plenty to choose from, including vegetarian dishes. Seafood is the speciality of the house in the summer months - fresh oysters with sweet chilli dip, prawn & monkfish gratin in garlic butter, wild salmon with Madeira & chanterelle sauce - and there's an emphasis on giving good value; even the supplement for lobster, from McSwynes Bay, is very reasonable. In winter, when seafood is less plentiful, there are more red meats, poultry and game. The wonderful location, helpful staff and consistently good cooking make this a place people keep coming back to. The wine list leans towards the Old World, particularly France, and offers some non-alcoholic wines and an unusually extensive selection of half bottles. **Seats 60.** Not suitable for children. D daily in summer 6.30-9.30, L Sun only 1.30-3.30; D from €46.00 (depending on choice of main course); Set Sun L €26; house wine €19; No SC. Restaurant closed Mon & Tue low season. Hotel closed mid Jan-mid Feb. MasterCard, Visa, Laser. **Directions:** Situated on the N56, 8km from Killybegs, 20 km from Donegal Town on the coast road to St Johns Point; first left outside Dunkineely village.

Greencastle
👻 BAR/RESTAURANT

Kealys Seafood Bar

The Harbour Greencastle Co Donegal
Tel: **074 93 81010** Fax: 074 93 81010 Email: kealys@iol.ie

 The ferry between the fishing port of Greencastle and Magilligan Point in Northern Ireland now brings many new visitors to an area that used to seem quite remote - and those in the know plan their journeys around a meal at James and Tricia Kealy's excellent seafood restaurant. It's a low key little place where simplicity has always been valued and, even if it's just to pop in for a daytime bowl of Greencastle chowder and some home-baked chowder, don't miss the opportunity of a visit to Kealys - if we did

an award for seafood chowder, theirs would take the prize! James's approach to seafood is creative and balanced, seen in dishes which are modern in tone but also echo traditional Irish themes, and in which delicious local organic vegetables are used with fish to make the most of both resources. Typical dishes might include baked fillet of hake on braised fennel with a tomato & saffron butter sauce and, perhaps, a classic Irish partnership of baked Atlantic salmon with a wholegrain mustard crust served on Irish spring cabbage and bacon. There will be at least one meat or poultry dish offered every day and there's always an imaginative vegetarian dish too - Gubbeeen cheese & almond fritters, on a seasonal salad with honey & mustard dressing, for example. James is also a great baker and makes a variety of breads - you might find that one of them makes a perfect partner for one of their range of Irish farmhouse cheeses, typically Gubbeen, St Killian, Boilié and Cashel Blue. Service, under Tricia's direction, is smart and friendly - and a compact but appealing wine list offers good value, and includes a small selection of half and quarter bottles. Children welcome until 9pm. **Seats 65.** L Tue-Sun, 12.30-2.45pm; D Tue-Sun, 7-9.30 (Sun to 8.30); Set D €35, also à la carte. House wine €15. Closed Mon, 2 weeks Nov, 25 Dec, Good Friday. Amex, MasterCard, Visa, Laser. **Directions:** Harbour at Greencastle.

Laghey
🏛 COUNTRY HOUSE

Coxtown Manor

Laghey Co Donegal
Tel: **074 973 4575** Fax: 074 973 4576
Email: coxtownmanor@od1dpost.com Web: www.coxtownmanor.com

 Just a short drive from the county town, this welcoming late Georgian house set in its own parkland is in a lovely, peaceful area close to Donegal Bay. Belgian proprietor, Edward Dewael - who fell for the property some years ago and is still in the process of upgrading it - personally ensures that everything possible is done to make guests feel at home. A pleasant wood-panelled bar with an open fire is well-stocked, notably with Belgian beers and a great selection of digestifs to accompany your after dinner coffee - and it extends into a

pleasant conservatory on one side and a drawing room on the other. Accommodation is divided between a recently converted coach house at the back where the new bedrooms are very spacious, with plenty of room for golf kits and large items of luggage, and have excellent bathrooms to match - yet many guests still prefer the older rooms in the main house, for their character; some have countryside views and open fireplaces and they are large, comfortable and well-proportioned, with recently renewed bathrooms. Children welcome (under 12 free in parents' room; cot available without charge, baby-sitting arranged). Walking; garden. **Rooms 9** (2 junior suites, 9 en-suite, 1 shower only). B&B €99 pps, ss €20. **Dining Room:** The elegant and well-appointed period dining room is the heart of the house, and is - like the food served here - attractive yet not too formal. Friendly staff promptly offer aperitifs and presentation of menus which are priced by course and offer about four mostly classic dishes with an emphasis on seafood (scallops from Donegal Bay, clams and mussels from Lissadell, for example), also Thornhill duck and local Charolais beef - a sound foundation for proficient cooking: starters will certainly include at least one shellfish dish (trio of Donegal Bay lobster, fresh crab and prawns on organic salad, perhaps); main course choices are also likely to favour seafood (wild Donegal Bay salmon with creamy herb sauce), but may include less usual dishes like squab pigeon (served de-boned, with caramelised apples). The produce is mostly local - and of superb quality - but the style is Belgian, offering a different experience from other dining options in the area. Belgian chocolate features strongly on the dessert menu but there are lighter options. Dining at Coxtown is now mainly for residents (but non residents are welcome by reservation when there is room), and good food and great service from friendly staff ensure that will be an enjoyable experience. **Seats 25.** Restaurant open to limited numbers of non-residents by reservation. D Tue-Sat; Set D €46; also short a la carte. House wine €21.50. Breakfast buffet 8-10am; (cooked options include delicious Fermanagh dry-cured black bacon.) Closed Sun, Mon, Nov 1 - Feb 10. Amex, MasterCard, Visa, Laser. **Directions:** Main sign on N15 between Ballyshannon & Donegal Town.

Letterkenny
🏛️👁️ HOTEL/RESTAURANT

Castle Grove Country House Hotel

Letterkenny Co Donegal
Tel: 074 91 51118 Fax: 074 91 51118
Email: reservation@castlegrove.com Web: www.castlegrove.com

Parkland designed by "Capability" Brown in the mid 18th-century creates a wonderful setting for Raymond and Mary Sweeney's lovely period house overlooking the lough. Although new hotels in Letterkenny have brought competition, Castlegrove remains the first choice for discerning visitors to the area: it is, as Mary Sweeney says, an oasis of tranquillity. Constant improvement is the policy and the last few years have seen major changes, including a new conservatory, a larger new restaurant and, most recently, the adjoining coach house has been developed to make seven lovely bedrooms - all carefully designed and furnished with antiques to feel like part of the main house - and a small conference room. The original walled garden is also under restoration as part of an on-going development of the gardens which will continue for several years. Bedrooms are spacious and elegantly furnished to a high standard with antiques, and bathrooms are gradually being upgraded where practical, to provide walk-in showers as well as full bath. Good breakfasts include a choice of fish as well as traditional Irish breakfast, home-made breads and preserves. Mary Sweeney's personal supervision ensures an exceptionally high standard of maintenance and housekeeping, and staff are friendly and helpful. Two boats belonging to the house are available for fishing on Lough Swilly and there is a special arrangement with three nearby golf clubs. Conference/banqueting (25/50). House available for private use (family occasions, board meetings etc) Not suitable for children under 12. No pets. **Rooms 14** (1 suite, 2 junior suites, 2 shower only, 2 disabled, all no-smoking) B&B about €80 pps, no ss. *Weekends/ short breaks available. Open all year except Christmas. Not suitable for children under 10 after 7pm. **Seats 50** (private room, 15). B'fst 8-9.30 daily, L 12.30-2 Mon-Sat, D 6.30-9 daily. Set L from about €22, light L about €15; Set D about €30-48, D also à la carte; house wines from €15; sc discretionary. Reservations required. Closed L Sun; 23-29 Dec. Amex, Diners, MasterCard, Visa, Laser. **Directions:** R245 off main road to Ramelton.

Lough Eske
HOTEL/RESTAURANT

Harvey's Point Country Hotel

Lough Eske Donegal Co Donegal
Tel: 074 972 2208 Fax: 074 972 2352
Email: info@harveyspoint.com Web: www.harveyspoint.com

Blessed with one of Ireland's most beautiful locations, on the shores of Lough Eske, this hotel was first opened by the Gysling family in the late 1980s, with chalet-style buildings linked by covered walkways and pergolas creating a distinctly alpine atmosphere reminiscent of their native Switzerland - a style that suited the site well, with the open low-level design allowing views of the lough and mountains from most areas of the hotel. Guests re-visiting today will find many changes, and a far more luxurious establishment - rooms in the new forty room extension do not all have a lake view, but acres of space, six foot beds and a circular bath the size of a small swimming pool will please many guests. However, the older rooms - which are tucked away in front of the extension, along the ground floor corridor - may be of much more interest to those in the know; although less luxurious, they will appeal if you would enjoy being closer to the countryside, and with access to the lough. **Restaurant:** The bar and restaurant areas are unchanged: a welcoming log fire sets the tone in the bar, where menus are promptly offered by friendly staff, and the restaurant - a large room, extending right down to the foreshore, where classically appointed tables are set up to take advantage of the beautiful view - seems more appealing than ever. Head chef Franck Pasquier's menus offer an extensive choice and, while there are no surprises, the tone is refreshingly classical - salmon with tarragon beurre blanc, black sole on the bone, chicken chasseur are all typical - and M. Pasquier's classic French cooking is always a treat. The restaurant is also open for lunch, every day except Saturday. **Seats 100** (private room, 20). Air conditioning. Toilets wheelchair accessible. L 12.30-2.30 (Sun 12-6) & D 6-9.30, daily in summer. [Nov-Mar: open only Wed D-Sun L]. Set D €50, Set L €25; house wine from €19.50; no SC. Off season (Nov-Mar), closed D Sun, all Mon & Tue. Amex, Diners, MasterCard, Visa, Laser. **Directions:** N15 /N56 from Donegal Town - take signs for Lough Eske & hotel. (6km from Donegal Town.)

Lough Eske
B&B

Rhu-Gorse

Lough Eske Co Donegal **Tel: 074 972 1685** Fax: 074 972 1685
Email: rhugorse@iol.ie Web: www.lougheske.com

Beautifully located, with stunning views over Lough Eske (and windows built to take full advantage of them), Grainne McGettigan's modern house may not be not architecturally outstanding but it has some very special attributes, notably the warmth and hospitality of Grainne herself, and a lovely room with picture windows and a big fireplace, where guests can relax. Bedrooms and bathrooms are all ship-shape and residents can have afternoon tea as well as breakfast, although not evening meals; however Harvey's Point is very close,(see entry), and Donegal town is only a short drive. Animals are central to Rhu-Gorse, which is named after a much-loved pedigree dog bred by Grainne's father-in-law (a descendant now follows her around everywhere), and one of her special interests is breeding horses: not your average B&B, but a comfortable, hospitable and very interesting base for a walking holiday or touring the area. Golf nearby. Children welcome (under 4s free in parents' room, baby sitting arranged). Pets allowed in some areas. Garden. **Rooms 3** (2 en-suite, shower only; 1 with private bath; all no smoking). B&B €40, ss €10. Closed 31 Oct-31 Mar. MasterCard, Visa, Laser. **Directions:** Take N15 /N56 from Donegal Town. Take signs for Lough Eske & Harvey's Point Hotel. Pick up signs for Rhu-Gorse.

Portsalon
👁 💶 B&B

Croaghross

Portsalon Letterkenny Co Donegal
Tel: 074 915 9548 Fax: 074 915 9548
Email: jkdeane@croaghross.com Web: www.croaghross.com

John and Kay Deane's latter-day country house enjoys a lovely location on the Fanad peninsula, overlooking Lough Swilly. It is a very pleasant house, surrounded by beautiful gardens, the Deanes are natural hosts and it's close to Ballydaheen Gardens and Glenveagh National Park. A comfortable guests' sitting room with lovely view across gardens and the lough provides plenty of relaxing seating for guests, and guest rooms are attractively positioned - three open onto a sun terrace, while two side rooms overlook a landscaped rock garden. Breakfast is the only meal served, but the Deanes will direct you to the most suitable local restaurant for dinner. Although officially closed in winter, bookings can be made by arrangement - this is an attractive option for a group, as the house is centrally heated throughout and the living room has a big open fire. The Deanes also have a new 3 bedroomed single storey house available next door, which is available for self-catering or B&B, and a 3-bedroomed self-catering cottage nearby. Special golf rates are available for guests - Croaghross is within 5 minutes walk of Portsalon golf club. Golf nearby - special rates available for Croaghross guests. Children welcome (under 5s free in parents' room, cot available without charge; baby sitting arranged). Pets permitted. Garden. **Rooms 5** (all en-suite & no smoking, 2 shower only, 1 for disabled). B&B from €35 pps, ss €10.00. Closed 1 Oct-17 Mar. MasterCard, Visa, Laser. **Directions:** Letterkenny - Ramelton- R246 (Milford direction) through Kerrykeel to Portsalon; opposite golf course turn up hill.

Rathmullan
 COUNTRY HOUSE/RESTAURANT

Rathmullan House

Rathmullan Co Donegal
Tel: 074 91 58188 Fax: 074 91 58200
Email: info@rathmullanhouse.com Web: www.rathmullanhouse.com

Set in lovely gardens on the shores of Lough Swilly, this gracious nineteenth century house is fairly grand with public areas which include three elegant drawing rooms, but it's not too formal - and there's a cellar bar which can be very relaxed. It was built as a summer house by the Batt banking family of Belfast in the 1800s, and has been run as a country house hotel since 1961 by the Wheeler family and, under the current energetic management of William and Mark Wheeler, and Mark's wife, Mary, an impressive extension has recently been completed. The design is in sympathy with the surroundings and they now have ten very desirable, individually decorated new bedrooms, and The Gallery, a state of the art conference facility for up to 80 delegates. Bedrooms in the original house vary in size, decor, outlook and cost, but all are comfortably furnished in traditional country house style. Donegal has an other-worldliness that is increasingly hard to capture in the traditional family holiday areas and, although now larger, Rathmullan House still retains a laid-back charm and that special sense of place. Conference/banqueting (80). Swimming pool, steam room, tennis. Children welcome; cot €15 (free under 6 months), baby sitting arranged. Pets permitted by arrangement. Gardens. **Rooms 32** (19 with separate bath & shower, 9 ground floor, 2 for disabled). B&B €110 pps, ss €45, SC 10%. **The Weeping Elm:** The dining room has been revamped and extended, but the famous tented ceiling (designed by the late Liam McCormick, well known for his striking Donegal churches) has been retained. It is a pleasant room that makes the most of the garden outlook - including a formal garden beside the extension, which is settling in nicely - and provides a fine setting for Peter Cheesman's modern Irish cooking, as well as the tremendous breakfasts for which Rathmullan is justly famous. Cooking here is upbeat traditional and carefully-sourced menus offer a wide choice - including specialities like Fanad Head crab plate, loin of Rathmullan lamb with cauliflower purée and rosemary jus and, perhaps, a compôte of garden fruits with carrageen pudding. The carrageen is equally at home at breakfast too - each morning a tremendous buffet is laid out, offering a huge variety of juices, fruits, cooked ham, smoked salmon and farmhouse cheeses, home-bakes and preserves - plus a menu of hot dishes. cooked to order. (Rathmullan was the Ulster winner of our Irish Breakfast Awards in 2002). The Rathmullan wine list is exceptionally informative, listing many interesting bottles and giving suggestions as to the best wine and food partnerships. **Seats 100.** D daily 7.30-8.45 (Sat 7-9); Set D €45/50 house wine from €23; SC 10%. *Informal meals are available in Batts Bar & Café and the Cellar Bar: L, 1-2.30pm daily (Batts 1-7 for residents); Early D is also available in The Cellar Bar, 5-8pm daily in summer; children's menu available. Closed 17th - 27th December. Amex, MasterCard, Visa, Laser. **Directions:** Letterkenny to Ramelton - turn right to Rathmullan at the bridge, through village and turn right to hotel.

Rossnowlagh

Sand House Hotel

👁 HOTEL/RESTAURANT

Rossnowlagh Co Donegal **Tel: 071 985 1777**
Fax: 071 985 2100 Email: info@sandhouse.ie Web: www.sandhouse.ie

Perched on the edge of a stunning sandy beach two miles long, the Britton family's famous hotel lost its trademark crenellated roof-line a few years ago, but emerged with an extra storey and an elegant new look, reminiscent of a French chateau. Wonderful sea views and easy access to the beach have always been the great attractions of The Sand House, which started life as a fishing lodge in the 1830s and completed its latest metamorphosis with a new floor of bedrooms, a panoramic lift (who will bother with the stairs when the lift has the best view in the house?), a new boardroom and a marine spa, where seaweed products are used for a range of exclusive body and skincare treatments. Existing bedrooms were also refurbished and upgraded and many have a superb outlook; all are very comfortable, with excellent bathrooms - and everyone can enjoy the view from the new sun deck which has replaced the Atlantic Conservatory, and allows a sheltered retreat from which to soak in the sea view. Things that haven't changed at the Sand House include the ever-burning welcoming fire in the foyer, exceptional housekeeping - and the hospitality of the Britton family and staff, which is the real appeal of this remarkable hotel. Golf is a major attraction for guests at The Sandhouse, which is a member of The Emerald Triangle (three strategically places establishments offering great golf experiences: the other two are Rathsallagh, Co Wicklow, and Glenlo Abbey, Co Galway, see entries). Also partners in 'Play 3 Great Golf Courses in Ireland's North-West' (Donegal GC, Bundoran, Castle Hume). Spa; fishing, cycling, tennis, walking, tennis on site; horse riding, boating and many other activities available nearby. Details on application. Conferences (100). Children welcome (under 7s free in parents' room, cots available without charge, baby sitting arranged). Pets permitted by arrangement. **Rooms 60** (1 suite, 2 junior suites, 5 executive, 5 shower only, 50 no-smoking, 1 disabled). Lift. 24 hour room service. B&B €90pps, ss €30. SC 10%, Closed Dec & Jan. **Seashell Restaurant:** The restaurant is rather unexpectedly at the front of the hotel (and therefore faces inland) but is well-appointed, in keeping with the rest of the hotel. John McGarrigle, who has been with the hotel since 1995, presents seasonal 5-course dinner menus, changed daily; fresh seafood and locally sourced lamb and beef (also game, in season) provide the foundation for a traditional repertoire which is quite conservative but offers plenty of choice on all courses. Finish with a choice of Irish cheeses or hotel-style desserts. Staff are helpful and attentive. Good choice of wines by the glass. *Soup and sandwiches are also available in the bar at lunchtime, every day except Sunday. **Seats 110** (private room, 8). Children welcome. D daily 7-8.30, L Sun only, 1-2. Set D €50/55, Set Sun L €25-27.50; house wines from €20. SC 10%. Closed Dec & Jan. Amex, Diners, MasterCard, Visa, Laser. **Directions:** Coast road from Ballyshannon to Donegal Town.

COUNTY GALWAY

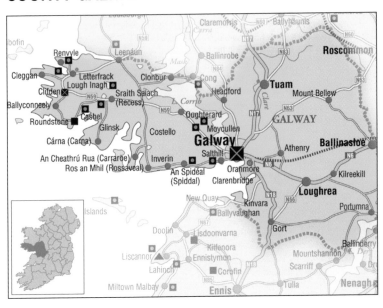

Galway City
🏛️ 🆂🅵 HOTEL/RESTAURANT

Glenlo Abbey Hotel

Bushypark Galway Co Galway
Tel: 091 526 666 Fax: 091 527 800
Email: info@glenloabbey.ie Web: www.glenlo.com

féile bia Originally an eighteenth century residence, Glenlo Abbey is just two and a half miles from Galway city yet, beautifully located on a 138-acre estate, with its own golf course and Pavilion, it offers all the advantages of the country. Although it is not a very big hotel, the scale is generous: public rooms are impressive, and large, well-furnished bedrooms have good amenities and marbled bathrooms. The old Abbey has been restored for meetings and private dining, with business services to back up meetings and conferences. For indoor relaxation the Oak Cellar Bar serves light food and, in addition to the classical River Room Restaurant - a lovely bright room with tables tiered to take full advantage of lovely views over Lough Corrib and the surrounding countryside. Conference/banqueting 120/160. Golf (9 & 18 hole); fishing, equestrian, cycling, walking. Children welcome (cot available, baby sitting arranged). No pets. Garden. Boutique. **Rooms 46** (3 suites, 1 junior suite, 17 executive, 1 shower only, 1 for disabled, all no-smoking). Wheelchair access. Lift. B&B €137pps, no ss. Ample parking. Helipad. Open all year except Christmas. **River Room Restaurant:** D daily 7-10. A la carte. **Pullman Restaurant:** This is perhaps the country's most novel dinner venue; four carriages, two of them from the original Orient Express that featured in scenes from "Murder on the Orient Express", filmed in 1974. Adapting it to restaurant use has been achieved brilliantly, with no expense spared in maintaining the special features of a luxurious train. There is a lounge/bar area leading to an open dining carriage and two private 'coupes' compartments, each seating up to six. Background clackity-clack and hooting noises lend an authenticity to the experience and the romance is sustained by discreetly piped music of the 1940s and 50s. The view from the windows is of a coiffeured golf course, Lough Corrib and Connemara hills in the distance. Welcome by smart staff is pleasant, service throughout exemplary. Tables are set up as on a train, with silver cutlery, simple glassware and white linen (although napkins are paper); the food is suitably inclined to Asian influences and, while not cutting edge, it is very enjoyable. In line with the fun of the theme, you could begin your meal with a Pullman Summer Salad - and even end it with Poirot's Pie (apple tart); more typically, try an excellent 'Assiette of Oriental

Appetisers' includes sushi,sashimi, prawn tempura, smoked salmon, and mini spring roll soy sauce and wasabi - and follow with a main course of 'Beijing Kao Ya', deliciously crisp-skinned roast half duck with a home-made barbecue & pomegranate sauce. Short, well-chosen wine list. Recommended as much for its unique, special occasion experience as for the fare - but the cooking is reliable and a visit is always enjoyable. **Seats 66.** D daily 6.30-10. A la carte. Amex, Diners, MasterCard, Visa, Laser. **Directions:** 4 km from Galway on N59 in the Clifden direction.

Galway City
€ CAFÉ

Goya's

2/3 Kirwans Lane Galway Co Galway
Tel: 091 567010 Email: goyas@eircom.net Web: www.goyas.ie

If only for a cup of cappuccino or hot chocolate and a wedge of chocolate cake or a slice of quiche, a restorative visit to this delightful contemporary bakery and café is a must on any visit to Galway. There's something very promising about the cardboard cake boxes stacked up in preparation near the door, the staff are super, there's a great buzz and the food is simply terrific. What's more, you don't even have to be in Galway to enjoy Emer Murray's terrific baking - contact Goya's for her seasonal mail-order catalogues "Fabulous Festive Fancies" (Christmas cakes, plum pudding, mince pies etc) and "Easter Delights" (simnel cake and others); wedding cakes also available. If you're wondering where to start, why not try a speciality: Goyas 3-layer chocolate gateau cake. Open all day Mon-Sat. MasterCard, Visa, Laser. **Directions:** Behind McDonaghs Fish Shop, off Quay Street.

Galway City
🏛 🍴 COUNTRY HOUSE

Killeen House

Bushy Park Galway Co Galway
Tel: 091 524 179 Fax: 091 528 065
Email: killeenhouse@ireland.com Web: www.killeenhousegalway.com

Catherine Doyle's delightful, spacious 1840s house enjoys the best of both worlds: it's on the Clifden road just on the edge of Galway city yet, with 25 acres of private grounds and gardens reaching right down to the shores of Lough Corrib, offers all the advantages of the country, too. Catherine's thoughtful hospitality and meticulous standards make a stay here very special, beginning with tea on arrival, served on a beautifully arranged tray with fine linen and polished silver - a house speciality extending to the usually mundane tray provided in your bedroom. Guest rooms are luxuriously and individually furnished, each in a different period, e.g. Regency, Edwardian and (most fun this one) Art Nouveau; the bedding is exquisite, bathrooms are lovely and there are many small touches to make you feel at home. And, although the menu is not exceptionally extensive, breakfast is a delight. Not suitable for children under 12. Garden; walking. No pets.* Killeen House was our Guesthouse of the Year in 2003. **Rooms 6** (1 shower only). Lift. B&B €90pps, ss €50. Closed 23-27 Dec. Amex, Diners, MasterCard, Visa. **Directions:** On N59 between Galway city and Moycullen village.

Galway City
€ RESTAURANT

Oscars Restaurant

Dominick Street Galway Co Galway **Tel: 091 582180**
Email: oscarsgalway@eircom.net Web: www.oscarsgalway.com

féile bia This is a love-it-or-loathe-it place: the decor is wildly wacky, with overloud jazz and dim lighting giving it a night clubby atmosphere - but few would question Michael O'Meara's position as Galway's most innovative chef. The menu, in an old-fashioned wine list cover, is extensive: cooking influences are eclectic, leaning towards Thailand and the East, although some dishes are quite European in style (roast rabbit with prunes) or even traditional Irish (fish cakes in an oatmeal crust); a starter platter for two might consist of onion badjis, spiced chicken wings, mushrooms in garlic butter, fish cake, spare ribs and dip, yet Japanese style chicken yakatori is another option. Staff are very interested and attentive - and, while it's difficult to know what to make of the place at first, all the signs indicate something serious going on in the kitchen. Dishes enjoyed on a recent visit include a starter of tiger prawns tossed in garlic and lemon butter, with toasted rice and salad and, another prawn dish, a Malaysian style prawn and chilli samble - served very dramatically, as is the house style; but, despite the high drama, the cooking is very good, flavours are delicious and less adventurous diners can rely on a really good steak, or rack of Connemara lamb (served boulangère perhaps, with a wild crabapple reduction). Portions are large, including desserts which tend more towards the classics: nectarines poached with star anise and cinnamon, with a raspberry compôte and vanilla ice cream, perhaps. The wine list favours Europe, with some choice also from Australia, Chile, and California. Despite the wackiness of the room and presentation, everything on Oscars' extensive menu is prepared and cooked to order - and Michael O'Meara's expressive, confident cooking has earned a following in Galway. **Seats 45.** D Tue-Sun, 6.30-10 (5.30 Sat/5.30-9 Sun). Earlybird D €20 until 7 (6.30 Sat); also A la carte. House wines from €19.50. Closed Mon. MasterCard, Visa, Laser.

Galway City
🏛 HOTEL

Park House Hotel

Forster St. Eyre Square Galway Co Galway
Tel: 091 564 924 Fax: 091 569 219
Email: parkhousehotel@eircom.net Web: www.parkhousehotel.ie

téite bia This hotel just off Eyre Square has the individuality that comes with owner-management and provides an exceptionally friendly and comfortable haven from the bustle of Galway, which seems to be constantly in celebration. Warmly decorated public areas include a well-run bar with lots of cosy corners where you can sink into a deep armchair and relax, and a choice of dining options - The Park for formal dining, and The Blue Room for informal meals. Guest rooms are spacious, very comfortably furnished and well-equipped for business travellers, with a desk, internet access and safe; generous, well-planned bathrooms are quite luxurious, with ample storage space and Molton Brown toiletries. Good breakfasts include a buffet selection (with a delicious fresh fruit salad), plus a choice of hot dishes, including fish - a perfectly cooked plaice, and undyed smoked haddock attracted praise on a recent visit. And you know you're in Galway when you find oysters on the room service menu... If you want a thoroughly Irish welcome in the heart of Galway, you could not do better than stay at this cosy and central hotel: the prices are very reasonable - and private parking for residents is a real plus. Park Room Restaurant (D daily & L Sun); bar food L&D daily. Children welcome (under 12s free in parents' room, cots available). No pets. **Rooms 57** (2 junior suites, 1 for disabled). Lift. 24 hour room service. B&B €150 pps, ss €65. Closed 24-26 Dec. Amex, Diners, MasterCard, Visa, Laser. **Directions:** Located adjacent to Eyre Square.

Galway City
🏛 🌟 HOTEL

Radisson SAS Hotel Galway

Lough Atalia Road Galway Co Galway **Tel: 091 538300** Fax: 091 538380
Email: sales.galway@radissonsas.com Web: www.galway.radissonsas.com

téite bia Ideally situated on the waterfront, overlooking Lough Atalia, this fine contemporary hotel is more central than its scenic location might suggest, as the shops and restaurants off Eyre Square are only a few minutes walk. An impressive foyer with unusual sculptures, audacious greenery and a glass-walled lift raise the spirits, and attractive public areas include the cosy Backstage Bar and a pleasant lounge, in a sunny position looking over the roman-style leisure centre towards Lough Atalia. Guest rooms are furnished to a very high standard throughout with excellent bathrooms and facilities; luxurious 'Level 5' suites have superb views, individual terraces and much else besides - all of which, plus services such as 3-hour express laundry, make this the ideal business accommodation. [Radisson SAS Hotel Galway was our Business Hotel of the Year for 2005]. Excellent facilities for conferences and meetings are matched by outstanding leisure facilities, including a destination spa, Spirit One, which offers a range of beauty treatments, pamper programmes and spa break packages (details on application). Friendly, helpful staff are a great asset in every area of the hotel. Children welcome (under 16s free in parents' room; cot available without charge, baby sitting arranged) Conference/banqueting (1000/680). Video-conferencing, business centre. Leisure centre (17m pool, children's pool, gym, sauna, steam bath, Jacuzzi, outdoor hot tub); spa, beauty salon. No pets. Underground car park. Helipad. **Rooms 217** (2 suites, 2 junior suite, 16 executive, 184 no smoking, 11 for disabled.) Lift. B&B €120, ss €100. **Restaurant Marinas:** The dining experience in this large split-level restaurant has an understandably Scandinavian tone (including a buffet option), but decor in blues and browns is inspired by Lough Atalia and there is a sense of style and confidence about the room that is reflected in capable, friendly service. An extensive à la carte menu is international in style and flavours, although non fish eaters will find enduring favourites like chargrilled beef fillet, rack of lamb, and a vegetarian dish such as couscous stuffed bell peppers. Although there is little mention of local produce, wheat free and vegetarian dishes are highlighted, and also healthy eating options for guests attending Spirit One spa. But Marinas also offers the less usual option of a Scandinavian style buffet, which is an attractive choice if you are dining early, while everything is fresh. The best thing about the buffet is the varied selection of marinated salads and vegetables, cold meats, smoked fish, served with a wide choice of condiments and dressings; although some dishes will deteriorate while keeping hot, the buffet is good value and an enjoyable experience in such pleasant surroundings. The wine list is well thought out and includes about a dozen wines by the glass and nine half bottles - a boon for business guests dining alone. The restaurant works equally well next morning, for its famous Scandinavian buffet breakfast. *The Atrium Bar Menu has a more Irish tone, and offers an informal dining option, including a very reasonably priced 4-course buffet lunch. **Seats 200** (private room 90). Air conditioning. Toilets wheelchair accessible. Children welcome. D daily, 6-10.30, L Daily 12.30-3 (Sun 1-3). Set L €15, D €22/40, also à la carte. Set Sun L, €28. House wines from €22. Guests dining in the hotel are entitled to a 35% discount on usual rates in the underground car park. Amex, Diners, MasterCard, Visa, Laser. **Directions:** 3 minutes walk from bus & train station.

Galway City
Ⓔ RESTAURANT

The Malt House Restaurant

Olde Malt Mall High Street Galway Co Galway
Tel: 091 567 866 Fax: 091 563 993
Email: fergus@themalthouse.ie Web: www.malt-house.com

féile bia This old restaurant and bar in a quiet, flower-filled courtyard off High Street is a cosy oasis, away from the often frenetic buzz of modern Galway. It has character - enhanced by low lighting, candles, background jazz and the sound of happy diners at night - and is well-managed, with bar and waiting staff coping seamlessly, even at the busiest of times. Informal meals are served in the bar, and the restaurant is comfortably set up with well-spaced tables smartly dressed in white and maroon (the Galway colours). Brendan Keane, who has been head chef since 1997, offers several menus (including a 5-course Seafood Sampler menu) and, although fairly traditional, there are occasional contemporary notes; and the restaurant is developing areas of speciality - beginning, perhaps, with the range of cocktails offered as aperitifs in the bar, then in menus which demonstrate a desire to offer a genuine choice from the usual line-up, including gluten-free dishes and vegetarian choices. Native Galway oysters are properly served, with a small salad and excellent breads, brown soda and walnut; other dishes recently enjoyed include oven roasted duck breast with sautéed sweet potatoes, caramelised oranges and Grand Marnier sauce (arbitrarily served well done, but crisp skinned and delicious nonetheless), classic Dover sole on the bone, and a feathery chocolate fondant, with tarragon crème anglaise. Service is snappy and attentive - and wine buffs will enjoy mulling over a wide-ranging list, presented by grape variety, with extensive notes; there are some bargains to be had, often including each week's featured wine. In addition to the main dinner menus, there is an evening bar menu, a lunch menu that extends through the afternoon and a pre-theatre menu that offers outstanding value. After years of ticking over, there is a sense of something more ambitious at work here - and it remains a relaxed restaurant, where people come to have a good time. **Seats 70** (private room, 20; also outdoor dining for 24). Children welcome but not after 8pm. Air conditioning. L & D Mon-Sat: L 12-5, Set L €24 (value L €9.95). D 6-10, early bird €19.90 (6-7pm) Also à la carte L&D available, house wine from €18; no SC. Closed Sun & Dec 25-Jan 5. Amex, Diners, MasterCard, Visa, Laser. **Directions:** Located in a courtyard just off High Street.

Aran Islands

€ ⊚ B&B

Man Of Aran Cottages

Kilmurvey Inis Mór Aran Islands Co Galway
Tel: 099 61301 Fax: 099 61324
Email: manofaran@eircom.net Web: www.manofarancottage.com

Despite its fame - this is where the film Man of Aran was made - Joe and Maura Wolfe make visiting their home a genuine and personal experience. The cottage is right beside the sea and Kilmurvey beach, surrounded by wild flowers, and Joe has somehow managed to make a productive garden in this exposed location, so their meals usually include his organically grown vegetables (even artichokes and asparagus), salads, nasturtium flowers and young nettle leaves as well as Maura's home-made soups, stews and freshly-baked bread and cakes. Dinner is served in the little restaurant but there are benches in the garden, with stunning views across the sea towards the mountains, where you can enjoy an aperitif, or even eat outside on fine summer evenings. Packed lunches are available too. **Seats 20.** D at 7.30 (one sitting) is mainly for residents, but non-resident guests are also welcome by reservation. Set D about €30; wine list, about €16-33. No SC. No regular weekly closures, but check availability of meals when booking. Closed Nov-Feb. **Accommodation:** The three little bedrooms are basic but full of quaint, cottagey charm and they're very comfortable, although only one is en-suite. Breakfast will probably be a well cooked full-Irish - made special by Joe's beautifully sweet home-grown cherry tomatoes if you are lucky - although they'll do something different if you like. Children welcome (under 4s free in parents room). No pets. Children welcome (under 4s free in parents' room). No pets. Garden, walking. **Rooms 3** (1 en-suite, all no smoking). B&B €40, ss €10. Closed Nov-Feb. **No Credit Cards.**

Cashel

🏛 🍷 ⊚ HOTEL/RESTAURANT

Cashel House Hotel

Cashel Co Galway
Tel: 095 31001 Fax: 095 31077
Email: info@cashel-house-hotel.com Web: www.cashel-house-hotel.com

Dermot and Kay McEvilly were among the pioneers of the Irish country house movement when they opened Cashel House as an hotel in 1968. The following year General and Madame de Gaulle chose to stay for two weeks, an historic visit of which the McEvillys are justly proud - look out for the photographs and other memorabilia in the hall. The de Gaulle visit meant immediate recognition for the hotel, but it did even more for Ireland by putting the Gallic seal of approval on Irish hospitality and food. The gardens, which run down to a private beach, contribute greatly to the atmosphere, and the accommodation includes especially comfortable ground floor garden suites, which are also suitable for less able guests (wheelchair accessible, but no special grab rails etc in bathrooms). Relaxed hospitality combined with professionalism have earned an international reputation for this outstanding hotel and its qualities are perhaps best seen in details - log fires that burn throughout the year, day rooms furnished with antiques and filled with fresh flowers from the garden, rooms that are individually decorated with many thoughtful touches. Service (with all day room service, including all meals) is impeccable, and delicious breakfasts include a wonderful buffet display of home-made and local produce (Cashel House was the Connaught winner of our Irish Breakfast Awards in 2001). Conference/banqueting (15/80). Children welcome; cot available (€10); baby sitting arranged; playroom. Pets permitted in some areas. Walking, tennis, garden.* Self-catering accommodation is also available nearby; details on application. **Rooms 32** (13 suites, 4 family rooms, 6 ground floor, 1 shower only). B&B €125pps, no ss; SC12.5%. **Restaurant:** A large conservatory extension makes the most of the outlook onto the lovely gardens around this well-appointed split-level restaurant, which is open to non-residents. Although ably assisted by a well-trained staff, including Arturo Amit who has been head chef since 2000, Dermot McEvilly has overseen the kitchen personally since the hotel opened, providing a rare consistency of style in five-course dinners that showcase local produce, notably seafood. Despite occasional world influences - in a tasting plate of seafood in a green chilli and coconut broth, for example - the tone is classic: roast Connemara lamb is an enduring favourite and there is an emphasis on home-grown fruit and vegetables, including some fine vegetarian dishes and homely desserts, such as rhubarb or apple tart, or strawberries and cream - then farmhouse cheeses come with home-baked biscuits. The personal supervision of Kay McEvilly and restaurant manager Ray Doorly ensures caring service, and an extensive and informative wine list includes many special bottles for the connoisseur - yet there are also plenty of well-chosen, more accessible wines (under EU30), and a good choice of half bottles. * A short à la carte bar lunch menu offers interesting snacks and sandwiches, but also hot meals, including Irish stew or even lobster if desired; afternoon teas are also served daily in the bar. (Bar L12.30-2.30, Afternoon Tea 2.30-5). Restaurant **Seats 80.** D daily 7-8.30 (Sun-9), L 12-2.30 (Sun 12.30-2.30). Set D €48. Set Sun L €30; also à la carte. House wine €24.12.5% s.c. Closed 5 Jan-5 Feb. Amex, MasterCard, Visa, Laser. **Directions:** South off N59 (Galway-Clifden road), 1 mile west of Recess turn left.

Cashel

🏨 ⊙ HOTEL/RESTAURANT

Zetland Country House

Cashel Bay Cashel Co Galway **Tel: 095 31111**
Fax: 095 31117 Email: zetland@iol.ie Web: www.zetland.com

Originally built as a sporting lodge in the early 19th century, Zetland House is on an elevated site, with views over Cashel Bay and still makes a good base for fishing holidays. This is a charming and hospitable house, with a light and airy atmosphere and an elegance bordering on luxury, in both its spacious antique-furnished public areas and bedrooms which are individually decorated in a relaxed country house style, and include two lovely newer rooms, more recently opened. The gardens surrounding the house are very lovely too, greatly enhancing the peaceful atmosphere of the house. Its unusual name dates from the time when the Shetland Islands were under Norwegian rule and known as the Zetlands - the Earl of Zetland (Lord Viceroy 1888-1890) was a frequent visitor here, hence the name. Conference/banqueting (30/75). Tennis, cycling, walking. Snooker, Children welcome (cot available, €10; baby sitting arranged). Pets permitted by arrangement in certain areas. Garden. **Rooms 20** (2 family rooms, 1 shower only, 3 ground floor, all no smoking) B&B €110pps, ss €25. **Restaurant:** Like the rest of this lovely hotel, the dining room is bright, spacious and elegant. Decorated in soft, pretty shades of pale yellow and peach that contrast well with antique furniture - including a fine sideboard where plates and silver are displayed - the restaurant is in a prime position for enjoying the view and makes a wonderful place to watch the light fading over the mountains and the sea. A warm welcome and quietly efficient service from staff who are clearly happy in their work greatly enhances the pleasure of dining here. The kitchen makes good use of the vegetables and herbs grown in the hotel garden, along with the best of local produce, notably lobster - and also game in season. From a menu offering about five equally enticing dishes on each course, a typical meal might be Connemara crab & cucumber risotto, pink grapefruit and gin sorbet and chargrilled rump of lamb (served, perhaps, with a goats cheese and potato mousse and tapenade jus); finish with Irish cheeses with apple chutney, or a classic dessert such as warm dark chocolate fondant with whiskey ice cream. Excellent breakfasts are also served in the restaurant - home-made preserves are an especially delicious feature. Non residents welcome by reservation; children welcome. *Snack lunches available, 12-2 daily. Restaurant SC 12.5%. Amex, Diners, MasterCard, Visa, Laser. **Directions:** N59 from Galway. Turn left after Recess.

Clifden

⊙ HOTEL/RESTAURANT

Ardagh Hotel & Restaurant

Ballyconneely Road Clifden Co Galway
Tel: 095 21384 Fax: 095 21314
Email: ardaghhotel@eircom.net Web: www.ardaghhotel.com

féile bia Beautifully located, overlooking Ardbear Bay, Stephane and Monique Bauvet's family-run hotel is well known for quiet hospitality, low key comfort and good food. Public areas have style, in a relaxed homely way: turf fires, comfortable armchairs, classic country colours, and a plant-filled conservatory area upstairs are pleasing to the eye and indicate that peaceful relaxation is the aim here. Bedrooms vary according to their position but are well-furnished with all the amenities required for a comfortable stay, and have been recently renovated. (Not all have sea views - single rooms are at the back with a pleasant countryside outlook). Bedrooms include some extra large rooms, especially suitable for families. Children welcome (cot available without charge, baby sitting arranged). Pets allowed by arrangement. Garden, walking; snooker, pool table. **Rooms 17** (2 suites, 2 family rooms, all no smoking). Room service (all day). B&B €87.50 pps, ss €30.* Short / off-season breaks available. **Restaurant:** This long-established restaurant is a well-appointed light-filled room on the first floor, with stunning lake and mountain views - and a warm reception is sure to set the tone for an enjoyable evening. Monique Bauvet's menus are wide-ranging: an excellent choice of local seafood usually includes oysters, mussels, scallops, wild salmon, crab, lobster, and a variety of fish including black (Dover) sole, and there will be a fair choice of meats too, including local lamb - a roast rack, perhaps, with roasted celeriac mash and a rosemary & thyme jus - along with some poultry and at least one imaginative vegetarian choice. Cooking is generally reliable and delicious home-made breads, well-flavoured soups (including the creamy house chowder), interesting vegetables, home-grown salads and home-made ice creams are among the details that stand out, and there is also a good cheese selection, served with grapes, celery and crackers. Home-made petits fours will follow with your coffee (or tea/tisane). Relaxed service, under the direction of Stéphane Bauvet, contributes to an atmosphere of confident profes-sionalism that greatly enhances a meal here. A fairly priced wine list strong on old world wines, especially Bordeaux and Burgundy, also has an interesting choice from South Africa and offers eight half bottles and several magnums. **Seats 50.** D 7-9.15 daily, Set D €49.50, à la carte also available; house wine €21.50; sc discretionary. Closed Nov-Easter. Amex, Diners, MasterCard, Visa, Laser. **Directions:** 2 km outside Clifden on Ballyconneely Road.

Clifden

🏛🎗👁 COUNTRY HOUSE

Dolphin Beach Country House

Lower Sky Road Clifden Co Galway
Tel: 095 21204 Fax: 095 22935
Email: dolphinbeach@iolfree.ie Web: www.connemara.net/dolphinbeachhouse

The Foyle family's stunning beachside house is set in 14 acres of wilderness, which makes a wonderful contrast to the style and comfort within. The house, which has an early 19th century farmhouse at its heart, was renovated and extended by Billy and Barbara Foyle, who then opened for guests in 1998. Those familiar with the old Foyle magic (Rosleague Manor, Quay House) will find it a-plenty here, where the family talent for creating original interiors is seen especially in Billy's unusual woodwork - bedheads, mirror frames, anything that takes his fancy - which brings a delightfully quirky element to the fresh style of this warm and friendly house. There's a wonderful feeling of quality throughout: bedrooms are finished to a very high standard, with antique furniture, pristine bedlinen, lovely bathrooms and underfloor heating; television and tea/coffee making facilities are available on request. Now that Billy and Barbara's daughters Clodagh (managing) and Sinead (cooking) have key roles, they bring new energy and enthusiasm to this unique house and the atmosphere is delightful. The family grow their own organic vegetables too, and these, together with other local produce, notably seafood and Connemara lamb, are used for Sinead's lovely evening meals, which are served in a dining room overlooking the beach (ask about dinner when booking your room). Breakfast follows the same philosophy - you can even collect your own free-range eggs for breakfast. (Dolphin Beach was winner of our Irish Breakfast Award for Connacht in 2003). Non-residents are welcome for dinner by reservation, and there is a small wine list, all under €35. Not suitable for children. No pets. Walking, garden, safe swimming off rocky beach. **Rooms 9** (5 shower only, all no smoking). B&B €85 pps, ss €5. D 7-8pm, €39 (booking essen-tial); house wine €25. Closed Dec-Jan. MasterCard, Visa, Laser. **Directions:** Left off Sky Road, about 3 miles from Clifden.

Clifden

 GUESTHOUSE

The Quay House

Beach Road Clifden Co Galway
Tel: 095 21369 Fax: 095 21608
Email: thequay@iol.ie Web: www.thequayhouse.com

GUESTHOUSE OF THE YEAR
BEST BREAKFAST - NATIONAL WINNER

In a lovely location - the house is right on the harbour, with pretty water views when the tide is in - The Quay House was built around 1820. It has the distinction of being the oldest building in Clifden and has also had a surprisingly varied usage: it was originally the harbourmaster's house, then a convent, then a monastery; it was converted into a hotel at the turn of the century and finally, since 1993, has been relishing its most enjoyable phase as a guesthouse, in the incomparable hands of long-time hoteliers, Paddy and Julia Foyle. It's a fine house, with spacious rooms - including a stylishly homely drawing room with an open fire, that makes a relaxing place to read, or to come back to after an evening out. And the accommodation is exceptionally comfortable, in airy, wittily decorated and sumptuously furnished rooms that include not only two wheelchair-friendly rooms, but also seven newer studio rooms, with small fitted kitchens, balconies overlooking the harbour and, as in the original rooms, all have excellent bathrooms with full bath and shower. Breakfast is served in a charming conservatory, decorated with a collection of silver domes and trailing Virginia creeper criss-crossing the room on strings, and it is simply superb. A buffet is laid out to tempt you as you enter - succulent melons and other fresh fruit, poached apricots, rhubarb and prunes, yoghurt and cheeses, including a goat log (non dairy), freshly baked breads and home-made marmalade and preserves...and (how nice to see the priorities here) orders for your tea or coffee are taken even before you sit down at a table beautifully set up with individual jugs of freshly squeezed orange juice, chevron-patterned butter in little china dishes, Maldon salt and coarse-ground pepper. There's no written menu, but hot dishes are likely to include a perfectly cooked traditional Irish, scrambled eggs with smoked salmon, kedgeree and pan-fried lemon sole, all served with crisp toast (crusts removed) and freshly-baked breads and scones straight from the Aga - and fresh top-ups of tea and coffee. Excellent service under Julia's supervision too: all round, about as perfect as breakfast could be. Although officially closed in winter it is always worth inquiring. Children under 12 free in parents' room (cots available without charge, baby sitting arranged). No pets. Garden. Walking. **Rooms 14** (all with full bathrooms, 2 on ground floor, all no smoking). B&B €70pps, ss €40. Closed Nov-mid Mar. MasterCard, Visa, Laser. **Directions:** 2 minutes from town centre, overlooking Clifden harbour - follow signs to the Beach Road.

Clifden

€ CAFÉ

Two Dog Café

1 Church Hill Clifden Co Galway **Tel: 095 22186** Fax: 095 22195
Email: kennel@twodogcafe.ie Web: www.twodogcafe.ie

This smashing little café just off the square in Clifden is a gem, combining home-made cakes, gourmet sandwiches and aromatic Illy coffee with charming service, a laid-back newspaper-reading atmosphere and an Internet cafe upstairs. They do several imaginative soups - an unusual sweet potato & mulato soup with honey and cream came in for praise on a recent visit - and a wide range of gourmet sandwiches, wraps, paninis and quiches just the sort of thing for a light daytime bite. Try their quesadillas (tangy cheddar cheese, sliced scallions & chopped chillis pan-toasted between two four tortillas, then served with soured cream and spicy salsa) or a classic quiche lorraine, perhaps. But, luscious as all the wholesome savoury choices may be, it's really the display of home bakes that proves irresistible to any with the slightest hint of a sweet tooth. Scones, brownies, apricot crumble cake, orange & almond cake (flourless - ideal for coeliacs) and light and tasty raspberry cake...Just like granny used to make - magic! A must for daytime visitors to Clifden. Children welcome. **Seats 30.** Open daytime (Sun 12.30-4). No reservations. Closed Sun-Mon Nov-May MasterCard, Visa. **Directions:** Pff Market Square.

Craughwell

N ⛰ ☆ 👁 COUNTRY HOUSE/RESTAURANT

St. Clerans Country House

Craughwell Co Galway
Tel: 091 846070 Fax: 091 846600
Email: stclerans@iol.ie Web: www.merv.com

Once the home of the film director John Huston, St Clerans is a magnificent 18th century manor house on 45 acres of gardens and grounds, beautifully located in rolling countryside. It was carefully restored some years ago by the current owner, the American entertainer Merv Griffin, and decorated with no expense spared to make a sumptuous, hedonistically luxurious country retreat and restaurant. There's a great sense of fun about the furnishing and everything is of the best possible quality; reception rooms include a magnificently flamboyant drawing room and spacious bedrooms that are individually decorated and have peaceful garden and countryside views; most are done in what might best be described as an upbeat country house style, while others - particularly those on the lower ground floor, including John Huston's own favourite room, which opens out onto a terrace with steps up to the garden - are restrained, almost subdued, in atmosphere. All are spacious, with luxuriously appointed bathrooms (one has its original shower only) and a wonderful away-from-it-all feeling. Housekeeping is immaculate, and there was a discernible sense of purposeful new management on recent visits by the Guide. **Rooms 12** (6 junior suites, 6 executive. 1 shower only, 4 gound floor). B&B €210 pps. Children under 11 years free in parents room. Cots available free of charge. **Restaurant:** The restaurant, which is open to non-residents by reservation, provides an elegant setting for cooking by Japanese head chef Hisashi Kumagai (Kuma). The room has lovely views of pastoral east Galway, including a fine tree which dominates a near meadow, and is floodlit at night; a crimson carpet and heavy, matching drapes set a slightly decadent tone but appointments are otherwise quite classical, with plain white linen-clad tables, fine glassware, silver, and china and gold candle holders. Aperitifs are served in the drawing room by a turf fire, to muted strains of Chopin and Beethoven (but not from the grand piano that suits the room so well). Unpriced 4-course set dinner menus, printed on parchment-like paper tied with ribbon, offer a choice of 4 or 5 dishes on each course. Kuma is an accomplished chef, his ingredients are only the very best and his food is beautifully presented. A spring roll of oak-smoked salmon and avocado with sesame seed & hoisin sauce is an outstanding example of Kuma's oriental/western fusion cooking, and an outstanding main course is roulade of local lamb with prosciutto ham with mint-scented rosemary sauce - the description does not do justice to this dish of poached lamb, a stunning tribute to Connemara lamb; the inclusion of old fashioned floury new potatoes with a modern al dente selection is delightful. Desserts are perhaps a little less impressive, but well-executed nonetheless - and might include an unusual green tea ice cream. The wine list is shortish for an establishment of this status, but includes some interesting white burgundies and a good choice of half bottles. Service by local staff is charming and attentive and, overall, local diners are fortunate to have this rare gem within striking distance of Galway city. **Seats 30.** D 7-9pm daily, €65. SC discretionary. Closed 24-26 Dec. Amex, Diners, MasterCard, Visa, Laser. **Directions:** 2 miles off N6 between Loughrea and Craughwell.

Kilcolgan

🏠 🍷 👁 RESTAURANT/ATMOSPHERIC PUB

Moran's Oyster Cottage

The Weir Kilcolgan Co Galway
Tel: 091 796 113 Fax: 091 796 503
Email: moranstheweir@eircom.net Web: www.moransoystercottage.com

This is just the kind of Irish pub that people everywhere dream about. It's as pretty as a picture, with a well-kept thatched roof and a lovely waterside location (with plenty of seats outside where you can while away the time and watch the swans floating by). People from throughout the country beat a path here at every available opportunity for their wonderful local seafood, including lobster, but especially the native oysters (from their own oyster beds) which are in season from September to April. Willie Moran is an ace oyster opener, a regular champion in the famous annual competitions held in the locality. Farmed Gigas oysters are on the menu all year. Then there's chowder and smoked salmon and seafood cocktail and mussels, delicious crab salads - and lobster, with boiled potatoes & garlic butter. Private conference room. The wine list is not over-extensive, but carefully selected, informative and fairly priced. Morans was the Guide's Seafood Pub of the Year in 1999. **Seats 100** (private rooms, 8 and 12; outdoor seating, 50/60). Air conditioning. Toilets wheelchair accessible. Meals 12 noon -10pm daily. House wine from €18. Closed 3 days Christmas & Good Fri. Amex, MasterCard, Visa, Laser. **Directions:** Just off the Galway-Limerick road, signed between Clarenbridge and Kilcolgan.

Leenane

🏛👁 COUNTRY HOUSE

Delphi Lodge

Leenane Co Galway **Tel: 095 42222** Fax: 095 42296
Email: stay@delphilodge.ie Web: www.delphilodge.ie

COUNTRY HOUSE OF THE YEAR

téile bia One of Ireland's most famous sporting lodges, Delphi Lodge was built in the early 19th-century by the Marquis of Sligo, and is magnificently located in an unspoilt valley, surrounded by the region's highest mountains (with the high rainfall so dear to fisherfolk). Owned since 1986 by Peter Mantle - who has restored and extended the original building in period style - the lodge is large and impressive in an informal, understated way, with antiques, fishing gear and a catholic collection of reading matter creating a stylish yet relaxed atmosphere. The guest rooms are all quite different, but they have lovely lake and mountain views, good bathrooms (some recently upgraded), and are very comfortably furnished. Dinner, for residents only, is taken house-party style at a long oak table - traditionally presided over by the person lucky enough to catch the day's biggest salmon. The set menu begins with an amuse-bouche (homemade game sausage, perhaps, with herb champ & red onion marmalade), and is cooked by Cliodhna Prendergast, who has earned a reputation that reaches far beyond the valley for her cooking of a "range of dishes that is vast and eclectic" - some traditional, others modern, or oriental. Home made ravioli of wood pigeon is a speciality, served with wild mushrooms & a light Parmesan sauce - also nephrops from Killary Bay, which come with warmed rocket butter. Coffee and home-made chocolates round off the feast in the Piano Room, where, perhaps, the good company of other guests may keep you from your bed. The famous Delphi Fishery is the main attraction, but many people come for other country pursuits, painting, or just peace and quiet. A billiard table, the library and a serious wine list (great bottles at a very modest mark-up) can get visitors through a lot of wet days. *Five restored cottages close to the lodge offer self-catering accommodation. Private house parties from €220 pp. Not suitable for children. No pets. Garden, fishing, walking, cycling, snooker. *Short breaks (eg 2DB&B from €220pps); also fly fishing tuition courses (weekends, €750); off season food & wine weekends with an emphasis on game Oct-Dec from €395. **Rooms 12** (all executive standard). B&B €95 pps, ss €30. Meals 1-2 pm and 8pm. Residents L €16, D €49; 8 well-chosen house wines, all €22; SC discretionary. Closed Dec 20 - Jan 6. MasterCard, Visa, Laser. **Directions:** 8 miles northwest of Leenane on the Louisburgh road.

Letterfrack

🏛👁 COUNTRY HOUSE

Rosleague Manor Hotel

Letterfrack Co Galway **Tel: 095 41101** Fax: 095 41168
Email: info@rosleague.com Web: www.rosleague.com

téile bia This lovely, graciously proportioned, pink-washed Regency house looks out over a tidal inlet through gardens planted with rare shrubs and plants. Although the area also offers plenty of energetic pursuits, there is a deep sense of peace at Rosleague and it's hard to imagine anywhere better to recharge the soul. The hotel changed hands within the Foyle family a few years ago and it now has an energetic young owner manager, Mark Foyle, who is gradually working his way through a major renovation programme: the conservatory bar, restaurant and a number of bedrooms (and their bathrooms) have now been completely refurbished (two have four-poster beds), and the gardens (already extensive, and listed in the Connemara Garden Trail) were further developed to make new paths and establish a wild flower meadow. This is a very pleasant, peaceful place to stay; there are two lovely drawing rooms with log fires and the restaurant - a lovely classical dining room, with mahogany furniture and a fine collection of plates on the walls - is open to non-residents by reservation. Head chef Pascal Marinot, who has been at Rosleague since 2000, offers a daily-changing dinner menu in a quite traditional style - starters like oysters with shallot vinegar & lemon, or home-made chicken liver paté with cranberry sauce & Melba toast, a soup course, and straightforward main courses such as black sole on the bone. For dessert, Rosleague chocolate mousse is an inherited speciality, going back to Mark's uncle, Paddy Foyle's, time in the kitchen. Children welcome (cot available free of charge, baby sitting arranged) Garden, tennis, fishing, walking. Pets permitted by arrangement. **Rooms 20** (4 junior suites). B&B €110pps, ss €30. Restaurant **Seats 50** (Private Room seats 10). L 12-3, D 7.30-9 daily, non-residents welcome by reservation; Set D €45. House wine €21. Closed Dec- Mar. Amex, MasterCard, Visa, Laser. **Directions:** On N59 main road, 7 miles north-west of Clifden.

Oranmore

Flamme Bay

 RESTAURANT The Galway Bay Resort Renville Oranmore Co Galway
Tel: 091 388639 Email: flammebay@eircom.net Web: www.flammebay.com

Michel Flamme, well known from his previous position as executive head chef at the K Club, took on the lease of the restaurant at the Galway Bay Golf Resort in 2005. The dining room has wonderful views of Galway Bay and, although still due for refurbishment at the time of going to press, Michel's skills in the kitchen and the exceptional location mark this out as a must-visit destination. And, (temporarily) dowdy dining room aside, the food side of a visit here should not disappoint, as Michel's concise menus offer great dishes - including his famous speciality starter of crispy wonton of Galway prawns, and fine main courses such as seared cod with peas and smoked bacon cream, or fillet of beef with braised ox cheek in red wine - and the standard of food in the Spike Bar has also improved under his management. **Seats 80** (Private Room seats 30), outdoor dining for 35, Reservations required; D daily 6.30-10 (closed Sun D), L Sun only 1-4.30. D Gourmet Menu €60. House Wine € 19.50. Closed Mon-Tue. *The Spike Bar opens all day, all week for Brasserie style food (9-8.30). Spike Bar may close for winter.

Oughterard

Currarevagh House

COUNTRY HOUSE Glann Road Oughterard Co Galway **Tel: 091 552 312** Fax: 091 552 731
Email: mail@currarevagh.com Web: www.currarevagh.com

Tranquillity, trout and tea in the drawing room - these are the things that draw guests back to the Hodgson family's gracious, but not luxurious early Victorian manor overlooking Lough Corrib. Currarevagh, which was built in 1846 as a wedding present for Harry Hodgson's great, great, great grandfather, is set in 150 acres of woodlands and gardens with sporting rights over 5,000 acres. Guests have been welcomed here for nearly half a century; the present owners, Harry and June Hodgson, are founder members of the Irish Country Houses and Restaurants Association ('Ireland's Blue Book'), and recently joined by their son Henry. Yet, while the emphasis is on old-fashioned service and hospitality, the Hodgsons are adamant that the atmosphere should be more like a private house party than an hotel, and their restful rituals underline the differences: the day begins with a breakfast worthy of its Edwardian origins, laid out on the sideboard in the dining room; lunch may be one of the renowned picnic hampers required by sporting folk. Then there's afternoon tea, followed by a leisurely dinner. Fishing is the ruling passion, of course - notably brown trout, pike, perch and salmon - but there are plenty of other country pursuits to assist in building up an appetite again for June's good home cooking, all based on fresh local produce. Her 5-course dinner menus might begin with a salad of air dried lamb (a local speciality from McGeough's butchers in Oughterard), then a crab and watercress soup, followed by medallions of pork rolled in pistachio nuts and finally a dessert such as chocolate truffle, and Irish cheeses; there is no choice but menus are changed daily and there is quite an extensive, fairly priced wine list. Non-residents welcome by reservation. Not suitable for children under 5. Garden, walking, tennis. **Rooms 15** (all en-suite). B&B €95, ss €35. No SC. D €42.50, at 8pm (non residents welcome by reservation). Wines from €17.50. Closed mid Oct- Apr. MasterCard, Visa, Laser, Switch. **Directions:** Take N59 to Oughterard. Turn right in village square and follow Glann Road for 4 miles.

Oughterard Area

 CAFÉ

Brigit's Garden Café

Pollagh Rosscahill Co Galway **Tel: 091 550 905** Fax: 091 550 491
Email: info@brigitsgarden.ie Web: www.brigitsgarden.ie

Jenny Beale's beautiful themed garden near Oughterard reflects the Celtic festivals and, in addition to woodland trails, ring fort and stone chamber has a café that is worth a visit in its own right. A pine-ceilinged modern room that also acts as reception/shop has a small kitchen open to view at one end, and is set up with tables covered in old-fashioned oil cloth; everything's very simple, with plain white crockery and stainless cutlery and paper serviettes and, in fine weather, there is seating outside too. A short (vegetarian) blackboard menu offers a daily soup: chunky, wholesome vegetable with thyme, perhaps, a meal in itself with brown bread & butter), and a special such as home-grown chard and blue cheese pasta. Lovely toasted sandwiches are generously filled salad and a choice of fillings (egg mayonnaise, goats cheese & herb, hummus & olive, cheese & scallion), and great home bakes include delicious scones with jam & cream, a luscious, walnut & apricot carrot cake, which is nutty and moist. Good coffee, tea or tisanes, and soft drinks like cranberry or lemon juice - just the kind of place you need to know about when exploring the area. Good toilets too, including baby changing facilities. **Seats 35** (+20 outdoors). Open 11-5 daily. Closed Oct - mid Apr. MasterCard, Visa, Laser. **Directions:** Just off the N59 between Moycullen and Oughterard.

Recess

HOTEL/RESTAURANT

Ballynahinch Castle Hotel

Recess Co Galway **Tel: 095 31006** Fax: 095 31085
Email: bhinch@iol.ie Web: www.ballynahinch-castle.com

Renowned as a fishing hotel, this crenellated Victorian mansion enjoys a most romantic position in 450 acres of ancient woodland and gardens on the banks of the Ballynahinch River. It is impressive in scale and relaxed in atmosphere - a magic combination which, together with a high level of comfort and friendliness (and an invigorating mixture of residents and locals in the bar at night), all combine to bring people back. The tone is set in the foyer, with its huge stone fireplace and ever-burning log fire (which is a cosy place to enjoy afternoon tea) and the many necessary renovations and extensions through the years have been undertaken with great attention to period detail, a policy also carried through successfully in furnishing both public areas and bedrooms, many of which have lovely views over the river. A stay here is a restorative treat and, after a restful night's sleep, a Ballynahinch breakfast will give you a good start ahead of a day's fishing, wilderness walks on the estate, or simply touring the area. (Ballynahinch was the Connaught winner of our Irish Breakfast Awards in 2002.) **Owenmore Restaurant:** This bright and elegant room has the classic atmosphere of a splendidly old-fashioned dining room, and is carefully organised to allow as many tables as possible to enjoy its uniquely beautiful river setting, where you can watch happy fisherfolk claiming the last of the fading daylight on the rocks below. Head chef Robert Webster's daily dinner menus have plenty of fine local produce to call on - wild salmon, of course, also sea fish, Connemara lamb and prime Irish beef (supplied by the renowned butcher, McGeough's of Oughterard) - a great basis for specialities with enduring popularity like poached wild Atlantic salmon, baked Connemara lamb cutlets and lobster. Vegetarians are well looked after too - home-made pasta is a speciality, papardelle served with artichoke hearts, garlic and Parmesan cheese, perhaps. A thoughtfully assembled wine list offers an unusual range of house wines and a good choice of half bottles. *Excellent meals are also served in the hotel's characterful bar - a mighty high-ceilinged room with a huge fireplace, and many mementoes of the pleasures of rod and hunt. An informal alternative to the Owenmore experience - and a great place for non-residents to drop into for a bite when touring Connemara. Fishing: 3 miles of private fly fishing for Atlantic salmon, sea trout and brown trout. Landscaped gardens and wilderness walks on 450 acres; members of Connemara Garden Trail. Small conferences (12). Cycling, walking; Children welcome (under 3s free in parents' room; cots available without charge, baby sitting arranged). No pets. Walking, cycling, tennis. fishing. Golf nearby. **Rooms 40** (3 suites, 40 with separate bath & shower.) No lift. 24 hr room service. B&B €120 pps, ss €30; sc 10%. Short/special interest/off season breaks offered - details on application. Owenmore Restaurant open daily, D only 6.30-9 (Set D €49), house wines from €25.20. Bar meals 12.30-3 & 6.30-9 daily. SC 10%. Closed Christmas & Feb. Amex, Diners, MasterCard, Visa, Laser. **Directions:** N59 from Galway - Clifden; left after Recess (Roundstone road), 2 km.

Recess
ⓜ◉ HOTEL

Lough Inagh Lodge

Recess Co Galway **Tel: 095 34706** Fax: 095 34708
Email: inagh@iol.ie Web: www.loughinaghlodgehotel.ie

Maire O'Connor's former sporting lodge on the shores of Lough Inagh makes a delightful small hotel, with a country house atmosphere. It has large, well-proportioned rooms, interesting period detail and lovely fireplaces with welcoming log fires, as well as all the modern comforts. Public areas include two drawing rooms, each with an open fire, and a very appealing bar with a big turf fire and its own back door and tiled floor for wet fishing gear. Bedrooms, which include one recently added room and several with four-posters, are all well-appointed and unusually spacious, with views of lake and countryside. Walk-in dressing rooms lead to well-planned bathrooms and tea/coffee-making facilities are available in rooms on request. While it has special appeal to sportsmen, Lough Inagh makes a good base for touring Connemara and is only 42 miles from Galway; in addition to fishing, golf, pony trekking and garden visits are all nearby. Off-season breaks offer especially good value. **Finisglen Room:** This handsome dining room has deep green walls and graceful spoonback Victorian mahogany chairs, and non-residents are welcome for dinner by reservation. Fiona Joyce has been head chef since 2002, and the food in both the restaurant and the bar is excellent; alongside the popular dishes like smoked salmon, pan-fried steaks, wild salmon and lobster (when available) you may find less usual choices including starters of grilled fish sausage, or air-dried Connemara lamb. Desserts, including a wide range of ices, are home made, service is friendly, and portions generous. The wine list includes a fair range of half bottles, some non alcoholic wines and, unusually, a rosé among the house wines. *Tempting bar menus are also offered for lunch, dinner and afternoon tea. Small conferences/banqueting (15/36). Children welcome (under 3s free in parents' room, cots available without charge, baby sitting arranged). Pets permitted. Garden, walking, cycling. **Rooms 13** (5 junior suites, 10 no smoking); room service (24 hr). B&B €113 pps, ss €20. **Restaurant:** L 12.30-4.30; D daily 7-9 (reservations required), Set D €42; alos A la Carte and Vegetarian Menu. House wine €21; Bar meals 10-9 daily. SC10%. Closed mid Dec-mid Mar. Amex, Diners, MasterCard, Visa, Laser. **Directions:** From Galway city travel on N59 for 40 miles. Take right N344 after Recess; 3 miles on right.

Renvyle
◉ HOTEL

Renvyle House Hotel

Renvyle Co Galway **Tel: 095 43511** Fax: 095 43515
Email: info@renvyle.com Web: www.renvyle.com

CREATIVE USE OF VEGETABLES AWARD

féile bia In one of the country's most appealingly remote and beautiful areas, this famous Lutyens-esque house has a romantic and fascinating history, having been home to people as diverse as a Gaelic chieftan and Oliver St John Gogarty - and becoming one of Ireland's earliest country house hotels, in 1883. In good weather it is best approached via a stunning scenic drive along a mountain road with views down into a blue-green sea of unparalleled clarity. Once reached, the hotel seems to be snuggling down for shelter and, although it has limited views, there is a shift of emphasis to the comforts within, a feeling reinforced by the cosy atmosphere of the original building, with its dark beams, rug strewn floors and open fires - and a snug conservatory where guests can survey the garden, and the landscape beyond. Photographs and mementoes recording visits from the many famous people who have stayed here - Augustus John, Lady Gregory, Yeats and Churchill among them - keep guests happily occupied for hours, but there is plenty to distract you from this enjoyable activity, including a heated outdoor swimming pool, tennis, trout fishing, golf (9 hole), and croquet - while the surrounding area offers more challenging activities including archaeological expeditions, horse riding, hill walking, scuba diving and sea fishing. Just loafing around is perhaps what guests are best at here, however, and there's little need to do much else. Head chef Tim O'Sullivan looks after the inner man admirably in lovely dinners featuring local seafood and Connemara produce, including Renvyle rack of lamb, local lobster and vegetables in season - and the hotel's bar food is also excellent. All this, plus the scent of a turf fire and a comfortable armchair, can be magic. The grounds and gardens around the hotel are a special point of interest at Renvyle, and come as a delightful contrast to the magnificently rugged surrounding scenery. Special breaks (midweek, weekend and bank holiday) are very good value and Renvyle makes an excellent conference venue. (conference/banqueting 200); secretarial services. Children welcome (under 4s free in parents' room, cots available without charge; crèche, playroom, children's playground, children's tea, baby sitting arranged). Archery, all-weather tennis court, clay pigeon shooting, croquet, lawn bowls, snooker. **Rooms 69** (6 suites, 40 no smoking, 1 for disabled). B&B €115, no ss, no SC. Restaurant open 7-9 daily (Set D €45). Bar meals 11-7 daily (excl 25 Dec, Good Fri). Closed Jan. Amex, Diners, MasterCard, Visa, Laser. **Directions:** 12 miles north of Clifden.

Roundstone Area

€ ◎ COUNTRY HOUSE

The Angler's Return

Toombeola Roundstone Co Galway

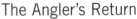

Tel: 095 31091 Email: Web: www.anglersreturn.com

This charming and unusual house near Roundstone was built as a sporting lodge in the eighteenth century and, true to its name, fishing remains a major attraction to this day. But you don't have to be a fisherperson to warm to the special charms of The Anglers Return: peace and tranquillity, the opportunity to slow down in a quiet, caring atmosphere in this most beautiful area - this is its particular appeal. The house is set in three acres of natural gardens (open every day in spring and summer; best in late spring) and makes a good base for the Connemara Garden Trail - and, of course, for painting holidays. Bedrooms are bright and comfortably furnished in a fresh country house style, although only one is en-suite (the other four share two bathrooms between them); this is not a major problem and the overall level of comfort is high. However, bathroom arrangements are gradually being improved - one now features a restored Victorian ball & claw cast-iron bath, and an extra shower is due to be installed soon. As well as fishing, there is golf nearby, and riding and boat trips can be arranged for guests - and there are maps and information for walkers too. No television but there are lots of books to read - and tea or snacks are available at any time during the day or evening, (out in the secluded back garden in fine weather, or beside the fire in the soothing drawing room, perhaps); dinner is available for groups staying several days, otherwise bookings can be made in nearby restaurants. Breakfast will include freshly baked breads, home-made yoghurts, marmalade and jams, and freshly picked herb teas from the garden - and you are even invited to collect your own egg. Not suitable for children. Walking, fishing, garden. **Rooms 5** (1 en-suite, 4 with shared bathrooms; all no smoking). B&B €48, ss by arrangement. * Special interest breaks offered (painting, walking); details on application. Closed 30 Nov-1 Mar. **No Credit Cards. Directions:** From Galway, N59 Clifden road; turn left onto R341 Roundstone road for 4 miles; house is on the left.

COUNTY KERRY

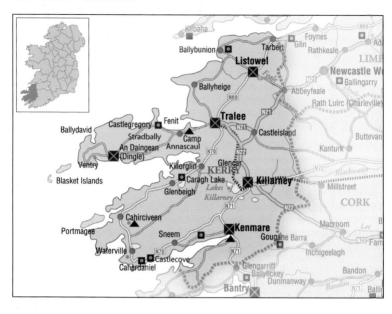

Ballybunion
🏨 GUESTHOUSE

Teach de Broc

Links Road Ballybunion Co Kerry **Tel: 068 27581** Fax: 068 27919
Email: teachdebroc@eircom.net Web: www.ballybuniongolf.com

You don't have to play golf to appreciate this highly popular guesthouse, but it certainly must help as it is almost within the boundaries of the famous Ballybunion links. Aoife and Seamus Brock offer an extremely high standard of comfort, with satellite television in all rooms, and there is a commitment to constant upgrading and improvement: recent additions include a new guest lounge and a wine/coffee bar, four more fine bedrooms, and the introduction of an electric massage chair for easing golfers' aches and pains after a long day on the links. Yet, however comfortable and well-located this exceptional guesthouse may be, it's the laid-back and genuinely hospitable atmosphere created by this energetic and dedicated couple that really gets them coming back for more. Always keen to provide the best possible service for the discerning golfer, an excellent breakfast is served from 6am, with freshly baked scones and croissants among the good things offered. Light evening meals are available to residents, and have proved a popular alternative to going into town to eat; home-made gourmet pizzas are the speciality of the house - a 12" thin crust with olive oil, chorizo, bacon, red onion, goats cheese & herbs, for example...also other simple dishes like traditional cottage pie. Wine licence. *Stay & Play golf breaks offered; details on application. Masseuse on call. Laundry service. Horse riding nearby. Own parking. Garden. Masseuse on call. Secretarial services. Laundry service. Horse riding available nearby. Own parking. Garden. Not suitable for children. No pets. Wine licence. **Rooms 14** (all en-suite, 4 with separate bath & shower, 2 shower only, all no-smoking, 1 for disabled). Lift. Turndown service. B&B €80pps, ss €40. Closed 1 Nov - 15 Mar. MasterCard, Visa, Laser. **Directions:** Directly opposite entrance to Ballybunion Golf Club.

Caherdaniel
🔧👁 HOTEL/RESTAURANT

Derrynane Hotel

Caherdaniel Co Kerry **Tel: 066 947 5136** Fax: 066 947 5160
Email: info@derrynane.com Web: www.derrynane.com

féile bia If only for its superb location on the seaward side of the Ring of Kerry road this unassuming 1960s-style hotel would be well worth a visit, but there is much more to it than the view, or even its waterside position. The accommodation is quite modest but very comfortable, the food is good and, under the excellent management of Mary O'Connor and her well-trained staff, this hospitable, family-friendly place provides a welcome home from home for many a contented guest. Activity holidays are a big draw - there are beautiful beaches, excellent fishing with local fisherman Michael Fenton (who supplies all necessary equipment and has a fully licensed boat), Waterville Golf Course offers special rates at certain times - and the hotel has published its own walking brochure. Don't leave the area without visiting Daniel O'Connell's beautiful house at Derrynane or the amazing Ballinskelligs chocolate factory. Children welcome (under 4s free in parents' room, cots available without charge, baby sitting arranged; playroom) Heated outdoor swimming pool, tennis, pool table. Walking. Garden. **Rooms 70** (all en-suite, 15 family rooms, 33 ground floor, 50 no smoking). B&B from about €65 pps. *Special breaks offered: details on application. Closed Oct-mid Apr. **Restaurant:** Beautifully located, overlooking the heated outdoor swimming pool and the hotel's gardens (which reach down to the shore), the restaurant enjoys stunning sea views - be sure to ask for a table by the sea, as the view is a major part of the experience; on a warm summer evening the huge plate glass windows slide back to let in purest Atlantic sea air - a rare treat. While not a fine dining experience, good food has always been a feature of the hotel and there is a commitment to high quality ingredients, local where possible (a detailed list of suppliers is given). Healthy Options are highlighted on 4-course dinner menus that offer a good choice of simply presented popular dishes like smoked salmon, duck or chicken liver mousse, Kerry lamb or beef, and duckling - and a very reasonably priced children's menu is offered separately. Attentive staff do everything possible to make a meal here a pleasant experience - and a helpful wine list is clearly presented, with excellent descriptions of each bottle. *A light bar menu is also available every day, 11am-9pm. **Seats 100.** D 7-9 daily, Set D from about €30. also A la C, sc discretionary. House wine about €20. * All day salad bar avalable for light meals. Hotel closed mid Oct- Apr. Amex, Diners, MasterCard, Visa, Laser. **Directions:** Midway on Ring of Kerry.

Cahirciveen
🔧 BAR/RESTAURANT

QC's Seafood Bar & Restaurant

3 Main Street Cahirciveen Co Kerry **Tel: 066 947 2244**
Fax: 066 947 2244 Email: info@qcbar.com Web: www.qcbar.com

With its rugged stone wall, old counter, enormous fireplace, nautical antiques and pictures of local interest, Kate and Andrew Cooke's bar and restaurant on the main street has great style and atmosphere - and, once you know how delicious the food is, and how warm the ambience, you'll find it impossible ever to drive straight through Cahirciveen again. Nothing stands still here - they opened in 2000 and, having recovered from the initial renovation programme, Kate and Andrew turned their attention to a sheltered courtyard at the back (now charmingly set up for barbecues and al fresco dining), refurbished the restaurant area - which, in typical Kerry style, is an extension of the bar - and in the next phase they hope to add accommodation. Meanwhile, delicious local seafood is the main attraction, supplied by the family company, Quinlan's Kerry Fish at Renard's Point. It's cooked, Basque-style, on a charcoal grill especially imported from Spain, so expect delicious chargrills, with lots of olive oil and garlic: shellfish cooked with garlic, chilli, Spanish onion & tomato, is a speciality for example - prawns (langoustines) or fresh crab claws and crabmeat are served sizzling in a Spanish cazueala (traditional terracotta dish); another speciality is pan-seared baby squid, served with caramelised onions and salsa verde, while wild Kerry salmon is smoked in the family factory and served simply with a caper and red onion salad and home-made brown bread - then there are chargrilled steaks, Kerry lamb and vegetarian dishes (Ardsallagh goat cheese parcel, wild mushroom risotto) to balance up all that seafood. The most pleasing aspect of the food is its immediacy - everything is ultra-fresh, simply prepared and full of zest. And, of course, there's a wine list majoring in Spain to match. Simply irresistible. [* Accomodation is planned for 2006/7; Andrew also runs a yacht charter service, see www.YachtCharterKerry.com] An interesting wine list leans strongly towards Spain, especially the reds, although house wines are from France & Chile; it is good to see sherry listed as a mainstream wine rather than relegated to aperitif status. €17.50. Children welcome. **Seats 60.** (Outdoor seating, 30). Meals: (Summer 7 days, Winter Thu-Sun) L 12-2.30 (closed Sun L) & D 6-9.30; Closed 25 Dec, Good Fri; annual closure 8 Jan - Mid Feb. Minimum credit card charge, €25. MasterCard, Visa, Laser. **Directions:** In the centre of Caherciveen.

Caragh Lake
COUNTRY HOUSE/RESTAURANT

Caragh Lodge

Caragh Lake Killorglin Co Kerry
Tel: 066 976 9115 Fax: 066 976 9316
Email: caraghl@iol.ie Web: www.caraghlodge.com

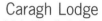 Less than a mile from the Ring of Kerry, Mary Gaunt's lovely Victorian house and gardens are nestling on the shores of the startlingly beautiful Caragh Lake, and it is an idyllic place, with views of Ireland's highest mountains, the McGillicuddy Reeks. The house which is elegantly furnished with antiques but not too formal makes a cool, restful retreat, and afternoon tea taken in one of the two lovely drawing rooms (each with an open fire), or on the lawn, is a treat indeed. Bedrooms in the main house have that indefinable atmosphere that comes as a house gently ages, but the newer 'garden' rooms are all furnished in a similar country house style and have lovely bathrooms, wonderful views and their own entrance and sitting room (complete with open log fire). Salmon and trout fishing, boating and swimming are all available at the bottom of the garden. Not suitable for children under 12. No pets. Banqueting (50). **Rooms 15** (1 suite, 6 junior suites, 8 superior, all no smoking). B&B €97.50, ss €42.50. Closed mid Oct-mid Apr. **Restaurant:** In this elegant dining room overlooking the lake, local produce such as freshly caught seafood, often including wild salmon from Caragh Lake, Kerry lamb and home-grown vegetables, takes pride of place - and Mary's real love of cooking shines through. Wide-ranging menus tempt with starters like tian of crab and avocado with gazpacho sauce, followed by soup (cream of scallop perhaps) or sorbet (possibly raspberry) of the day then main courses such as wild salmon on a bed of olive oil scented potato purée, Caragh Lodge crispy half duck with plum sauce or roast cannon of Kerry lamb with pea and mint purée and herb jus. Fish cookery is a particular strength, and also baking - not only in delicious home-baked breads, but also baked desserts and treats for afternoon tea, including recipes handed down by Mary's family through the generations. **Seats 34** (private room, 12). D daily, 7-8.30; about €40 (average, à la carte). Good wine list, unusually strong on South African wines. House wine €24. SC discretionary. Open to non-residents by reservation. Not suitable for children under 12. Establishment closed mid Oct-mid Apr. Amex, Diners, MasterCard, Visa. **Directions:** N70 from Killorglin, Glenbeigh direction, second road signed Caragh Lake; left at end road.

Caragh Lake
COUNTRY HOUSE/RESTAURANT

Carrig Country House & Restaurant

Caragh Lake Killorglin Co Kerry
Tel: 066 976 9100 Fax: 066 976 9166
Email: info@carrighouse.com Web: www.carrighouse.com

At the heart of Frank and Mary Slattery's sensitively extended Victorian house lies a hunting lodge once owned by Lord Brocket - and he chose well, as it is very attractive and handsomely set in fine gardens with the lake and mountains providing a dramatic backdrop. The house is welcoming and well-maintained, with friendly staff (Frank himself carries the luggage to your room) and a relaxed atmosphere, notably in a series of sitting rooms where you can chat beside the fire or have a drink before dinner. This is a place where you can lose yourself for hours with a book, or playing chess, cards or board games in the games room, or boating out on the lake. Some of the large, airy bedrooms have their own patios, and all are furnished with antiques, and have generous, well-designed bathrooms with bath and shower - an impressive Presidential Suite has a sitting room with panoramic views across the lake to the Magillicuddy Reeks, two separate dressing rooms and jacuzzi bath. The extensive gardens are of great interest - a map is available, and personalised tours can be arranged. Not suitable for children under 8 except small babies (under 1 free of charge, cot available, baby sitting arranged). Dogs allowed in some areas. Swimming (lake), fishing (ghilly & boat available), walking, garden, croquet. **Rooms 16** (1 suite, 1 junior suite, 3 no smoking) B&B about €80 pps, ss €50. Closed Dec-Feb. **Lakeside Restaurant:** Beautifully situated overlooking the lake, the restaurant is a fine big room with well-spaced tables and, like the rest of the house, a relaxed atmosphere. A strong kitchen team is led by head chef Helen Vickers, and pastry chef Patricia Teahan, who have been steadily building the reputation of Carrig House as a dining destination since 2003. Extensive menus offer a balanced choice, with fresh Kerry seafood and Kerry lamb the main specialities; starters like freshly shucked Cromane oysters with cucumber relish and salmon, and potted Valentia Island crab with melba toast are typical and, among the dozen or so main courses offered (and served with home grown vegetables from their own walled kitchen garden) there may be an unusual dish such as a chargrilled loin of lamb with a mini shepherd's pie and about four fish dishes, some with oriental tones. Vegetarian dishes are changed daily. Be sure to save some room for Patricia Teahan's desserts, a choice of at least half a dozen classical treats that please the eye as much as the palate. **Seats 55** (private room, 15) Outdoor dining for 20. D daily, 7-9. Extensive à la carte. House wine €25. SC discretionary. Non-residents welcome (booking essential). Establishment closed Dec-Feb. Diners, MasterCard, Visa, Laser. **Directions:** Left after 2.5 miles on Killorglin/Glenbeigh Road N70 (Ring of Kerry), then turn sharp right at Caragh Lake School (1.5 miles), half a mile on the left.

Caragh Lake

🏛 ◉ HOTEL/RESTAURANT

Hotel Ard-na-Sidhe

Caragh Lake Co Kerry **Tel: 066 976 9105** Fax: 066 976 9282
Email: ardnasidhe@eircom.net Web: www.killarneyhotels.ie

Set in woodland and among award-winning gardens, this peaceful Victorian retreat is in a beautiful mountain location overlooking Caragh Lake. Decorated throughout in a soothing country house style, very comfortable antique-filled day rooms provide plenty of lounging space for quiet indoor relaxation and a terrace for fine weather all with wonderful views. Bedrooms shared between the main house and some with private patios in the garden house are spacious and elegantly furnished in traditional style, with excellent en-suite bathrooms. This is a sister hotel to the Hotel Europe and Dunloe Castle (see entries), whose leisure facilities are also available to guests. Dooks, Waterville, Killeen and Mahony's Point golf courses are all within easy reach. **Rooms 18** (3 suites,1 family room, 5 ground floor, 6 no smoking). Under 2s free in parents' room; cots available free of charge. No pets. B&B €85 pps (ss €50), SC included. Limited room service. **Fairyhill Restaurant:** Like the rest of the hotel, the dining room has intimacy and character and, after a fireside drink and a look through Eileen O'Brien's menus, this is a delightful place to spend an hour or two. Eileen - well-known chef at the former Killarney restaurant, The Strawberry Tree, now re-located to Co Wicklow (see entry) - offers unusually earthy menus for an hotel, with the emphasis on local ingredients and updated interpretations of traditional Irish themes. Specialities include the house boxty (traditional Irish potato cake with an onion and mustard sauce), for example, and a main course of Kerry mountain lamb, that is baked with vegetables in mint scented pastry and served with panfried lamb cutlets - a dish reminiscent of the traditional Kerry pie most closely associated with Dingle. Other choices are wide-ranging and include several fish dishes, although there is a stronger emphasis on meats than is usual in the area. This is quite hearty food, and may not leave a lot of room for desserts, which include speciality ice creams (served imaginatively, on a slab of ice), or the Irish cheese plate. Coffee and petits fours can be served beside the drawing room fire. Non residents are welcome by reservation. Closed (restaurant usually closes on Sun), Oct- Apr. Amex, Diners, MasterCard, Visa, Laser. **Directions:** Off N70 Ring of Kerry road, signed 5 km west of Killorglin.

The Chart House

Dingle
☆ 🏆 RESTAURANT

The Mall Dingle Co Kerry **Tel: 066 915 2255** Fax: 066 915 2255
Email: charthse@iol.ie Web: www.charthousedingle.com

Even in an area so well-endowed with good eating places, Jim McCarthy's attractive stone-built restaurant is outstanding. There's a smart little bar just inside the door - where Jim, the perfect host, always seems to be meeting, seating and seamlessly ensuring that everyone is well looked after and generally having a good time. And head chef Noel Enright leads a talented kitchen team: his menus are based on the best of local ingredients, sometimes in dishes with an international tone - a superb speciality starter of Annascaul black pudding, for example, is wrapped in filo pastry and served with apple and date chutney and hollandaise sauce, while roast breast of Skeaghanore duck comes with crispy polenta, minted yoghurt and chilli garlic oil; other dishes are just gently updated - rack of Kerry mountain lamb, for example, is accompanied by a butter bean purée and bay leaf jus; accurate, confident cooking lends these traditional foods a new character, and a large selection - perhaps half a dozen or more - of simple, perfectly cooked side vegetables are the ideal complement. Seafood is well represented, of course - three or four seafood choices might include a less usual fish dish like herb crusted skate, with leek & truffle risotto, salsa verde and balsamic reduction, and mainstream vegetarian dishes - possibly two or more on each course - have wide appeal. Desserts include classics like a basket of home-made ice creams, or luscious lemon scented pannacotta, with a wild berry compôte and shortbread biscuits: superb! But those with a savoury tooth will still feel that the smart money is on the Irish cheeses (Ardrahan, Gubbeen, Cashel Blue, perhaps, all in perfect condition), which are cannily offered with a glass of vintage port and served with delicious home-made oat biscuits and two varieties of grapes. Terrific hospitality, top class ingredients and gimmick-free creative cooking - great restaurant. Prices are fairly moderate (starters around €8.75, main courses average €22). An interesting wine list includes South African wines imported directly, and has helpful tasting notes as well as a clear layout of country of origin and vintages - and, of course, there's always a Chateau MacCarthy in stock. *Jim McCarthy was the Guide's Host of the Year in 2003. **Seats 45.** Children welcome. Air conditioning. D 6.30-10, daily in summer (Jun-Sep), restricted opening in winter - please phone ahead to check; à la carte. SC discretionary. House wine €19.50. Closed 7 Jan-13 Feb. MasterCard, Visa, Laser. **Directions:** Left at roundabout as you enter the town.

Doyle's Seafood Restaurant & Townhouse

Dingle
◉ : RESTAURANT WITH ROOMS

5 John Street Dingle Co Kerry
Tel: 066 915 1174 Fax: 066 915 1816
Email: cdoyles@iol.ie Web: www.doylesofdingle.com

Originally a small pub built in 1790, Doyles was established as a restaurant over a quarter of a century ago - and was one of the first in a town which is now renowned for good eating places. Currently in the hospitable hands of Charlotte Cluskey and her son John, it's a cosy, characterful place with an old kitchen range and natural materials - stone floor, kitchen tables and sugar chairs, a real wooden bar and high stools - which all create a relaxed country atmosphere in keeping with its history. Local seafood is the main attraction - nightly specials depend on the day's landings - and lobster, selected from a tank in the bar, is a speciality. Aside from lobster, speciality seafood dishes include hot oysters glazed with a horseradish sabayon, a West Coast platter and baked fish pie 'Doyle's style' (a tasty mixture of fish in a creamy wine sauce with crumb & cheese crust). There are, however, one or two concessions to non-seafood eaters such as Kerry mountain lamb done various ways (roast rack and leg with braised puy lentils, roast garlic & thyme jus is a favourite) or traditional beef & Guinness stew, and vegetarian dishes are available. Puddings are nice and traditional or there's a plated selection of farmhouse cheeses to finish. Accommodation is also offered. **Seats 45.** Air conditioning. D only, Mon-Sat 6-10. Early D €35 (6-7.15pm); also à la carte; house wine from €19.95; sc 10%. Closed Sun.

Accommodation: Quality accommodation includes a residents' sitting room as well as spacious bedrooms with well-designed en-suite bathrooms. B&B €72 pps, ss €65. Establishment closed 3 weeks Dec, mid Jan-mid Feb. Amex, Diners, MasterCard, Visa, Laser. **Directions:** On entering Dingle, take third exit from roundabout into The Mall; turn right into John Street.

Dingle
🏛 COUNTRY HOUSE

Emlagh House

Dingle Co Kerry **Tel: 066 915 2345** Fax: 066 915 2369
Email: info@emlaghhouse.com Web: www.emlaghhouse.com

The Kavanagh family's luxurious guesthouse is tucked into a site close to the Dingle Skellig Hotel, on the sea side of the road; it has been built with exceptional attention to detail and is maturing gracefully as the landscaping fills in. The style throughout the house is gracious, in large, well-proportioned rooms furnished in traditional country house style but with a contemporary streak that gives it a welcome lightness of touch. Bedrooms (most of which have harbour views) are elegant and extremely comfortable, with fresh flowers, fruit and chocolates to greet guests on arrival and many features, including individually controlled heating/air conditioning, trouser press with iron, direct dial phone with modem, satellite TV, video, radio & CD - the latter wired to luxurious marbled bathrooms with underfloor heating, separate shower and bath, double basins, heated mirror and towel rails and thick bathrobes. Some interconnecting rooms are available to provide private accommodation for groups. Hosts Marion and Gráinne Kavanagh do everything possible to make guests comfortable, and their attention to detail includes an evening turndown service. Evening meals are not offered, as the restaurants of Dingle are so near, but excellent breakfasts are served in a stylish dining room where contemporary influences in the decor are skilfully blended with antiques. A new conservatory overlooking the harbour is under construction as we go to press, providing another place for guests to read and relax. Many activities (golf, fishing, sailing, equestrian) available nearby. Not suitable for children. No pets. Own parking (20). **Rooms 10** (all no smoking, 1 for disabled). Lift. B&B €100pps, ss €40. Residents D Mon-Sat, 6.30-8. No D on Sun. A la carte. House wine from €24. Closed 1 Nov-15 Mar. MasterCard, Visa, Laser, Switch. **Directions:** Upon entering Dingle, take first left after petrol station.

Dingle
🏛🍽 GUESTHOUSE

Greenmount House

Upper John Street Dingle Co Kerry
Tel: 066 915 1414 Fax: 066 915 1974
Email: info@greenmount-house.com Web: www.greenmount-house.com

Just five minutes walk from the centre of Dingle, John and Mary Curran have run one of Ireland's finest guesthouses since the mid-70s. It's an exceptionally comfortable place to stay, quietly located on the hillside, with private parking and uninterrupted views across the town and harbour to the mountains across the bay. The spacious, well-appointed bedrooms are mainly junior suites with generous seating areas and particularly good amenities, including fridges as well as tea/coffee-making trays, phone and TV (and, in most cases, also their own entrance and balcony). There's a comfortable residents' sitting room with an open fire, and a conservatory overlooking the harbour, where wonderful breakfasts are served. Greenmount and won our Irish Breakfast Award (Munster Region) in 2001, and it has always been a point of pride: the aroma of home baking is one of the things that gives this house a special warmth, and all the preserves are home-made too; there's a wonderful buffet - laden down with all kinds of fresh and poached fruits, juices, yogurts, cheeses, freshly baked breads - as well as an extensive choice of hot dishes, including the traditional full Irish breakfast. The wonder is that anyone ever leaves this place of a morning at all. Not suitable for children under 8. No pets. Garden, walking. Parking (15). **Rooms 9** (7 junior suites, 1 shower only, all no smoking). B&B €50pps, ss €40, SC discretionary. Closed 20-27 Dec. MasterCard, Visa, Laser. **Directions:** Turn right and right again on entering Dingle.

Dingle
☕ BAR/RESTAURANT

Lord Baker's Restaurant & Bar

Dingle Co Kerry **Tel: 066 915 1277**
Email: info@lordbakers.ie Web: www.lordbakers.ie

féile bia Believed to be the oldest pub in Dingle, this business was established in 1890 by a Tom Baker. A popular businessman in the area, a colourful orator, member of Kerry County Council and a director of the Tralee-Dingle Railway, he was known locally as "Lord Baker" and as such is now immortalised in John Moriarty's excellent bar and restaurant in the centre of Dingle. A welcoming turf fire burns in the front bar, where bar food such as chowder and home-baked bread or crab claws in garlic butter is served. At the back, there's a more sophisticated dining set-up in the restaurant proper (and, beyond it, a walled garden). Seafood (notably lobster from their own tank) stars, of course, and speciality dishes include monkfish wrapped in bacon, with garlic cream sauce and classic seafood mornay; but there's also a good choice of other dishes using local mountain lamb (roast rack or braised shank, perhaps), also Kerry beef, chicken and local duckling all well-cooked and served in an atmosphere of great hospitality. In addition to the main menu there are chef's specials each evening - and an unusual house speciality features on the dessert menu: traditional plum pudding with brandy sauce! Sunday lunch in the restaurant is a particularly popular event and very well done (booking strongly advised); on other days, the lunchtime bar menu, plus one or two daily specials such as a roast, can be taken in the restaurant. An informative wine list includes a Connoisseur's Selection of ten wines. John is an excellent host, caring and watchful - no detail escapes his notice, ensuring that every guest in Dingle's largest restaurant will leave contented. **Seats 120.** L Fri-Wed, 12.30-2; D Fri-Wed, 6-10. Early D €18.50 (6-7), Set D €24, also à la carte; light lunch, €9.80. Closed Thurs, 23-28 Dec & Good Friday. Amex, MasterCard, Visa, Laser. **Directions:** Town centre.

Dingle
👁 GUESTHOUSE

Milltown House

Dingle Co Kerry **Tel: 066 915 1372** Fax: 066 915 1095
Email: info@milltownhousedingle.com Web: www.milltownhousedingle.com

The Kerry family's attractive guesthouse on the western side of the town is set in immaculate gardens running down to the water's edge and enjoys beautiful views of the harbour and distant mountains - for those who value a quiet situation this is perhaps the best-located house in Dingle, as it is well off the road. Day rooms include an informal reception room, a comfortably furnished sitting room and a conservatory breakfast room overlooking the garden - breakfast is quite an event, offering everything from fresh juices and fruit, through cold meats and cheeses, freshly baked breads and an extensive cooked breakfast menu. The bedrooms all very comfortable and thoughtfully furnished with phone, TV with video channel, tea/coffee making facilities and iron/trouser press - include two with private patios. Constant upgrading is the policy at this hospitable house: a number of rooms have recently been increased in size and a new lounge, with sea and mountain views, was added to the front of the house. Not suitable for children. No pets. Garden. **Rooms 10** (6 junior suites, all with full bath en suite, all no smoking). B&B about €75 pps, ss €55. Room service (limited hours). Closed Nov-mid Apr. Amex, MasterCard, Visa, Laser. **Directions:** West through Dingle town, 0.75 miles from town centre.

Dingle
€ B&B

Number Fifty Five

55 John Street Dingle Co Kerry **Tel: 066 915 2378**
Email: stelladoyle@eircom.net Web: www.stella.thewub.com

Stella Doyle's charming B&B in the centre of Dingle offers accommodation with character - and a high level of comfort at a very affordable price. Although the frontage seems small from the road, it is larger than it looks: the two guest bedrooms are on the ground floor and delightfully furnished in a fresh country house style, with television and full bathrooms (bath and power shower). But there is a surprise in store when you go upstairs to the first floor and find a light and spacious open plan living room, which has great style and, like the rest of the house, is furnished with antiques and original art. There's a large seating area at one end and, at the other, a dining area with large windows looking out to fields at the back of the house; here Stella, who spent most of her working life as a chef, serves delicious breakfasts for guests; no menu - 'anything you like, really'. Guests are welcomed to this hospitable haven with a cup of tea on arrival - and breakfast is sure to send them happily on their way. Not suitable for children. No pets. **Rooms 2** (both en-suite with full bath & no smoking). B&B €35, ss €15. Closed 30 Sep-mid Apr. **No Credit Cards. Directions:** At main road roundabout, turn right up the mall; turn right up John Street - the house is at the top on the left side.

Dingle
🍷 RESTAURANT

Out of the Blue

Waterside Dingle Co Kerry **Tel: 066 915 0811**
Email: info@outoftheblue.ie Web: www.outoftheblue.ie

Tim Mason's deli and seafood restaurant is an absolute delight. Discerning locals know how lucky they are to have such an exciting little place on their doorstep and it's just the kind of thing that visitors dream of finding - it is not unusual to find a different language spoken at every table. Although its brightly-painted exterior has a kind of temporary look from the road, once you get inside it is obvious that this is a highly focused operation, where only the best will do: there's a little wine bar at the front and, in the simple room at the back, seriously delicious seafood cookery is the order of the day for those lucky enough to get a table. Everything depends on the fresh fish supply from the boats that day and menus - changed twice daily, at lunch and dinner - are given on blackboards: if there's no fresh fish, they don't open. Head chef Jean-Marie Vireaux cooks wonderful classics, sometimes with a modern twist - examples might include Glenbeigh mussels 'marinières', traditional French-style soups (with home-made brown bread), Dublin Bay prawns (langoustines) with garlic butter, perhaps, or sweet chilli sauce, and there may be less usual fish like pollock. Lobster is very reasonably priced and so is crayfish, which is a rarity on Irish menus; either might be cooked 'en casserole' with cognac, or chargrilled with thyme & olive oil, then served with garlic butter. A short but skilfully assembled wine list complements the food perfectly - and has a dozen fish named in four languages on the back: this place is a little gem. **Seats 28** (+ 16/20 outdoors). L & D Thu-Tue,L 12.30-3, D 6.50-9.30 (Sun 6-8). Reservations accepted (required for D). A la carte. House wines from €17. Closed Wed ('usually'), also days when fresh fish is unavailable & Nov-Feb. MasterCard, Visa, Laser, Switch. **Directions:** Opposite the pier on Dingle harbour.

Dingle Area

♈ ◉ GUESTHOUSE/RESTAURANT

Gorman's Clifftop House & Restaurant

Glaise Bheag Ballydavid Dingle Peninsula Co Kerry
Tel: 066 915 5162 Fax: 066 915 5003
Email: info@gormans-clifftophouse.com Web: www.gormans-clifftophouse.com

féile bia Beautifully situated near Smerwick Harbour on the Slea Head scenic drive and Dingle Way walking route, Sile and Vincent Gorman's guesthouse is, as they say themselves "just a great place to relax and unwind". It's also a very comfortable place to do this, as the whole premises has recently been virtually rebuilt and upgraded to a high standard. Natural materials and warm colours are a feature throughout the house and open fires, newspapers and books in two generous lounging areas (and a lot of pottery from the nearby Louis Mulcahy workshops) create a welcoming laid-back atmosphere. Bedrooms include some on the ground floor with easy access from the parking area, and four superior rooms with jacuzzi bath, safes suitable for laptops, CD players and ironing facilities; but all rooms are attractively furnished in country style and very comfortable, with beautiful satin cotton sheets, broadband, TV and thoughtfully finished bathrooms with extra large Turkish bath sheets - and most rooms now have king size beds. The Gormans are knowledgeable and helpful hosts too, giving personal advice where it's needed. Breakfast - an excellent buffet with home-baked breads, freshly squeezed juices, fruits, cheeses and cold meats as well as hot dishes cooked to order - is a treat that will set you up for the day. Gorman's was our Guesthouse of the Year in 2002. Children welcome (under 3s free in parents' room, cot available free of charge). No pets. Garden, cycling, walking. **Rooms 9** (2 junior suites, 2 superior, 1 for less able, 1 shower only, all no smoking). B&B €75 pps, ss €35. *Short breaks offered - details on application. **Restaurant:** With large windows commanding superb sea views and, on fine evenings, spectacular sunsets, this is a wonderful place to enjoy Vincent Gorman's good cooking. Begin with a fresh seafood chowder or apple, celery & tomato soup, perhaps - or an attractive speciality of potato cake & Annsacaul black pudding sandwich with mushroom & bacon sauce, which is lighter than it sounds; main courses include several seafood dishes (trio of plaice, John Dory and prawns with carrot & dill sauce, perhaps) and the ever-popular sirloin steak (house style, with scallion mash, mushroom & brandy sauce); vegetarian choices are always given - a main course of grilled aubergine and roasted pepper mille feuille with spinach & goats cheese is a speciality - and copious dishes of delicious vegetables are left on the table for guests to help themselves. Desserts are a strong point too: home-made ice creams, chocolate nemesis, and rhubarb & strawberry crumble are just a few of the temptations on offer, or you can finish with an Irish cheese plate. Sile, who is a warm and solicitous host, supervises front of house. A well thought out wine list includes organic house wines and a good choice of half bottles. **Seats 40.** D Mon-Sat, 6-9. Set D € 33/38. House wine from €18.50. Restaurant closed Sun. House closed 24-26 Dec; weekends only by reservation Nov-Mar. MasterCard, Visa, Laser. **Directions:** 8 miles from roundabout west of Dingle Town - sign posted An Fheothanach. Keep left at V.

Kenmare
€ CAFÉ

Jam

6 Henry St Kenmare Co Kerry **Tel: 064 41591**
Fax: 064 40790 Email: info@jam.ie Web: www.jam.ie

James Mulchrone's delightful bakery and café has been a great success since the day it opened, in March 2001 and, unlikely as this may seem in a town that has some of the best eating places in Ireland, it brought something new and very welcome. Affordable prices, friendly service and an in-house bakery have proved a winning combination; everything is made on the premises using the best of local produce and you can pop into the self-service café for a bite at any time all day. To give a flavour of the wide range offered, lovely main course choices include salmon & spinach baked in pastry with horseradish and a selection of quiches (roast vegetable with goats cheese, basil & pinenuts, for example, or bacon, onion & cheddar). If you're planning a day out, they have all you could want for a delicious picnic here, including a wide range of sandwiches and salads, terrines and all sorts of irresistible cakes and biscuits. The café menu changes daily and party platters and celebration cakes are made to order (48 hours notice required for special orders.). The stated aim is "to provide fresh, quality, imaginative food at affordable prices in nice surroundings"; this they are doing very well both here and in their branch on High Street, Killarney. *Also at: 77 High Street, Killarney; Tel: 064 31441. **Seats 60.** Air conditioning. Open Mon-Sat, 8am-5pm. Closed Sun, 3 days Christmas. **No Credit Cards. Directions:** Lower Henry Street on the left.

Kenmare
👁 RESTAURANT

Lime Tree Restaurant

Shelburne Street Kenmare Co Kerry
Tel: 064 41225 Fax: 064 41839
Email: limetree@limetreerestaurant.com Web: www.limetreerestaurant.com

Tony and Alex Daly's restaurant is in an attractive cut stone building built in 1832 and set well back from the road. An open log fire, exposed stone walls, original wall panelling and a minstrels' gallery (which provides an upper eating area) all give character to the interior and there is a contemporary art gallery on the first floor, which adds an extra dimension to a visit here - fine original artwork in the restaurant gives a hint of what may be for sale. There can be a real buzz once the room fills up, and this is perhaps a restaurant to be visited for the overall experience rather than outstanding cooking. A la carte menus offer plenty of choice, plus daily specials (including vegetarian options) - less emphasis on local seafood than might be expected but, among several fish dishes, a speciality is seafood potpourri "en papillotte", a selection of fish cooked plainly in parchment paper, with fish stock and wine. Some dishes have a world cuisine tone but, judging by recent visits, the main stream choices are more successful: aged Bellingham Blue cheese tartlet makes a delicious starter, for example (lovely crisp pastry topped by caramelised onion and lightly baked cheese), and a gently updated main course of oven-roasted Kerry lamb is served on lightly sautéed potato and marries well with traditional flavours in the accompanying rosemary scented cherry tomatoes. Desserts range from the homely (apple & blackberry crumble with vanilla custard), to tweaked classics (crème brulée 'en tasse'). Service, under the direction of restaurant manager Maria O'Sullivan, is professional and relaxed; a user-friendly wine list is organised by style ('light, crisp and appealing', 'soft bodied and fruity'...) and includes some interesting bottles. And remember that it might be wise to budget a little extra for dinner here - you could be taking home a modern masterpiece; gallery open from 4pm. Toilet wheelchair accessible. Air conditioning. Not suitable for children after 7 pm. **Seats 60.** D daily 6.30-10; à la carte (average main course about €23). House wine €20; sc discretionary. Closed-Nov-Mar. MasterCard, Visa, Laser. **Directions:** Top of town, next to Park Hotel.

Kenmare
☆ RESTAURANT

Mulcahys Restaurant

36 Henry Street Kenmare Co Kerry
Tel: 064 42383 Fax: 064 42383 Email: mulcahys@hotmail.com

If you are ever tired of finding the same old dishes on every menu, just head for Kenmare and refresh your palate at Bruce Mulcahy's original, efficiently run and friendly contemporary restaurant. A light-filled room is spacious and stylish, with smart modern table settings, funky cutlery and delicious breads on a pretty little bamboo tray. Far from being yet another copy-cat chef playing with world cuisines, Bruce has gone to the source to learn his skills - he learned about fusion food in Thailand, for example, and studied the art of sushi making in Japan; but the secret of this restaurant's great success is that, although many dishes are highly unusual, exciting menus cater for conservative tastes as well as the adventurous palate. Bruce's skills are best seen in house specialities such as sushi & sashimi (Japanese nori sheets filled with local seafood and served with wasabi, pickled ginger & mirin dip) or, in a style that is closer to home, an assiette of lamb (a salt and rosemary crusted cutlet with parsnip purée, a braised lamb shank parcel and roast sausage of lamb's tongue). All produce used here is certified organic, vegetarians get a dish of the day on the blackboard and, not only is the cooking inspired, but service is charming and knowledgeable - and there's also a magical wine list to match. The early dinner menu is great value and, at the other end of the spectrum, Mulcahy's offers a 6-course Tasting Menu, which is a real treat. **Accommodation:** Virginia's Guesthouse (Tel: 064 41021; email: Virginia's@eircom.net; www.virginias-kenmare.com). The restaurant and guesthouse share an entrance, but are run quite separately. Neil and Noreen Harrington have eight comfortable rooms, all with phone, television, safe and tea/coffee trays - and en-suite power showers. And their breakfasts are a point of honour, offering fresh orange juice and pressed apple juice, porridge (with or without whiskey cream), free range eggs and Kenmare smoked salmon among many other temptations. B&B €40-60 (Room service, limited hours). Toilets wheelchair accessible. **Seats 50.** D daily, 6-10; L Sun only, 12.30-3. Table D'hote D €30. Gourmet menu €60. Set Sun L €20. L & D also à la carte. House wines from €19.50. SC discretionary. Closed 23-26 Dec. Amex, Diners, MasterCard, Visa, Laser. **Directions:** Halfway down Henry Street, on the righthand side.

Kenmare
☆ ❦ RESTAURANT

Packie's

Henry Street Kenmare Co Kerry **Tel: 064 41508** Fax: 064 42135

téile bia In a town blessed with an exceptional choice of wonderful eating places, the Foley family's buzzy little restaurant has long been a favourite for returning visitors. The long main room has a little reception bar with a couple of stools shoehorned into it, and a dividing stone feature wall with foliage-filled gaps in it provides both privacy and, along with candlelight, mirrors and framed pictures, makes for a warm, relaxed atmosphere - an impression immediately confirmed by welcoming staff, who are exceptionally friendly and efficient, keeping everyone at the closely packed tables happy throughout the evening. Head chef Martin Hallissey's menus (plus each evening's specials) are based mainly on local ingredients, notably organic produce and fish - and, although there's clear interest in international trends, combinations tend to be based on traditional themes, such as classic Irish stew with fresh herbs, which is a speciality. Close examination of menus will probably reveal more dishes that have stood the test of time than new ones, but what remains impressive is the basic quality of the food, especially local seafood. Finish with Irish farmhouse cheeses or good desserts, including home-made ice creams. An interesting and well-priced wine list offers plenty to choose from, with some available by the glass. Children welcome. Toilets wheelchair accessible. **Seats 35.** D Mon-Sat, 6-10; à la carte. House wine from €16.90; sc discretionary. Reservations advised. Closed Sun; mid Jan- end Feb. Amex, MasterCard, Visa, Laser. **Directions:** Town centre.

Kenmare
★ 🏛🏛 ❦ ◉ HOTEL/RESTAURANT

Park Hotel Kenmare

Kenmare Co Kerry
Tel: 064 41200 Fax: 064 41402
Email: info@parkkenmare.com Web: www.parkkenmare.com

This renowned hotel enjoys a magnificent waterside location in the midst of Ireland's most scenic landscape, with views over gardens to the everchanging mountains across the bay - yet it's only a short stroll to the Heritage Town of Kenmare. Many travellers from all over the world have found a home from home here since the hotel was built in 1897 by the Great Southern and Western Railway Company as an overnight stop for passengers travelling to Parknasilla, 17 miles away. The current proprietor, Francis Brennan, re-opened the hotel in 1985, and has since earned international acclaim for exceptional standards of service, comfort and cuisine; it is a most hospitable and relaxing place, where a warm welcome and the ever-burning fire in the hall set the tone for a stay in which guests are discreetly pampered by outstandingly friendly and professional staff. And since 2004 that pampering has been taken to new heights in the hotel's deluxe destination spa, Sámas, which translates from the Gaelic as 'indulgence of the senses'. Unlike anything else offered in Ireland, Sámas adjoins the hotel on a wooded knoll and is designed to rejuvenate the body, mind and spirit; there are separate male and female areas (also two day suites for couples) and guests can choose from over forty holistic treatments, designed by a team of professionals to meet individual needs. Lifestyle programmes incorporating spa treatments with other activities in the area - walking on the Kerry Way, golf, fishing, horse trekking - offer a unique way to enjoy the deeply peaceful atmosphere of this luxurious hotel. Then, innovative as always, the folk at the Park have come up with yet another little treat for guests, the Reel Room, which is a private 12-seater cinema. As for the guest accommodation, spacious suites and bedrooms are individually furnished to the highest standards, with personally selected antiques and many special details. And, in line with the excellence which prevails throughout the hotel, the outstanding breakfasts served at the Park make a great way to start the day. [Park Hotel Kenmare was the national winner of our Hotel Breakfast of the Year Award in 2005.] Golf club adjacent (18 hole). Garden, tennis, croquet, cycling, walking, snooker. Horse riding, sea and game angling, mountain walks and stunning coastal drives are all nearby. **Rooms 46** (9 suites, 24 junior suites, 8 family rooms, 8 ground floor, 1 disabled, 46 no smoking). Lift. 24 hour room service. Children welcome (under 4 free in parents' room, cots available without charge). No pets (but kennels available on grounds). B&B about €215 pps, (single occupancy €242); holistic retreats from €855 (3 days, low season) offer very good value. Hotel closed Dec-mid Feb except Christmas/New Year. **Restaurant:** The more contemporary restaurants become the norm in Ireland, the more precious the elegance of this traditional dining room seems - and the views from window tables are simply lovely. Ensuring that the food will match the surroundings is no light matter but a stylishly restrained classicism has characterised this distinguished kitchen under several famous head chefs, and Joe Ryan - who has been head chef since 1995 - maintains this tradition admirably. His menus are not over-extensive yet allow plenty of choice and, although there's an understandable leaning towards local seafood, including lobster (try the house selection of Kenmare Bay seafood with leeks, lemon beurre blanc), at least one imaginative vegetarian dish is offered on each course. Kerry lamb and local Skeaghanore duck are also enduring specialities: a treat of a dish for two people is roast Skeaghanore duck with sautéed mouli & pomme paille with Kenmare honey & sherry vinegar sauce. Superb attention to detail - from the first trio of nibbles offered with aperitifs in the bar, through an intriguing amuse-bouche served at the table, well-made breads, punctilious wine service and finally the theatrical little Irish coffee ritual and petits fours at the end of the meal - all this contributes to a dining experience that is exceptional. The wine list, although favouring the deep-pocketed guest, offers a fair selection in the €30-40 bracket and includes a wine suitable for diabetics. Service is invariably immaculate. A short à la carte lounge menu is available, 11am-6pm. Not suitable for children under 8 after 8 pm. **Seats 80** (private room, 60, outdoor dining 40). D, 7-9 daily; Set D menus €49-67; also à la carte. House wine from €32.50; sc discretionary. Amex, MasterCard, Visa. **Directions:** Top of town.

Kenmare

 BAR/RESTAURANT

The Purple Heather

Henry Street Kenmare Co Kerry **Tel: 064 41016**
Fax: 064 42135 Email: oconnellgrainne@eircom.net

Open since 1964, Grainne O'Connell's informal restaurant/bar was among the first to establish a reputation for good food in Kenmare, and is a daytime sister restaurant to Packie's. It's a traditional darkwood and burgundy bar that gradually develops into an informal restaurant at the rear. as is the way in many of the best Kerry bars, and what they aim for and achieve, with commendable consistency is good, simple, home-cooked food. Start with refreshing freshly squeezed orange juice, well-made soups that come with home-baked breads, or salad made of organic greens with balsamic dressing. Main courses include a number of seafood salads, vegetarian salads (cold and warm), pâtés including a delicious smoked salmon pâté plus a range of omelettes, sandwiches and open sandwiches (Cashel Blue cheese and walnut, perhaps, or crabmeat with salad) or Irish farmhouse cheeses (with a glass of L.B.V Offley port if you like). This is a great place, serving wonderfully wholesome food in a relaxed atmosphere - and it's open almost all year.* Grainne O'Connell also has self-catering accommodation available nearby. **Seats 40.** Bar open Mon-Sat,11-6; meals, 10.45-7. Closed Sun, Christmas, bank hols. Visa, Laser, Switch. **Directions:** Town centre - mid Henry Street (on right following traffic flow).

Kenmare

🏛️🏛️★ 🍴👁️ HOTEL/RESTAURANT

Sheen Falls Lodge

Kenmare Co Kerry
Tel: 064 41600 Fax: 064 41386
Email: info@sheenfallslodge.ie Web: www.sheenfallslodge.ie

féile bia Set in a 300-acre estate just across the river from Kenmare town, this stunning hotel made an immediate impact from the day it opened in April 1991; it has continued to develop and mature most impressively since. The waterside location is beautiful, and welcoming fires always burn in the handsome foyer and in several of the spacious, elegantly furnished reception rooms, including a lounge bar area overlooking the tumbling waterfall. Decor throughout is contemporary classic, offering traditional luxury with a modern lightness of touch and a tendency to understatement that adds up to great style; accommodation in spacious bedrooms - and suites, which include an extremely impressive presidential suite - is luxurious: all rooms have superb amenities, including video/DVD and CD players, beautiful marbled bathrooms and views of the cascading river or Kenmare Bay. Outstanding facilities for both corporate and private guests include state-of-the-art conference facilities, a fine library (with computer/internet), an equestrian centre (treks around the 300 acre estate) and The Queen's Walk (named after Queen Victoria), which takes you through lush woodland. A Health & Fitness Spa includes a pretty 15 metre pool (and an extensive range of treatments including seaweed wraps and aromatherapy massages) and, alongside it, there's an informal evening bar and bistro, 'Oscars', which has its own separate entrance as well as direct access from the hotel. But it is the staff, under the guidance of the exceptionally warm and hospitable General Manager, Adriaan Bartels, who make this luxurious and stylish international hotel the home from home that it quickly becomes for each new guest: nothing is ever too much trouble to ensure that guests get the best possible enjoyment and relaxation from a stay at Sheen Falls. [Adriaan Bartels was our Host of the Year in 2004.] * Two luxuriously appointed self-contained two-bedroomed thatched cottages, Little Hay Cottage and Garden Cottage, and a 5-bedroomed house on the estate, are also available to rent. Conference/banqueting (120/140); business centre, secretarial services, video-conferencing. Health & Fitness Spa (swimming pool, jacuzzi, sauna, steam room, treatments, beauty salon), boutique, snooker, equestrian, walking, fishing, gardens, tennis, cycling. Children welcome (cots available, €25, baby sitting arranged; playground). No pets. **Rooms 66** (1 presidential suites, 11 suites, 8 junior suites, 14 ground floor rooms, 10 no-smoking bedrooms, 1 disabled). Lift. 24 hour room service; turndown service. B&B €215 pps, ss €90. **La Cascade:** This beautifully appointed restaurant is designed in tiers to take full advantage of the waterfalls floodlit at night and providing a dramatic backdrop for an exceptional fine dining experience. Aidan McGrath, who has been Head Chef since 2004, continues the modern Irish cooking which is the hallmark of this lovely restaurant, backed up by faultless service under the supervision of restaurant manager Adrian Fitzgerald. An admirably concise table d'hôte menu offers only three or four choices on each course - of which two of the starters, and one or two main courses may be seafood - crab from Castletownbere and wild salmon from the estate, perhaps - and both pigeon and rabbit are all also popular. Cooking is consistently impressive and the dishes offered often include variations on a number of specialities: Kerry lamb is almost de rigeur, of course, and predictably delicious, also duck - a seared breast may be served with fine green beans, girolles, fondant potato and exotic flavourings of Tahitian vanilla jus and Argan oil. Speciality desserts include updated classics like hot soufflés (caramel, with Baileys sabayon & malt milk ice cream perhaps) and farmhouse cheeses, served with scrumptious parmesan biscuits. The atmospheric wine cellar is a particular point of pride - guests can visit it to choose their own bottle, and port may also be served there after dinner - wine buffs will enjoy the wine list and should make a point of seeing it well ahead of dining if possible, as it details around 950 wines, with particular strengths in the classic European regions, especially Burgundy and Bordeaux, and a fine collection of ports and dessert wines. *Light lunches (smoked salmon, club sandwiches etc) and afternoon tea are available in the sun lounge, 12-6 daily, and the informal Oscar's Bar & Bistro offers an extensive à la carte dinner menu, including a children's menu, every evening, 6-10pm. Restaurant **Seats 120** (private room, 24; outdoor seating, 50). Pianist, evenings. Toilets wheelchair accessible. D daily 7-9.30. Set D €65. House wines from about €32. SC discretionary. Hotel closed all Jan. Amex, Diners, MasterCard, Visa, Laser. **Directions:** Take N71 Kenmare (Glengariff road); turn left at Riversdale Hotel.

Kenmare
🏛🍷 GUESTHOUSE

Shelburne Lodge

Cork Road Kenmare Co Kerry
Tel: 064 41013 Fax: 064 42135
Email: shelburne@kenmare.com Web: www.kenmare.net/shelburne/

Tom and Maura Foley's fine stone house on the edge of the town is well set back from the road, in its own grounds and lovely gardens. It is the oldest house in Kenmare and has great style and attention to detail; spacious day rooms include an elegant, comfortably furnished drawing room with plenty of seating, an inviting log fire and interesting books for guests to read - it is really lovely, and the feeling is of being a guest in a private country house. Spacious, well-proportioned guest rooms are individually decorated and extremely comfortable; everything (especially beds and bedding) is of the highest quality and, except for the more informal conversion at the back of the house, which is especially suitable for families and has neat shower rooms, the excellent bathrooms have full bath. But perhaps the best is saved until last, in the large, well-appointed dining room where excellent breakfasts are served: tables are prettily laid with linen napkins and the menu offers all kind of treats, beginning with freshly squeezed juices, a choice of fruits (nectarine with strawberries, perhaps) with extras like natural yoghurt, honey and nuts offered too, lovely freshly-baked breads, homemade preserves, leaf tea and strong aromatic coffee, and - as well as various excellent permutations of the full traditional Irish breakfast - there's fresh fish (sole, perhaps, with lemon butter), and Irish farmhouse cheeses too. Simply delicious. [Shelburne Lodge was our Guesthouse of the Year in 2005, and also winner of the Best Guesthouse Breakfast Award.] No evening meals are served, but residents are directed to the family's restaurant, Packie's (see entry). Children welcome (under 4s free in parents' room, cot avilable without charge, baby sitting arranged). Garden, tennis. Own parking. No pets. **Rooms 9** (2 shower-only). B&B €75, ss €15. Closed Dec 1-mid Mar. MasterCard, Visa. **Directions:** on Cork road R569.

Killarney
🏛🏛🍷👁 HOTEL/RESTAURANT

Aghadoe Heights Hotel

Killarney Co Kerry
Tel: 064 31766 Fax: 064 31345
Email: info@aghadoeheights.com Web: www.aghadoeheights.com

A few miles out of town, this famous low-rise hotel, dating from the '60s, enjoys stunning views of the lakes and the mountains beyond and also overlooks Killarney's two 18-hole championship golf courses. It is now one of Ireland's most luxurious hotels and, under the caring management of Pat and Marie Chawke and their welcoming staff, it is a very special place. Major refurbishments have recently been undertaken and, while the controversial exterior remains a subject of debate, the renovation of the interior - including 24 new junior suites, a palatial glass-fronted two-bedroom penthouse suite and a superb new spa & wellness centre - is now complete. Contemporary, stylish public areas are airy and spacious, with lots of marble, original artwork, and a relaxed, open ambience and, from the foyer, hints of the stunning view that invite exploration - perhaps into the chic bar which links up with a new terrace and the swimming pool area (lots of lounging space for sunny days), or up to the first floor open-plan lounge area, where a delicious traditional Afternoon Tea is served (2-5.30pm). Accommodation is seriously luxurious, in spacious rooms with balconies and lake views, large sitting areas, plasma screen televisions, video, DVD (library downstairs, also Internet booth) and a host of extras. Bathrooms are equally sumptuous, with separate shower and all the complimentary toiletries you could wish for. The new 10,0000 sq ft spa is among Europe's best and offers couples suites, where couples may enjoy treatments together, and some treatments - including 'Ayervedic Precious Stone therapy' in a custom built Aromatherapy cabin - are unique. But at the heart of all this luxury it is the caring hands-on management of Pat and Marie Chalke who, with their outstanding staff, make everyone feel at home. And you will leave on a high too, as breakfast is another especially strong point. [Aghadoe Heights was our Hotel of the Year in 2005.] Conference/banqueting (110/100); business centre. Leisure centre, swimming pool, spa, hair salon. Garden, tennis, walking. Children welcome (Under 2s free in parents' room; cot available, €20, baby sitting arranged). No pets. **Rooms 75** (2 suites, 24 junior suites, 10 family rooms, 27 ground floor rooms, 2 for disabled, 72 non smoking). Lift. Turn down service. 24 hour room service. B&B about €140 pps, ss €65. Closed Jan & Feb. **Restaurant:** The restaurant is on an upper floor, integrated into an open plan area, with distant views over the lakes and mountains; it is a bright and elegant space, with beautifully appointed tables and fresh flowers providing an appropriate setting for dining in a hotel of this standard. The original team led by Executive Head Chef Robin Suter, who has been at the hotel since 1990, is still in place, and continues the classic French style of food and service for which the hotel is famous. The tone is quite conservative, offering updated variations of many well-loved dishes - tian of avocado and crab may come with a dill & yoghurt dressing, for example, and fillet of beef with wild mushrooms and roasted shallot - and there will also be the great classics, like grilled chateaubriand sauce béarnaise and sole meunière. There is generosity in the cooking - portions are noticeably larger than usual in fine dining restaurants which, like the relaxed dress code and the family-friendliness, reflects the policy of the hotel generally to welcome everyone - and their hearty appetites. A pianist sets the scene at dinner time, and also at the hotel's renowned Sunday lunch buffet. An extensive and informative wine list includes a good range of classics, several magnums and an unusually good choice of half bottles. **Seats 120** (private room available). Reservations required. Children welcome, but not after 7pm. D daily.6.30-9.30, L Sun only 12-2. Set D €60, also à la carte; Set Sun L €45. House wines from €22. Closed Jan-Feb. Helipad Amex, Diners, MasterCard, Visa, Laser. **Directions:** Two miles north of Killarney; signposted off N22.

Killarney
COUNTRY HOUSE

Coolclogher House
Mill Road Killarney Co Kerry
Tel: 064 35996 Fax: 064 30933
Email: info@coolclogherhouse.com Web: www.coolclogherhouse.com

Mary and Maurice Harnett's beautiful early Victorian house is just on the edge of Killarney town and yet, tucked away on its 68 acre walled estate, it is an oasis of peace and tranquillity. The house has been extensively restored in recent years and has many interesting features, including an original conservatory built around a 170 year-old specimen camellia - when camellias were first introduced to Europe, they were mistakenly thought to be tender plants; it is now quite remarkable to see this large tree growing under glass. It is an impressive yet relaxed house, with well-proportioned, spacious reception rooms stylishly furnished and comfortable for guests, with newspapers, books, fresh flowers - and open fires in inclement weather - while the four large bedrooms have scenic views over gardens, parkland and mountains. Gazing out from this peaceful place, it is easy to forget that the hustle and bustle of Killarney town is just a few minutes' drive away; it could just as well be in another world. Mary and Maurice enjoy sharing their local knowledge with guests to help them get the most of their stay at what they quite reasonably call 'perhaps the most exclusive accommodation available in Killarney'. The house is also available for private rentals. Children over 5 welcome (free in parents' room under 10). No pets. Garden, walking. Golf, fishing nearby; garden visits nearby. **Rooms 4** (all en-suite, all no smoking). B&B €95, ss €50.*Coolclogher House is also offered as a weekly rental (from €4,500) for special occasions, suits groups of 10-12; staff can be arranged if required. *Golf breaks offered (B&B or rental). MasterCard, Visa, Laser. **Directions:** Leaving Killarney town, take (Muckross Road) onto Mill Road; take first left turn into Mill Road (after metal bridge); gates on right after 0.5 mile.

Killarney
GUESTHOUSE

Earls Court House

Woodlawn Junction Muckross Road Killarney Co Kerry
Tel: 064 34009 Fax: 064 34366
Email: info@killarney-earlscourt.ie Web: www.killarney-earlscourt.ie

A neat, functional exterior does little to prepare first-time visitors for the comfort and character to be found at this purpose-built guesthouse quite near the town centre, which offers exceptionally comfortable accommodation at moderate prices and is run with warmth and professionalism by Roy and Emer Moynihan. A welcoming open fire burns in the large beautifully furnished foyer which, together with an adjoining guest sitting room, has plenty of comfortable seating for guests - an ideal rendez-vous, or simply a place to relax -
and, as elsewhere in the house, antiques, books, paintings and family photographs are a point of interest and emphasise the personality of this spacious home from home. Emer's personal attention to the details that make for real comfort - and the ever-growing collection of antiques that guarantees individuality for each room - are the hallmarks of the outstanding accommodation offered, which includes four rooms with canopy beds. All the bedrooms are well-planned and generously-sized, with double and single beds, well finished bathrooms, phone and satellite TV; tea/coffee-making facilities are available on request. Guests are directed to restaurants in the town for evening meals, but superb breakfasts are served in a large, antique-furnished dining room, where guests are looked after with charm and efficiency. Earls Court was our Guesthouse of the Year for 2004. Fully certified for disadvantaged access. Children welcome (under 3s free, cot available without charge, baby siting arranged). Pets allowed in some areas. Garden. Parking. **Rooms 24** (4 suites, 2 for disabled, all no smoking). Lift. Room service (limited hours). B&B €60 pps, ss €40. Closed 14 Nov-14 Feb. Amex, MasterCard, Visa. **Directions:** Take the first left at the traffic lights on Muckross road (signed), then 3rd premises.

Killarney
HOTEL/RESTAURANT

Killarney Park Hotel

Kenmare Place Killarney Co Kerry
Tel: 064 35555 Fax: 064 35266
Email: info@killarneyparkhotel.ie Web: www.killarneyparkhotel.ie

féile bia Situated in its own grounds, a short stroll from the town centre, the Treacy family's luxurious, well run hotel is deceptively modern - despite its classical good looks, it only celebrated its first decade in March 2002. However it has already undergone more than one transformation, indeed, constant improvement is so much a theme here that it is hard to keep up with developments as they occur. The exceptionally welcoming atmosphere strikes you when the doorman first greets you, as you pass through the outer lobby to Reception and then into a series of stylish seating areas, with fires and invitingly grouped sofas and armchairs; the same sense of comfort characterises the Garden Bar (which has a sheltered terrace for fine days) and also the quiet Library, which provides a relaxing haven. Elegant public areas are punctuated by a sweeping staircase that leads to bedrooms luxuriously furnished in a choice of two strongly contrasting styles, with great attention to detail in each case. Spacious traditional suites have a private entrance hall and an elegant sitting area with a fireplace creating a real home from home feeling, and all the older rooms are also furnished in a similar warm country house style, with judiciously selected antiques. But a major renovation programme recently completed has seen the conversion of eight deluxe rooms to junior suites in a dramatically contemporary style, and the refurbishment of others along similar lines - like every room in the hotel, they have been thoughtfully and individually designed, with air conditioning, well-planned bathroomss and the many small details that make a hotel room really comfortable, and they certainly have a new wow factor. Housekeeping is never less than immaculate and, most importantly, of course, the staff at this wonderful hotel are committed to looking after guests with warmth and discretion, making it an ideal choice for both business and pleasure. A stunning health spa opened within the hotel recently, with eight treatment rooms, outdoor hot tub, plunge pool and jacuzzi; the menu of treatments offered is seriously seductive and it may well happen that some guests never feel the need to leave the hotel at all during their stay. [Park Hotel Killarney was our Hotel of the Year in 2002.] *The much older sister property, the Ross Hotel, nearby is under reconstruction at the time of going to press, given the Treacy family track record at Killarney Park Hotel, it will be a resounding success. Conference/banqueting (150/150); business centre; video conferencing (on request). In-room safe. Spa, hot tub, jacuzzi. Leisure centre, swimming pool (20m), sauna, plunge pool, jacuzzi pool. Library; billiard room. Garden, walking, cycling. Children welcome (under 2 free in parents room; cots available without charge, playroom, baby sitting arranged). No Pets. **Rooms 72** (3 suites, 26 junior suites, all no-smoking, 1 for disabled). Lift. 24 hour room service. Turndown service. B&B €192.50 pps, ss €192.50; no sc. Closed 24-27 Dec. **The Park Restaurant:** This large and opulent room has the essential elements of grandeur - the ornate ceiling, glittering chandeliers - but has recently been lightened by a contemporary tone in the furnishings. Odran Lucey, who has been head chef since 1999, has earned a reputation for this restaurant as a dining destination in its own right, making it a great asset to this fine hotel. Although they are not overlong or unnecessarily wordy, plenty of choice is offered on appealing menus which make up a five course dinner or, as dishes are priced individually, also allow à la carte choices. The underlying style is classical but this is creative food, cooked with panache. An enduring house speciality that illustrates the style is a starter of pan-seared foie gras served with Clonakilty black pudding, apple compôte toasted brioche and prune syrup, which is a nicely judged combination of classical and modern influences - and a main course of roast breast of Skeghanore duck with a fig & apple samosa and turnip fondant shows the same skilful blending of traditional partnerships and innovative additions. But when it comes to a real classic - Dover sole - it is cooked classically, 'meunière' and served with parsley potatoes - and what a joy to find lobster offered simply, with butter and lemon juice. Courteous service and the presence of a pianist, who plays throughout dinner, add to the sense of occasion. A wide-ranging wine list includes many of the classics and, not only a fair choice of half bottles, but also a sommelier's choice of the week, offering half a dozen good wines by the glass. An interesting feature of the restaurant is an open wine cellar, which guests are free to browse.* Odran Lucey is also responsible for the excellent bistro style food served The Garden Bar where - as elsewhere in the hotel - children are made very welcome. Restaurant seats 150 (private room,40). Reservations required. Air conditioning. Toilets wheelchair accessible. D daily 7-9.30; Set D €57.50; also à la carte. House wines from €28. SC discretionary. * Food is also served in the bar, 12 noon-9pm daily. Hotel closed 24-27 Dec. Amex, MasterCard, Visa, Laser. **Directions:** Located in Killarney town - all access routes lead to town centre.

Killarney
🏨 HOTEL

Killarney Royal Hotel

College Street Killarney Co Kerry Tel: **064 31853** Fax: 064 34001
Email: royalhot@iol.ie Web: www.killarneyroyal.ie

Another of Killarney's unrivalled collection of fine hotels, this family-owned establishment is a charming older sister to the luxurious Hayfield Manor Hotel in Cork city (see entry). Joe and Margaret Scally have recently lavished care and investment on it and the impressive result is a beautifully furnished hotel in an elegant period style that is totally appropriate to the age and design of the building. No expense has been spared on the highest quality of materials and workmanship, air conditioning has been installed throughout the hotel and rooms have been individually designed, all with sitting areas and marble bathrooms. But what is most remarkable, perhaps, is the warm and friendly atmosphere that prevails throughout the hotel, conveyed partly through the soft warm tones chosen for furnishing schemes, but also through the attentive attitude of friendly, caring staff under the direction of General Manager, Nicola Duggan. Interesting modern food is served every day in the bar, which is popular meeting place for an informal meal, while the main dining room - also recently refurbished - is more traditional and reservations are required; however, in addition to the roast rack of lamb which is quite rightly - de rigeur in these parts, lobster is a speciality in both areas. Conference/banqueting (50/100); secretarial services. Wheelchair accessible. Children welcome (cots available without charge, baby sitting arranged). Pets permitted by arrangement. No on-site parking (arrangement with nearby car park). **Rooms 29** (5 junior suites, 5 no-smoking, 1 disabled). Lift. 24 hour room service. B&B €110 pps, ss €50. Restaurant **Seats 80** (reservations advised): L daily, 12.30-2.30; D daily, 6.30-9.30. Early D €20 (6.30-7.30), Set D €20/30; Set L €25. Also à la carte. Closed 23-26 Dec. Amex, Diners, MasterCard, Visa, Laser, Switch. **Directions:** In Killarney town centre on College Street, off the N22.

Killarney
Ⓔ RESTAURANT

Mentons @ The Plaza

Killarney Plaza Hotel Kenmare Place Killarney Co Kerry
Tel: 064 21150 Fax: 064 41839
Email: info@mentons.com Web: www.mentons.com

Gary Fitzgerald's smashing first-floor restaurant in bustling downtown Killarney has two entrances - one up a rather grand flight of steps from the street (asserting its independence), the other through the hotel (up stairs or on the lift) but, either way, it's all a pretty impressive beginning for a dining experience which should prove to be a delightful surprise. It's a bright contemporary space on two levels and several areas, with classy modern table settings and a surprisingly luxurious atmosphere - all helped by welcoming staff, who clearly want everyone to have a wonderful time. It's especially popular for lunch, when informal menus offer a range of light dishes such as Mentons Caesar salad, steamed Cromane mussels in coriander, lemon and coconut broth, and hot panini, and more substantial choices like Cronin's jumbo spicy sausages with roast garlic mash and thyme jus. Evening menus are more structured and begin with an early dinner that offers outstanding value; but, at any time, it's the sheer quality of ingredients used that stands out - and the deft confidence of Gary's cooking: expect excellent details like delicious home made breads, and dishes with great textures and gorgeous flavours. An imaginative vegetarian starter, for example, might consist of a generous chunk of grilled goats cheese served on top of a caramelised apple ring and a delicious crisp-outside-soft-inside hazelnut blini, with a well-dressed beetroot salsa - pretty and oh-so-tasty. A recent visit by the Guide showed that this restaurant is living up to its early promise and offering tip-top quality, accomplished cooking and smart service at very fair prices. **Seats 65.** Air conditioning. Children welcome. L daily 12.30-5, D daily 6-9. Earlybird D 6-7 € 23.95. ALso A la C L&D. Closed last 2 weeks Jan. MasterCard, Visa. **Directions:** Killarney town centre.

Killarney
Ⓔ RESTAURANT

Old Presbytery Restaurant

Cathedral Place Killarney Co Kerry **Tel: 064 30555** Fax: 064 30557
Email: oldpresbytery@eircom.net Web: www.oldpresbytery.com

féile bia Gerry Browne and Mary Rose Hickey's impressive restaurant is in a beautifully restored 3-storey building and has earned its place as one of the area's leading fine dining establishments. The restaurant is divided into elegant, well-appointed dining areas on two floors - the ground floor space is broken up into several small areas, while the first floor provides a large dining room which can be used for private parties. Friendly, efficient reception and a comfortable bar area for aperitifs bode well, and head chef Christina Cotter's promising modern Irish menus offer plenty of choice, including several appealing vegetarian choices. Classically based cooking with international influences produces some interesting and attractive dishes, such as a starter of chicken liver paté with walnut & raisin brioche and ruby port dressing or a fish main course of roast monkfish with lemon beurre blanc and citrus and ginger couscous. Braised Kerry lamb shank is perennially popular, served with colcannon mash, roast root vegetables and a whiskey mustard sauce. Desserts are particularly good - a speciality worth waiting for (it takes 15 minutes) is a divine warm melting chocolate cake, with white chocolate sauce and vanilla ice cream - and, of course, there are cheeses (Irish and continental). A high standard of ingredients and accomplished cooking are enhanced by pleasing surroundings and highly professional staff who provide outstanding service. A well-balanced wine list includes half a dozen house wines and a good selection of half bottles. Children welcome. Private car park. **Seats 65** (private room, 50). Reservations accepted. Air conditioning. Toilets wheelchair accessible. D Wed-Mon, 6.30-10. Early D €25 (6.30-7); otherwise à la carte; house wines, €21. SC discretionary. Closed Tue all year; 24-25 Dec, Good Fri and 6 Jan-6 Feb. Amex, Diners, MasterCard, Visa, Laser. **Directions:** Opposite St Mary's Cathedral.

Killarney Area

IIII.III. ◉ HOTEL

Hotel Dunloe Castle

Beaufort Killarney Co Kerry **Tel: 064 44111** Fax: 064 44583
Email: sales@kih.liebherr.com Web: www.killarneyhotels.ie

féile bia Sister hotel to the Hotel Europe (Fossa) and Ard-na-Sidhe (Caragh Lake), this beautifully located hotel is mainly modern (although the original castle is part of the development) and has much in common with the larger Europe: the style is similar, the scale is generous throughout, and standards of maintenance and housekeeping are exemplary. Like the Europe, the atmosphere is distinctly continental; some of the exceptionally spacious guest rooms have dining areas, and all have magnificent views, air conditioning and many extras. The surrounding park is renowned for its unique botanical collection, which includes many rare plants. Golf is, of course, a major attraction here and there is an equestrian centre on site, also fishing on the River Laune, which is free of charge to residents. Conference/banqueting (150/180). Leisure centre, swimming pool. Snooker, pool table. Garden, fishing, walking, tennis, equestrian. Children welcome (under 2s free in parents' room, cot available without charge; playroom, playground). No pets. **Rooms 110** (1 suite, 40 no smoking). Lift. B&B from about €95 (weekend specials from about €210). Closed 1 Oct-mid April. Amex, Diners, MasterCard, Visa. **Directions:** Off main Ring of Kerry road.

Killarney Area

IIII.III. ◉ HOTEL

Hotel Europe

Fossa Killarney Co Kerry **Tel: 064 71300** Fax: 064 37900
Email: sales@kih.liebherr.com Web: www.killarneyhotels.ie

féile bia Although now around thirty five years old, this impressive hotel was exceptionally well built and has been so well maintained through the years that it still outshines many a new top level hotel. Public areas are very large and impressive, comfortably furnished and make full use of the hotel's wonderful location, and bedrooms follow a similar pattern, with lots of space, quality furnishings, beautiful views and balconies all along the lake side of the hotel. Leisure facilities include a 25-metre swimming pool, fitness suite and sauna; the hotel adjoins the three Killarney golf clubs - Killeen, Mahony's Point and Lackabane - and the two nine hole courses, Dunloe and Ross, are nearby. The hotel's continental connections show clearly in the style throughout but especially, perhaps, when it comes to food - breakfast, for example, is an impressive hot and cold buffet. Housekeeping is exemplary and, perhaps unexpectedly, this is a very family-friendly hotel. Excellent conference and meeting facilities include a 450-seat auditorium with built-in microphones and translation system. Leisure centre, swimming pool, beauty and hair salons. Equestrian, fishing, (indoor) tennis, snooker. Children welcome (under 12s free in parents room, cot available without charge; playroom, playground). No pets. Lift. **Rooms 204** (8 suites, 60 no smoking, 154 twin rooms). B&B from about €99, SC incl. Closed end Oct -mid Mar. **Panorama Restaurant:** This aptly-named restaurant is beautifully situated and elegantly appointed - views over the Lakes of Killarney with the mountains beyond providing a haunting backdrop, a fine setting for classic European cooking which makes full use of local produce like Kerry lamb and salmon through wide-ranging international menus, which offer something to please everyone, including vegetarians. Westphalian ham from the excellent German butchers shop across the road (which is well worth a visit) might be among the starters, followed by marinated local salmon (with rösti & horseradish cream, perhaps) and there could be some less usual main courses, such as suckling pig in caraway jus. Delicious desserts - chocolate marquise with redcurrants, maybe, or cherry clafoutis with Black Forest ice cream - then a slow coffee as you watch the light fading behind the mountains... Details are good - lovely breads are made in-house, for example, and there's a very extensive range offered at breakfast. Service is pleasant and very efficient. [*A separate informal restaurant, The Brasserie, offers popular all day food, 11am-11pm daily.] **Seats 450.** Pianist Thu-Sat. D daily, 7-9.30. Set 4-course D about €54. House wine €28. Hotel closed mid Nov-mid Mar. Amex, MasterCard, Visa, Laser. **Directions:** On main Ring of Kerry road.

Killorglin
👁 RESTAURANT

Nick's Seafood Restaurant & Piano Bar

Lr Bridge Street Killorglin Co Kerry
Tel: 066 976 1219 Fax: 066 976 1233 Email: info@nicks.ie

This is one of the famous old restaurants of Ireland and Nick Foley's is clearly thriving. It consists of two attractive stone-faced townhouses - one a traditional bar with a piano and some dining tables, where arriving guests can linger over a drink and place their orders, the other the main dining area. With quarry tiles, darkwood furniture, heavily timbered ceiling, wine bottles lining a high shelf around the walls - and piano playing drifting through from the bar - the diningroom has great atmosphere. Nick's cooking of classic French with an Irish accent has earned a special reputation for his way with local seafood and - although there are always other choices, notably prime Kerry beef and lamb - it is for classic seafood dishes like grilled Cromane mussels, home cured gravadlax, lobster thermidor, and Valentia scallops mornay that his name is synonymous throughout Ireland. And, if you want to see what that much-maligned item the speciality seafood plate is like at its best, make the journey to Nick's - for sheer quality, variety and attention to detail), it's unbeatable: individual sauces highlight the character of each sumptuous morsel, bringing out the subtle sea flavours. Irish seafood at its best, and very good value for money. Desserts, all home-made and changed weekly, may well be little more than an afterthought after such savoury delights - perhaps a shared tasting plate is the best solution - and there's a good cheeseboard too. Although it would be a shame to come here without enjoying such exceptional seafood, vegetarians aren't forgotten either and the service is outstanding, and the music and great atmosphere as beguiling as ever. An extensive wine list, hand-picked by Nick and with many bottles imported directly, includes interesting house wines and an unusual choice of half bottles. Children welcome. **Seats 90** (private room,40). Air conditioning. Live Piano nightly. D Wed-Sun 6.30-9.45 in winter, daily in summer (to 9.30 Sun). Set D €45. Extensive wine list; house wine from €19.50; sc discretionary. Closed all Nov and 2 weeks Dec, Mon-Tue in Dec-Mar & Christmas. MasterCard, Visa, Laser. **Directions:** On the Ring Road of Kerry, 20 km from Killarney.

Listowel
€ BAR/RESTAURANT WITH ROOMS

Allo's Restaurant, Bar & Bistro

41/43 Church Street Listowel Co Kerry
Tel: 068 22880 Email: allosbar@eircom.net

féile bia Named after the previous owner ("Alphonsus, aka Allo"), Helen Mullane's café-bar seems much older than it is, as the whole interior was reconstructed with salvaged materials (the flooring was once in the London Stock Exchange). It is brilliantly done with the long, narrow bar divided up in the traditional way, with oilcloth-covered tables along the side and at the back, now extending into a restaurant in the house next door which can have great atmosphere on a busy evening. A team of six talented chefs cook delicious bistro food at lunch and dinner, and a meal here is always fun - expect lively combinations of traditional and new Irish cooking with some international influences, based on carefully sourced ingredients. Theme nights are often held. **Seats 50** (private room, 20). Open Tue-Sat, L12-7, D 7-9 L & D à la carte; House wine €20. Closed Sun & Mon, 25 Dec & Good Fri. D reservations required. **Accommodation:** There are three beautiful guest bedrooms. Spacious and stylishly furnished with antiques, they have four-poster beds, luxurious Connemara marbled bathrooms and tea/coffee making facilities. **Rooms 3** (1 shower only). Room Rate, €70-130 (depending on the time of year, festivals etc); breakfast available at local café/hotel. Amex, MasterCard, Visa, Laser. **Directions:** Coming into Listowel on the N69, located half way down Church Street on the right hand side (almost opposite Garda Station).

Sneem

👁 GUESTHOUSE

Tahilla Cove Country House

Tahilla Cove Sneem Co Kerry
Tel: 064 45204 Fax: 064 45104
Email: tahillacove@eircom.net Web: www.tahillacove.com

Although it has been much added to over the years and has a blocky annexe in the garden, this family-run guesthouse has an old house in there somewhere. There's a proper bar, with its own entrance (which is used by locals as well as residents) and this, together with quite an official looking reception desk just inside the front door, makes it feel more like an hotel than a guesthouse Yet this is a refreshingly low-key place, and it has two very special features: the location, which is genuinely waterside, is really lovely and away-from-it-all; and the owners, James and Deirdre Waterhouse. Tahilla Cove has been in the family since 1948, and run since 1987 by James and Deirdre who have the wisdom to understand why their many regulars love it just the way it is and, apart from regular maintenance (and some recent major refurbishment) little is allowed to change. Comfort and quiet relaxation are the priorities. All the public rooms have sea views, including the dining room and also a large sitting room, with plenty of armchairs and sofas, which opens onto a terrace (where there are patio tables and chairs overlooking the garden and the cove with its little stone jetty). Accommodation is divided between the main house and the annexe, which is very close by; rooms vary considerably but all except two have sea views, many have private balconies, and all are en-suite, with bathrooms of varying sizes and appointments (only one single is shower-only). All rooms have phone, TV, hair-dryer and individually controlled heating. Food is prepared personally by James and Deirdre and, although the dining room (20) is mainly intended for residents, others are welcome to share their Irish home cooking when there is room; simple 5-course menus change daily. It's also a lovely place to drop into for a cup of tea overlooking the little harbour. Garden; walking; fishing. Children welcome (under 2s free in parents' room, cot available without charge). Pets allowed in some areas. **Rooms 9** (1 shower only, all no smoking). B&B €70 pps, ss €25. D at 7.45; Set D €30. Non-residents' welcome by reservation. Closed for D Tue-Wed; house closed mid Oct-Easter. Amex, MasterCard, Visa, Laser. **Directions:** 11 miles west of Kenmare and 5 miles east of Sneem (N70).

Tralee

🏨 HOTEL

Meadowlands Hotel

Oakpark Rd Tralee Co Kerry **Tel: 066 718 0444** Fax: 066 718 0964
Email: info@meadowlands-hotel.com Web: www.meadowlands-hotel.com

féile bia This hotel in a peaceful part of the town is set in 3 acres of grounds and landscaped gardens, yet within walking distance of the town centre. Open since 1998, the high quality of materials and workmanship is now paying off as the building mellows and takes on its own personality - and this, together with caring service from well-trained staff, is ensuring its position as one of the area's leading hotels. The interior layout and design of the hotel are impressive; notably the whole hotel is wheelchair friendly and furniture, commissioned from Irish craft manufacturers, is interesting, well-made and practical. Stylish, well-designed bedrooms are spacious and comfortable, with striking decor - and the suites have jacuzzis. The main restaurant, An Pota Stóir, is open for dinner only (except Sunday - lunch only) and booking is advised as it is popular with locals as well as residents. Informal meals (notably seafood, from the proprietor's fishing boats) are available in the bar, Johnny Franks, every day (12.30-9). Conference/banqueting (200/180). Golf nearby. Garden. Children welcome (under 3s free in parents' room, cots available free of charge, baby sitting arranged). Wheelchair accessible. No pets. **Rooms 58** (2 suites, 10 superior rooms, 25 no smoking, 2 for disabled). Lift. 24 hour room service. B&B €100 pps, ss €25. Off-season value breaks available. Closed 24-26 Dec. Amex, MasterCard, Visa, Laser. **Directions:** 1km from Tralee town centre on the N69, but usually accessed by N21/N22: go straight through the last two roundabouts and turn right at each of the next two traffic lights; the hotel is on the right.

Tralee
☆ RESTAURANT

Restaurant David Norris

Ivy House Ivy Terrace Tralee Co Kerry **Tel: 066 718 5654**
Fax: 066 712 7392 Email: restaurantdavidnorris@eircom.net

Creative cooking, welcoming and very professional staff, an informative but sensibly limited wine list and value for money have all won Tralee's leading restaurant many friends, and it has a loyal local following. Although there is little about David Norris's premises to suggest a special experience, once you get up the stairs to the reception area you'll soon sense the excitement and energy in his seasonal menus, which are beautifully balanced with clever combinations - and simply written, with a refreshing directness.

The restaurant is a simple room, with plates on the walls, lightwood furniture in the Charles Rennie Macintosh style, and well-spaced tables dressed with quality linen, plain glasses and white china, and fresh flowers. All the niceties of a special meal are observed, from the first delicious amuse-bouche to that last luscious petit four, but the aim is to offer the best of food at reasonable prices, and this it does very well: presentation is beautiful, but the main emphasis throughout is on taste and everything served, including breads, pasta and ice cream, is hand-made on the premises. Seafood is well-represented, as would be expected in this area, but Kerry beef might also top the bill, or an imaginative vegetarian dish with mainstream appeal. Other dishes with a difference served here might include a starter cassoulet of venison sausage with chorizo and a brioche and herb crust, or a ragoût of lamb and baby onions with a balsamic sabayon and a honey-mustard dressing. A perfectly cooked starter of crisp-fried calamari with a spicy tomato and chilli sauce attracted praise on a recent visit, and also a lemon and thyme flavoured roast breast of guinea fowl and a confit of its leg, accompanied by a delicious pea and chive cream. And, while not extensive, the wine list contains some nice surprises. The early dinner menu (Tue-Fri) offers outstanding value. **Seats 40.** D Tue-Sat, from 5pm; early D €24.95 (5-7); also à la carte. House wine €19.95; sc discretionary, except 10% (charged on food only) on parties of 10+. Closed Sun, Mon, all bank hols, 1 week Oct, 2 weeks Jan/Feb. Amex, MasterCard, Visa, Laser. **Directions:** Facing Siamsa Tire, across from Brandon Hotel.

Waterville
◉ RESTAURANT

Paddyfrogs Gourmet Restaurant

The New Line Waterville Co Kerry **Tel: 066 947 8766**
Fax: 066 947 8767 Email: paddyfrogs@eircom.net

Sandra Foster and chef Max Lequet's purpose-built restaurant is in a lovely situation, with views over Waterville Bay. The design, by local architect Albert Walsh, combines an attractive traditional exterior with a spacious and surprisingly sumptuous interior that reflects the beauty of the area, with original artwork, subdued lighting, plush chairs in rich shades of red and green, copper candelabra reminiscent of curly sheep's horns and driftwood mirrors - and thoughtful table settings to set off a special meal. A pleasant glass-front reception has several tables outdoors and a view of the Atlantic - a lovely place to enjoy a drink and look at menus. Sandra and her team are very welcoming and, with a nice blend of Irish hospitality and French cooking, the emphasis throughout is on quality, welcome and relaxation. Menus are not overlong but offer a wide choice, with a slight bias towards seafood but plenty else beside, including, of course, Kerry lamb - Max takes pride in using the best of local ingredients and this comes through on the plate, in dishes that combine local flavours with French flair; an example particularly enjoyed on a recent visit was a starter brioche of Sneem black pudding on sautéed sweet apples with traditional cider sauce. The cooking is skilful and every dish served here has personality, with the flavours, colours and textures of individual ingredients allowed their say, and great attention to detail in saucing and presentation - and, in an especially generous gesture from a Frenchman, only Irish cheeses are served. This is a restaurant which has matured dramatically since it opened in 2004, and is now earning a reputation well beyond the immediate area. Wheelchair Accessible. Ample parking. Set D €39.50, also à la carte or Vegetarian Menu. There's a Paddyfrogs D daily 6.30-10. Closed Oct-Mar. MasterCard, Visa, Laser, Switch. **Directions:** Ring of Kerry - right on the waterfront in Waterville.

COUNTY KILDARE

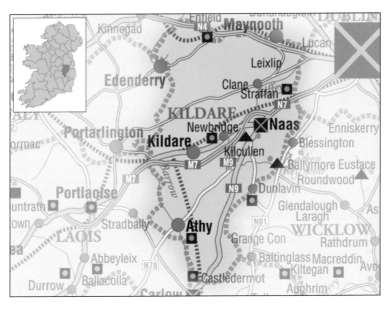

Athy

👁 COUNTRY HOUSE

Coursetown Country House

Stradbally Road Athy Co Kildare
Tel: 059 863 1101 Fax: 059 863 2740

Jim and Iris Fox's fine 200 year old house just off the Stradbally road is attached to a large arable farm. The house is welcoming, immaculately maintained and very comfortable, with some unusual attributes, including Jim's natural history library (where guests are welcome to browse) and extensive, well-tended gardens stocked with many interesting plants, including rare herbaceous plants, and old roses and apple trees. Bedrooms vary according to their position in the house, but all are thoughtfully furnished in a pleasantly homely country house style and have direct dial phones, tea/coffee facilities and hair dryers. Iris takes pride in ensuring that her guests have the comfort of the very best beds and bedding - and the attention to detail in the pristine shower rooms is equally high, with lots of lovely towels and quality toiletries. (A bathroom is also available for anyone who prefers to have a good soak in a tub.) Another special feature is a ground floor room near the front door which has been specially designed for wheelchair users, with everything completed to the same high standard as the rest of the house. Then there is breakfast - again, nothing is too much trouble and the emphasis is on delicious healthy eating. The wide selection offered includes fresh juices and fruit salad, poached seasonal fruit (plums from the garden, perhaps) pancakes, French toast with banana & maple syrup, Irish farmhouse cheeses, home-made bread and preserves - and the traditional cooked breakfast includes lovely rashers specially vacuum-packed for Iris by Shiel's butchers, in Abbeyleix. Small weddings catered for (20). Not suitable for children under 12 and older children must have their own room. No smoking house. Pets allowed in some areas by arrangement. Garden. **Rooms 4** (all with ensuite shower, all no smoking, 1 for disabled). B&B €60pps ss €15. 10% discount on breaks of 2 nights or more. Closed 16 Dec- 6 Jan. MasterCard, Visa. **Directions:** Just outside Athy, on R428. Turn off N78 at Athy, or N80 at Stradbally; well signposted.

Ballymore Eustace
PUB/RESTAURANT

The Ballymore Inn

Ballymore Eustace Co Kildare **Tel: 045 864 585**
Fax: 045 864 747 Email: theballymoreinn@eircom.net

féile bia It's the fantastic food that draws people to the O'Sullivan family's pub and it's wise to book well ahead to get a taste of the wonderful things this fine country kitchen has to offer, especially at weekends. The building gives out a few hints about what's in store as you approach - the neatly painted cream and navy exterior, the clipped trees in tubs flanking the front door - and the blackboard menu just inside - all bring a sense of anticipation. Inside, there two interesting bar areas where unusual craft furniture, original artwork and striking fresh flowers and plants all add up to the kind of place where details count so the menu, when it arrives, fits into the pattern. Top quality ingredients have always been at the heart of the food operation here, so you will find Penny Lange's local organic vegetables, also beef, lamb, bacon, chicken and eggs that come only from recognised quality assured Irish farms, and Irish farmhouse cheese from Sheridans Cheesemongers in Dublin, who ensure that every cheese is correctly ripened before delivery. Immaculate sourcing, careful cooking and a relaxed ambience have proved a winning formula - so much so that, as we go to press, renovations and expansion are under way again. Meanwhile, the business of providing some of Ireland's best informal food goes on, and continues to improve - a new Express Lunch Menu has recently been introduced, for example, offering real food for customers in a hurry: a delicious home-made soup with home-made breads (baked twice daily), perhaps, or their renowned Kildare sandwich, with baked ham, vintage cheddar & apricot chutney, or a simple hot dish like Spanish omelette, or lamb meatballs with spaghetti and pesto. Regular menus have more choice, including the house speciality - crisp-based modern pizzas such as Fresh Tomato, Buffalo Mozzarella (or ricotta), Seranno Ham, Rocket and Pesto, based on artisan products and baked in a special pizza oven. Vegetarian dishes can be very tempting, and exellent fish cookery always includes some blackboard specials, but this is beef country so why not have a well-aged sirloin steak, chargrilled and served with a smoked paprika dressing and crispy onions, some of Thomas Doyle's potatoes - gratin, sauté or champ. (Just keep off the Ballymore Inn home fries: they're addictive.) Delicious, homely desserts include a gorgeous apricot & almond tart, served warm with home-made ice cream. Children welcome to 10pm. **Seats 50.** Air conditioning. Food served daily, 12.30-9 (Sun to 7). House wines €17.50; sc discretionary. Closed 25 Dec & Good Fri. Amex, MasterCard, Visa, Laser. **Directions:** From Blessington, take Baltinglass road. After 1.5 miles, turn right to Ballymore Eustace.

Curragh
COUNTRY HOUSE

Martinstown House

Curragh Co Kildare **Tel: 045 441 269** Fax: 045 441 208
Email: info@martinstownhouse.com Web: www.martinstownhouse.com

Just on the edge of the Curragh, near Punchestown, Naas and The Curragh race courses, this delightful 200 year old house was built by the famous architect Decimus Burton who also designed the lodges in the Phoenix Park, Dublin, and is the only known domestic example of this 'Strawberry Hill' gothic architectural style in Ireland. It is on a farm, set in 170 acres of beautifully wooded land, with free range hens, sheep, cattle and horses, an old icehouse and a well-maintained walled kitchen garden that provides vegetables, fruit and flowers for the house in season. Meryl Long welcomes guests to this idyllic setting, aiming to offer them 'a way of life which I knew as a child (but with better bathrooms!), a warm welcome, real fires and good food.' It is a lovely family house, with very nicely proportioned rooms - gracious but not too grand - open fires downstairs, and bedrooms that are all different, each with its own special character and very comfortably furnished, with fresh flowers. A stay here is sure to be enjoyable, with the help of a truly hospitable hostess who offers a delicious afternoon tea on arrival - and believes that holidays should be fun, full of interest and with an easy-going atmosphere. Croquet lawn. Golf and equestrian activities nearby. Not suitable for children under 12. No pets. **Rooms 4** (3 en-suite, 1 with private bathrooms, all no smoking) B&B from €90 pps, ss €20. Residents D €45 (by arrangement - book the previous day). House wine about €22.50. Closed mid Dec-early Jan. Amex, MasterCard, Visa. **Directions:** Kilcullen exit off M9 then N78 towards Athy. Sign at 1st crossroads.

Leixlip
🏨 HOTEL/RESTAURANT

Leixlip House Hotel

Captains Hill Leixlip Co Kildare
Tel: 01 624 2268 Fax: 01 624 4177
Email: info@leixliphouse.com Web: www.leixliphouse.com

Up on a hill overlooking Leixlip village, just eight miles from Dublin city centre, this fine Georgian house was built in 1722 and is furnished and decorated to a high standard in period style and, with gleaming antique furniture and gilt-framed mirrors in thick carpeted public rooms decorated in soft country colours, the atmosphere is one of discreet opulence. Bedrooms include two suites furnished with traditional mahogany furniture; the strong, simple decor particularly pleases the many business guests who stay here and there is a welcome emphasis on service - all day room service, nightly turndown service with complimentary mineral water and chocolates - and a shoe valet service. Hotel guests have complimentary use of a nearby gym. Conference/banqueting (70/140). Secretarial services. Children welcome. No pets. **Rooms 19** (5 executive, 14 shower only). All day room service. B&B from about €82.50 pps, ss about €52.50. **The Bradaun Restaurant:** The commitment to quality evident in the hotel as a whole is continued in the restaurant, a bright, high-ceilinged, formally appointed dining room. Consistently good modern Irish cooking is offered through wide-ranging menus, based on fresh seasonal produce and well executed with pleasing attention to detail. Set menus offer particularly good value for money and there's an attractive lounge menu for those who prefer an informal meal. An extensive, informative and carefully chosen wine list would make good bedtime reading. Not suitable for children after 7.30pm. **Seats 45.** D Tue-Sun, 6.30-10 (Sun to 8.30); L (Sun only, except group bookings on other days) 12.30-4; Restaurant closed Mon (except for group bookings). Hotel closed 25-26 Dec. Amex, Diners, MasterCard, Visa, Laser. **Directions:** Leixlip exit off M4 motorway. Take right in Leixlip village at traffic lights.

Maynooth
🏨 HOTEL/RESTAURANT

Moyglare Manor

Maynooth Co Kildare **Tel: 01 628 6351** Fax: 01 628 5405
Email: info@moyglaremanor.ie Web: www.moyglaremanor.ie

Only eighteen miles from Dublin and a very short distance from the K Club, Norah Devlin's classical Georgian manor is approached by a tree-lined avenue, allowing the arriving guest to appreciate this imposing stone built house to the full. Mrs Devlin's love of antiques is famous - gilt-framed mirrors and portraits are everywhere, shown to advantage against deep-shaded damask walls, and chairs and sofas of every pedigree ensure comfortable seating, even at the busiest times; no wonder a visit here is sometimes described it as 'like being in an antique shop'. Spacious bedrooms and suites are also lavishly furnished in period style, some with four-poster or half tester beds, and all have well-appointed bathrooms. Golf nearby (four courses within 10 miles), also Tennis and Horse Riding locally. Small conferences/banqueting (30); secretarial services. Not suitable for children under 12. No pets. Garden; Walking. **Rooms 16** (1 suite, 4 exec., 2 disabled). B&B from €115 pps, ss €25. **Restaurant:** Dining in the traditionally appointed Restaurant is always a treat: grand and romantic, it's just the place for a special occasion. Edward Cullen, who has been head chef since 2003, has maintained the house style of country house coking, and both lunch and dinner menus offer a nicely balanced combination of traditional favourites and sophisticated fare, with an emphasis on seafood and game in season - and a fine wine list to match. As well as golf (four courses within 10 miles), there is also tennis and horse riding nearby. Garden; walking. Not suitable for children under 12. Restaurant **seats 70** (private room, 25). L Daily 12.30-2 (12-2.30 Sun); D daily 7-9 (8.30 Sun). Set L €34.95. Set D €60, also à la carte. House wine from about €22. Pianist 4 evenings a week. House closed Good Friday, 5 days over Christmas. Amex, Diners, MasterCard, Visa, Laser. **Directions:** From Dublin, N4 west; exit for Maynooth, keep right at church; after 2 .5 miles, turn left at Moyglare crossroads, then next right.

Straffan

⛫ HOTEL/RESTAURANT

Barberstown Castle

Straffan Co Kildare **Tel: 01 628 8157** Fax: 01 627 7027
Email: barberstowncastle@ireland.com Web: www.barberstowncastle.ie

féile bía Steeped in history through three very different historical periods, Barberstown Castle has been occupied continuously for over 400 years. It now includes the original keep in the middle section of the building, a more domestic Elizabethan house (16th century), a 'new' Victorian wing added in the 1830s by Hugh Barton (also associated with nearby Straffan House, now The K Club, with whom it shares golf and leisure facilities) and, most recently, a large new wing added by the current owner, Kenneth Healy, which is built in keeping with its age and style. Some of the individually decorated rooms and suites are in the oldest section, the Castle Keep, others are more recent, but most are stylish and spacious, and some have four-posters. Public areas include two drawing rooms and an elegant bar, and there are big log fires everywhere. Conference/banqueting 150/230. Garden, walking. Golf. Children welcome (cot available). No pets. **Rooms 59** (16 junior suites, 17 premier rooms, 21 ground floor, 1 shower only, 3 disabled, all no smoking.) Lift. Closed 24-26 Dec. **Restaurant:** Fine dining of character is offered in The Castle Restaurant, where head chef Bertrand Malabat, who joined the castle in 1999, presents a number of menus including a six-course Tasting Menu (served to complete parties only) and a seasonal à la carte with about seven choices on each course. The style is classic French with the occasional nod to international fashions; local beef or lamb usually feature, also game in season, and there will be several appealing fish dishes and at least one imaginative vegetarian dish. Finish with a classic sweet like vanilla crème brulée with an almond tuile - or a selection of Irish farmhouse cheeses and home-baked breads. Very professional service. * Light meals are available in the Tea Rooms, 10am-7pm daily. Not suitable for children under 12. **Seats 100** (private room 32). Reservations advised. D 7-9.30 (Sun, 6-8); L Sun only 12-2.30. Set Sun L €32.50. Set D €60 (6-course Tasting Menu); à la carte D also available. House wine €22.50; sc discretionary (but 10% on parties of 7+). Light meals available in the Tea Rooms daily 10-7. Closed 24-26 Dec. Amex, Diners, MasterCard, Visa, Laser. **Directions:** West N4 - turn for Straffan exit/ South N7 - Kill Exit.

Straffan

⛫⛫★ 🏆 HOTEL/RESTAURANT

K Club - Kildare Hotel & Golf Club

Straffan Co Kildare
Tel: 01 601 7200 Fax: 01 601 7298
Email: hotel@kclub.ie Web: www.kclub.ie

féile bía The origins of Straffan House go back a long way - the history is known as far back as 550 AD - but it was the arrival of the Barton wine family in 1831 that established the tone of today's magnificent building, by giving it a distinctively French elegance. It was bought by the Smurfit Group in 1988 and, after extensive renovations, opened as an hotel in 1991. Set in lush countryside, and overlooking formal gardens and its own pair of championship golf courses, the hotel boasts unrivalled opulence. The interior is magnificent, with superb furnishings and a wonderful collection of original paintings by famous artists, including Jack B.Yeats, who has a room devoted to his work. All suites and guest rooms are individually designed in the grand style, with sumptuous bathrooms, superb amenities and great attention to detail. In preparation for the 2006 Ryder Cup, major developments were undertaken by the hotel, including a new bedroom extension, an extension to the Byerley Turk Restaurant, and a spa - and, even while these improvements were in progress, the hotel has always been run with apparently effortless perfection. Although most famous for its golf, the hotel also offers river fishing for salmon and trout and coarse fishing with a choice of five stocked lakes (equipment bait and tackle provided; tuition available). For guests interested in horticulture there is a mapped garden walk, with planting details. On site amenities include: swimming pool; specialist therapies; beauty salon. Tennis; walking; fishing; cycling; equestrian. Snooker; pool table. 24 hour concierge; 24 hour room service; twice daily housekeeping. **Rooms 92.** Lift. *Legends Restaurant (stylish informality and European cuisine at the clubhouse of the Arnold Palmer Course): 12.30-9.30 daily; Monza Restaurant (casual Irish/Italian fare at the clubhouse of the new Michael Smurfit course): open 7am-10.30, meals from noon daily. **The Byerly Turk:** Beside the K Club's premier restaurant, a pleasantly clubby bar opens onto an elegant terrace with a distinctly French tone - here, on fine summer evenings, guests can consider menus over an aperitif and admire the new golf course across the river before heading in to the restaurant, where tall, dramatically draped windows, marble columns, paintings of racehorses, tables laden with crested china, monogrammed white linen, gleaming crystal and silver all create an impressive background for the hotel's fine food, using the best of local and estate-grown produce. The Menu du Jour is concise, but all the little touches - a complimentary amuse-bouche, home-made petits fours with the coffee - that make a special dining experience memorable will be in place. A seasonal à la carte menu is also offered, and a surprise "Tasting Menu" (on request), for complete parties. Service is friendly as well as professional - and, given the intertwined history of Straffan House and the Barton family, it is appropriate that the Bordeaux Reserve from Barton and Guestier should be the label chosen for the hotel's house wine. Children welcome. **Seats 115** (private room 14). Air conditioning. Pianist in the evening. D 7-9.30 (Tue-Sat). Set D about €70; also à la carte. House Wine from €26; sc discretionary. *Excellent less formal dining options are available at the two golf Clubs: Legends Restaurant offers European cuisine at the original Palmer course (12.30-9.30 daily); Monza, is the Italian restaurant at the new Smurfit course (7-10.30 daily). Amex, Diners, MasterCard, Visa, Laser. **Directions:** 30 mins south west of Dublin airport and city (M50 - N4).

COUNTY KILKENNY

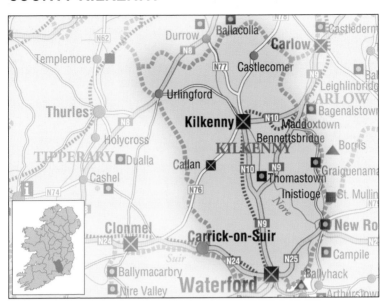

Callan

 COUNTRY HOUSE

Ballaghtobin

Ballaghtobin Callan Co Kilkenny
Tel: 056 772 5227 Fax: 056 772 5712
Email: catherine@ballaghtobin.com Web: www.ballaghtobin.com

Set in parkland in the middle of a five hundred acre working farm, this immaculately maintained house has been in the Gabbett family for three hundred and fifty years. Graciously proportioned rooms are beautifully furnished and the spacious bedrooms - which Catherine Gabbett has decorated stylishly - all have antique furniture and every comfort, including lovely bathrooms with bath and overbath shower, and tea/coffee trays. The house is surrounded by large gardens, with a hard tennis court, croquet lawn - and even a ruined Norman church - for guests' use. No dinners, but there are good restaurants within a short drive. Including The Motte at Inistioge (see entry). Children welcome (under 3s free in parents' room; cot availablewithout charge). Pets allowed by arrangement. Garden, walking, tennis, croquet. **Rooms 3** (all en suite & no smoking). B&B €45, ss 10. Closed at Christmas. MasterCard, Visa. **Directions:** Past Golf Club on left, 2.3 miles, bear left; bear left at junction, entrance on left opposite Gate Lodge.

Graiguenamanagh

Waterside

🍷 ⓔ 👁 RESTAURANT/GUESTHOUSE

The Quay Graiguenamanagh Co Kilkenny
Tel: 059 97 24246 Fax: 059 97 24733
Email: info@watersideguesthouse.com Web: www.watersideguesthouse.com

An attractive old stone warehouse on the quayside of this charming village on the River Barrow makes a characterful setting for Brian and Brigid Roberts' well-run restaurant and guesthouse. On fine summer days there are tables outside, then a comfortable reception area leads into the restaurant, where Brigid offers modern European food on varied and enticing menus - in very pleasant waterside surroundings. She uses fresh local produce wherever possible, sometimes including a speciality starter of Graiguenamanagh smoked eel with side salad & horseradish sauce - the eel fishery at Graiguenamanagh dates back to the Cistercian monks who built the town and weirs on the river, and is now active again. Aside from a range of mainstream choices (salmon, pork steak, striploin beef steaks) game might be offered in season (venison fillet in a redcurrant & wild berry sauce, perhaps) and interesting vegetarian choices, such as puff pastry parcel with seasonal vegetables Knockdrinna goat cheese, marjoram and white wine sauce, are always included. Finish with a nice homely dessert such as warm pear & almond cake, served with fresh cream. There's always an an Irish cheese plate too, with a choice of half a dozen ports to accompany, if you wish. Sunday lunch menus are more extensive, cleverly integrating casual choices like paninis and sandwiches alongside more substatial dishes. Service is friendly and willing under Brian's supervision - and the wine list, which is extensive for a country restaurant, is interesting and fairly priced. An early dinner menu offers outstanding value for money. **Seats 40.** Outdoor Dining available in the Summer. D 6.30-9.30 daily; L Sun only 12.30-3. Set L €19, Early D €20 (6.30-7.45). Set D €37, also à la carte. House wine, €19.75. No SC. * In summer there's also a light Daytime Menu available, 11-4. **Accommodation:** Ongoing renovations are gradually upgrading the accommodation, which is quite simple but comfortable, with direct dial phones, tea/coffee making facilities and TV in all rooms. Some rooms at the top of the building are especially spacious and all overlook the river. Book lovers may be interested in weekend book sales at Waterside, which is the home of the Graiguenamangh Book Festival and booktown project (details from Brian). Hillwalking holidays for small groups are offered (guide, maps, packed lunch, transport etc all arranged). Children welcome (under 3 free in parents' room, cot available without charge, baby sitting arranged). No pets. **Rooms 10** (all shower only) B&B €49pps, ss €15. *Weekend packages/ short breaks from €79 pps. No lift. Closed Jan. Amex, MasterCard, Visa, Laser. **Directions:** 17 miles south east of Kilkenny on Carlow/Kilkenny border.

Kilkenny

Kilkenny Design Centre

🍷 ⓔ RESTAURANT

Castle Yard Kilkenny Co Kilkenny
Tel: 056 772 2118 Fax: 056 776 5905
Email: info@kilkennydesign.com Web: www.kilkennydesign.com

féile bia Situated in what was once the stables and dairy of Kilkenny Castle - and overlooking the craft courtyard - this deservedly popular first floor self-service restaurant is situated above temptations of a different sort, on display in the famous craft shop. Wholesome and consistently delicious fare begins with breakfast for guests staying at Butler House, as well as non-resident visitors. The room is well-designed to allow attractive and accessible display of wonderful food, all freshly prepared every day: home baking is a strong point and, although there is plenty of hot food to choose from as well, salads, are a particular strength, always colourful and full of life - fresh beetroot, asparagus, spinach, red onion, coriander & crumbly Lavistown local cheese makes a salad worth travelling for, for example, and the selection changes all the time. Wines and beers are available, also gourmet coffees and herbal teas. Very reasonably priced too - well worth a visit. Toilets wheelchair accessible. Lift. **Seats 180.** Meals daily: Mon-Sat, 11-7, Sun & bank hols 11-3.30. Self service. Closed Sun & banks hols off-season (Jan-Mar). Amex, Diners, MasterCard, Visa, Laser. **Directions:** Opposite Kilkenny Castle.

Kilkenny
RESTAURANT WITH ROOMS

Lacken House

Dublin Road Kilkenny Co Kilkenny
Tel: 056 776 1085 Fax: 056 776 2435
Email: info@lackenhouse.ie Web: www.lackenhouse.ie

féile bia Jackie and Trevor Toner's period house on the edge of Kilkenny city is best known as a restaurant, but also appeals to those who want the comfort of an hotel with the hospitality of a smaller establishment (including excellent breakfasts). The restaurant offers a combination of traditional and modern fine dining - most importantly the head chef, Barry Foley's philosophy is to use only the best local produce and mainly organic vegetables and fruit: there's a formal commitment to the Féile Bia Charter on menus, and suppliers are credited: lamb and beef come from Kenna's butchers, fresh fish and seafood from Kikenny Fish Centre (both of Friar Street, Kilkenny), while pork and poultry are supplied by J.J. Cullen, of John Street. The cooking style is a combination of traditional and modern fine dining, and menus offered include a vegtarian one (on request) and an à la carte which includes specialities, some of them luxurious - foie gras terrine, roast suckling pig, roast crispy duckling and rack of Kilkenny lamb all feature. Menus are well-balanced, with more seafood than might be expected in a midlands restaurant and one or two unexpected ingredients, such as ostrich fillet, but local meats are exceptional: Kilkenny beef is renowned and there will always be at least one dish amongst the specialities highlighted on the menu - a fillet, perhaps, served with with parsnip & truffle purée, spiced onion rings and Madeira jus. A nice feature of the menu is the option of tasting selections - a Lacken House House Platter, for example, offers mini-portions of several starters, and then of course there are desserts or cheese plates too - the farmhouse cheese selection includes the lovely local cheese, Lavistown, and comes with scrumptious home-baked biscuits. An interesting wine list includes six house wines, about a dozen half bottles and an unusually extensive choice of dessert wines. Private parties and functions are also catered for (conference/banqueting 25/45). Children welcome. **Seats 45.** (Private room, 25). D Tue-Sat, 6.30-9.30; also Sun of bank hol weekends & in summer (1 Jun-30 Sep); Earlybird D €35 (6-7.30). Set D €50; house wine €21. Closed Mon (also Sun during winter except bank hol weekends); 24-27 Dec. **Accommodation:** Guest bedrooms vary in size and outlook but all have been extensively refurbished recently, effectively recreating Lacken House as a boutique hotel, with appeal to those who want the comfort of an hotel with the hospitality of a smaller establishment. Excellent breakfasts are served in the restaurant. Room service (limited hours); in-room treatments and massage. Children welcome (under 4 free in parents' room, cot available free of charge, baby sitting arranged). No pets. Garden. **Rooms 11** (2 junior suites, 5 power shower only, 1 family room, all no smoking). B&B €70 pps, ss €25. Amex, MasterCard, Visa, Laser. **Directions:** On N10 Carlow/Dublin Road into Kilkenny City.

Kilkenny
ATMOSPHERIC PUB

Marble City Bar

66 High Street Kilkenny Co Kilkenny
Tel: 056 776 1143 Fax: 056 776 3693 Web: www.langtons.ie

féile bia The Langton family's historic bar was redesigned by the internationally acclaimed designer, David Collins, a few years ago. Although initially controversial (especially the ultra-modern stained glass window which now graces an otherwise traditional frontage), it is a wonderful space to be in and attracts a varied clientèle. Everyone enjoys the vibrant atmosphere, and the excellent ingredients-led contemporary European bar food: a dish like confit of pork sausages with creamy potatoes and red wine onion gravy, for example, will probably be based on the superb lean sausages hand-made nearby by Olivia Goodwillie (who also makes Lavistown cheese), and the fresh cod'n'chips in a crispy beer batter will be just in from Dunmore East. More recently the bar has reinvented itself again and they have now introduced the Marble City Tea Rooms, below the main restaurant area, where lighter food like coffees, teas and pastry are available, 9-7 daily - and there's outdoor seating for a couple of dozen people. Good service, even at busy times; well chosen small wine list. Bar food served from 10 am, daily. Food service begins with breakfast, from 10am daily; main menus from 12 noon-9 pm (Sun: L 12-3; D 3-9). A la carte. House wine €20 (€5 per glass). Closed 25 Dec & Good Fri. Amex, Diners, MasterCard, Visa, Laser. **Directions:** Ample car parking at rear. Main Street, city centre.

Kilkenny
⒠ HOTEL/RESTAURANT

Zuni Restaurant & Townhouse
26 Patrick Street Kilkenny Co Kilkenny **Tel: 056 772 3999**
Fax: 056 775 6400 Email: info@zuni.ie Web: www.zuni.ie

Although Zuni is an hotel ('boutique' style, and offering a more youthful style of accommodation than other comparable establishments), the atmosphere is more restaurant with rooms: an oasis of contemporary chic in this bustling city, it is well established as an in-place for discerning Kilkenny diners. The room is large and airy, overlooking a courtyard (alfresco dining in fine weather) and there's a separate restaurant entrance so you don't have to go through the hotel. Maria Raftery's menus are based on local ingredients but international in tone, with a dish like teryaki salmon with Asian vegetables and sweet soy beurre blanc offered alongsde chargrilled Irish sirloin with seasoned potato wedges, crispy oyster mushroom and peppercorn sauce. Attractively presented food is always full of flavour: smart salads make sassy starters and Maria, who cooks with panache in view of diners, is a cool and accomplished chef. Menus to note include a 'Dinequick' lunch menu which includes bowl food and shared platters as well as more conventional dishes, an 2 or 3-course early dinner menu which offers a good choice and gives great value for money - and an upbeat contemporary variation on the traditional lunch which packs them in on Sundays. *Zuni Espress, a café nearby, offers coffees and gourmet sandwiches with a global flavour; you can pre-order on 056 779 5899 - just the thing for a picnic lunch, perhaps. Toilets wheelchair accessible. Children Welcome. **Seats 70** (Outdoor seating, 24). (Breakfast); L Tue-Sun 12.30-2.30 (Sun 1-3), D daily 6.30-10 (Sun 6-9). Early D €18.95 2 or € 25 3 course (6.30-7.30). Otherwise à la carte. House wine from €20.95. SC 12.5% added to parties 6+. **Accommodation:** This boutique hotel offers a more youthful style of accommodation than other comparable establishments; the minimalist decor is difficult to keep immaculate, but major refurbishment (painting, replacement of bathroom fittings, carpets and soft furnishings) has recently been completed. Rooms have direct dial phones, AC, Iron/Trouser Press, ISDN lines and TV, tea/coffee-making facilities. Breakfast is served in the restaurant. Children welcome (under 10s free in parents' room; cot available without charge). No pets. Private parking, but guests must get the receptionist to open the security bar (best to use the mobile phone, perhaps). **Rooms 13** (8 shower only, 5 no smoking,1 for disabled). Lift. B&B €60ps, ss €20. Hotel closed 23-27 Dec. Amex, MasterCard, Visa, Laser. **Directions:** On Patrck Street - leads to Waterford road; 200 yards from Kilkenny Castle.

Thomastown
⏛ HOTEL/RESTAURANT

Mount Juliet Conrad
Thomastown Co Kilkenny
Tel: 056 77 73000 Fax: 056 77 73019
Email: mountjulietinfo@conradhotels.com Web: www.mountjuliet.com

Lying amidst 1500 acres of unspoilt woodland, pasture and formal gardens beside the River Nore, Mount Juliet House is one of Ireland's finest Georgian houses, and one of Europe's greatest country estates. Even today it retains an aura of eighteenth century grandeur, as the elegance of the old house has been painstakingly preserved. Suites and bedrooms in the main house have period decor with all the comfort of modern facilities and there's additional accomodation in the Club Rooms at Hunters Yard, which is very close to the main house, and where most of the day-to-day activities of the estate take place. There is also self-catering accommodation offered, at the Rose Garden Lodges (close to Hunters Yard) and The Paddocks (at the tenth tee). Although now best known for golf the hotel is well located for exploring this beautiful area and there is plenty for non-golfers to do: gardens and woodlands to wander, new sports to try, Spa & Health Club for pampering. In order to build on their growing reputation as a destination for activity breaks, a new equestrian centre is under way as we go to press, and also a new spa; Mount Juliet has also recently launched a range of Master Classes in a number of disciplines, including fishing, painting, salsa and wellness. There is a choice of fine dining in the Lady Helen Dining Room (see below), or an equally attractive contemporary option in the stylish Kendals restaurant at Hunters Yard. Conference/banqueting (140/140). Children welcome (under 12s free-sharing with 2 adults, but extra bed costs e65; Cot available e50, Baby sitting arranged; Childrens play area). No pets. Gardens. Equestrian; Angling. Clay pigeon shooting, Archery, Tennis, Croquet, Cycling, Walking, Trails. Spa and Health Club (15m Swimming Pool; Treatments; Hair Dressing). Rooms 58 (2 suites, 8 junior suites, 8 superior, 1 disabled; all no smoking). No Lift. Room rate about €265 sc discretionary. Open all year. **Lady Helen Dining Room:** Although grand, this graceful high-ceilinged room, softly decorated in pastel shades and with sweeping views over the grounds, is not forbidding and has a pleasant atmosphere. To match these beautiful surroundings, classic daily dinner menus based on local ingredients are served, including wild salmon from the River Nore, vegetables and herbs from the Mount Juliet garden and regional Irish farmhouse cheese. Service is efficient and friendly. Extensive international wine list. **Seats 60** (private room 25). Toilets wheelchair accessible. D daily 7-9.30. A la carte. House wine from €28. * It can be difficult to get a reservation at the Lady Helen Dining Room, especially for non-residents, so booking well ahead is advised. A very attractive alternative dining option is offered at the newer contemporary restaurant, Kendals, which is open for breakfast, & also for dinner (6-10) daily, *Informal dining is available in The Club, Presidents Bar (12am-9pm). Amex, Diners, MasterCard, Visa, Laser. **Directions:** M7 from Dublin, then M9 towards Waterford, arriving at Thomastown on the N9 via Carlow and Gowran. (75 miles south of Dublin, 60 miles north of Rosslare).

COUNTY LAOIS

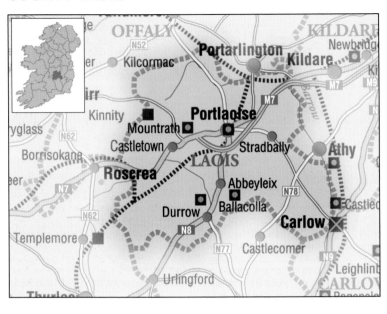

Abbeyleix
🌱 RESTAURANT WITH ROOMS

Preston House

Main Street Abbeyleix Co Laois
Tel: 0502 31432 Fax: 0502 31432
Email: prestonhouse@eircom.net

téite bia A sign on the pavement outside Michael and Allison Dowling's attractive creeper-clad house welcomes people to their friendly and informal country-style restaurant. A short but tempting à la carte lunch menu offers something very unusual in restaurants: the real flavour and textures of home cooking: soups with freshly-baked brown bread, chicken liver paté with toast and salad followed, perhaps, by fish of the day or a vegetarian dish like grilled goats cheese with salad and relish. For desserts there are sophisticated classics like crème brûlée but also simple, wholesome options too, like apple crumble or fresh fruits with yoghurt. Dinner brings a three course menu with a choice of at least five dishes on each course, and also an à la carte menu. Allison's good home cooking shines in lovely classics like coq au vin, grilled wild salmon fillet with hollandaise and a tasty vegetarian option like pasta with tomato, basil and courgette sauce. A well-chosen list of about twenty wines includes good house wines and two champagnes. A first-floor ballroom runs across the whole width of the building and, with a library area up a few stairs at one end providing comfortable seating for non-participants and a minstrels' gallery at the other, it makes a superb venue for local events. Preston House offers deliciously wholesome food at accessible prices, and was selected for our Happy Heart Eat Out Award in 2002. Not suitable for children after 7 pm. **Seats 35.** Private room available. Restaurant toilet wheelchair accessible. L Tue-Sat, 12.30-2.30; D Thu-Sat 7-9. Set D €40; also à la carte. House wine €20 sc discretionary (10% on parties of 6+). Closed Sun & Mon; Christmas period. **Accommodation:** The four large, high-ceilinged bedrooms are interestingly furnished with antiques, and unusual en-suite facilities have been cleverly incorporated without spoiling the proportions of these fine rooms by hiding them in what appears to be a long wardrobe but which opens up to reveal a row of individual facilities shower, WC etc. Children welcome (under 4 free in parents' room). No pets. No smoking establishment. **Rooms 4** (all shower only, all no smoking). Room service (limited hours). B&B €60 pps, ss €10. MasterCard, Visa, Laser. **Directions:** In the village, a few doors down from Morrisey's.

Durrow
🏛 HOTEL/RESTAURANT

Castle Durrow

Durrow Co Laois **Tel:** 0502 36555 Fax: 0502 36559
Email: info@castledurrow.com Web: www.castledurrow.com

féile bia Peter and Shelley Stokes' substantial 18th century country house midway between Dublin and Cork is an impressive building with some magnificent period features, and offers comfort and relaxation with style. A large marbled reception area with fresh flowers gives a welcoming impression on arrival, and public rooms include a large drawing room/bar, where informal meals are served, and a lovely dining room with a gently pastoral outlook at the back of the house (see below). Very spacious, luxurious accommodation is in high-ceilinged, individually decorated rooms and suites in the main house (some with four posters), with views over the surrounding parkland and countryside; some more contemporary but equally luxurious ground floor rooms are in a wing - particularly suitable for guests attending the weddings which have become a speciality, as they are convenient to the banqueting suite and avoid disturbing other guests. Conference/banqueting (160/170). Children welcome (under 5s free in parents' room, cot available without charge, baby sitting arranged, children's playground). Pets allowed by arrangement. Garden, walking, tennis (all weather, floodlit), cycling, snooker. Golf, fishing, equestrian all nearby. Hairdressing, beauty salon. **Rooms 24** (3 ground floor, 4 family rooms, all no smoking). B&B €100 pps, ss €40. 24 hr room service. Turn down service. Closed Christmas & 2 weeks in Jan. **Castle Restaurant:** Candles are lit in the foyer and restaurant at dusk, giving the whole area a lovely romantic feeling. Head chef David Rouse policy is for careful sourcing of all food, and the quality shows. Fish dishes, especially, have come in for praise on recent visits; wild Irish venison is a speciality in season, and a well-balanced cheese plate, might include the delicious local Lavistown cheese, from Kilkenny. Staff are very pleasant and helpful. **Seats 50** (private room, 20). Reservations required. Toilets wheelchair accssible. Breakfast 8-10, D daily, 7-9 (5-8 Sun; Early Bird D avail 5-6 S only, €35). Bar meals also available, 12-7 daily. Set D €50; Bar L à la carte. SC discretionary. House wines €20. Closed 24-26 Dec; 31 Dec-18 Jan. Amex, MasterCard, Visa, Laser. **Directions:** On main Dublin-Cork road, N8.

Mountrath
👁 COUNTRY HOUSE

Roundwood House

Mountrath Co Laois **Tel:** 0502 32120 Fax: 0502 32711
Email: roundwood@eircom.net Web: www.roundwoodhouse.com

It is hard to see how anyone could fail to love this unspoilt early Georgian house, which lies secluded in mature woods of lime, beech and chestnut, at the foot of the Slieve Bloom mountains. A sense of history and an appreciation of genuine hospitality are all that is needed to make the most of a stay here. Forget about co-ordinated decor and immaculate maintenance, just relax and share the immense pleasure and satisfaction that Frank and Rosemarie Kennan derive from the years of renovation work they have put into this wonderful property. Although unconventional in some ways, the house is extremely comfortable and well-heated (with central heating as well as log fires) and all the bathrooms have been recently renovated (all have full bath, some also with over-bath shower). Each bedroom has its particular charm, although it might be wise to check if there is a large group staying, in which case the bedroom above the drawing room may not be the best option. Restoration is an ongoing process and an extraordinary (and historically unique) barn is possibly the next stage; this enterprise defies description, but don't leave Roundwood without seeing it. Children, who always love the unusual animals and their young in the back yard, are very welcome and Rosemarie does a separate tea for them. Dinner is served at 8 o'clock, at a communal table, and based on the best local and seasonal ingredients (notably locally reared beef and lamb); Rosemarie's food suits the house - good home cooking without unnecessary frills, and Frank is an excellent host. A relatively extensive wine list includes a generous choice of half bottles. Children welcome (under 3 free in parents' room, cot available without charge; playroom; baby sitting arranged). Garden, croquet, boules, walking - there is a mile long walk in the grounds and garden renovation is ongoing. Stabling available at the house; horse riding nearby. Golf nearby. No Pets. **Rooms 10** (all en-suite & 4 no-smoking). B&€75 pps, ss €25. No sc. D at 8pm; 5-course set D, €45 (non-residents welcome by reservation if there is room); please book by noon. House wine €15.50. Dining room closed Sun & Mon except for resident guests, 25 Dec & month of Jan. Amex, Diners, MasterCard, Visa, Laser, Switch. **Directions:** On the left, 3 miles from Mountrath, on R440.

Portlaoise
 GUESTHOUSE

Ivyleigh House

Bank Place Church Street Portlaoise Co Laois
Tel: 0502 22081 Fax: 0502 63343
Email: info@ivyleigh.com Web: www.ivyleigh.com

This lovely early Georgian house is set back from the road only by a tiny neatly box-hedged formal garden, but has a coachyard (with parking), outhouses and a substantial lawned garden at the back. It is a listed building and the present owners, Dinah and Jerry Campion, have restored it immaculately and furnished it beautifully in a style that successfully blends period elements with bold contemporary strokes, giving it great life. Two sitting rooms (one with television) are always available to guests and there's a fine dining room with a large communal table and a smaller one at the window for anyone who prefers to eat separately. Bedrooms are the essence of comfort, spacious, elegant, with working sash windows and everything absolutely top of the range including real linen. Large shower rooms have power showers and many excellent details, although those who would give anything for a bath to soak in will be disappointed. But it is perhaps at breakfast that this superb guesthouse is at its best. An extensive menu shows a commitment to using quality local produce that turns out to be even better than anticipated: imaginative, perfectly cooked and beautifully presented. As well as a full range of fresh juices, fruits, yogurts, cereals and porridge, speciality hot dishes include Cashel Blue cheesecakes - light and delicious, like fritters - served with mushrooms and tomatoes. And through it all Dinah Campion (who must rise at dawn to bake the bread) is charming, efficient and hospitable. This is one of Ireland's best guesthouses, and was Leinster winner of our Irish Breakfast Awards in 2002. No evening meals, but the Campions direct guests to good restaurants nearby. Not suitable for children under 8. No pets. Garden. Golf & garden visits nearby. **Rooms 6** (all shower only & no smoking); phone, tea/coffee facilities. B&B €62.50, ss €12.50. Closed Christmas period. MasterCard, Visa. **Directions:** Centre of town follow signs for multi storey car park, 30 metres from carpark.

Portlaoise
€ RESTAURANT/SHOP

The Kitchen & Foodhall

Hynds Square Portlaoise Co Laois
Tel: 0502 62061 Fax: 0502 62075

Jim Tynan's excellent restaurant and food shop is definitely worth a little detour. Delicious home-made food, an open fire, relaxed atmosphere - a perfect place to break a journey or for a special visit. The foodhall stocks a wide range of Irish speciality food products (and many good imported ones as well) and also sells products made on the premises: home-made terrines and breads for example (including gluten-free breads - which are also available in the restaurant) lovely home-bakes like Victoria sponges, crumbles and bread & butter pudding, and home-made chutneys and jams. You can buy home-made ready meals too and any of the extensive range of wines from the shop can be bought for the restaurant without a corkage charge. The restaurant offers a great choice of wholesome fare, including at least three vegetarian dishes each day - old favourites like nut roast, perhaps and others like feta cheese tart and broccoli roulade. Hereford premium beef is typical of the Irish produce in which such pride is taken - and self-service lunches come with a wholesome selection of vegetables or salads. It's well worth making a special visit here in the autumn, to stock up their home-made and speciality Christmas food. **Seats 200.** Open all day Mon-Sat, 9-5.30; L12-2.30. Value L €10.50. A la carte & Vegetarian Menu. House wine from €10.99. Wheelchair access. Closed Sun, 25 Dec-5 Jan. Amex, MasterCard, Visa, Laser. **Directions:** In the centre of Portlaoise, beside the Courthouse.

COUNTY LEITRIM

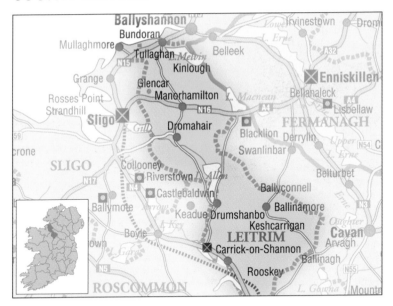

Carrick-on-Shannon
🏛 COUNTRY HOUSE

Hollywell Country House

Liberty Hill Cortober Carrick-on-Shannon Co Leitrim
Tel: 071 962 1124 Fax: 071 962 1124
Email: hollywell@esatbiz.com Web: www.hidden-ireland.com/hollywell

After many years as hoteliers in the town (and a family tradition of inn-keeping that goes back 200 years), Tom and Rosaleen Maher moved some years ago to this delightful period house on a rise across the bridge, with its own river frontage and beautiful views over the Shannon. It's a lovely, graciously proportioned house, with a relaxed family atmosphere. Tom and Rosaleen have an easy hospitality (not surprisingly, perhaps, as their name derives from the Gaelic "Meachar" meaning hospitable), making guests feel at home very quickly and this, as much as the comfort of the house and its tranquil surroundings, is what makes Hollywell special. Bedrooms are all individually furnished in period style, with tea and coffee making facilities, and delicious breakfasts are worth getting up in good time for: fresh juice, fruits and choice of teas, coffees and herbal teas, freshly-baked bread, home-made preserves, lovely choice of hot dishes - anything from the "full Irish" to Irish pancakes with maple syrup or grilled cheese & tomato with black olive pesto on toast. No evening meals, but Tom and Rosaleen advise guests on the best local choices and there's a comfortable guests' sitting room with an open fire to gather around on your return. A pathway through lovely gardens leads down to the river; fishing (coarse) on site. Lots to do in the area - and advice a-plenty from Tom and Rosaleen on the best places to visit. Not suitable for children under 12. Pets allowed by arrangement. **Rooms 4** (2 junior suites, 2 shower only). B&B about €60 pps, ss about €30. Closed early 1 Nov-28 Feb. Amex, MasterCard, Visa, Laser. **Directions:** From Dublin, cross bridge on N4, keep left at Gings pub. Hollywell entrance is on left up the hill.

Carrick-on-Shannon

ATMOSPHERIC PUB/RESTAURANT

The Oarsman Bar & Café

Bridge Street Carrick-on-Shannon Co Leitrim
Tel: 071 962 1733 Fax: 071 962 1734
Email: info@theoarsman.com Web: www.theoarsman.com

féile bia This attractive and characterful pub moved into a new era when Conor and Ronan Maher took it over in 2002. The brothers are sons of Tom and Rosaleen Maher (see entry for Hollywell), and clearly have what's known as "the hotelier's gene": numerous visits by the Guide at different times of day and days of the week have invariably found everything spick-and-span, very welcoming and efficiently run, even at busy times. The bar - which is very pleasantly set up in a solidly traditional style with two fires, comfortable seating arrangements for eating the excellent bar meals, and an occasional gesture towards contemporary tastes in the decor - leads off towards a sheltered patio at the back, which makes a spot for a sunny day and gives the bar an open atmosphere; just the place for one of their delicious Illy coffees with a complimentary house chocolate. New partner Lorcan Fagan joined the team in 2005, and there are various plans afoot, including extending the hours of food service, to offer simple, tasty bar bites; meanwhile, a strong kitchen team led by head chef Shaun Hanna produce consistently excellent food, offered on sassy lunchtime bar menus (warm wraps, healthy options and enticing organic pastas - Noodle House, made locally - and main course salads) and exciting à la carte evening menus offered upstairs three evenings a week. Here you might have a great meal beginning with two of the best farmhouse cheeses - baked Ardrahan in filo pastry and deep-fried Cooleeney - served with roasted cherry tomatoes & warm honey dressing; an unusual soup like butternut squash, ham hock & barley broth, or the Oarsman seafood chowder; any one of eight terrific main courses, say roast loin of venison, with red onion & courgette chutney, honey glazed pears and red wine jus ... And don't forget to save a space for a wonderful ending - such as warm chocolate fondant with lemon & coriander anglaise sauces and pistachio ice cream. This is one of the country's pleasantest pubs and they have a fine restaurant - definitely worth a detour. Bar meals: L Mon-Wed 12-3.30, Thu-Sat 12-2.30. A la carte. Restaurant **Seats 35** (private room 7). Reservations required. D Thu-Sat 6.45-9.45. A la carte. House wine from €17. Not suitable for children after 9pm. Restaurant closed Sun-Wed (D); no bar L Sun. Bar closed 25 Dec, Good Fri. MasterCard, Visa, Laser. **Directions:** Town centre: coming from Dublin direction, turn right just before the bridge.

COUNTY LIMERICK

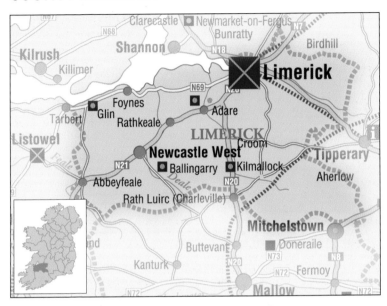

Limerick
Ⓔ RESTAURANT

Brûlées Restaurant

Corner of Henry St & Mallow St Limerick Co Limerick
Tel: 061 319931 Email: brulees@eircom.net

Donal and Teresa Cooper's restaurant is on a busy corner, with window tables given a glimpse of the River Shannon and County Clare across the bridge. The interior is well-appointed, with little dining areas on several levels that break groups up nicely and are elegantly furnished in a simple classic style that makes the most of limited space. For some years this has been the first choice in the city, for discerning local diners and visitors alike. A soothing ambience and nice details - real linen napkins, olives and freshly baked breads to nibble - make a good start while you look at appealing menus which show pride in using the finest of ingredients, both local and imported in imaginative, colourful modern Irish cooking, which is as good as it sounds - a speciality starter of pan-fried goats cheese & pancetta parcels with mixed leaves and pecan oil makes a good beginning, or a vegetarian dish like a tartlet of cherry tomato, buffalo mozzarella, pine nut & basil drizzled with truffle oil might be a tempting option. Main courses offer a balanced combination of ingredients in sound modern Irish cooking, such as a speciality dish of pan-fried escalope of pork in a herb crumb, with caramelised apples, baby spinach and a mustard & caper fruit sauce. Menus are consistently appealing - vegetarian dishes are invariably imaginative, also fish and seafood, which will always include daily specials, which Donal describes to guests very accurately, with prices - Donal's hospitality and thoughtful, professional service are an important part of the experience here. Teresa's cooking is accurate, the presentation attractive without being fussy and, with main courses averaging around €24, this is good value for the high quality of food served. Side dishes are simple, there's a good cheese selection - and puddings always include, of course, a classic crème brûlée, served with a crunchy brandysnap. Lunch menus offer especially good value. Interesting, fairly priced wine list. **Seats 30.** L 12.30-2.30 (Thu-Fri only); D 6.30-9.30. Early Bird D €30 (5-7), also à la carte. House wine €20; SC discretionary (12.5% on groups of 6+). Closed Sun, Mon; 25 Dec-1 Jan. Amex, Diners, MasterCard, Visa, Laser. **Directions:** On the corner of Henry Street and Lower Mallow Street, near Jurys Inn roundabout.

Limerick

🏨👁 HOTEL

Clarion Hotel

Steamboat Quay Limerick Co Limerick
Tel: 061 444100 Fax: 061 444101
Email: info@clarionhotellimerick.com Web: www.clarionhotellimerick.com

féile bia This dramatic cigar-shaped 17-storey hotel right on the River Shannon waterfront in the centre of Limerick enjoys panoramic views over the city and the Shannon region. Like other recently built sister hotels, clean-lined contemporary elegance is the theme throughout and there is a semi-open plan arrangement of foyer, bars and dining spaces, which take full advantage of the location. Business facilities are excellent and bedrooms - which vary more than usual in hotels due to the unusual shape of the building - are offered in several pleasingly simple, modern colour schemes (although a high-silled window design means you must stand to enjoy the view). All rooms have striking maple furniture, air conditioning, and everything that makes an hotel room the perfect retreat, including many nice little extras, and the top two floors have suites and penthouses available for long lets. Residents have unlimited use of leisure facilities - there is a health and fitness club on the first floor - and several decked balconies and terraces at different levels encourage guests to take full advantage of fine weather. Apart from the Malaysian/Thai all-day menu offered in the hotel's Kudos Bar, all meals are served in the well-appointed Sinergie Restaurant, a very attractive contemporary room with river views. Menus are lively and generally well-executed; at its best, a meal here can be a most enjoyable experience. Although this landmark building is easily located, gaining access to the hotel can be tricky for those unfamiliar with the city's one-way system; a nearby car park is used by the hotel and it is advisable to get clear instructions before arrival. (There is a moderate charge for parking.) Conference/banqueting (120/120). Secretarial services. Video-conferencing. Leisure centre; swimming pool. **Rooms 123.** (1 suite, 31 junior suite, 21 executive, 90 no smoking, 5 disabled). Lift. 24 hour room service. Children welcome (under 2 free in parents' room; cot available without charge). B&B 70pps, ss €30. **Sinergie Restaurant:** B'fst 7-10 (cooked €15, continental €10); L Sun-Fri,12.30-2.30; D daily, 7-9.45; (closed L Sat). Set Sun L €25; Set D €39; also à la carte. **Kudos Bar** serves Asian food, 12-9 daily. Short breaks (inc golfing breaks) offered; details on application. Closed 24-25 Dec Amex, Diners, MasterCard, Visa, Laser, Switch.
Directions: Take Dock Road exit off the Shannon Bridge Roundabout, first right.

Adare

🏨🏨👁 HOTEL/RESTAURANT

Adare Manor Hotel & Golf Club

Adare Co Limerick **Tel: 061 396566** Fax: 061 396124
Email: reservations@adaremanor.com Web: www.adaremanor.com

féile bia The former home of the Earls of Dunraven, this magnificent neo-Gothic mansion is set in 900 acres on the banks of the River Maigue. Its splendid chandeliered drawing room and the glazed cloister of the dining room look over formal box-hedged gardens towards the Robert Trent Jones golf course. Other grand public areas include the Gallery, named after the Palace of Versailles, with its unique 15th century choir stalls and fine stained glass windows. Luxurious bedrooms have individual hand carved fireplaces, fine locally-made mahogany furniture, cut-glass table lamps and impressive marble bathrooms with powerful showers over huge bathtubs. Quite recent additions include a new clubhouse in the grounds (complete with full conference facilities) and a "golf village" of two and four bedroom townhouses which provides a comfortable accommodation option for longer stays, large groups and families. Conference/banqueting (220/150). Leisure centre, swimming pool, spa treatments; beauty salon; hairdressing. Shop. Golf (18), equestrian; fishing; walking; cycling. Garden. Children welcome (cots available without charge, baby sitting arranged). No pets. **Rooms 63** (1 state room, 5 suites, 8 junior suites, 15 ground floor rooms). Lift. 24 hour room service. Room rate from €395. SC discretionary. Open all year. **Restaurant:** The beautifully appointed Oak Room Restaurant provides a fine setting for Mark O'Donoghue's modern classical cuisine, which is cooking based on seasonal produce, including vegetables from the estate's own gardens. Local ingredients feature - roast fillet of local beef with horseradish mash and onion sauce is a popular example, and vegetarian dishes such as spinach and blue cheese lasagne with roast baby beetroot and sweet potato wedges are offered menu on the main menu. **Seats 60** D (6.30-10) daily; Set D €56; house wine from €25; SC discretionary. *More informal bistro style dining is offered all day at the Carriage House Restaurant, 7am -9.30 pm daily. Open all year. Amex, Diners, MasterCard, Visa, Laser. **Directions:** On N21 in Limerick.

Adare   # Dunraven Arms Hotel

🏨 🍷 HOTEL/RESTAURANT   Adare Co Limerick **Tel: 061 396 633** Fax: 061 396 541
Email: reservations@dunravenhotel.com   Web: www.dunravenhotel.com

féile bia Established in 1792, the Murphy family's large hotel has somehow retained the comfortable ambience of a country inn. A very luxurious inn nevertheless, especially since the recent completion of 12 new junior suites: under the personal management of Bryan and Louis Murphy, the furnishing standard is superb throughout, with antiques, private dressing rooms and luxurious bathrooms, plus excellent amenities for private and business guests, all complemented by an outstanding standard of housekeeping. It's a great base for sporting activities - equestrian holidays are a speciality and both golf and fishing are available nearby - and also ideal for conferences and private functions, including weddings (which are held beside the main hotel, with separate catering facilities). In recent times the hotel has earned an unrivalled reputation for the quality and value of short breaks offered, and there is an ongoing determination to provide personal service and quality in all aspects of its operation which makes Dunraven Arms an outstanding example of contemporary Irish hospitality at its best. *Dunraven Arms was the our Hotel of the Year in 2004. Equestrian; hunting; fishing; shooting; archery. Bike hire; walking. Leisure centre, indoor swimming pool, beauty salon. Walking. Garden. No pets. **Rooms 86** (6 suites, 24 junior suites, 56 executive, 30 ground floor, 1 family room, all no smoking). Lift. 24 hour room service. Turndown service. B&B €132.50 pps, no ss. Room-only rate €200. SC12.5% . Open all year. **Maigue Restaurant:** Named after the River Maigue, which flows through the village of Adare, the restaurant is delightfully old fashioned - more akin to eating in a large country house than in an hotel. A new head chef, Colin Greensmith, joined the hotel in 2005 and continues the tradition of pride in using the best of local produce. Menus offer a balanced selection of about half a dozen dishes on each course and, although particularly renowned for their roast rib of beef (carved at your table from a magnificent trolley), other specialities like River Maigue salmon and local game in season, especially pheasant, are very popular. Menus are not overlong but may offer some dishes not found elsewhere - a main course of pan-fried calves liver on a bed of colcannon with shallots and lardons of bacon, perhaps - and little home-made touches add an extra dimension - farmhouse cheeses are served with home-made biscuits as well as grapes and an apple And date dressing, for example. Service, under the direction of John Shovlin, who has been restaurant manager since 1980, is exemplary - as elsewhere in the hotel. A wide-ranging wine list offers some treats for the connoisseur as well as plenty of more accessible wines. Restaurant not suitable for children under 12 after 7pm. **Seats 70** (private room 40). Reservations required. D daily 7-9.30, L Sun only 12.30-1.30. Set Sun L €27, D à la carte. House wine from about €20, SC 12.5%. [*The Inn Between, across the road in one of the traditional thatched cottages, is an informal brasserie style restaurant in common ownership with the Dunraven Arms; D Tue-Sat, 6.30-9.30. * Light bar food (soup and sandwiches) available daily, 12-7.] Amex, MasterCard, Visa, Laser. **Directions:** First building on right as you enter the village coming from Limerick (11 miles).

Adare
👁 RESTAURANT

The Wild Geese Restaurant

Rose Cottage Main Street Adare Co Limerick
Tel: 061 396451 Fax: 061 396451
Email: wildgeese@indigo.ie Web: www.wild-geese.com

féile bia David Foley and Julie Randles' restaurant is in one of the prettiest cottages in the prettiest village in Ireland - and, with consistently good modern Irish cooking and caring service, it's an irresistible package. David Foley is a fine chef who sources ingredients with care - seafood comes from west Cork, there are local meats, poultry and game in season; everything comes from a network of small suppliers built up over the years. Menus offered include a shortish 'Value' menu (no time restriction), a semi à la carte which is considerably priced by course, and a separate vegetarian menu, on request. All the niceties of a special meal are observed - delicious home-baked bread (mustard seed, perhaps) is delivered with an amuse-bouche, such as a shot glass of asparagus soup, The cooking style is sophisticated - a luxurious main course speciality is ravioli of Castletownbere lobster on a bed of Savoy cabbage, with basil and chive hollandaise, although a more homely rack of Adare lamb with traditional accompaniments such as potato & garlic gratin and rosemary jus is an enduring favourite. Like everything else in your meal, desserts (including ice creams) are freshly made on the premises. Friendly staff and an informative wine list add greatly to the dining experiences. Not suitable for children after 8 pm. **Seats 60** (private room 30). D Tue-Sun 6.30-10 (Sun 9.30). Set D €30/36 (2/3 course), also à la carte. House wines €22. Closed Mon May-Sep; also Sun off-season (Oct-Apr). Closed 1st 3 weeks Jan. Amex, Diners, MasterCard, Visa, Laser, Switch. **Directions:** From Limerick, at top of Adare village, opposite Dunraven Arms Hotel.

Ballingarry
🏛☆ 🐐 COUNTRY HOUSE/RESTAURANT

The Mustard Seed at Echo Lodge

Ballingarry Co Limerick
Tel: 069 68508 Fax: 069 68511
Email: mustard@indigo.ie Web: www.mustardseed.ie

féile bia Dan Mullane's famous restaurant The Mustard Seed started life in Adare in 1985, then moved just ten minutes drive away to Echo Lodge, a spacious Victorian country residence set on seven acres of lovely gardens, with mature trees, shrubberies, kitchen garden and orchard - and very luxurious accommodation. Elegance, comfort and generosity are the hallmarks - seen through decor and furnishings which bear the mark of a seasoned traveller whose eye has found much to delight in while wandering the world. As well as offering accommodation in the main house, the conversion of an old schoolhouse in the garden now provides three newer superior suites, a residents' lounge and a small leisure centre with sauna and massage room - this stylish development offers something quite different from the older accommodation and is in great demand from regular guests who make Echo Lodge their base for golf and fishing holidays. Small conferences (20); banqueting (65). Children welcome (under 2s free in parents' room, cots available without charge, baby sitting arranged). Pets allowed by arrangement. Garden, walking. Sauna, massage room. **Rooms 16** (2 suites, 8 shower only, 1 family room, 2 ground floor, 1 for disabled, 8 no smoking,). Turndown service. B&B €90 pps, ss €20. Special winter breaks offered, depending on availability. Closed Christmas week, 2 wks Feb. **Restaurant:** Food and hospitality are at the heart of Echo Lodge and it is in ensuring a memorable dining experience, most of all, that Dan Mullane's great qualities as a host emerge (he was our Host of the Year in 2001). The evening begins with aperitifs in the Library, prettily served with a tasty amuse-bouche - and this attention to detail is confirmed in the beautiful dining room, where fresh flowers on each table are carefully selected to complement the decor. Head chef Tony Schwartz cooks in a modern Irish style, and the wonderful organic kitchen gardens supply him with much of the produce for the restaurant - do allow time to see them before dinner and, perhaps, hazard a guess as to what will be on the menu - while other ingredients are carefully sourced from organic farms and artisan food producers. Menus are wide-ranging and very seasonal - the components of a delicious salad will be dictated by the leaves and herbs in season. Plum tomatoes and asparagus, in mid summer perhaps, accompanied by a parmesan, basil and a balsamic reduction, and the soup course - typically of roast vegetable - is also likely to be influenced by garden produce. Main courses such as pan seared salmon with crushed new potatoes are based on the best local meats, seafood just up from the south-western fishing ports and seasonal game. With such an abundance of garden produce, vegetarians need have no fear of being overlooked - every course features an unusual vegetarian offering. Finish with Irish farmhouse cheeses at their peak of perfection, or gorgeous puddings, which are also likely to be inspired by garden produce. Finally, irresistible home-made petits fours are served with tea or coffee, at the table or in the Library. All absolutely delicious - and, with service that is professional and efficient, yet always relaxed and warm, the hospitality here is truly exceptional. After dinner, take a stroll through the lushly planted pleasure garden; there is even a special route - of just the right length - marked out for smokers. *(The Mustard Seed was selected for our Natural Food Award in 2005, presented in association with Euro-Toques.) Not suitable for children. **Seats 55.** Reservations required; non residents welcome. D 7-9.30. Earlybird D €35 (7-8); 4-course D, €52. House wine €26. Closed 24-27 Dec, 2 weeks Feb. Amex, MasterCard, Visa, Laser. **Directions:** From top of Adare village take first turn to left, follow signs to Ballingarry - 8 miles; in village.

Glin

🏛️ 🌸 ◉ CASTLE

Glin Castle

Glin Co Limerick **Tel: 068 34173** Fax: 068 34364
Email: knight@iol.ie Web: www.glincastle.com

Surrounded by formal gardens and parkland, Glin Castle stands proudly on the south bank of the Shannon; the FitzGeralds, hereditary Knights of Glin, have lived here for 700 years and it is now the home of the 29th Knight and his wife Madame FitzGerald. The interior is stunning, with beautiful rooms enhanced with decorative plasterwork and magnificent collections of Irish furniture and paintings. But its most attractive feature is that everything is kept just the same as usual for guests, who are magnificently looked after by manager Bob Duff. Guest rooms and suites are decorated in style, with all the modern comforts, plus that indefinable atmosphere created by beautiful old things; accommodation was originally all in suites - huge and luxurious, but not at all intimidating because of the lived-in atmosphere that characterises the whole castle - but additional rooms -"smaller, friendly, with a family atmosphere"- were more recently opened (no need for this family to haunt the auctions in order to furnish the extra rooms!). And there are many small thoughtfulnesses - the guests' information pack, for example, lists possible outings and itineraries under different interests (gardens, historical etc) and how much time you should allow. When the Knight is at home he will take visitors on a tour of the house and show them all his pictures, furniture and other treasures; interested guests will also relish the opportunity to enjoy the famous gardens, including the 2 acre walled kitchen garden which provide an abundance of seasonal produce for the castle kitchens. There is tennis on site, also an interesting shop - and make sure you fit in a visit to O'Shaughnessy's lovely old pub, just outside the castle walls. The menu at Glin Castle changes daily with the seasons and as the head chef, Lionel, is Malaysian the menus for dining residents also reflect his Asian talents, seen in varied menus with a hint of the exotic. *Glin Castle was our Country House of the Year in 2005. The garden and house are open to the public at certain times. Small conferences/private parties (20/30). Not suitable for children under 10 except babies (cot available without charge, baby sitting arranged). Pets permitted by arrangement in certain areas. Gardens, walking, tennis. **Rooms 15** (3 suites; all no-smoking). B&B €140 pps. Dinner is available for residents by reservation; an attractive menu with about four choices on each course is offered. Dining Room **Seats 30.** D 7-9.30, Set D €48. House wine from about €21; sc discretionary. Closed Dec-Mar 1 Amex, Diners, MasterCard, Visa, Laser. **Directions:** 32 miles west of Limerick on N69, 4 miles east Tarbert Car Ferry; drive up main street of Glin village, turn right at the top of the square.

Kilmallock
Ⓔ FARMHOUSE

Flemingstown House

Kilmallock Co Limerick **Tel: 063 98093** Fax: 063 98546
Email: info@flemingstown.com Web: www.flemingstown.com

Imelda Sheedy King's welcoming farmhouse is on the family's dairy farm just two miles from the medieval village of Kilmallock; well-signed at the entrance, it sits well back from the road up a long drive flanked by fields of grazing cattle, and leading to an immaculately maintained garden in front of the house. The original house dates back to the 18th century and has been sympathetically extended down through the years, to make a large and well-proportioned family home with pleasingly spacious, comfortably furnished reception rooms - and huge bedrooms, furnished with antique furniture and unfussy neutral decor that contrasts well with the dark furniture. En-suite facilities don't include baths, but have power showers - and, like the rest of the house, everything is well maintained and immaculate. Imelda is a great host, offering genuinely warm and welcoming hospitality - and she's also a great cook, as guests discover at a wonderful breakfast spread that includes a selection of her sister's Bay Lough farmhouse cheeses, home-baked bread and scones, home-made preserves and even their own farm butter. The menu also offers several choices of prepared fresh seasonal fruit (much of it home-grown, of course), a choice of cereals and, in addition to the "full Irish", you may choose from kippers, smoked salmon with scrambled eggs, pancakes with fruit, or a platter of cheese. Dinner is also available, by prior arrangement - there's a choice of two or three dishes on each course, including treats like chicken liver paté with Cumberland sauce, or cucumber soup garnished with smoked Irish salmon, Slaney Valley leg of lamb (carved at the table) with timbales of garlic & herb potato, and apple tart with crème anglaise. This is a lovely place to stay and, aside from the many things to do and see nearby, is well placed to break a journey to or from the south-west. Children welcome (under 2 free in parents' room, cot available, baby sitting arranged). **Rooms 5** (all shower only & no smoking). B&B €55pps. ss €15. D €40 (residents only). Packed L on request. Closed Nov-Mar. MasterCard, Visa. **Directions:** R512 to Kilmallock from Limerick; then towards Fermoy for 2 miles. House set back from road, on left.

COUNTY LONGFORD

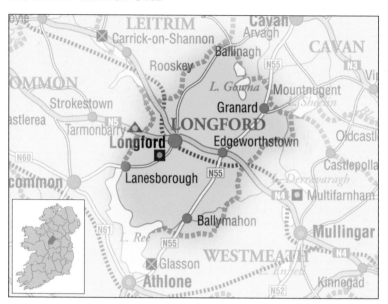

Longford
🏛 COUNTRY HOUSE/RESTAURANT

Viewmount House

Dublin Road Longford Co Longford
Tel: 043 41919 Fax: 043 42906
Email: info@viewmounthouse.com Web: www.viewmounthouse.com

James and Beryl Kearney's lovely 1750s Georgian house just on the edge of Longford town was once owned by Lord Longford, and is set in four acres of beautiful wooded gardens. It really is a delightful house and has been sensitively restored with style, combining elements of grandeur with a human scale that makes guests feel very comfortable. Its warmth strikes the first-time visitor immediately on arrival in the hall, which has a welcoming open fire and a graceful white-painted staircase seen against warm red walls. An elegant period drawing room and the six guest bedrooms all have their particular charm (one is especially large, but all are delightful); but perhaps the handsomest room of all is the unusual vaulted dining room, where an extensive breakfast menu is served. This is a most appealing house, with old wooden floors, rugs, antique furniture - and, most importantly, a great sense of hospitality. The original intention was to operate a restaurant here and that is due to happen shortly after we go to press, not in the main house but in one of the classic stone outbuildings, which have been under restoration for some time, and already include self-catering accommodation. The restaurant was nearing completion on the Guide's last visit - a fine room of great character overlooking a Japanese garden with water features - and the gardens, which are of great interest and designed as a series of rooms, are also nearing completion. Golf nearby. Children welcome (under 4 free in parents' room). Gardens. No pets. **Rooms 6** (1 suite, 3 bath & shower, 3 shower only, all no smoking). B&B €55, ss €10. *Self-catering also available - details on application. Amex, MasterCard, Visa. **Directions:** From Longford R393 to Ardagh. 7 miles, up sliproad to right following signs. Entrance 200m on right.

COUNTY LOUTH

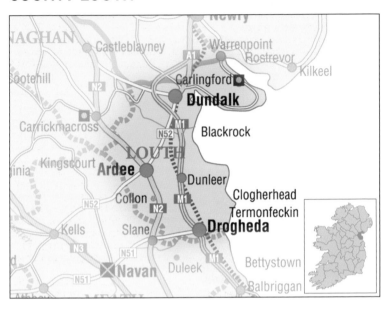

Carlingford
 COUNTRY HOUSE/RESTAURANT

Ghan House
Carlingford Co Louth
Tel: **042 937 3682** Fax: 042 937 3772
Email: ghanhouse@eircom.net Web: www.ghanhouse.com

Conveniently located just an hour from Dublin or Belfast airports, the Carroll family's 18th century house is attractively situated in its own walled grounds on the edge of Carlingford village, with views across the lough to the Mountains of Mourne. A proper little bar offers a relaxing space where guests can mingle - in a more convivial atmosphere, perhaps, than beside the drawing room fire, although that too has its moments; it's very pleasant for residents to return to, and especially welcoming for non-residents just coming in for dinner. Accommodation is in four rooms of character in the main house, each with sea or mountain views, and eight newer bedrooms in a separate building, which have been finished to a fairly high standard. And there's even more to it than comfortable accommodation and the delicious meals you will enjoy for dinner or breakfast, as the Carrolls also run a cookery school on the premises. Conference/banqueting (55/85); house available for exclusive use. Garden; walking. Children welcome (under 5s free in parents' room; cots available without charge; baby sitting arranged). No pets. **Rooms 12** (1 shower only, 3 superior, 2 family, 4 ground floor all no-smoking) B&B Single Room €65; Double Room €85/95 pps, ss from €5-40. (Discounts applied on stays of 2 or more nights.) Open all year except Christmas & New Year. **Restaurant:** Dinner is, of course, a high priority at Ghan House. The style is contemporary, based mainly on quality home-grown (vegetable, fruit and herbs), home-made (breads, ice creams, everything that can be made on the premises) and local produce, notably Cooley lamb and beef, dry cured bacon, free range eggs - and seafood: oysters are synonymous with Carlingford (there are also mussels from the lough and lobster from Ballagan, while smoked salmon and crab come from nearby Annagassan). A user-friendly set dinner menu with about five choices on each course is also priced by course, allowing considerable flexibility without having a separate à la carte: typical dishes on a late summer menu might include warm terrine of scallops and salmon with a saffron dressing, a duo of free-range Cooley beef (an interesting dish of slow cooked shin and pan seared fillet) with red wine sauce, button onions, mushrooms and mash - or perhaps, local red legged partridge, with braised cabbage & chateaux potatoes. Finish with Irish farmhouse cheese or a classic dessert - terrine of dark chocolate & coffee, perhaps, with home-made pistachio ice cream. Interesting, fairly priced wine list. Non-residents are welcome by reservation. **Seats 55** (private room 34). D only, Fri & Sat 7-9.30 (other times by arrangement); D "most days"; Set D €47; special 8-course Gourmet Night menu €68 (available six times a year); L Sun only 12.30-4. House wine €17.50; sc discretionary. Children welcome. House closed 24/25 Dec and 31 Dec-6 Jan. Amex, MasterCard, Visa, Laser. **Directions:** 15 minutes from main Dublin - Belfast Road N1.10 metres after 30 mph sign on left hand side after entering Carlingford from Dundalk direction.

Collon
Ⓔ RESTAURANT WITH ROOMS

Forge Gallery Restaurant
Church Street Collon Co Louth
Tel: 041 982 6272 Fax: 041 982 6584
Email: info@forgegallery.ie Web: www.forgegallery.ie

This charming two-storey restaurant has been providing good food, hospitality and service for over twenty years now - and still retains a well-earned reputation as the best eating place for miles around. It's a most attractive place; the exterior is invariably immaculate when seen from the road and, as you enter under a fine old arch, an equally impeccably landscaped parking area is revealed - and also a pretty garden area outside the attached accommodation, and a neat smokers' area outside the entrance. The building itself has loads of character, and has been furnished and decorated with flair, providing a fine setting for food that combines country French and New Irish styles, with a few other influences along the way. Seasonal produce stars, much of it local especially seafood, but also game in season, vegetables and fruit - and this quality produce, plus sound cooking, excellent service and an interesting ambience make for an enjoyable dining experience. Favourite starters include very attractive tian of wild oak smoked salmon with chive crème fraîche and a delicious warm salad of Dublin Bay prawns with salad leaves and fresh herbs - followed, perhaps, by main courses of roast duckling (a great house speciality, served on a bed of pak choi, with spring onion, soy and ginger sauce) or a combination dish of beef fillet with Boyne salmon, with a tarragon sauce. Although menus - which are quite extensive - seem quite conservative, there's some contemporary flair in the kitchen, and presentation is stylish. A short vegetarian menu is also offered, and a tempting dessert menu might include Kath's bread and butter pudding, and a seasonal crème brulée - and, of course, Irish cheeses. An interesting wine list, strong on clarets, includes a dozen house wines and an unusually wide choice of half bottles. Private parking (9). **Seats 60.** Air conditioning. L Tue-Fri (& Sun by booking only) 12.30-2.30. D Tue-Sat, 7-9.30. Set D €50; à la carte also available. House wine from €24; sc discretionary (except 10% on parties of 6+). Accommodation details on application. Closed Sun Night & Mon; Christmas & 1 week Jan. Amex, Diners, MasterCard, Visa, Laser. **Directions:** On N2, 35 miles from Dublin due north, midway between Slane and Ardee, in centre of village.

COUNTY MAYO

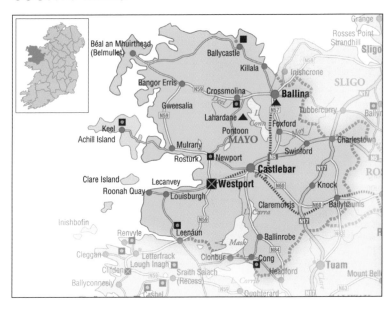

Achill Dugort

👁 GUESTHOUSE

HOST OF THE YEAR

Gray's Guest House

Dugort Achill Island Co Mayo
Tel: 098 43244/ 43315

Vi McDowell has been running this legendary guesthouse in the attractive village of Dugort since 1970, and nobody understands better the qualities of peace, quiet and gentle hospitality that have been bringing guests - especially artists and writers - here for the last hundred years. Mrs McDowell is very involved with the cultural life of the island - especially the Desmond Turner Achill Island School of Painting, and the cottage where Nobel prize-winning author Heinrich Böll once lived, which now offers a haven for artists and writers - and is an extraordinarily interested and hospitable hostess. This an unusual establishment, occupying a series of houses, and each area has a slightly different appeal: there's a large, traditionally furnished sitting room with an open fire, comfortable leather lounge furniture, and several conservatories for quiet reading. Bedrooms and bathrooms vary considerably due to the age and nature of the premises, but the emphasis is on old-fashioned comfort; each of the three houses now has a fitted kitchen with everything you need to rustle up a light lunch, also a washing machine and tumble dryer, and the rooms all have tea & coffee-making trays; phones for incoming calls were introduced quite recently and there are extra shared bathrooms in addition to en-suite shower facilities. Children are welcome and have an indoor playroom and safe outdoor play area, plus pool and table tennis for older children. Dinner for residents is served in a large, quite formally appointed dining room, where lovely old-fashioned menus are offered - dishes like smoked mackerel with gooseberry sauce or celery & apple soup, roast lamb or beef, poached Keem Bay salmon with hollandaise sauce, Eve's pudding with whiskey sauce or fresh strawberry meringue. Packed lunches are also available on request. Pets permitted in some areas by arrangement. Children welcome (under 3s free in parents' room). Garden, fishing, walking. Pool table. **Rooms 15** (all en-suite, 1 with bath & shower, 14 shower only). B&B €55 pps, ss €4, SC discretionary. D 7pm. Set D €32, house wine €18. Closed 24-26 Dec. Personal cheques accepted. **No Credit Cards. Directions:** Castlebar, Westport, Newport, Achill Sound - Dugort!

Achill Keel

€ ◉ B&B

Bervie

Keel Achill Island Co Mayo **Tel: 098 43114** Fax: 098 43407
Email: bervie@esatclear.ie Web: www.bervieachill.com

John and Elizabeth Barrett's magical beachside house was once a coast guard station and, since 1932, has been the ultimate escape for the many guests who have stayed here. It's a low, tucked-in kind of a place with a little wicket gate giving direct access to the beach, and an other-worldliness which is very rare these days. Elizabeth was born here and, aside from the location and the charm of the house itself - which has style without being at all 'decorated' - it is the sense of continuity that makes it special; and, of course, she has the 'hotelier's gene' which makes hospitality come naturally. Bedrooms, while not especially large, are comfortably furnished with everything you need to feel at home, there is a large dining room, where Elizabeth serves a home-cooked dinner with several choices on each course, and plenty of room for sitting around the turf fire; while meals are primarily for residents, there's a natural hospitality here - beginning with the hot-buttered scones and home-made jam Elizabeth makes for afternoon tea - and a willingness to fit in extra guests if there is room. Children welcome (cot available without charge). Pets allowed in some areas. Pool table, playroom, garden. **Rooms 14** (all en-suite & no smoking, 11 shower only). Room service (limited hours). B&B €45-60 pps. ss €15-25. Weekend Dining Room seats 32. D €30-40 (reservations required; non-residents welcome if there is room). Closed Nov-Mar. MasterCard, Visa. **Directions:** Follow signs to Keel from bridge onto island; turn left in village, towards beach.

Achill Keel

€ CAFÉ/RESTAURANT

The Beehive

Keel Achill Island Co Mayo
Tel: 098 43134/43018 Fax: 098 43018

At their informal restaurant and attractive craft shop in Keel, husband and wife team Michael and Patricia Joyce take pride in the careful preparation and presentation of the best of Achill produce, especially local seafood such as fresh and smoked salmon, mussels, oysters and crab. Since opening, in 1991, they have extended both the menu and the premises more than once and now offer great all-day self-service food, which you can have indoors, or take out to a patio overlooking Keel beach in fine weather Everything is homemade, and they make delicious soups such as cheddar & onion, courgette & onion, leek & mussel, seafood chowder and traditional nettle soup (brotchán neantóg) all served with homemade brown scones. As baking is a speciality, there's always a tempting selection of cakes, bracks, teabreads, fruit tarts, baked desserts and scones with home-made preserves or you can simply have a toasted sandwich, or an Irish farmhouse cheese plate (with a glass of wine perhaps). * The family also has accommodation on the island; details from the restaurant. **Seats 100** (outdoor seating, 50; private room, 50). Toilet wheelchair accessible; children welcome, baby changing facility. Meals 11-6 daily, Easter-early Nov. A la carte; wine licence: house wines from €16.95 (plus large selection of quarter bottles, around €4.50). Sc discretionary. Closed Nov-Easter Amex, MasterCard, Visa, Laser. **Directions:** Situated in the centre of Keel overlooking beach and Minuan cliffs.

Gaughans

Ballina
🍺 ATMOSPHERIC PUB

O'Rahilly Street Ballina Co Mayo
Tel: 096 70096 Email: edgaug@eircom.net

féile bia This is one of the great old pubs of Ireland and has a gentle way of drawing you in, with the menu up in the window and a display of local pottery to arouse the curiosity. It's a fine old-fashioned bar, with everything gleaming and a great sense of the pride taken in its care. Michael Gaughan opened the pub in November 1936 and his son, Edward, took over in 1972. Edward's wife Mary is a great cook and, once they started doing food in 1983 they never looked back; everybody loves the way they run the place and Mary still does all the cooking. Her specialities (all good home cooking) include home-made quiche Lorraine with salad, lovely old-fashioned roasts - roast stuffed chicken with vegetables and potatoes, perhaps, or baked gammon, and local seafood, when available: fresh crab is served from May to the end of August, wild sea salmon from 1st June to the second week in July, and smoked salmon all year round - such respect for seasonality is rare enough these days, and it is good to see it. There's always a daily special (€9) and old favourites like lemon meringue pie and pineapple upside down pudding for dessert. Lighter options on the menu include open smoked salmon or crab sandwich (in season), smoked salmon salad, ploughman's lunch, and it's all great wholesome fare. And, charmingly listed along with the Bewley's tea and coffee, the wine and Irish coffee "Glass of spring water: Free." Now that's style. Children welcome. Opening hours: Mon-Sat from 11 am (Mon-Thu to 11.30; Fri & Sat to 12.30) Sun 8-11pm. Bar food served Mon-Sat, 11am-5pm. Closed 25 Dec & Good Fri. Diners, MasterCard, Visa, Laser. **Directions:** Up to the post office, on the left.

Enniscoe House

Ballina Area
🏛🌳 COUNTRY HOUSE

Castlehiill Crossmolina Ballina Co Mayo
Tel: 096 31112 Fax: 096 31773
Email: dj@enniscoe.com Web: www.enniscoe.com

In parkland and mature woods on the shores of Lough Conn, Enniscoe can sometimes seem stern and gaunt, as Georgian mansions in the north-west of Ireland tend to be, but this hospitable house has great charm: with family portraits, antique furniture, crackling log fires, warm hospitality and good home cooking, it makes a lovely place to come back to after a day in the rugged countryside. It was built by ancestors of the present owner, Susan Kellett, who settled here in the 1660s, and is a very special place for anglers and other visitors with a natural empathy for the untamed wildness of the area. Large public rooms include a fine drawing room, with a big log fire and plenty of seating, and a more intimate dining room (which can accommodate some extra non-resident guests nevertheless). Susan's wholesome 5-course dinners change daily and make good use of local produce in dishes like timbales of smoked salmon (from Clarkes of Ballina) with cucumber salad, curried courgette soup and - a delicious house speciality - roast free-range pork with apricot and walnut sauce. Homely desserts to finish (rhubarb and orange crumble, perhaps) and cheeses laid out on the sideboard as they are again next morning, as part of an excellent breakfast. Traditionally furnished bedrooms are large, very comfortable and, like their en-suite bathrooms, regularly refurbished. And there is also much of interest around converted outbuildings at the back of the house, including a genealogy centre (The Mayo North Family History Research Centre, Tel: 096 31809), a small but expanding agricultural museum with working blacksmith, and conference facilities. The house is surrounded by woodlands, where Susan has built a network of paths, and major renovations have recently taken place in the walled gardens, which are open to the public and have tea-rooms and a shop stocking quality "non-tourist" items, collectables, and garden plants. There is brown trout fishing on Lough Conn and other trout and salmon fishing nearby; boats, ghillies, tuition and hire of equipment can be arranged. Golf (three courses within easy reach) and equestrian nearby. Children welcome (under 2s free in parents' room, cot available without charge, baby sitting arranged), and dogs are also allowed by arrangement. Gardens open at all times for residents (without charge). * Self-catering units also available. Small conferences (50). **Rooms 6** (all en-suite, 2 no smoking) B&B €88 pps, ss €12. Turndown service. Restaurant: **Seats 20.** D daily, 7.30-8.30pm; reservations accepted; non residents welcome by reservation. 3-course Set D €45; house wines €18-22. Closed 1 Nov-1 Apr. MasterCard, Visa, Laser. **Directions:** 2 miles south of Crossmolina on R315.

Ballycastle
€ RESTAURANT

Mary's Bakery & Tea Rooms

Main Street Ballycastle Co Mayo **Tel: 096 43361**

Mary Munnelly's homely little restaurant is the perfect place to stop for some tasty home cooking. Baking is the speciality but she does "real meals" as well - a full Irish breakfast, which is just the thing for walkers, home-made soups like mushroom or smoked bacon & potato, wild salmon various ways (in season) and free range chicken dishes. And, if you strike a chilly day, it's very pleasant to get tucked in beside a real fire too. There's also a garden with sea views for fine weather - and home-made chutneys and jams on sale to take home. **Seats 30** (also outdoor seating for 12). Toilets wheelchair accessible. Open 10am-6pm daily in summer (may open later - to 8-ish - in high season; shorter hours off season); Closed Sun off-season (Oct-Easter), & first 3 weeks Jan. **No Credit Cards. Directions:** From Ballina - Killala - main road to Ballycastle, on way to Ceide Fields.

Ballycastle
🏛 🏵 ◉ HOTEL/RESTAURANT

Stella Maris Hotel

Ballycastle Co Mayo **Tel: 096 43322** Fax: 096 43965
Email: info@stellamarisireland.com Web: www.stellamarisireland.com

HIDEAWAY OF THE YEAR

Built in 1853 as a coast guard regional headquarters, this fine property on the edge of the wonderfully away-from-it-all village of Ballycastle was later acquired by the Sisters of Mercy, who named it Stella Maris, and it now makes a very special small hotel, restored by proprietors Terence McSweeney and Frances Kelly, who have created a warm and stylish interior where antiques rub shoulders with contemporary pieces. There's a welcome emphasis on comfort throughout public areas, including a cosy bar - but the location is this hotel's major asset and a conservatory built all along the front takes full advantage of it, allowing guests to relax in comfort and warmth while drinking in the majestic views of the surrounding coastline and sea. Accommodation blends understated elegance with comfort in uncluttered rooms that have magnificent views and are furnished with antiques but - with complimentary broadband, modern bathrooms and power showers - offer the best of both worlds. Children welcome (under 3s free in parents' room; baby sitting arranged). Walking; fishing. Garden. No pets. **Rooms 12** (1 suites, 6 shower only, 1 ground floor, 1 disabled, all no smoking). B&B €102.50 pps, ss €42.50. **Restaurant:** Dinner - cooked under Frances' direct supervision - is a very enjoyable experience, based on local ingredients as far as possible, including organic produce from nearby Enniscoe (see entry) and also from the hotel's own new gardens. Menus are well-balanced and imaginative, without being over-influenced by fashion: sautéed lambs kidneys (in season), carrot & orange soup, rack of Mayo lamb with puy lentils and sage-flavoured jus are all typical and there is usually a choice of two fish dishes (vegetarian option on request). Classic desserts include refreshing seasonal fruits - poached plums with vanilla ice cream, glazed Italian meringue & mango coulis, perhaps - and there will always be an Irish farmhouse cheese plate - then it's back to the conservatory for a digestif... The wine list, while relatively short, has been chosen with care. Residents also have a treat in store each morning, as the Stella Maris breakfast is worth lingering over: lashings of freshly squeezed juice, a beautiful fruit plate, gorgeous freshly-baked brown bread, hand-made preserves and perfect hot food cooked to order, be it a traditional Irish or a special like creamy scrambled eggs with smoked salmon; not a grand display, but exceptionally delicious. Stella Maris was selected as Connaught winner of our Irish Breakfast Awards in 2004. This is indeed a wonderful retreat. Short breaks offered - details on application. Banqueting (24). **Seats 24.**

Reservations required; non-residents welcome. D 7-10 (Mon residents' only), L Sun only, 1-3; D à la carte, Sun L €25; house wine €21. Restaurant closed Mon (to non-residents); hotel closed Oct-Apr. *Complimentary broadband access in all rooms. MasterCard, Visa, Laser. **Directions:** West of Ballina on R314; 1.5 miles west of Ballycastle.

Castlebar
€ RESTAURANT

Café Rua

New Antrim Street Castlebar Co Mayo
Tel: 094 902 3376 Email: aran@iol.ie

Aran and Colleen McMahon's attractive little restaurant is well located near the Linenhall Arts & Exhibition Centre and you can't miss it, with its cheerful red frontage. The same light-hearted tone prevails inside too - it's not a very large room but pine tables (some covered in red oilcloths) are quite well-spaced and most have a good view of the large blackboard menu that lists all kinds of good things to raise the spirits of weary shoppers and culture vultures. Wholesome, home-made fresh food is the order of the day here, and careful sourcing of ingredients is a point of pride - so pasta dishes are based on the excellent Noodle House pastas from Sligo, Irish farmhouse cheeses and other speciality ingredients are supplied by Sheridans cheesemongers, fish comes from Clarkes of Ballina and pork from Ketterich's of Castlebar. Organic vegetables are supplied by a nearby organic scheme in summer, Macroom stoneground oats go into the porridge that is served with home-made apple compôte in winter - and ingredients for the full Irish come from the renowned butchers, Kellys of Newport. Regular dishes like home made chicken liver paté, warm chicken salad with chilli mayonnaise and ratatouille crostini Are announced on one blackboard, while another gives hot specials like potato & parsley soup, roast loin of pork with champ, braised red cabbage and turnip purée and wild salmon with fennel and new season potatoes. There's an interesting drinks menu (wines, juices, hot chocolate with marshmallows) and 'because we know that they love food too', there's also a special children's menu, one of many thoughtful touches. Luscious desserts and good home bakes too: great little place. Children welcome. Wheelchair accessible. **Seats 35.** Open all day Mon-Sat, 9.30-5.30. Closed Sun; 1 week at Christmas. MasterCard, Visa, Laser. **Directions:** Opposite Tourist Information Office.

Cong
★ HOTEL/RESTAURANT

Ashford Castle

Cong Co Mayo
Tel: 094 954 6003 Fax: 094 954 6260
Email: ashford@ashford.ie Web: www.ashford.ie

Ireland's grandest castle hotel, with a history going back to the early 13th century, Ashford is set in 350 acres of beautiful parkland. Grandeur, formality and tranquillity are the essential characteristics, first seen in immaculately maintained grounds and, once inside, in a succession of impressive public rooms that illustrate a long and proud history - panelled walls, oil paintings, suits of armour and magnificent fireplaces. Accommodation varies considerably due to the size and age of the building, and each room in some way reflects the special qualities of the hotel. The best guest rooms, and the luxurious suites at the top of the castle - many with magnificent views of Lough Corrib, the River Cong and wooded parkland - are elegantly furnished with period furniture, some with enormous and beautifully appointed bathrooms, others with remarkable architectural features, such as a panelled wooden ceiling recently discovered behind plasterwork in one of the suites (and now fully restored). The hotel's exceptional amenities include a neo-classical fitness centre, and sporting activities are detailed in a very handy little pocket book. The castle has two restaurants: The Connaught Room, which is mainly for residents, is the jewel in Ashford Castle's culinary crown and one of Ireland's most impressive restaurants, and the much larger George V Dining Room. Conference/banqueting (110/65); business centre; secretarial services; video conferencing. Fitness centre, beauty salon, hairdressing. Children welcome: under 12 free in parents' room (deluxe rooms only), cot available without charge, baby sitting arranged. No pets.

Rooms 83 (6 suites, 5 junior suites, 32 executive, some no smoking). Lift. 24 hour room service. Turn down service. Room rate about €420 (max 2 guests); SC 15%. Short/off-season breaks offered - details on application. **The Connaught Room:** This small room is one of Ireland's most impressive restaurants. The acclaimed Executive Head Chef, Stefan Matz, who joined the team in 2003, oversees the cooking for both this and the George V Dining Room. The style is broadly classical French, using the best of local ingredients - Atlantic prawns, Galway Bay sole, Cleggan lobster, Connemara lamb, and speciality produce like James McGeough's wonderful cured Connemara lamb from Oughterard, in sophisticated dishes that will please the most discerning diner. If at least two people (preferably a whole party) are agreed, a 7-course Menu Surprise tasting menu is available - and after dinner you will be presented with a souvenir copy of the Menu Surprise: a wonderful way to commemorate a special occasion. Typical dishes might include an elegant starter of chilled prawn tails set in Sauternes consommé, and a main course medallion of veal with foie gras & broad beans - paired interestingly with Ma De Daumas Gassac 2000 - while Irish farmhouse cheeses and warm soufflés are among the tempting endings for luxurious meals which are, as always, greatly enhanced by meticulous attention to detail. Service is discreet and extremely professional. **Seats 20.** D only, 7-9 (usually residents only). **George V Dining Room:** Lunch and dinner are served in this much larger but almost equally opulent dining room, where a combination of fine food and attentive service, under the direction of Maitre d'Hôtel Seamus Judge, promise an outstanding dining experience. A five-course dinner menu offers a choice of about five dishes on the first and main courses, including some tempting vegetarian suggestions. Lunch offers a shortened and somewhat simplified version of the dinner menu, but the same high standards apply: every meal bears the hallmarks of confident cooking and a light touch that, while classically correct, is thoroughly modern as well. Dishes particularly enjoyed on a recent visit includes a starter of duck foie gras with melted figs and Sauternes jelly - a light, gently flavoured salad; a clear seafood broth spiked with balsamic vinegar which exemplified real ability in the kitchen, as did a strawberry & green peppercorn sorbet - and a dessert of lavender & olive oil infused peaches with raspberry sorbet & caramelised puff pastry: original and superb. All the little niceties of a special meal are observed including appetisers, a range of excellent home-made breads and wonderful petits fours (by pastry chef Bernd Strauss). The wine list is a 37 page tome that remains a stunning example of an old-fashioned, grand hotel list. Although unarguably expensive, the dining experience at Ashford castle gives value for money - and Sunday Lunch is very reasonable for the quality of food, service and surroundings. *A light daytime menu is also available in The Gallery. *All meals in the castle are by reservation, but Afternoon Tea is served at The Cottage, for day visitors to the grounds. **Seats 130.** L daily 12.30-2, D daily 7-9.30. Set L €36, Set D €80 Tasting Menu (Connaught Room only). A la carte D also available; house wines from €28. SC.15%. *All meals in the castle are by reservation, but Afternoon Tea is served at The Cottage, for day visitors to the grounds. Amex, Diners, MasterCard, Visa, Laser. **Directions:** 30 miles north of Galway on Lough Corrib.

Mulrany

🏛️👁️ B&B

Rosturk Woods

Mulrany Westport Co Mayo **Tel: 098 36264** Fax: 098 36264
Email: stoney@iol.ie Web: www.rosturk-woods.com

Beautifully located in secluded mature woodland and gardens, with direct access to the sandy seashore of Clew Bay, Louisa and Alan Stoney's delightful family home is between Westport and Achill Island, with fishing, swimming, sailing, walking, riding and golf all nearby. It is a lovely, informal house; the three charming guest bedrooms are all en-suite with pretty, individualistic bathrooms, and very comfortably furnished. There is also an elegantly relaxed sitting room for guests' use, and an abundance of local low-down from the Stoneys, who will direct you to all the best places to eat nearby and make sure you get the most from a visit to this beautiful area. Self-catering accommodation is also offered - details on inquiry. Children welcome (under 4 free in parents' room, cot available without charge, baby sitting arranged). Garden. Pets allowed by arrangement. **Rooms 3** (all en-suite & no-smoking, 1 shower only). B&B €50 pps, ss €20. Self-catering cottages also available. Closed Nov-Mar. **No Credit Cards. Directions:** 7 miles from Newport on Achill Road.

Newport

🏛 🌐 COUNTRY HOUSE/RESTAURANT

Newport House

Newport Co Mayo
Tel: 098 41222 Fax: 098 41613
Email: info@newporthouse.ie Web: www.newporthouse.ie

For two hundred years this distinctively creeper-clad Georgian House overlooking the river and quay, was the home of the O'Donnells, once the Earls of Tir Connell. Today it symbolises all that is best about the Irish country house, and has been especially close to the hearts of fishing people for many years. But, in the caring hands of the current owners, Kieran and Thelma Thompson, and their outstanding staff, the warm hospitality of this wonderful house is accessible to all its guests not least in shared enjoyment of the club-fender cosiness of the little back bar. And, predating the current fashion by several centuries, pure spring water has always been piped into the house for drinking and ice-making The house has a beautiful central hall, sweeping staircase and gracious drawing room, while bedrooms, like the rest of the house, are furnished in style with antiques and fine paintings. The day's catch is weighed and displayed in the hall - and the fisherman's bar provides the perfect venue for a reconstruction of the day's sport. Newport was our Country House of the Year in 1999, and also selected for our annual Wine Award in 2004. Fishing, garden, walking, snooker. **Rooms 18** (2 with private (non connecting) bathrooms, 2 with bath & separate shower, 4 ground floor, 1 disabled). Children welcome (under 2s free in parents' room; cots available, baby sitting arranged). Limited wheelchair access. Pets allowed in some areas. B&B €151, ss €26, no S.C. Closed mid Oct-mid Mar. **Restaurant:** High-ceilinged and elegant, this lovely dining room makes the perfect backdrop for "cooking which reflects the hospitable nature of the house" in fine meals made with home-produced and local foods. Home smoked salmon is a speciality and fruit, vegetables and herbs come from a walled kitchen garden that has been worked since 1720 and was established before the house was built, so that fresh produce would be on stream for the owners when they moved in. John Gavin has been head chef since 1983 and his 5-course menus feature fresh fish, of course freshwater fish caught on local lakes and rivers, and also several varieties of fish delivered daily from nearby Achill island; wild salmon is from the house smoking room (prepared to a secret recipe...), but carnivores will be equally delighted by charcoal grilled local beef or roast spring lamb, and perhaps game in season. To finish, there are Irish farmhouses cheeses with fresh fruit, and classic desserts, often using fruit from the garden. And then there is Kieran's renowned wine list that, for many, adds an extra magic to a meal at Newport. It includes classic French wines about 150 clarets from 1961-1996 vintages, a great collection of white and red burgundies, excellent Rhônes and a good New World collection too. The foundations of this cellar go back many decades to a time when Kieran was himself a guest at Newport; great wines are a passion for him and, while acknowledging that they are irreplaceable, he offers them to guests at far less than their current retail value. Great lists of this scale and quality are almost a thing of the past, so is a matter of celebration that such a collection should belong to a generous spirit like Kieran, who takes pleasure in allowing others to share his passion. **Seats 38.** D daily, 7-9. Set D €59; house wine from €21. Toilets wheelchair accessible. Non-residents welcome by reservation. Amex, Diners, MasterCard, Visa, Laser. **Directions:** In village of Newport.

Westport

🏛 HOTEL/RESTAURANT

Ardmore Country House Hotel

The Quay Westport Co Mayo
Tel: 098 25994 Fax: 098 27795
Email: ardmorehotel@eircom.net Web: www.ardmorecountryhouse.com

BEST HOTEL BREAKFAST

féile bia Pat and Noreen Hoban's small family-run hotel is quietly located in immaculately maintained gardens near Westport harbour, with views over Clew Bay, and it offers warm hospitality, very comfortable accommodation and good food. Spacious, individually decorated guest rooms are all furnished to a very high standard; the style is luxurious and the range of facilities - which includes an iron and ironing board and, in many rooms, a separate bath and shower - is impressive. Guests are given the choice of seaview or back of house rooms, allowing for a less expensive option; this also applies to short breaks offered. An outstandingly good breakfast includes (amongst other equally tempting items) a choice of freshly squeezed juices in generous glasses, fresh fruit (correctly prepared according to type, eg skinned grapefruit segments), delicious cafetière coffee, a perfectly-cooked, simple version of 'the full Irish', and a superb fish plate (perhaps a combination of monkfish and seabass fillets, and 'a few scallops' if you are lucky). Great details too - freshly baked breads, home-made preserves and prompt service. Not suitable for children. No pets. Garden. **Rooms 13** (all superior; 2 ground floor; all no smoking). Room service (limited hours); turndown service. B&B €95 pps, ss €35. Closed 1 week Christmas, all Jan & Feb. **Restaurant**: The restaurant - a well-appointed irregularly shaped room with a sea view over the front gardens, and some useful corners for têtes-à-tête conversations - is the heart of this house, and owner-chef Pat Hoban presents pleasingly classic menus which make good reading over an aperitif in the comfortable bar and include a wide range of meat and poultry but have a strong emphasis on local seafood, including shellfish such as scallops and lobster when available. From a strong selection of starters, chicken liver terrine served with Cumberland sauce and toasted brioche attracted praise on a recent visit - dramatically presented with big pieces of brioche used like bookends, this was an imaginative (and tasty) re-interpretation of an old classic. Staff, some of whom may recently have arrived from abroad, employ charm and determination to ensure that an enjoyable evening is had by all. **Seats 50.** D 7-9 (daily in summer, Tue-Sat low season). A la carte (3-course D €45). House wine €20. Closed Sun & Mon in low season, 1 week Christmas, Jan & Feb. Amex, MasterCard, Visa, Laser. **Directions:** 1.5 kms from Westport town centre, on the coast road.

Westport
🏛 HOTEL/RESTAURANT

Knockranny House Hotel

Knockranny Westport Co Mayo **Tel: 098 28600**
Fax: 098 28611 Email: info@khh.ie Web: www.khh.ie

féile bia Set in landscaped grounds on an elevated site overlooking the town, this privately owned Victorian-style hotel opened in 1997. A welcoming open fire and friendly staff at reception create an agreeably warm atmosphere: the foyer sets the tone for a hotel which has been built on a generous scale and is full of contrasts, with spacious public areas balanced by smaller ones - notably the library and drawing room - where guests can relax in more homely surroundings. Bedrooms are also large - the suites have four poster beds and sunken seating areas with views - and most are very comfortable (some with jacuzzi baths). A health spa with nine treatment rooms, swimming pool, gym, and hair salon opened shortly before we went to press. Snooker room. **Rooms 54** (3 suites, 9 deluxe, 3 executive, 3 shower only, some no smoking, 2 for disabled.) Lift. Room service. B&B about €120, ss about €50. Closed 22-26 Dec. **La Fougère:** Contemporary Irish cooking is offered in the hotel dining room, La Fougère ("the fern"), which is at the front of the hotel, with views across the town to Clew Bay and Croagh Patrick. Menus are wide-ranging, in a classic/modern style; there is pride in local produce, including the renowned organic Clare Island salmon and Mayo lamb - specialities include home-smoked salmon (on a herb & potato pikelet with wasabi vinaigrette, for example). Even in a town with plenty of good restaurants to choose from, this is pleasant place for an outing - there is a sense of the restaurant being well-run, with friendly interaction between staff and guests which adds greatly to the enjoyment of a good meal. A user-friendly wine list blends entertainment and information in various ways, including colour coding different weights of wine; there's a good choice of mid-range wines, and plenty available by the glass. **Seats 100.** D 6.30-9 (Sun 7-9). L 12-2.30 (Sun1-2.30). Set D €45; Set Sun L €24.95. House wines from €20. SC discretionary. Hotel closed 22-26 Dec. Amex, MasterCard, Visa, Laser. **Directions:** Take N5/N60 from Castlebar. Hotel is on the left just before entering Westport.

Westport

👁 RESTAURANT

Quay Cottage Restaurant

The Harbour Westport Co Mayo **Tel: 098 26412** Fax: 098 28120
Email: quaycottage@eircom.net Web: www.quaycottage.com

Kirstin and Peter MacDonagh have been running this charming stone quayside restaurant just outside Westport since 1984, and it never fails to delight. It's cosy and informal, with scrubbed pine tables and an appropriate maritime decor, which is also reflected in the menu (although there is also much else of interest, including steaks, honey roast duckling and imaginative vegetarian options). But seafood really stars, typically in starters of chowder or garlic grilled oysters and main courses like tandoori monkfish tail, served on fresh tagliatelle with riata dressing - or baked fillet of salmon with fresh buttered asparagus and creamy saffron & lime sauce. Daily specials are often especially interesting (langoustine, halibut, scallops, lobster for example) and there are nice homely desserts, like rhubarb pie with real custard or a plated farmhouse cheese selection such as Cashel Blue, smoked Gubbeen and an Irish brie, with fresh fruit and biscuits. Freshly-brewed coffee by the cup to finish. There's a great atmosphere in this immaculately maintained restaurant, and Kirstin supervises a friendly front of house team. The compact, reasonably priced wine list is well-chosen. Children welcome. **Seats 80** (private room, 40/15; outdoor seating, 4). Air conditioning. Toilets wheelchair accessible. D 6-10 (daily in summer, Tue-Sat in winter). 'Value' D €25, Set D €35; also à la carte; house wine €16.50; SC discretionary (except 10% on parties of 6+). Closed Sun & Mon in winter, Christmas, all Jan. Amex, MasterCard, Visa, Laser. **Directions:** On the harbour front, at gates to Westport House.

COUNTY MEATH

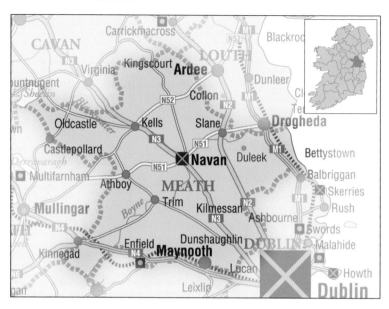

Duleek
 RESTAURANT

The Spire Restaurant

Church Lane Duleek Co Meath **Tel 041 982 3000**
Email: info@www.thespirerestaurant.ie Web: www.thespirerestaurant.ie

Shay and Deborah Kendrick's converted church in the historic village of Duleek - which is the site of many an interesting item including Ireland's oldest and largest lime tree - was formerly St Kienan's Church of Ireland and, together with the adjacent St Mary's Abbey, it makes a specular sight when lit up at light. From a virtual ruin, the church has been given a clean-lined contemporary look, with clear glass windows, uncluttered pale walls lit by big torchon style sconce lamps, some modern paintings, large plants that break up the space, and a mezzanine floor that virtually doubles the dining space and makes a perfect venue for private functions. Darkwood tables are set up simply in quality modern style, and Shay's well-balanced menus offer plenty of treats, including a strong vegetarian option and delicious starters, which might include a sophisticated chicken and smoked duck terrine. Menus are admirably seasonal so, for example, comforting cuisine gran'mère dishes like pot-roasted lamb and delicious beef cassoulet with root vegetables are offered in the colder months. Accomplished cooking, caring staff, great atmosphere and fair prices should ensure that this restaurant does well. **Directions:** Situated near the M1 south of Drogheda.

Enfield
HOTEL

Marriott Johnstown House Hotel

Enfield, Co Meath **Tel 046 954 0000**
Email: info@johnstonhouse.com Web: www.johnstonhouse.com

féile bia This recently developed hotel and spa is close to the motorway, but it has a carefully restored mid-18th century house at its heart and something of its country house atmosphere lives on. Although the original house is only a small part of the hotel, it is the focal point and an unusually fine feature is a drawing room with a ceiling by the renowned Francini brothers, who were responsible for some of Ireland's finest plasterwork in great houses of the time. The Guide's most recent visit coincided with major changes at the hotel and it was not at its best. However, it is a pleasing and well-appointed place to stay and, given the recent appointment of a new General Manager with previous experience at the renowned Sheen Falls Lodge in Co Kerry, improvements can confidently be expected. Conference/banqueting (900/500). Spa. Garden, walking; golf nearby. **Rooms 126** (1 presidential suite, 4 suites, 8 junior suites, 10 no smoking rooms, 4 disabled). B&B about €90pps, ss about €45. Lift. 24 hr room service. Amex, Diners, MasterCard, Visa, Laser.

Navan B&B

Killyon House

Dublin Road Navan Co Meath **Tel: 046 907 1224** Fax: 046 907 2766
Email: info@killyonguesthouse.ie Web: www.killyonguesthouse.ie

You couldn't miss Michael and Sheila Fogarty's modern guesthouse, with its striking array of colourful flowers and hanging baskets. Furnished with antiques, with modern double-glazing to reduce the noise of traffic, it has gardens leading down to the banks of the Boyne, King the back of the house unexpectedly tranquil, and the dining room overlooks the river, giving guests the added interest of spotting wildlife, sometimes including otters and stoats, along the bank from the window. The Fogartys are extremely hospitable hosts, rooms are very comfortable and nothing (even preparing a very early breakfast) is too much trouble. There's also a separate guests' sitting room and, although they are too close to the restaurants of Navan to make evening meals a viable option, they do a particularly good breakfast - and, of course, the Fogartys will direct you to the best local restaurant for your needs. Children welcome (under 5 free in parents' room; cots available without charge, baby sitting arranged). No pets. Garden, walking; fishing. Parking **Rooms 6** (4 shower only, all no smoking). Room service (limited hours). B&B about €40 pps, ss about €10. Open all year except Christmas.

Kilmessan HOTEL

Station House Hotel

Kilmessan Co Meath **Tel: 046 902 5239** Fax: 046 902 558
Email: info@thestationhousehotel.com Web: www. thestationhousehotel.com

féile bia The Slattery family's unique establishment is an old railway junction, which was closed in 1963, and all the various buildings were converted to a make an hotel of character. It is an interesting and unusual place to visit, with lovely gardens, and makes a good base for buisness, or for exploring this fascinating county. The restaurant attracts diners from a wide area - their traditional Sunday lunch is especially renowned (L&D daily, except Sat L). Conference/banqueting (350/180). Children welcome. **Rooms 20** (1 suite, 1 executive, 20 no-smoking, 2 disabled). B&B about €95, ss €25. Amex, Diners, MasterCard, Visa. **Directions:** Follow signs from Dunshaughlin.

COUNTY MONAGHAN

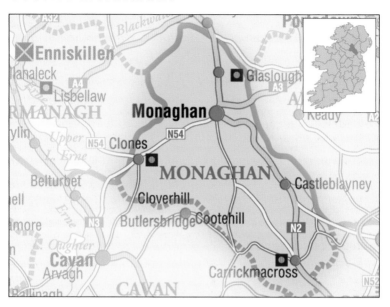

Carrickmacross
☆ 🌎 HOTEL/RESTAURANT

Nuremore Hotel & Country Club

Carrickmacross Co Monaghan
Tel: 042 966 1438 Fax: 042 966 1853
Email: nuremore@eircom.net Web: www.nuremore.com

féile bia This fine owner-managed country hotel just south of Carrickmacross is set in a parkland estate, with its own 18-hole golf course, and serves the sporting, leisure and business requirements of a wide area very well. As you go over the little bridge ("Beware - ducks crossing") and the immaculately maintained hotel and golf club open up before you, worldly cares seem to recede - this is a place you can get fond of. The hotel invariably gives a good impression on arrival and this sense of care and maintenance is continued throughout. Spacious, comfortably arranged public areas and generous bedrooms with views over the gardens and lakes are regularly refurbished. It would make an excellent base to explore this little known area - and there is plenty to do on site. The superb country club has a full leisure centre and a wide range of related facilities - including a gymnasium and spa - and there are conference and meeting rooms for every size of gathering, with state-of-the-art audio-visual equipment available. Conference/banqueting (600/400); business centre, secretarial services on request, video conferencing. Leisure centre, swimming pool, spa; beauty salon; golf (18), fishing, walking, tennis, garden; snooker. Children welcome (cots available, €13; baby sitting arranged). No pets. **Rooms 72** (7 junior suites, 11 executive, 5 family, 42 no smoking). 24 hr room service. B&B €130 pps, ss €50. *Short breaks offered, including spa and golf breaks; details on application. Open all year. **Restaurant:** Although not aspiring to fashionable decor, the restaurant is well-appointed in a fairly formal country house style, with generous white-clothed tables and a couple of steps dividing the window area and inner tables, allowing everybody to enjoy the view over golf course and woodland. Not only is The Restaurant at Nuremore well established as the leading restaurant in the area, but the head chef, Raymond McArdle, has earned a national reputation for the hotel, which is now on the must-visit destination list for discerning travellers in Ireland. Proprietress Julie Gilhooly has lent every possible support to this talented protegé since his arrival here in 2000, and his spacious, state-of the art kitchen is the envy of chefs throughout the country. Raymond sources ingredients meticulously, using local produce as much as possible in top rank daily set lunch and dinner menus, a separate vegetarian menu, a 'grown-up' children's menu, and an evening à la carte. Recent visits by the Guide have invariably confirmed the consistent excellence and innovativeness of the cooking, seen in perfectly executed and well-flavoured dishes like an innovative starter of West Cork tuna with red charred salad, braised baby artichokes, crisp ventrèche, citrus & soy dressing. From a choice of six or seven equally appealing main courses on the dinner menu, dishes like roast Wexford sea scallops with sautéed cèpe, creamed cauli-flower, organic spinach, truffle & chive vie with other house specialities such as a glorious celebration of pork - sauté fillet of black pig, with crisp spiced belly, braised ham hock & parsley, with choucroûte, apple chutney & Calvados jus. Everything, it seems, is similarly impressive - and, on the dessert menu, difficult choices must be made between half a dozen equally desirable and beautifully presented dishes. A selection of French and Irish cheeses comes with a walnut and apricot brioche - and wonderful petits fours are served with cappuccino or espresso. This is exceptional cooking and, under the supervision of restaurant manager Frank Trutet, service is in line with the high standard of food. There's many a treat in store on the extensive and well-organised wine list, which includes a good house wine selection and a further Sommelier Recommendation in the €30-60 bracket, an unusually wide choice of dessert wines and half bottles, a fair number of magnums and a menu of Caterède armagnacs going back to 1920. This is a restaurant offering outstanding value for money, especially at lunch time. *Raymond McArdle was the Guide's Chef of the Year in 2005. **Seats 100** (private room, 50). Air conditioning. L Sun-Fri, 12.30-2.30; D daily 6.30-9.30 (Sun to 9). Set L €25 (Set Sun L, €30); Set D €48 (Vegetarian Menu about €25, Children's Menu €17.50); Prestige Menu €80. House wine from €26; sc discretionary. Closed L Sat. Open all year. Amex, Diners, MasterCard, Visa, Laser. **Directions:** Just south of Carrickmacross, 55 miles from Dublin on N2 ot take M1 from Dublin and turn off at Ardee/Derry exit.

Clones

 HISTORIC HOUSE

Hilton Park
Clones Co Monaghan
Tel: 047 56007
Email: mail@hiltonpark.ie Web: www.hiltonpark.ie

Once described as a "capsule of social history" because of their collection of family portraits and memorabilia going back 250 years or more, Johnny and Lucy Madden's wonderful 18th century mansion is set in beautiful countryside, amidst 200 acres of woodland and farmland. With lakes, Pleasure Grounds and a Lovers' Walk to set the right tone, the house is magnificent in every sense and the experience of visiting it a rare treat. Johnny and Lucy are natural hosts and, as the house and its contents go back for so many gener-

ations, there is a strong feeling of being a privileged family guest as you wander through grandly-proportioned, beautifully furnished rooms. Four-posters and all the unselfconscious comforts that make for a very special country house stay are part of the charm, but as visitors from all over the world have found, it's the warmth of Johnny and Lucy's welcome that lends that extra magic. The gardens are also of particular interest - formal gardens have recently been restored to their former glory and Lucy, an enthusiastic organic gardener and excellent cook, supplies freshly harvested produce for meals in the house, while other ingredients are carefully sourced from trusted suppliers of organic and free-range products. Dinner for residents is served in a beautiful dining room overlooking the gardens and lake - and memorable breakfasts are taken downstairs in the Green Room next morning. This is exceptional hospitality, with an Irish flavour and, in recognition, Hilton Park was selected for our International Hospitality Award in 1999. Not suitable for children under 8 (except babies under 1 year, free in parents' room, cot available), playroom for older children. Pets allowed by arrangement. Gardens, boating, fishing (own lake), walking, cycling. Golf nearby. * Self catering accommodation also available - details on inquiry. * Hilton Park is available for group bookings - family celebrations, small weddings and small conferences. **Rooms 6** (all en-suite & no smoking). B&B €125 pps, ss €40 (children 8-14, 50% disc). Residents D Tue-Sat, €55 at 8 pm (Fri, 8.30); please give 24 hours notice.Interesting short wine list; house wine €20/23. SC discretionary. Closed - none specifically, please ring ahead during off-season. MasterCard, Visa. **Directions:** 3 miles south of Clones on Scotshouse Road.

Glaslough

🏛️ 👁️ CASTLE/RESTAURANT

Castle Leslie

Glaslough Co Monaghan **Tel: 047 88100** Fax: 047 88256
Email: info@castleleslie.com Web: www.castleleslie.com

téile bia During the three centuries that this extraordinary place has been in the Leslie family it has changed remarkably little - and its fascinating history intrigues guests as much as the eccentricity of Castle Leslie as they find it today. Once inside the massive front door (guarded by family dogs who snooze in beds flanking the stone steps) there is no reception desk, just a welcoming oak-panelled hall (and afternoon tea in the drawing room), and there are no phones, television sets or clocks in the rooms, although concessions to the 20th century have been made in the form of generous heating and plentiful hot water. The bedrooms are all different, furnished and decorated around a particular era, with en-suite bathrooms a feature in their own right with huge baths, wacky showers and outrageous toilets, all done in a tongue-in-cheek style, reflecting the family's eccentric history and the wonders of Victorian plumbing. In a charming reverse of circumstances, the family lives in the servants' wing, so guests can enjoy the magnificence of the castle to the full it has all the original furniture and family portraits. The estate has wonderful walks, and pike fishing; boating and picnic lunches on the estate are available by arrangement. Due to the nature of the castle (and the fact that the Leslies see it as a wonderful refuge from the outside world for adults) this is not a suitable place to bring children. However, children are very welcome at the Hunting Lodge & Castle Leslie Equestrian Centre, which is just inside the castle gates; various equestrian programmes are offered and accommodation is more reasonably priced. There is also an informal restaurant at the Hunting Lodge, which is open to non-residents. Despite the extreme eccentricity suggested by details such as the answering machine ("please leave your message after the (scream)", this is actually a professionally run business and a little more 'hotel-like' than the publicity suggests. Cookery School. Conferences/banqueting (60/98). Gardens, walking, fishing, tennis. No children (except at Hunting Lodge). Pets allowed by arrangement. Garden, walking, fishing, equestrian. **Rooms 20** (3 suites; 5 ground floor, all no smoking). Turndown service; no room service; no lift. B&B €135pps, ss €35; 2-night bookings only at weekends. [Hunting Lodge: B&B €75 pps, ss €25]. Short breaks offered, including Christmas at the castle, or equestrian Christmas breaks, at the Hunting Lodge. Open all year. **Restaurant:** The dining experience is a high point of any visit to Castle Leslie and non-residents are welcome to come for dinner, by reservation. It is all done in fine old style with pre-dinner drinks in the drawing room (or the Fountain Garden in summer) and dinner, which is served in rooms including the original dining room, unchanged for over a century, by waitresses wearing Victorian uniforms. However, despite the obvious oddities of faded grandeur - tables with a slight list, chairs and sofas which have long since lost their stuffing - Noel McMeel, executive head chef since 2000, is essentially offering a restaurant dining experience rather than a country house dinner; the list of signature dishes is quite extensive and includes freshly smoked Irish salmon, with black pepper, sea salt, lavender honey, mustard, chive cream and basil oil - served with a glass of Madfish unwooded Chardonnay - and roasted shank of sprig lamb with traditional Irish champ, roasted vegetables & rosemary jus. Separate vegetarian menu available. Many entertaining wine and food events are held during the year - contact the Castle for details and the Castle Leslie range of preserves and speciality foods is available from the castle and Brown Thomas, in Dublin. **Seats 70.** Reservations required. D daily 6-9; Set D €52 (Gourmet Menu €57, 5 course Eclectic Menu €60), Vegetarian Menu also available. House wine from €20.50. Amex, MasterCard, Visa, Laser. **Directions:** 10 mins from Monaghan Town: Monaghan-Armagh road-Glaslough.

COUNTY OFFALY

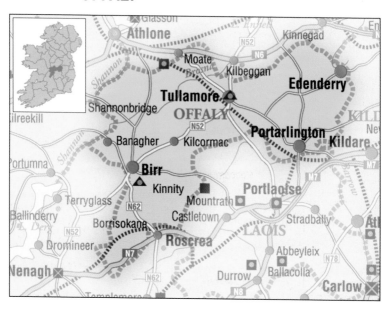

Birr
🏺 RESTAURANT/PUB

The Thatch Bar & Restaurant

Crinkle Birr Co Offaly **Tel: 0509 20682** Fax: 0509 21847
Email: thethatchcrinkle@eirom.net

This characterful little thatched pub and restaurant just outside Birr shows just how good a genuine, well-run country pub with imaginative, freshly cooked food can be. Des Connole, proprietor since 1991, has achieved a well-earned reputation for the immaculate maintenance and atmosphere of the pub, and for good food - in the restaurant, where both set menus and an à la carte are offered, and for imaginative bar food. Expect a mixture of traditional dishes such as ever-popular sirloin steaks (with garlic mash, braised wild mushrooms & rosemary jus) and more unusual things plenty of seafood for a midland restaurant, and exotics like ostrich (which is farmed in Ireland) and kangaroo; local produce is there as well, of course, in a house speciality of apricot & spinach stuffed pork fillet with a light creamy Irish whiskey sauce, for example, and there are some vegetarian options. Good food and warm hospitality make this one of the best eating places in the area. Children welcome. Parking. **Seats 50** (private room, 15-20). D 6.30-9.30 daily, Set D about €37, also à la carte; L Sun-12.30 & 2.30; Set Sun L about €20; early evening bar menu Mon-Sat 5-7.30 (except Jul-Aug), à la carte; house wine about €18; SC discretionary. Bar meals Mon-Sat, 12.30-3.30 & 5-7.30. Toilets wheelchair accessible. Restaurant closed D Sun, establishment closed 25 Dec, Good Fri. Diners, MasterCard, Visa, Laser. **Directions:** 1 mile from Birr (Roscrea side).

Tullamore
🅝🅥 BAR/RESTAURANT

The Wolftrap

William Street Tullamore Co Offaly **Tel: 0506 23374**

The brainchild of Gina Murphy and her husband Padraig McLoughlin (previously of the well-known bar and restaurant, Crockets on the Quay, in Ballina, Co Mayo, which is still run by members of the family), this large bar and 'informal fine dining' restaurant is named after a mountain in the nearby Slieve Blooms (the border between Laois and Offaly is at its peak), and occupies a large town centre building near the harbour, which they have renovated and furnished with flair. With its warm atmosphere, long opening hours, imaginative menus and great service, it's the in place - and head chef Ronan Fox's consistently good cooking (a judicious mixture of traditional and contemporary) is sure to hit the spot. The stylish first floor restaurant opened shortly before we went to press and, with food and service to match that in the bar downstairs was an immediate success. Traditional music every Tuesday (Padraig and Ronan are both musicians). Late bar with DJ Fri & Sat. Bar L 12-3 (light snacks 3-5), evening bar menu 5-8.30. Restaurant D 6-10.30 daily.

COUNTY ROSCOMMON

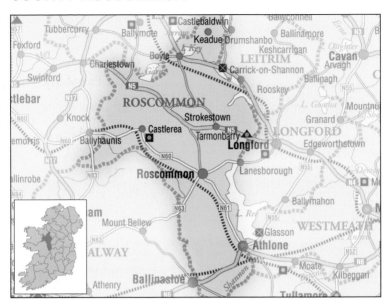

Castlerea
🏛 COUNTRY HOUSE

Clonalis House

Castlerea Co Roscommon **Tel: 094 962 0014**
Fax: 094 962 0014 Email: clonalis@iol.ie Web: www.clonalis.com

Standing on the land that has been the home of the O'Conors of Connacht for 1,500 years, this 45-roomed Victorian Italianate mansion may seem a little daunting on arrival, but it's magic - and the hospitable owners, Pyers and Marguerite O'Conor-Nash, enjoy sharing their rich and varied history with guests, who are welcome to browse through their fascinating archive. Amazing heirlooms include a copy of the last Brehon Law judgment (handed down about 1580) and also Carolan's Harp. Everything is on a huge scale: reception rooms are all very spacious, with lovely old furnishings and many interesting historic details, bedrooms have massive four poster and half tester beds and bathrooms to match and the dining room is particularly impressive, with a richly decorated table to enhance Marguerite's home cooking. Clonalis House is set amid peaceful parklands and is a good base from which to explore counties Roscommon, Galway, Mayo and Sligo. * Two attractive self-catering cottages are also offered, in the courtyard; details on application. A 10% reduction is offered for stays of three or more nights. Horse riding, fishing, shooting and golf (9) are all nearby. Unsuitable for children under 12 years. No pets. **Rooms 4** (3 ensuite, 1 with private bathroom; all no smoking). Garden, walking. Golf nearby. B&B €85 pps, ss €20. Residents D Tue-Sat, €40 (24 hrs notice required); wines about €20. (D not available Sun or Mon.) Closed Oct-mid Apr. MasterCard, Visa, Laser. **Directions:** N60, west of Castlerea.

Tarmonbarry
♟ BAR/RESTAURANT

Keenans Bar & Restaurant

Tarmonbarry (via Clondra) Co Roscommon **Tel: 043 26052**
Fax: 043 26198 Email: info@keenans.ie Web: www.keenans.ie

Just beside the bridge over the Shannon in Tarmonbarry, this well-run bar and restaurant is a favourite watering hole for river folk and makes a great place to break a journey between Dublin and the north-west. The bar is comfortably set up for food and informal meals - mostly quite traditional, but with more international influences in the more expensive evening dishes - are served all day; open sandwiches on home-made wholemeal or soda bread, toasted sandwiches, salads and scones with jam & cream are typical, plus half a dozen daily specials (including specialities such as smoked fish casserole and bacon & cabbage at lunch, perhaps, and more elaborate dishes like roast half duckling on an orange & redcurrant stuffing with a plum & sherry sauce in the evening). A la carte menus are similar in tone but more extensive - wholesome, hearty fare that pleases all age groups; the steak sandwich (served with onions, chips, garlic butter & home-made horseradish sauce) is not to be missed - while the set dinner menu is a little more formal. Good unpretentious food and cheerful, efficient service keep happy customers coming back. Restaurant seats 30. Food served daily 12.30-8.30; L 12.30-2.30, D 6.30-8.30. D A la C, Set Sun L €23.95. House wine €18.95. Restaurant closed D Sun. Establishment closed 25 Dec, Good Fri. Amex, MasterCard, Visa, Laser. **Directions:** On N5, west of Longford town.

COUNTY SLIGO

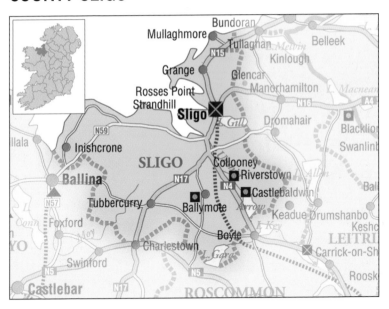

Ballymote
🏛️ ◉ COUNTRY HOUSE

Temple House
Ballymote Co Sligo
Tel: 071 918 3329 Fax: 071 918 3808
Email: stay@templehouse.ie Web: www.templehouse.ie

One of Ireland's most unspoilt old houses, this is a unique place - a Georgian mansion situated in 1,000 acres of farm and woodland, overlooking the original lakeside castle which was built by the Knights Templar in 1200 A.D. The Percevals have lived here since 1665 and the house was redesigned and refurbished in 1864 - some of the furnishings date back to that major revamp. Roderick and Helena Perceval have recently taken over from Roderick's parents, Sandy and Deb but, although there are ongoing improvements, there are no major changes envisaged. The whole of the house has retained its old atmosphere and, in addition to central heating, has log fires to cheer the enormous rooms. Spacious bedrooms are furnished with old family furniture (some also have some modern additions) and bathrooms are gradually being upgraded - not an easy task in a house of this age, but a high pressure water system has now been installed in most of them. Guests have the use of an elegant sitting room with open fires, and evening meals are served (every day except Sunday or Wednesday) in the very beautiful dining room and are a treat to look forward to, based on seasonal produce from the estate and other local suppliers. A typically delicious menu might include: smoked salmon vol au vents with a beurre blanc sauce, pork medallions in a brandy & apple sauce, with garden vegetables, and praline & honey ice cream with a blackcurrant coulis and roasted hazelnuts; there's always an Irish cheeseboard too - and home-made fudge with coffee in the Morning Room. Traditional Irish music and dancing sessions are often held nearby, in Ballintubber. Children welcome (babies free in parents' room; cots available, baby sitting arranged). No pets in the house. **Rooms 6** (5 en-suite, 2 shower only, 1 with private bathroom, all no smoking). B&B €85pps, ss €20. Residents D €42, 7.30pm (book by 1pm, not available Sun or Wed); house wine €14. Children's tea 6.30pm; SC discretionary. *Golf nearby, at Rosses Point and Strandhill - short breaks available. Closed 1 Dec-1 Apr. MasterCard, Visa, Laser. **Directions:** Signposted on N17, 7 miles south of N4 junction.

Castlebaldwin
🏨★ 🍷 👁 HOTEL/RESTAURANT

Cromleach Lodge

Castlebaldwin via Boyle Co Sligo
Tel: 071 **916 5155** Fax: 071 916 5455
Email: info@cromleach.com Web: www.cromleach.com

téile bia Quietly situated in the hills just above Lough Arrow, Christy and Moira Tighe's small hotel enjoys one of the finest views in Ireland - and it makes a luxurious retreat for the most discerning of guests. Cromleach is rightly renowned for exceptionally high standards of both food and accommodation - and, most importantly, the Tighe family and their staff have the magic ingredient of genuine hospitality, doing everything possible to ensure comfort and relaxation for their guests. Spacious bedrooms have an emphasis on comfort rather than fashion, and are thoughtfully furnished, with king-size and single beds, seating areas overlooking the lough with easy chairs to relax in, and well-planned bathrooms with lots of luxurious little extras and hospitality, housekeeping and attention to detail are all outstanding. The area around Cromleach is beautiful and unspoilt, and the Tighes like nothing better than to introduce guests to the many places of interest and activities nearby but, for many, just being here is more than enough. Small conferences (20). Children welcome (under 3 free in parents' room, cot available without charge, baby sitting arranged). Pets permitted by arrangement. Garden; walking; fishing. Golf nearby. **Rooms 10** (2 junior suites, 6 no-smoking). Room service (limited hours). Turndown service. B&B about €165 pps, ss about €45. Short breaks and off-season value breaks available. Closed Nov-Jan. **Restaurant:** Dinner is the high point of every guest's visit to this special place. The restaurant is arranged as a series of rooms, creating a number of individual dining areas for varying numbers of people - a system which tends to work better for groups than couples dining alone. Crisp linen, modern silver and crystal, fine china and fresh seasonal flowers - provide a beautifully understated setting for memorable meals. Moira Tighe and her personally trained kitchen team work superbly well together and the cooking style is modern Irish (without being slavishly fashionable), but it is Moira's scrupulously careful sourcing of ingredients, pride in local produce and outstanding cooking that makes this restaurant so special. Menus offered include an 8-course Tasting Menu ('intense flavours... light portions', for residents only) and a 5-course table d'hôte. Both menus are changed daily and always include some of the many house specialities - a simple, deeply-flavoured main course of marinated lamb fillet with creamed organic lentils & rosemary jus is typical. The dessert menu comes with helpful suggestions of dessert wines and ports to accompany: everything, from the first little amuse-bouche to the last petit four with your coffee is invariably a treat - and, as in all aspects of this wonderful place, service is flawless. Moira, who was the Guide's Chef of the Year in 2000, is an exceptional, totally dedicated chef - and well-trained, friendly, staff provide excellent service to complement the high standards of the kitchen. **Rooms 10.** Children welcome. Reservations required. **Seats 50** (private rooms, 4-24). D only, 6.30-8.30 daily. Set D about €65, also Residents' Tasting Menu; house wines from abou €24; sc discretionary. Toilets wheelchair accessible. Closed Nov-Jan. Amex, MasterCard, Visa, Laser. **Directions:** Signposted from Castlebaldwin on the N4.

Riverstown
🏨 COUNTRY HOUSE

Coopershill House

Riverstown Co Sligo Tel: 071 **916 5108** Fax: 071 916 5466
Email: ohara@coopershill.com Web: www.coopershill.com

téile bia Undoubtedly one of the most delightful and superbly comfortable Georgian houses in Ireland, this sturdy granite mansion was built to withstand the rigours of a Sligo winter but its numerous chimneys suggest there is warmth to be found within the stern grey walls. Peacocks wander elegantly on the croquet lawns (and roost in the splendid trees around the house at night) making this lovely place, home of the O'Hara family since it was built in 1774, a particularly perfect country house. Nothing escapes Brian O'Hara's disciplined eye: in immaculate order from top to bottom, the house not only has the original 18th century furniture but also some fascinating features, notably an unusual Victorian free-standing rolltop bath complete with fully integrated cast-iron shower 'cubicle' and original brass rail and fittings, all in full working order. Luxurious rooms are wonderfully comfortable and have phones and tea/coffee making facilities. Lindy runs the house and kitchen with the seamless hospitality born of long experience, and creates deliciously wholesome, country house home cooking which is served in their lovely dining room (where the family silver is used with magnificent insouciance even at breakfast). As well as their own neatly maintained vegetable garden, the O'Hara's have a deer farm: pot roast leg of venison with red wine is a house speciality. A surprisingly extensive wine list offers no less than six house wines - and has many treats in store. Coopershill is well placed for exploring this unspoilt area - and makes a good base for golfers too, with several championship courses, including Rosses Point within easy range. Tennis, cycling, boating, fishing, garden, croquet; snooker room. Children welcome (under 2 free in parents' room; cots available without charge, baby sitting arranged). No pets. **Rooms 8** (7 en-suite, 1 shower only, 1 private bathroom). Turndown service. B&B €111 pps, ss €19. Dining Room **Seats 16-20.** D 8.30 daily (non-residents welcome by reservation); Set D €40-€45, house wines from €14.50; sc discretionary.* 10% discount on stays of 3+ days. Closed end Oct-1 Apr. (Off season house parties of 12-16 people welcome.) Amex, Diners, MasterCard, Visa, Laser. **Directions:** Signposted from N4 at Drumfin crossroads.

Rosses Point

Austie's

👁 ATMOSPHERIC PUB

Rosses Point Co Sligo **Tel: 071 917 7020 / 917 7111**

This 200 year-old pub overlooking Sligo Bay has always been associated with a seafaring family and the old bar is full of fascinating nautical memorabilia. It has a very appealing ship-shape feeling about it and friendly people behind the bar, which was extended through to a very agreeable adjoining room recently, adding to the existing conservatory style dining room for the service of food - which is well above the usual bar food standard. Naturally enough, local seafood stars on menus, in starters like poached mussels in cream & garlic, for example, or delicious battered squid rings with sweet chilli sauce, and main courses like updated battered cod, or pan-fried John Dory in white wine sauce. There are lots of other choices, too including ever-popular steaks - expect wholesome food, with traditional appeal and a little gentle updating. A deck area looking across to Oyster Island was added quite recently - a pleasant spot for a sunny day. Traditional music at weekends. **Seats 60.** Children welcome to 9pm. Food served daily 5.30-9.30 in summer (also L Sun, 12.30-3.30). Bar Menu from 3pm. Times may vary off-season (Sept-Mar). A la carte menu; house wine from about €15; sc discretionary. Phone ahead to check opening off season. Closed 25 Dec & Good Fri. MasterCard, Visa, Laser. **Directions:** On the seafront.

Sligo

Atrium Café

🍴 € CAFÉ

The Niland Model Arts Centre The Mall Sligo Co Sligo
Tel: 071 914 1418 Email: info@modelart.ie Web: www.modelart.ie

If you are planning a visit to Sligo town, the Model Arts Centre is well worth a visit and it could make sense to arrange your day around a break here. Well-known chef Brid Torrades runs the delightful daytime restaurant, an open-plan café that spills out into the bright atrium area of the gallery - stylish, yet accessible, the perfect spot for seriously tempting simple, food with an emphasis on good quality and flavour: superb soups, for example, delicious omelettes or tuna & black olive bruschetta (both prettily presented with herbs and leaves from Rod Alston's Organic Centre, nearby) and hot daily blackboard specials. Pretty compôtes topped with cream - rhubarb, blackberry - are simply delicious, and there's good coffee too. * Another venue is planned quite soon. Parking is available, up the steep hill, behind the gallery. Parking (up the steep hill, behind the gallery). Meals: Tue-Sat 10-5 (lunch 12.15-3), also Sun Brunch 11-4; Veg menu avail. Closed Mon, 23 Dec-4 Jan, Easter weekend. **No Credit Cards. Directions:** Sligo town centre; prominent building on The Mall.

Sligo
Ⓔ RESTAURANT

Montmartre

Market Yard Sligo Co Sligo **Tel: 071 916 9901**
Fax: 071 914 0065 ӀEmail: montmartre@eircom.net

French run and staffed, this is the area's leading restaurant and has a strong local following, so reservations are strongly advised, especially at weekends. Although not big, there is a little bar area that doubles as reception and a bright and airy feeling, with potted palms, white crockery and smartly uniformed staff all emphasising the French style. Proprietor-chef Stéphane Magaud's varied menus offer imaginative French cuisine in a light, colourful style with local produce featuring in some dishes, especially seafood - Lissadell oysters and mussels, for instance, also lobster which is great value and served with an unusual saffron hollandaise; there may also be game in season, and there will always be imaginative vegetarian dishes . Sound cooking, attractive presentation and reasonable prices have brought this restaurant many friends. The wine list, which is mostly French with a token gesture to the New World, includes an unusually good selection of half bottles and wines by the glass. An early dinner menu offers exceptional value. **Seats 50.** Children welcome. Air conditioning. Toilets wheelchair accessible. D Tue-Sun, 5-11. Early D €15 (5-7pm), D a la carte. House wines from €18. Closed Mon, Christmas, 9-27 Jan. Amex, Diners, MasterCard, Visa, Laser, Switch. **Directions:** 150 yards from Hawks Well Theatre & Tourist Office.

Sligo
🏨 ◉ HOTEL

Radisson SAS Hotel Sligo

Ballincar Rosses Point Sligo Co Sligo
Tel: 071 914 0008 Fax: 071 914 0006
Email: info.sligo@RadissonSAS.com Web: www.radissonsas.com

This fine contemporary hotel out of town, towards Rosses Point, is not especially attractive from the road but, once inside the door it's a different story as it has that lovely light and appealing atmosphere that the new Radisson hotels seem to achieve especially well, and a huge welcoming flower arrangement in the large foyer to win over any waverers. Staff are keen to make guests feel at home, and clearly take pride in the hotel - and it's easy to see why. Simple lines and classy contemporary decor in quality materials and warm tones create a pleasing ambience, without distracting from the hotel's great attraction - the views over Sligo Bay. Bedrooms are well-sized and very comfortable, with all the facilities now expected of new hotels (TV options, voicemail, safe, mini bar, iron/ironing boar as well as trouser press, and so on), and there are various room combinations offered, including family rooms. **The Classsiebawn Restaurant**, which is an open-plan dining area along the front of the hotel (and gains in smart design and, especially, views anything it loses in lack of privacy) is an especially pleasant place for a weekend lunch, or dinner on a long summer evening, when the views can be enjoyed to the full. Conference/banqueting (900/590); business centre, video-conferencing on request. Leisure centre, swimming pool, spa. Golf nearby. **Rooms 132** (3 suites, 7 junior suites, 18 executive rooms, 6 disabled). 24 hr room service. Turndown service offered, Children welcome (under 17 free in parents' room; cots available without charge, baby sitting arranged). B&B €75pps, ss €20. Classiebawn Restaurant: D daily 7-10.30, L sat & Sun 12.30-2.30. Set 2/3 course D €32/40; set L from €15.50. Set Sun L €23.50. House wine, €20. Bar meals also available, 12-7 daily. No SC.* Short breaks offered; golf breaks are a speciality (3 championship courses nearby). Open all year. Amex, MasterCard, Visa. **Directions:** From Sligo town, follow signs for Rosses Point; the hotel is on the right after 2 miles.

COUNTY TIPPERARY

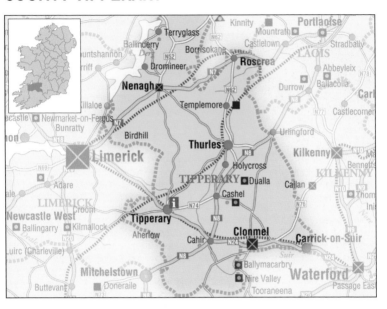

Ballinderry

Ⓔ RESTAURANT

Brocka-on-the-Water Restaurant

Kilgarvan Quay Ballinderry Nenagh Co Tipperary
Tel: 067 22038 Fax: 067 22955

Anthony and Anne Gernon's almost-waterside restaurant has attracted a following disproportionate to its size over the years and, although it has been extended at the back to include a high-ceilinged conservatory style room which opens onto a garden patio, it is still basically carved out of the lower half of a family home that is by no means huge. The atmosphere is very much a "proper restaurant" - yet with all the warmth of welcome that the family situation implies. There's a reception room with an open fire, comfy chairs, interesting things to read and look at (Anthony's a dab hand at wood carving) - and aperitifs served in generous wine glasses, while you read a menu that promises good things to come in the adjoining dining room and conservatory. Guests arriving in daylight will notice hens clucking around a garden well-stocked with fruit and vegetables - promising the best of all possible beginnings for your dinner. Seasonal menus depend on availability of course - if you are here in late spring, for example, you might be offered avocado pear with local goats cheese, yoghurt, capers & wild garlic - but there are always some specialities retained by popular demand, including Cooleeney cheese croquettes with home-made chutney (Cooleeney is one of Ireland's finest cheeses, made by Breda Maher on the family farm near Thurles). A late summer menu might include pork medallion in a herb crust with plum & cranberry - and there will always be home-grown vegetables in season. **Seats 30** (private room, 30). Air conditioning. Toilets wheelchair accessible. Reservations strongly advised. D 6.30-9 Mon-Sat in summer (call to check opening times off season). Set D about €40, also à la carte and a Vegetarian Menu. SC discretionary. House wine about €22. Closed Sun. **No Credit Cards. Directions:** Lough Derg drive, half way between Nenagh and Portumna.

Cahir

☆ BAR/RESTAURANT

Gannons Above The Bell

Pearse Street Cahir Co Tipperary **Tel: 052 45911**
Fax: 052 45531 Web: www.gannons-restaurant.com

Dermot Gannon has earned a loyal following at his attractive restaurant over The Bell pub, in a side street off the square in Cahir. Fresh flowers and a menu board at the door lead diners under an arch beside the pub, and upstairs to a restaurant of character on two floors: exposed brickwork, good lighting and smartly-appointed white linen-clad tables create a good first impression, quickly confirmed by a warm welcome and promptly presented menus which showcase local and specialist products: O'Briens potatoes, Delahunty mushrooms, Slaney Valley lamb, Grubb's cheeses and Connemara Smokehouse smoked salmon are all among those highlighted - and there is a mouthwatering choice of contemporary dishes to choose from. Seven starters, for example, include house favourites like baked Delahunty mushrooms with tomato relish, garlic mayo & Thai barbecue dips, and an aromatic salad of slow-roasted shredded Ballybrado organic pork, with Crozier blue cheese and hoi sin dressing; and, although Gannon's steaks take pride of place among the main courses, local lamb is sure to feature too - served with goats cheese crushed potatoes, petits pois, rosemary gravy and mint jelly. And, while this is really red meat country, a vegetarian dish - pasta with grilled marinated field mushrooms and parmesan cheese, perhaps - actually heads the bill and there will be a couple of fish dishes too. Dermot presents his dishes with style - oriental starters for example, are served in Chinese noodle bowls, and main courses in deep white pasta plates, fully garnished - and everything has great flavour. Portions are extremely generous, so the sweet-toothed should remember to leave room for gorgeous desserts that include a chocolate house speciality worth travelling for (a trio of excellent ganache, chocolate ice cream and chocolate mousse). Staff are pleasant and helpful and - although the standard of service can be uneven - Dermot Gannon is a seriously talented chef offering creative cooking that is worth a journey. It is also very good value for money - and so is a short but well-chosen wine list. * Bar meals downstairs are also supplied by the restaurant, and there is some overlap of menus. Children welcome, but not under 5s after 8pm. **Seats 50** (private room, 25). Reservations advised. D Tue-Sun, from 5.30-9. Early Bird D €26 (5.30-6.30), also A la carte. L Sun Only 12.30-2.30 (seasonal, phoning ahead is advised). Bar meals Tue-Sun, from 5.30. Closed Mon, 2 weeks off-season. House Wine €18. MasterCard, Visa, Laser. **Directions:** Off the town square - signposted.

Cashel

 RESTAURANT

Chez Hans

Moore Lane Cashel Co Tipperary **Tel: 062 61177** Fax: 062 61177

Although many others have since followed suit, the idea of opening a restaurant in a church was highly original when Hans-Peter Matthia did so in 1968. The atmosphere and scale - indeed the whole style of the place - is superb and provides an excellent setting for the fine food which people travel great distances to sample. Hans-Peter's son, Jason (who brought experience in great kitchens like Le Gavroche, La Tante Claire, and Restaurant Marco Pierre White) joined him in the business several years ago and this - together with the more recent opening of their excellent daytime restaurant, **Café Hans**, next door - has brought renewed energy, confirming its status as the leading restaurant in a wide area. Ably assisted by restaurant manager Louise Horgan and a strong kitchen brigade, Jason offers menus that include an early dinner menu which is definitely worth travelling for - with an outstanding choice of about ten excellent dishes on each course, it offers some of the best value to be found in Ireland. The à la carte offers an even wider range including many specialities - their famous cassoulet of seafood (half a dozen varieties of fish and shellfish with a delicate chive velouté sauce) for example, and classics like sole on the bone, imaginative vegetarian dishes - and, of course, the great lamb and beef for which the area is renowned. Finish perhaps with lemon tart and orange curd ice cream, and coffee with home-made chocolates. A wine list strong on classic old world wines offers some treats for the deep-pocketed as well as half a dozen special recommendations under about €25. Booking ahead is essential. **Seats 80** D Tue-Sat, 6-10. Early D 2/3 courses, €23/30 (6-7.30); also à la carte. House wines from €22.50. Closed Sun, Mon.1st week Sep, last 2 weeks Jan. MasterCard, Visa, Laser. **Directions:** First right from N8; at foot of Rock of Cashel.

Clonmel
☆ RESTAURANT

Clifford's Restaurant

29 Thomas Street Clonmel Co Tipperary
Tel: 052 70677 Fax: 052 70676

Michael and Deirdre Clifford's renowned restaurant is now well-established in its new premises in Clonmel, a fine old 3-storey stone building - formerly a CIE coal house - where their precious art collection and many well-earned accolades line the walls. The interior is light and bright, with smartly dressed tables, a chic little bar area - and also a paved area outside the restaurant, which is not just a smoking area, but set up with tables for outdoor dining in fine weather. Michael, who is a classical French chef with Irish influences, is known for the immense care he takes in sourcing his ingredients: meats come from a trusted butcher (Kennedy's of Cahir), organically grown vegetables are supplied by a local grower, and Deirdre's father also supplies home-grown garden produce. Menus offer a wide range of creative dishes, including many specialities which will be familiar to followers of this talented chef - starters will often include Michael's famous gateau of Clonakilty Black Pudding, for example, and among the main courses you may find his roast rack of Tipperary lamb with roasted pear & thyme sauce. And between the various menus offered - which include an extremely keenly priced early dinner, and a Sunday lunch which also offers great value - there are many other treats in store, ranging from an exceptionally good house chowder, to the homely flavours of an excellent beef & stout casserole or Michael's Gourmet Irish Stew, to more sophisticated dishes like gateau of fresh crab with fresh herbs, lemon & vermouth. Luscious desserts include the homely (fresh fruit crumble of the day) and the classic (raspberry torte, with raspberry coulis & fresh cream) and, of course, there are Irish farmhouse cheeses served in peak condition. A small but well-chosen wine list includes some lovely Spanish wines. Children welcome. Toilets wheelchair accessible. **Seats 60** (Private room, 25, outdoor seating 20). Reservations advised. Air conditioning. D Tue-Sun 5-10, Set L Sun, 12.30-4. Value D €18.50 (5-8), Gourmet Menu €48, D also à la carte. Set Sun L €25 (€10 Kids Menu). House wines from €21. SC discretionary (12% added to groups 6+). Pianist Fri-Sat. Closed Mon; Christmas Holiday. MasterCard, Visa, Laser. **Directions:** Around coner from bus & rail station.

Clonmel Area
 FARMHOUSE

Kilmaneen Farmhouse

Ardfinnan Newcastle Clonmel Co Tipperary **Tel: 052 36231**
Fax: 052 36231 Email: kilmaneen@eircom.net Web: www.kilmaneen.com

As neat as a new pin, Kevin & Ber O'Donnell's delightfully situated farmhouse is on a working dairy farm, surrounded by three mountain ranges - the Comeraghs, the Knockmealdowns and the Galtees - and close to the river Suir and the Tar, making it an ideal base for walking and fishing holidays. Kevin is trained in mountain skills and leads walking groups, and trout fishing in the Suir and Tar on the farm is free (hut provided for tying flies, storing equipment and drying waders). It's an old house, but well restored to combine old furniture with modern comforts. Bedrooms are not especially big, but they are very thoughtfully furnished (including tea/coffee facilities and iron/trouser press) and, like the rest of the house, immaculate. There's a great welcome and guests feel at home immediately - especially once they get tucked into Ber's delicious dinners. Don't expect any fancy menus or a wine list (you are welcome to bring your own wine), what you'll get here is real home cooking, based on fresh farm produce: home-produced beef, perhaps, or chicken stuffed with ricotta, spinach & parmesan and wrapped in cured ham, then apple pie for afters, perhaps - and breakfast are equally delicious, with stewed fruits from the garden and home-made breads and preserves as well as lovely porridge or the 'full Irish'. Genuinely hospitable hosts, homely comforts - including a log fire to relax beside after dinner and a large, well-maintained garden, where guests can enjoy the peaceful setting - all add up to a real country break. Kilmaneen was our

Farmhouse of the Year for 2005. Fishing, walking. *Self catering accommodation also available (with option of dinner at the farmhouse). **Rooms 5** (4 shower only, all en-suite & no smoking). B&B €40 pps, ss €5. Children welcome (under 2s free in parents' room, cots available without charge). Pets may be permitted by prior arrangement. Dining room seats 12. Residents' D 7pm except on Sun (must book in advance); Set D €25.00. No SC. Closed 20 Dec-7 Jan. MasterCard, Visa. **Directions:** In Ardfinnan, follow signs at the Hill Bar.

Fethard   # Mobarnane House
🏛 👁 COUNTRY HOUSE   Fethard Co Tipperary **Tel: 052 31962** Fax: 052 31962
Email: info@mobarnanehouse.com   Web: www.mobarnanehouse.com

Approached up a stylish gravel drive with well-maintained grass verges, Richard and Sandra Craik-White's lovely 18th century home has recently been restored to its former glory and makes a wonderfully spacious retreat for guests: the aim is to provide peace and quiet in great comfort, with very personal attention to detail. A large, beautifully furnished drawing room has plenty of comfortable seating for everyone when there's a full house - and the dining room, where Richard's good country cooking is served (usually at a communal table, although separate tables can be arranged on request), is a lovely room; everything served for dinner is freshly prepared on the day, allowing for any preferences mentioned at the time of booking. Accommodation is of the same high standard: all rooms have lovely views and comfortable seating (two have separate sitting rooms), quality bedding and everything needed for a relaxing stay, including tea/coffee making facilities, phones and television - and fresh flowers from the garden. Bathrooms vary somewhat (bedrooms without sitting rooms have bigger bathrooms), but all have quality towels and toiletries. An excellent breakfast gets the day off to a good start - and, as well as being well-placed to explore a large and interesting area blessed with beautiful scenery, an interesting history, local crafts and sports, there is tennis and croquet on site, and lovely lake and woodland walks in the grounds. Not suitable for children under 5 except babies (cot available without charge, baby sitting arranged). Pets by arrangement. **Rooms 4** (2 junior suites, all no smoking). B&B €80 pps, ss €30. Residents' 4-course D 8pm, €45; advance reservation essential. House wine €15. SC discretionary. Closed Nov-Mar. MasterCard, Visa. **Directions:** From Fethard, take Cashel road for 3.5 miles; turn right, signed Ballinure and Thurles; 1.5 miles on left.

Nenagh   # Country Choice Delicatessen & Coffee Bar
🍴 € CAFÉ/RESTAURANT   25 Kenyon Street Nenagh Co Tipperary
Tel: 067 32596 Fax: 067 32648 Web: www.countrychoice.ie

Food-lovers from all over the country plan journeys around a visit to Peter and Mary Ward's unique shop. Old hands head for the little café at the back first, fortifying themselves with simple home-cooked food that reflects a policy of seasonality if the range is small at a particular time of year, so be it. Meats, milk, cream, eggs, butter and flour: "The economy of Tipperary is agricultural and we intend to demonstrate this with a finished product of tantalising smells and tastes." Specialities developed over the years include Cashel Blue and broccoli soup served with their magnificent breads (made with local flours; a new of speciality yeast breads has recently been introduced) savoury and sweet pastry dishes (quiches, fruit tarts) and tender, gently-cooked meat dishes like Irish stew and Hereford beef and Guinness casserole. The shop carries a very wide range of the finest Irish artisan produce, plus a smaller selection of specialist products from further afield, such as olive oil and an unusual range of quality glacé fruits that are in great demand for Christmas baking (they make outstanding Christmas puddings too, for sale in the shop). Specialities that make this place so special include a great terrine, made from the family's saddleback pigs; the preserves - jam (Mary Ward makes 12,000 pots a year!) and home-made marmalade, based on oranges left to caramelise in the Aga overnight, producing a runny but richly flavoured preserve; then there is Peter's passion for cheese. He is one of the country's best suppliers of Irish farmhouse cheeses, which he minds like babies as they ripen and, unlike most shops, only puts on display when they are mature: do not leave without buying cheese. As well as all this, they run regular art exhibitions in the shop, wine courses and poetry readings. Definitely worth a detour. [Country Choice was the winner of our Natural food Award in 2004]. **Seats 40.** Picnic service available. Open all day (9-5.30); L 12-3 daily, à la carte; house wine - any bottle in the shop + €5 corkage; Vegetarian Menu available. Children welcome. Closed Sun, bank hols & Good Fri. MasterCard, Visa, Laser. **Directions:** Centre of town, on left half way down Kenyon Street.

Nenagh Area

🏛️ 🍷 👁️ HOTEL

Coolbawn Quay

Coolbawn Nenagh Co Tipperary **Tel: 067 28158** Fax: 067 28162
Email: info@coolbawnquay.com Web: www.coolbawnquay.com

Spas and retreats are appearing all over Ireland at the moment, but few could rival the beauty of this magic place. This unique resort on the eastern shores of Lough Derg is modelled on the lines of a 19th century Irish village with quietly understated luxurious accommodation in suites and rooms scattered throughout the cottages in the village - with hotel style service throughout, should you require it. The shoreside situation is truly lovely and there is a sense of being very close to the changing moods of nature, partly because the main building - which has a small traditional bar and a country style dining room - is only a few feet from the water, and partly because guests move around from building to building much more than in an ordinary hotel. Rooms are simple in style but furnished with everything you could wish for, including sound systems and - a very nice touch this - a turf-burning stove which is set up in advance, with matches at the ready, so you can have your own real fire whenever you like. The contrasts are wonderful here: whether you want to pamper yourself at the spa, hold a small conference or board meeting - or simply to unwind with style - this unusual village could be the ideal destination. And the inner man will be well looked after too, with excellent cooking by well known chef, Rob Oosterban. This is a romantic location for weddings, which can be held in a luxury banqueting marquee set by the water's edge. [*Coolbawn Quay was our Hideaway of the Year in 2005.] (Small conference/banqueting (40/225); lakeside marquee available for weddings or events. Spa; beauty treatments. Walking, fishing. Pool table. Children welcome (baby sitting arranged). Garden. No pets. Wheelchair accessible. **Rooms 48** (9 suites, 7 shower only, all no smoking). Room service (all day). B&B €95pps, ss €30. *Short / off season breaks offered. Restaurant **Seats 35.** Non residents welcome by reservation if there is room (not suitable for children under 10 after 6pm). D daily, 7-9; Set D €40, also small à la carte menu. Sun L by arrangement, for groups. Bar food daily in high season, 12.30-2,30 (residents & members only); also barbecues. House Wine from €15.95. * Luxury 3 & 4 bed cottages available with hotel-style service Amex, Diners, MasterCard, Visa, Laser. **Directions:** On eastern side of Lough Derg; access from N7.

Roscrea Area

🍷 RESTAURANT

Fiacrí Country House Restaurant & Cookery School

Boulerea Knock Roscrea Co Tipperary
Tel: 0505 43017 Fax: 0505 43018
Email: fiacrihouse@eircom.net Web: www.fiacrihouse.com

 Enda & Ailish Hennessy's lovely country house style restaurant and cookery school is not the easiest place to find (it is sensible to get directions when booking) but, once discovered, what a welcome sight their neat pink-painted farmhouse presents. Enda will be at hand to welcome guests, offering an aperitif beside the fire in the comfortably furnished bar, where you can look over Ailish's five-course menus, which are based on carefully sourced local and Quality Assured ingredients and credit suppliers on the first page. Menus are balanced, to include fish, poultry and vegetarian choices, but local meats are especially good, and large portions of seasonal vegetables are served separately - in

fact, as is to be expected in a farming area, generosity is a key feature here. House specialities include a delicious starter salad of baked Clonakilty black pudding & caramelised apple, and fairly traditional main courses like rack of Tipperary lamb with a pinenut and apricot stuffing, homemade mint sauce & rosemary jus, or the ever-popular grilled sirloin steak Diane, with roasted garlic mash. Like the bar, the restaurant has an open fire, and the style is pleasingly traditional - white linen, mahogany chairs, a warm green and red colour scheme - making a special yet a relaxed setting to enjoy a good meal. From a long list of desserts, you could try the excellent Assorted Dessert Plate - miniature servings of the day's desserts such as hazelnut meringue roulade, apple & summer fruit crumble, strawberry shortcake - or farmhouse cheeses. Caring service enhances the experience, and a compact, informative wine list offers good value. Ailish also offers cookery classes throughout the year. This is a very popular restaurant and advance booking is essential. *Fiacri was selected for our Féile Bia Award in 2004. Wheelchair accessible. **Seats 80.** Reservations required. Not suitable for children under 12. D Wed-Sat, 7-9.15. Set D €47. House wine €18. Full bar licence. Closed Sun, Mon,Tue and 24 Dec-Jan 10. * Cookery classes held Tue night. over a 5 week period (€140pp). In addition 1 day courses (€100) are held at such culinary demanding times as Christmas and Easter. Also BBQ evenings in the summer with Q&A. Classes are intimate and interactive and you get to eat it all after! Accommodation is available locally for the cookery classes. MasterCard, Visa, Laser.
Directions: Roscrea 6.5 miles, Erril 4.5, Templemore 8.

COUNTY WATERFORD

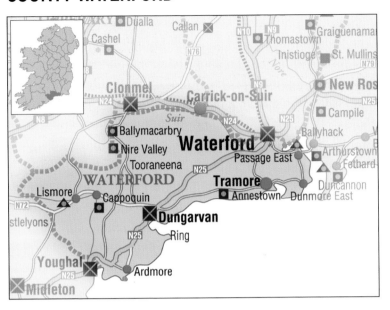

Ardmore
€ RESTAURANT

White Horses Restaurant

Ardmore Co Waterford **Tel: 024 94040**
Fax: 024 94040 Email: whitehorses@eircom.net

téile bia Christine Power and Geraldine Flavin's delightfully bright and breezy café-restaurant on the main street of this famous seaside village is one of those places that changes its character through the day but always has style. They're open for all the little lifts that visitors need through the day - morning coffee, afternoon tea - as well as imaginative lunches (plus their traditional Sunday lunch, which runs all afternoon) and a more ambitious à la carte evening menu. Vegetarian dishes feature on both menus - a pasta dish during the day perhaps, and spinach & mushroom crêpe with toasted brie in the evening - and there's a good balance between traditional favourites like steaks and more adventurous fare: a daytime fish dish could be deep-fried plaice with tartare sauce, for example, while its evening counterpart might be grilled darne Helvick salmon on asparagus, with a wine & cream sauce. Attractive and pleasant to be in - the use of local Ardmore pottery is a big plus on the presentation side, and emphasises the sense of place - this is a friendly, well-run restaurant and equally good for a reviving cuppa and a gateau or pastry from the luscious home-made selection on display, or a full meal. Even when very busy, service is well-organised and efficient. **Seats 50.** Air conditioning. In summer (May-Sep) open: Tue-Sun 11-11; L 12.30-3.30, D 6-10. In winter (Oct-Apr) open weekends only: Fri from 6 pm, Sat 11-11 & Sun 12-6. A la carte except Sun - Set L €25. Licensed; House Wine €117.50; sc discretionary. Closed Mon all year, except bank hols (bank hol opening as Sun), 1 Jan-13 Feb. MasterCard, Visa, Laser. **Directions:** Centre of village.

Ballymacarbry

🏛️🕐👁️ RESTAURANT/GUESTHOUSE

Hanora's Cottage

Nire Valley Ballymacarbry Co Waterford
Tel: 052 36134 Fax: 052 36540
Email: hanorascottage@eircom.net Web: www.hanorascottage.com

The Wall family's gloriously remote country guesthouse is now a very substantial building, yet they still actively nurture the spirit of the ancestral home around which Hanora's is built. This a very special place - equally wonderful for foot-weary walkers, or desk-weary city folk in need of some clear country air and real comfort - and the genuine hospitality of the Wall family is matched by the luxurious accommodation and good food they provide. Comfortably furnished seating areas with sofas and big armchairs provide plenty of room to relax, and the spacious thoughtfully furnished bedrooms all have jacuzzi baths (one especially romantic room is perfect for honeymooners); there's also a spa tub in a conservatory overlooking the garden, with views of the mountains. Overnight guests begin the day with Hanora's legendary breakfast buffet, which was the National Winner of our Irish Breakfast Awards in 2002; it takes some time to get the measure of this feast, so make sure you get up in time to make the most of it. Local produce and exotics (some of which you may not previously have encountered) jostle for space on the beautifully arranged buffet: fruits and freshly squeezed juices (including luscious Crinnaghtaun Apple Juice from Lismore), home-made muesli and porridge... a whole range of freshly-baked breads, including organic and gluten free varieties... local farmhouse cheeses, smoked salmon, home made jams - and all the cooked breakfast options you could wish for. This is truly a gargantuan feast, designed to see you many miles along the hills before you stop for a little packed lunch (prepared that morning) and ultimately return for dinner... Small weddings (40). **Rooms 10** (1 suite, 3 junior suites, all no smoking). Not suitable for children. No pets. B&B from €75 pps. Closed Christmas week. **Restaurant:** One of the best things about Hanora's is that people travel from far and wide to dine here, which adds an extra dimension to the atmosphere. How pleasant to mingle with residents at the fireside, have an aperitif and ponder on Eoin and Judith Wall's imaginative, well-balanced menus - then, difficult choices made, you move through to the restaurant, which overlooks a secluded garden and riverside woodland. Enthusiastic supporters of small suppliers, Eoin and Judith use local produce whenever possible and credit them on the menu - fresh fish from Dunmore East, free range chickens from Stradbally and local cheeses, for example. There's a separate vegetarian dinner menu on request as well as an à la carte which offers about seven dishes on each course, usually including some vegetarian options. Popular dishes include starters of sautéed lambs kidneys on a croustade with mushroom cream and stuffed mushrooms with walnuts, blue cheese & garlic mayonnaise, and main courses including beautifully fresh and accurately cooked fish or, as lamb is so abundant locally, the all-time favourite is roast rack of lamb (served, perhaps, with a delicious mint hollandaise). Desserts include classics like lemon tart with crème anglaise and good home-made ice creams - and, of course, there's always an Irish cheese selection. Not suitable for children under 12. Not suitable for children under 12. **Seats 30/40** D Mon-Sat, 7-9, Set D about €40, also à la carte. House wine about €14.50. Closed Sun, bank hols. MasterCard, Visa, Laser. **Directions:** Take Clonmel/Dungarvan (R671) road, turn off at Ballymacarbry.

Cappoquin

👁️ COUNTRY HOUSE/RESTAURANT

Richmond House

Cappoquin Co Waterford
Tel: 058 54278 Fax: 058 54988
Email: info@richmondhouse.net Web: www.richmondhouse.net

FEILE BIA AWARD

féile bia Genuine hospitality, high standards of comfort, caring service and excellent food are all to be found in the Deevy family's fine 18th century country house and restaurant just outside Cappoquin - no wonder this is a place so many people like to keep as a closely guarded secret. For returning guests, there's always a sense of pleasurable anticipation that builds up as you approach through parkland along a well-maintained driveway, which is lit up at night; after a brief pause to admire the climbing plants beside the door, you're into the fine high-ceilinged hall with its warming wood-burning stove and catch the scent of fires burning in the well-proportioned, elegantly furnished drawing room and restaurant opening off it. Claire or Jean Deevy will usually be there to welcome arriving guests, and show you to one of the nine individually decorated bedrooms; they vary in size and appointments, as is the way with old houses - some guests love the smallest cottagey bedroom, while others may prefer the larger ones - but all are comfortably furnished in country house style with full bathrooms. As well as serving wonderful dinners in the restaurant (see below), the Deevys make sure that you will have a memorable breakfast to see you on your way - it is a wonderful area to explore, and Richmond House makes an excellent base. Children welcome (under 3 free in parents' room, cot available without charge, baby sitting arranged). No pets. Garden; walking. Golf, garden visits nearby. *Six new rooms are planned shortly. **Rooms 9** (1 junior suite, all with full bathrooms & no smoking). B&B €75 pps, ss €20. Closed 23 Dec-12 Jan. **Restaurant:** The restaurant is the heart of Richmond House and non-residents usually make up a high proportion of the guests, which makes for a lively atmosphere. Warm and friendly service begins from the moment menus are presented over aperitifs - in front of the drawing room fire, or in a conservatory overlooking the garden. Paul is an ardent supporter of local produce and sources everything with tremendous care: Quality Assured meats (beef, lamb, bacon and sausages) come from his trusted local butcher, fresh seafood is from Dunmore East and Dungarvan herbs, fruit and vegetables are home grown where possible, and extra organic produce is grown nearby. There is a sureness of touch in Paul's kitchen, seen in stimulating menus that offer a balance between traditional country house cooking and more adventurous dishes inspired by international trends; dinner menus offering about five choices on each course are changed daily, and a slightly shorter separate vegetarian menu is also offered. House specialities include Helvick prawns (tempura, served with spicy avocado & tomato salsa, perhaps) and - a dish it would be hard to resist at Richmond House - roast rack of delicious West Waterford lamb; on a recent visit this was a memorable dish, perfectly cooked and beautifully presented on braised puy lentils and buttered green beans, with home-made mint jelly and rosemary & garlic jus; vegetables, served separately, are invariably imaginative and cooked 'au point'. Classic desserts are always a treat too, and pastry chef Anne Marie Hennessy includes plenty of imaginative and beautifully executed fruit-based choices to balance the richness of a fine meal here - a raspberry mille feuille perhaps, with lemon meringue ice cream and sauce anglaise - and, of course, there will always be Irish farmhouse cheeses with home-made biscuits. Service, under Claire's direction, is attentive and discreet. A carefully selected and fairly priced wine list includes interesting house wines, about twenty offered by the glass, and a good choice of half bottles. The early dinner menu offers particularly good value. Children welcome. **Seats 40** (private room, 16). D 6.30-9.30 (Sun 7-9) daily Set D €48, Early Bird €30 (Vegetarian Menu also avail); house wine €20; sc discretionary. Closed 23 Dec-12 Jan. Amex, Diners, MasterCard, Visa, Laser. **Directions:** Half a mile outside Cappoquin on N72.

Dungarvan
★ 🌸 RESTAURANT WITH ROOMS

The Tannery

10 Quay Street Dungarvan Co Waterford
Tel: 058 45420 Fax: 058 45814
Email: tannery@cablesurf.com Web: www.tannery.ie

Discerning diners from all over Ireland (and beyond) make a beeline for Paul and Maire Flynn's stylish contemporary restaurant, which is in an old leather warehouse - the tannery theme is imaginatively echoed throughout the light, clean-lined interior, creating a sense of history that adds greatly to the atmosphere. Pausing, perhaps, to have an aperitif in the little bar/reception area, arriving guests can see Paul and his team at work in the open kitchen on their way upstairs to the first-floor dining area, which is bright and welcoming, with dramatic paintings and fresh flowers. Menus are wonderfully simple, written with a confidence that transfers to the hungry guest: you just know that every dish will be an experience. While inspired to some extent by global trends and regional cooking - particularly of the Mediterranean countries - menus are based mainly on local ingredients, which Paul supports avidly and sources with care: local seafood stars in irresistible dishes like an unusual starter of crab crème brulée, and a main course of baked hake with steamed mussels and white wine & parsley broth. Pork and bacon supplied by local butcher JD Power are rightly another source of pride, as of course, is local lamb - rump of lamb is a speciality dish, served with chick pea purée with orange and aubergine salsa. And the perfect balance of Paul's menus is perhaps best seen in the strength of vegetarian choices, which make full use of the best farmhouse cheeses - in a main course of roasted asparagus with champ, truffle oil and Desmond cheese, for example. Dashing desserts are invariably tempting, and often appealingly simple too - strawberries in Cava with fromage blanc sorbet, for example... or an Irish farmhouse cheese platter, in perfect condition, makes a fine finale to the meal. The à la carte is very fairly priced for food of this quality, but the lunch and early evening menus (both changed daily) are outstandingly good value. Attentive and efficient service under Maire's direction, an interesting and kindly-priced wine list (with wines by the glass changed every week) and, above all, Paul's exceptional cooking, make for memorable meals. The Tannery was our Restaurant of the Year in 2004. Toilets wheelchair accessible. Children welcome before 8.30pm. **Seats 60** (private room up to 28). L Tue-Sun, 12.30-2.15 (Sun to 2.30); D Tue-Sat, 6.30-9.30 (also Sun in Jul & Aug, 6-9). Early D €27 (Tue-Fri, 6.30-7.30); Set Sun L €27; house wine €19.50; sc discretionary (10% on parties of 6+). Closed Mon, also D Sun off season; annual closure late Jan. **Rooms:** Accommodation is now offered in a boutique guesthouse just around the corner, in Church Street. Public areas of the house are very bright and funky but, while also contemporary, the six double rooms and a self-catering apartment are furnished more elegantly and to a very high standard. Ingenious breakfast arrangements provide the best of all possible worlds for the guest, without giving late night restaurant staff the problems of an early morning start - try it and see. Amex, Diners, MasterCard, Visa, Laser. **Directions:** End of lower main street beside old market house.

Lismore
🄴 RESTAURANT/WINE BAR

Barça Wine Bar & Restaurant

Main Street Lismore Co Waterford **Tel: 058 53810**
Fax: 058 53806 Email: barcawine@eircom.net

The spirit of a wonderful old bar in Lismore lives on in the Gormley sisters' chic tapas bar and restaurant, Barça. The frontage has been discreetly changed but, once inside the door, it's wonderful to find that - while this is clearly a contemporary rendition, with wine bottles lining the walls and the mandatory leather high stools - the essentials are still there, and the soft pastel tones are gently reminiscent of the way things were. A strong Spanish influence stems from the owners love of the Spanish relaxed, informal attitude to eating out - and the Spanish Tapas tradition has been adapted to use seasonal organic produce, preferably Irish; the front bar area is often buzzing with people waiting for tables in the restaurant at the back, or simply nibbling tapas from a selection of over a dozen little dishes offered at €3.50 each (deep fried calamari with garlic and saffron aioli, duck on toasted croûtons, smoked salmon with capers & red onion...). An in between area has armchairs and an open fire, and the restaurant is in two rooms towards the back of the building - opening onto a walled garden, with a deck and seating for fine weather. Simply decorated with some style, the restaurant has classy bare-topped tables, high-backed leather chairs and white walls hung with black and white photographs recording the changes to this fine old building. Friendly, relaxed, black-uniformed staff move quickly to ensure that food is piping hot each time a hand emerges from the kitchen hatch, ringing a little bell to announce that an order is ready. Tapas can be ordered as a larger appetiser portion, overlapping with a restaurant menu that offers a concise choice of main courses (from about €11), always including at least one tempting vegetarian option (a tartlet of caramelised red and white onion topped with goat cheese, perhaps). Desserts - just two perhaps, but oh-so-perfect - might be a dreamy vanilla pannacotta with berry & ginger compôte or flourless chocolate cake with whipped cream... Barça is realising its early potential - head chef Stéphane Tricot continues to do a great job and swift, friendly service is a match for his fine food. Don't miss this place if you're anywhere near Lismore. Not suitable for children after 7pm. **Seats 40** (outdoor seating, 20). Restaurant reservations required. Toilets wheelchair accessible. L Thu-Sat, 12.30-2.30 (Set L €10). D Thu-Sat, 6-10 (Set D €30), Open all day Sun (12.30-8); also A la carte. Closed Mon, Tue, Wed; Jan. MasterCard, Visa, Laser. **Directions:** At the east end of the main street in Lismore.

Lismore Area

RESTAURANT WITH ROOMS

Buggys Glencairn Inn

Glencairn Lismore Co Waterford
Tel: 058 56232 Fax: 058 56232
Email: info@buggys.net Web: www.buggys.net

Ken and Cathleen Buggy's dream of a country pub just oozes character - everything, from the little fire-lit bar to the beckoning old-world bedrooms, is full of charm. Ken is a talented artist - his delightfully quirky drawings have become symbolic of the West Waterford hospitality scene - but his artlessly rustic food (he describes it as "non-gourmet") is the main attraction here. Everything in this miniscule pub is based on top quality fresh ingredients and "made on the day" so be prepared for limited choice, especially towards the end of service. There's no obvious statement about local produce but you'll usually notice sources mentioned in the descriptions of many of the dishes - vegetables and salads grown locally are organic, Hederman of Cobh supplies smoked products and meats, poultry and game come from trusted butchers James Whelan (Clonmel) and O'Flynns (Cork). About six choices are offered on each course, and food is served in the bar as well as two little dining rooms charmingly set up with a stylish country informality. Paté de campagne is a favourite starter, full of texture and rich flavours, or there's something less usual like smoked eel, with horseradish sauce and salad (all served with home-made brown soda bread); this could be followed by fish (from Helvick) as available on the day - cooked simply in butter, olive oil and lemon juice - or pot-roasted guinea fowl, with wild herbs and apples, all served with crisp little home-made chips, vegetable of the day and a side salad. Finish up with something like fresh lime cake (with home-made ice cream), or farmhouse cheeses (Durrus, Milleens, Carrigaline, Cashel Blue & Dubliner), then cafetière coffee or an Irish coffee in the bar. An unusual wine list is not long, but carefully selected, under constant review and fairly priced. Cathleen supervises the restaurant, and service is both charming and efficient. Upstairs there are five delightful en-suite rooms, all no smoking (€62.50 pps, ss €7.50). Not suitable for children under 12. **Seats 40.** D daily in summer, 7-9, probably Wed-Sun in winter; à la carte; house wine €17.95; SC 10%. Usually closed Mon & Tue off season, Christmas period & occasionally throughout the year. (Times of opening are somewhat flexible - a phone call ahead is wise, especially off season; dinner reservations strongly advised).* Traditional cottage with 4 en-suite bedrooms, large kitchen, sitting room, study and gardens also available, for self-catering (not suitable for children under 12); details on application. MasterCard, Visa, Laser, Switch. **Directions:** 3 miles from Lismore off N72 Lismore/Tallow Road.

Millstreet

FARMHOUSE/CASTLE

The Castle Country House

Millstreet Dungarvan Co Waterford
Tel: 058 68049 Fax: 058 68099
Email: castlefm@iol.ie Web: www.castlecountryhouse.com

Set in 1.5 acres of recently landscaped gardens overlooking the River Finisk, the Nugent family's unusual and wonderfully hospitable farmhouse is in the 18th century wing of a 16th century castle. Although most of the house seems quite normal inside, it blends into the original building in places - so, for example, the dining room has walls five feet deep and an original castle archway. Spacious, comfortably appointed rooms have king size beds, television, tea/coffee facilities and neat shower rooms; (there is also a full bathroom available for any guest who prefers a bath). Meticulous housekeeping, a very pleasant guests' sitting room and fresh flowers everywhere all add up to a very appealing farmhouse indeed, and Joan uses their own produce - fruit, vegetables, meats and herbs - in her cooking. Excellent breakfasts, also dinner by arrangement: menus change daily and offer a choice; typical dishes might include blue cheese & onion tart with mixed leaves & soured cream; baked fillet of Helvick salmon with hollandaise sauce and home-grown apple tart with vanilla ice cream; there's also a choice of half a dozen wines. Children welcome (under 2 free in parents' room, cot available without charge). Pets permitted by arrangement. Garden, walking, fishing. **Rooms 5** (all en-suite, shower only and no smoking). B&B €45pps, ss €10. Dining Room **Seats 24**; Residents D €25. Closed 1 Nov-1 Mar. Diners, MasterCard, Visa. **Directions:** Off N72 on R671.

Tramore
🏛 RESTAURANT WITH ROOMS

Coast Restaurant & Townhouse

Upper Branch Road Tramore Co Waterford
Tel: 051 393646 Fax: 051 393647
Email: coastrestaurant@eircom.net Web: www.coast.ie

Turlough McNamara and Jenny McNally's gorgeous contemporary restaurant has a lovely bar area for pre-dinner drinks and the chic, smartly appointed dining room overlooking Tramore also has a fine terrace for outside dining. A warm welcome from friendly, well-trained staff and a glimpse of candle-lit polished tables, simply laid with crisp linen napkins, beautiful plates and fine glasses set the tone for a dining experience where details count. A la carte menus offer a well-balanced selection of six to eight dishes on each course, with a strong emphasis on seafood (presumably local, although not stated on the menu). Excellent breads are served with a choice of dips, and the cooking style is modern international - seen in starters like chorizo with buffalo mozzarella & sundried tomato risotto, and a deliciously retro Coast prawn cocktail, for example; Angus beef fillet comes in an updated classic style, with béarnaise sauce and shoe string potatoes, and vegetarian choices are persuasive - and a dish like homemade linguini with wild mushroom and wilted spinach velouté would tempt the most hardened carnivore. Finish with a luscious dessert - another retro inspiration like baked Alaska, perhaps - and a delicious Illy coffee. Cooking is accomplished, flavours well-judged and presentation appealing - small wonder that this gem of a restaurant has earned a loyal following. An interesting if rather pricey wine list offers about 50 bottles, including a house selection of half a dozen wines around €20, plus a further six marked as 'House Recommended', in the €24-30 range. Early dinner and Sunday lunch offer outstanding value. **Seats 45** (private room 15, outdoor seating 30). Children welcome. Toilets wheelchair accessible). D Tue-Sat 6.30-10 (also D Sun Jul-Aug), L Sun 1-3. Early D €26.50 (Tue-Fri, 6.30-7), Sun L €24.50, otherwise à la carte. House Closed Mon, D Sun off-season, all Jan. **Accommodation:** Four seriously stylish and beautifully appointed rooms are offered - as elsewhere at Coast, Turlough and Jennifer have demonstrated a confident sense of contemporary style, and the result is both beautiful and luxurious. Unusual features - notably the glass-walled bathrooms - will no doubt attract most comment but, as in the restaurant, it's actually the inspired blending of some old with the new that gives these rooms their special character: original artwork, great use of mirrors, well-planned lighting and a judicious mixture of ultra modern and antique furnishings all add up to a very special atmosphere. **Rooms 4** (2 junior suites, 2 executive, 2 shower only, all no smoking). Children welcome. No pets. B&B €50-80pps (depending on the room), ss €15. Closed Jan. Amex, MasterCard, Visa, Laser. **Directions:** From Waterford: right up hill after main roundabout, first right, restaurant on left.

Waterford
🏛 FARMHOUSE

Foxmount Country House

Passage East Road Waterford Co Waterford
Tel: 051 874 308 Fax: 051 854 906
Email: Info@foxmountcountryhouse.com Web: www.foxmountcountryhouse.com

For those who prefer a country house atmosphere, rather than an hotel, the Kent family's 17th century home on the edge of Waterford city is a haven of peace and tranquillity. The house is lovely, with classically proportioned reception rooms, and accommodation in five very different rooms which are all thoughtfully, and very comfortably, furnished - but, as peace and relaxation are the aim at Foxmount, don't expect phones or TVs in bedrooms, or a very early breakfast. However, Margaret Kent is a great cook and she loves baking, as guests quickly discover when offered afternoon tea in the drawing room - or in the morning, when freshly-baked breads are presented at breakfast. No evening meals are offered, but the restaurants of Waterford and Cheekpoint are quite close - and guests are welcome to bring their own wine and enjoy a glass at the log fire before going out for dinner. Children welcome (under 2s free in parent' room, cot available without charge). Pets by arrangement. Garden. **Rooms 5** (all with en-suite or private bathrooms, all no-smoking). B&B €55 pps, ss€15. Closed Nov-mid Mar. **No Credit Cards. Directions:** From Waterford city, take Dunmore Road - after 4 km, take Passage East road for 1 mile.

Waterford

🏛️👁️ HOTEL/RESTAURANT

Waterford Castle Hotel & Golf Club

The Island Ballinakill Waterford Co Waterford

Tel: 051 878 203 Fax: 051 879 316

Email: info@waterfordcastle.com Web: www.waterfordcastle.com

féile bia This beautiful hotel dates back to the 15th century, and is uniquely situated on its own 310 acre wooded island (complete with 18-hole golf course), reached by a private ferry. The hotel combines the elegance of earlier times with modern comfort, service and convenience - and the location is uniquely serene - its quietness (and the golf facility for off-duty relaxation) makes the castle a good venue for small conferences and business meetings, but it is also a highly romantic location and perfect for small weddings. All guest rooms have recently been refurbished and, although they inevitably vary in size and outlook, all are very comfortably furnished in a luxurious country house style. There are plans to extend the accommodation and add a health spa but, at the time of going to press, permissions have not yet been granted. Conference/banqueting (30/80). Golf, archery, clay pigeon shooting, fishing, tennis, walking, gardens. Pool table. Children welcome (under 4 free in parents' room; cots available; bay sitting arranged). **Rooms 19** (5 suites, 3 junior suites, 2 family, 4 ground floor, all no smoking). Lift. 24 hr room service. Turndown service. B&B €187.50pps, ss €77.50. Closed Jan. **Munster Room:** This beautiful dining room is appointed to the highest standard and head chef Michael Quinn and a fine kitchen brigade can be relied on to provide the food to match: menus are peppered with luxurious ingredients like lobster, foie gras, scallops, prawns, black sole, aged Irish beef and game, such as wild Irish venison; local produce is used as much as possible, including organic vegetables, and the cooking, in a modern classical style, is excellent. A set dinner menu is offered, but considerably priced by course, allowing for a semi à la carte selection. Children over 8 years welcome. **Seats 60.** D daily, 7-9, L Sun only (12.30-2); Set D €58, à la carte and vegetarian menu also available; Set Sun L €30. House wines €28. SC 10%. Pianist at dinner. Amex, Diners, MasterCard, Visa, Laser. **Directions:** Outskirts of Waterford City just off Dunmore East road.

Waterford Area

🏛️👁️ HOTEL

Faithlegg House Hotel

Faithlegg Co Waterford **Tel: 051 382000** Fax: 051 382010

Email: reservations@fhh.ie Web: www.faithlegg.com

féile bia Set in wooded landscape with magnificent views over its own golf course and the Suir estuary, this lovely 18th century house has a splendid Waterford Crystal chandelier to set the tone in the foyer, and public areas are elegant throughout. Accommodation, in the old house and a discreetly positioned new wing, is furnished to a high standard; the large, graciously proportioned rooms and suites in the old house are really lovely, while those in the new wing are more practical. (Self-catering accommodation is also offered in the grounds.) Aside from golf, the range of activities available on site includes a swimming pool, and numerous health and beauty treatments. There is a choice of restaurants nearby (Waterford city, or Cheekpoint, are each only a few minutes' drive), and the hotel's fine dining restaurant, The Roseville Rooms, offers classical cuisine. **Rooms 82**. **Roseville Rooms:** The bar is comfortably furnished in a clubby style - a good place to have an aperitif and look at the menu; orders may be taken here and you will be called through when your table is ready. Menus change daily, which is ideal for residents staying for several nights, and offers a balanced choice of about four on each course. The restaurant is shared between two lovely classical, formally appointed dining rooms and it is a very pleasant place to enjoy an evening meal. **Seats 90** (private room 40). Not suitable for children after 8.30pm. D daily, 6.30-9.30; L Sun only, 12.30-2.30. Set D €48, Set Sun L €28. House wines from €18. Amex, Diners, MasterCard, Visa, Laser. **Directions:** Off Dunmore East Road 6 miles outside Waterford city.

COUNTY WESTMEATH

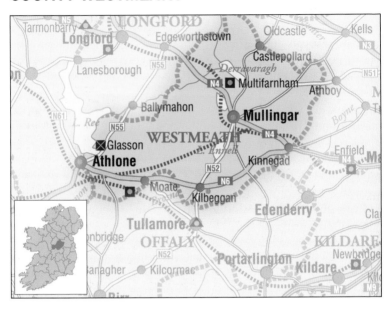

Athlone
☆ RESTAURANT

The Left Bank Bistro

Fry Place Athlone Co Westmeath
Tel: 090 649 4446 Fax: 090 649 4509
Email: info@leftbankbistro.com Web: www.leftbankbistro.com

Athlone makes a perfect break for anyone crossing the country, but it's much more than a handy stopover: it is now a destination town for discerning travellers. And, for many, it would be unthinkable to go through the area without a visit to Annie McNamara and Mary McCullough's elegant and spacious restaurant, where architectural salvage materials and interesting, subtle colours combine well with bare tables and paper napkins to convey an informal atmosphere that suits their lively food. Short, keenly-priced menus - plus specials chalked up on a blackboard - offer a wide range of delicious-sounding dishes with a multi-cultural stamp which, together with carefully sourced ingredients and snappy cooking, make this the number one choice for an informal meal in Athlone. Wraps, bruschetta, focaccia and pasta are typical lunch time dishes - try the tandoori chicken on focaccia - and vegetables are always colourful and full of zing. Fresh fish has its own menu (oysters baked with sweet chilli & coriander butter, and chargrilled citrus marinated tuna steak with cherry tomato & basil salsa are typical), and vegetarians can choose between blackboard specials and dishes from the regular menu, including favourites like Left Bank Salad (a gorgeous mixture of good things, with a wedge of foccacia) and vegetable spring rolls. Dinner menus are more extensive and tend to be based on more expensive ingredients, but the style is similar and they also include attractive vegetarian choices; delicious desserts are all home made and, of course, there's a farmhouse cheese plate too. A concise, well-chosen wine list offers a fair choice half bottles and several champagnes. For the quality of food and cooking, not to mention the sheer style of the place, a meal here is always good value - especially the early dinner menu. * A range of speciality products is now sold at the Left Bank: salamis, pestos, house dressing, oils, olives, pastas, and coffee are just a few examples. **Seats 60** (+ outdoor seating,16). Air conditioning. Toilets wheelchair accessible. Open Tue-Sat, 10.30-9.30: L 12-5 & D 5.30-9.30; Early bird D €25 (Tue-Fri 5.30-7.30), also à la carte; house wine €19. Closed Sun & Mon, bank hols & 10 days Christmas/New Year. MasterCard, Visa, Laser. **Directions:** Behind Athlone Castle, west side of the Shannon.

Glasson

⛪☆ 🌱 👁 RESTAURANT WITH ROOMS

Wineport Lodge

Glasson Co Westmeath
Tel: 090 643 9010 Fax: 090 648 5471
Email: lodge@wineport.ie Web: www.wineport.ie

GEORGINA CAMPBELL AWARD

féile bía Ray Byrne and Jane English's lovely lakeside lodge styles itself 'Ireland's first wine hotel' and the accommodation - which now includes a further ten beautiful rooms, hot tub and treatment rooms - is nothing less than stunning. A covered lakeside boardwalk leads to the front door: you enter your guest key card and step into a different world. A lofty residents lounge with a stove and its own bar simply oozes style and comfort, a hint of the high pamper quota waiting above in spacious suites and guest rooms, all with private balconies overlooking the lake. Superbly comfortable beds with goose down duvets and extra large pillows face the view, and seriously luxurious bathrooms have separate double-ended bath and walk-in shower. Wineport has a huge amount to offer discerning guests and has quickly become a hot choice for business and corporate events - every technological requirement has been thought of, and one look at meeting rooms which are dramatically planned to take full advantage of the beautiful location would sway anyone arranging a business event. Luxurious, romantic, beautiful, businesslike, this boutique hotel is a place of many moods: Wineport has everything. Ray and Jane were the Guide's Hosts of the Year in 1999, and Wineport was our Hideaway of the Year in 2003. It is in recognition of their dedication to quality, and a determination to present the very best hospitality that this country can offer, that Wineport was selected for the Georgina Campbell Award. Conference /banqueting 50/135. Children welcome (under 2 free in parents room, cot available free of charge, baby sitting arranged). Walking; fishing; garden. No pets. **Rooms 21** (3 suites, 2 junior suites, 4 superior, 1 family, 11 ground floor, 2 disabled, 2 shower only, all no smoking). B&B €97.50pps, ss €37.50; SC discretionary. No lift. Turndown service. All day room service. Masseuse (pre-booking required). Open all year except Christmas. **Restaurant:** Wineport Lodge began life as a restaurant, and faithful fans continue to beat a path to the door at the slightest excuse, to be treated to a fine meal, served with warmth and professionalism in this lovely contemporary restaurant - and what a setting! Regular guests find the combination of the view, the company and a good meal irresistible, and return bearing additions to the now famous Wineport collections (nauticalia, cats)... Head chef Feargal O'Donnell, who is a member of Euro-Toques and Féile Bia, presents well-balanced and strongly seasonal menus based on Quality Assured and local ingredients including game in season, eels, home-grown herbs and wild mushrooms. The number of dishes showcasing local and speciality produce is impressive, and constantly growing: local producers and suppliers listed on the menu include Abbey cheeses (Ballacolla, Co Laois), Reilly mushrooms (Glasson), Auburn Herbs (Athlone) and McBride's Butcher (Athlone) who is a specialist sausage maker, Donald Russell beef and lamb, Ballymahon - and, from further afield, Hick's pork products (Stillorgan), McGeough's smoked meats (Oughterad, Co Galway) and Lissadell Shellfish in Co Sligo. All this information, together with a stated commitment to the Féile Bia Charter is both interesting to read and very reassuring to guests, who will enjoy meals all the more in the knowledge that such care has been taken with sourcing the ingredients. The cooking style is diverse - international, with an occasional nod to traditional Irish themes - so you could begin a meal with a speciality starter such as McGeough's turf smoked lamb with wild rocket leaves & raspberries and bitter chocolate oil, or a delicious aromatic duck frisée salad with soft poached egg - and follow with dishes as diverse as baked turbot with cauliflower cream and oyster & mussel nage, or roast summer vegetables with herb gnocci & pesto butter. But this is beef country and it is fitting that a chargrilled 20 oz ribeye steak with smoked Ardrahan cheese & cracked pepper butter should top the bill, along with a mini-menu of beef (and lamb) dishes. After that you may well choose to finish with seasonal fruit and natural yoghurt or fromage frais as an alternative to a tempting selection of desserts... A separate children's menu is available. Wine is so closely intertwined with the history of Wineport that the list is very much a work in progress, but there are many suggestions for pairing wine and food throughout the menus offered; the main list include a value selection, organised by price. **Seats 100** (private room, 12; outdoor seating, 50). Toilets wheelchair accessible. Children welcome. Food service: Mon-Sat, 6-10; Sun 3-9; Set D €59, Gourmet Menu €75; otherwise à la carte; wines from €22. Closed 24-26 Dec. Amex, Diners, MasterCard, Visa, Laser. **Directions:** Midway between Dublin and Galway: take the Longford/Cavan exit off the Athlone relief road; fork left after 2.5 miles at the Dog & Duck; 1 mile, on the left.

Moate
👁 COUNTRY HOUSE

Temple Country House & Spa

Horseleap Moate Co Westmeath
Tel: 057 933 5118 Fax: 057 933 5008
Email: info@templespa.ie Web: www.templespa.ie

Relaxation is the essence of Declan and Bernadette Fagan's philosophy at Temple, their charming and immaculately maintained 200 year-old farmhouse in the unspoilt Westmeath countryside. On its own farmland where guests are welcome to walk close to peat bogs, lakes and historical sites, outdoor activities such as walking, cycling and riding are all at hand. Relaxation programmes and healthy eating have always been available at Temple, but when they introduced the Spa, this side of the operation moved into a new phase, offering yoga, hydrotherapy, massage, reflexology and specialist treatments such as Yon-Ka facial and seaweed body contour wraps. the success of the Spa led to extensive developments recently, which have extended the premises, adding new bedrooms, a hydropool, gym and quiet relaxation areas. Temple is a member of the Health Farms of Ireland Association, which means that special attention is given to healthy eating guidelines; vegetarian, vegan and other special diets are catered for, and the best of local produce lamb from the farm, garden vegetables, best midland beef, cheese and yoghurts are used in good home cooking. An atmosphere of calm, good food, comfortable surroundings, gentle exercise and pampering therapies all contribute to a relaxing experience here - and the wide range of programmes offered include pampering weekends, 24 hour escape breaks, mother & daughter breaks and his & her weekends. Garden, cycling, sauna, steam room, children's playground. **Rooms 23** (all en-suite, all no-smoking). Spa Package €235 pps, ss about €20 (min 2-night stay at weekends). Spa weekends from about €300 pps (ss about €40). Residents' D Tue-Sat, about €30 (book by 10 am; no D Sun, Mon). Wine licence. Closed Christmas-New Year. Amex, MasterCard, Visa, Laser. **Directions:** Just off N6, 1 mile west of Horseleap.

Mullingar
👁 RESTAURANT

The Belfry Restaurant

Ballynegall Mullingar Co Westmeath **Tel: 044 42488** Fax: 044 40094
Email: info@belfryrestaurant.com Web: www.belfryrestaurant.com

féile bía The tall spire will lead you to this unusual restaurant in a magnificently converted church near Mullingar. The design is brilliant, with (excellent) toilets near the entrance, perfect for a quick freshen up before heading up thickly carpeted stairs to a mezzanine lounge which is luxuriously furnished with big lounge-around leather sofas, striking lamps and fresh flowers. A second staircase descends to the dining area, which is very striking and extremely atmospheric, especially when seen in candlelight with a room full of people enjoying themselves, with background music from the grand piano where the altar used to be. Everything has been done to the very highest specifications, colours schemes are subtle and elegant - and the whole set-up is highly atmospheric. A new team, of head chef Damian Martin and front of house manager and sommelier Florence Servieres, took over The Belfry in 2005 and quickly earned a reputation well beyond the immediate area for first class modern classical cooking and warm, professional and efficient service - just what this stunning premises deserves. Damian offers well-priced lunch and early dinner menus and a more sophisticated à la carte; he is not afraid to have traditional dishes like oxtail, confit of belly pork or braised lamb neck on menus - and of course this is beef country, so offering tip top quality roast beef with Yorkshire pudding for Sunday lunch is a must - as well as the likes of foie gras en gelée with sweet & sour mango and brioche tuile, or seared salmon with crushed potato salad beetroot purée and sauce vierge. This down to earth quality in the cooking has won friends for the restaurant - and he has succeeded admirably in balancing the demands of an area where generous portions are de rigeur with the requirements of the fine dining guest. Florence is responsible for the wine list, which offers some treat and some interesting middle range bottles. Catering offered for private parties, small weddings (up to 75); private room for meetings. Cookery classes are offered - call the restaurant for details. **Seats 65** (private room 20). Air conditioning. Children welcome. D Wed-Sat, 6-9.30 (to 10 Fri/Sat); L Wed-Sat 12.30-2; Sun L only, 1-4. Early D from €22.50 (6-7.30), otherwise D à la carte, Set Sun L €29.50; house wines €21. Closed Mon,Tue & may close for 2 weeks in Jan. MasterCard, Visa, Laser. **Directions:** Castlepollard road, off the Mullingar bypass.

Mullingar
🌱 € CAFÉ

Ilia A Coffee Experience

28 Oliver Plunkett Street Mullingar Co Westmeath
Tel: 044 40300 Fax: 044 40050 Email: juliekenny@eircom.net

féile bia Julie Kenny's delightful 2-storey coffee house and informal restaurant in the centre of Mullingar is attractively set up - the first floor area is particularly pleasing, with a seating area of sofas, low tables and plants at the top of the stairs setting a relaxed tone and making a good place to wait for a friend, or to sip a cup of coffee while reading the paper at quiet times; the rest is more conventionally furnished in café style - and a more comfortable height for eating a real meal.

Menus cater for all the changing moods though the day, beginning with an extensive breakfast (everything from porridge with brown sugar and cream to traditional breakfast, to toasted bagels (their Bagel Combo - toasted bagel with crispy bacon, poached egg, topped with melted cheddar & tomato relish 'just walks out of the door'!), then there are the mid-day bites like home-made soup, paninis, steak baguettes, bruschetta, Ilia salad and much more (plenty for vegetarians) - and lots of pastries and desserts including a range of crêpes, both savoury and sweet. More predictably, there's a nice little drinks menu offering everything from big glasses of freshly squeezed orange juice through iced teas, smoothies, teas - and, of course, coffees (Java Republic), any way you like, including flavoured coffees. Everything is deliciously fresh and wholesome, staff are charming and efficient, prices reasonable - you'd be hard pushed to find much over €8. Takeaway also available. Wine licence.* "Ilia Gourmet" specialist food store is due to open across the road shortly after going to press. **Seats 60.** Children welcome. Toilets wheelchair accessible. Air conditioning. Open Mon-Sat 9am-5.30pm. Closed Sun, Christmas & bank hols. Amex, MasterCard, Visa, Laser. **Directions:** Centre of Town.

Multyfarnham
👁 COUNTRY HOUSE

Mornington House

Mornington Multyfarnham Co Westmeath
Tel: 044 72191 Fax: 044 72338
Email: stay@mornington.ie Web: www.mornington.ie

Warwick and Anne O'Hara's gracious Victorian house is surrounded by mature trees and is just a meadow's walk away from Lough Derravaragh where the mythical Children of Lir spent 300 years of their 900 year exile - the lough is now occupied by a pleasing population of brown trout, pike, eels and other coarse fish. This has been the O'Hara family home since 1858, and is still furnished with much of the original furniture and family portraits - and, although centrally heated, log fires remain an essential feature.

Bedrooms are typical of this kind of country house - spacious and well-appointed, with old furniture (three have brass beds) but with comfortable modern mattresses. Anne is well-known for her skills in the kitchen, and cooks proper country breakfasts and country house dinners for residents, using fresh fruit and vegetables from the walled garden and local produce (Westmeath beef cooked in Guinness is a speciality), while Warwick does the honours front-of-house. There is a wealth of wildlife around the house, and there are gardens and archaeological sites to visit nearby - this is a tranquil and restorative place for a short break. Pets allowed by arrangement. Garden, croquet; fishing. canoes, boats & bicylces can be hired. Equestrian: trekking & a cross-country course nearby. Golf nearby. Children welcome (cot available without charge, baby sitting arranged). **Rooms 5** (4 en-suite, 1 with private bathrooms, 2 shower only, all no smoking). Turndown service. B&B €70 pps, ss €20. Set residents D €40, at 8pm (book by 2pm). House wine €15.*Short breaks offered: 3-day stay (3 DB&B) from €275pps. Closed Nov-Mar. Amex, Diners, MasterCard, Visa, Laser. **Directions:** Exit N4 for Castlepollard.

COUNTY WEXFORD

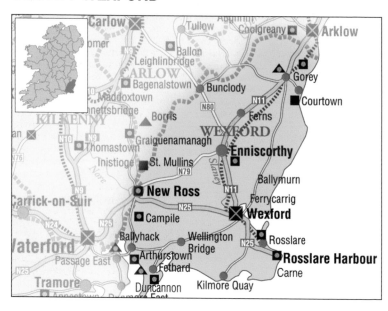

Arthurstown

🏛☆ 🍷 HOTEL/RESTAURANT

Dunbrody Country House Hotel & Cookery School

Arthurstown Co Wexford
Tel: 051 389 600 Fax: 051 389 601
Email: dunbrody@indigo.ie Web: www.dunbrodyhouse.com

féile bia Set in twenty acres of parkland and gardens on the Hook Peninsula, just across the estuary from Waterford city, Catherine and Kevin Dundon's elegant Georgian manor was the ancestral home of the Chichester family and the long tradition of hospitality at this tranquil and luxurious retreat is very much alive and well. Well-proportioned public rooms, which include an impressive entrance hall and gracious drawing room, are all beautifully furnished and decorated with stunning flower arrangements and the occasional unexpectedly modern piece that brings life to a fine collection of antiques. Spacious bedrooms, including those in a newer wing which blends admirably with the original building, generally have superb bathrooms and offer all the comforts expected of such a house - and fine views over the gardens. Constant improvement is the on-going quest at Dunbrody: recent developments include the conversion of outbuildings to create what must be Ireland's most stylish cookery school and, alongside it, a beautiful spa offering peace, relaxation and a full range of therapies and treatments. An outstanding breakfast offers a magnificent buffet - fresh juices, fruit compôtes, cheeses - as well as hot dishes from a tempting menu - and was the national winner of our Irish Breakfast Awards for 2004. While Dunbrody provides a wonderfully relaxing place for a leisure break, they also cater for business meetings, small conferences, product launches and incentive programmes (full details available on request). Conference/banqueting (30/110). Secretarial services; video conferencing. Cookery school. Spa & beauty salon. Garden, walking. Children welcome (under 5s free in parents' room; cot available without charge, baby sitting arranged). No pets. **Rooms 22** (7 suites, 7 junior suites, 7 superior). B&B €120 pps; ss €25. * A range of special breaks is offered (weekend, midweek, cookery, New Year); details on application. Open all year except Christmas. **The Harvest Room at Dunbrody:** The restaurant looks out onto a pleasure garden and, beyond, to a promisingly productive organic vegetable and fruit garden - an interesting place to browse around before dinner and, perhaps, hazard a guess as to what will be on the evening's menu. The dining room is a lovely well-proportioned room, with an open fire in winter and stunning flower arrangements all the time; it presents a striking blend of classic and contemporary style - bold choices which bring life to the room include some beautiful modern rugs, specially commissioned from Ceadogan Rugs at Wellington Bridge. Likewise, Kevin Dundon and his head chef, Phelim Byrne, offer tempting à la carte and set menus that combine classical and international influences with local produce and Irish themes - and suppliers are given full credit: fresh fish is delivered daily from nearby Duncannon harbour, and shellfish from Kilmore Quay, and meats are supplied by Wallace's butchers, of Wellington Bridge - and organic fruit, vegetables and herbs are home grown, as far as possible. Starters - which tend to showcase some unusual ingredients (tea-smoked chicken for example) and to be pretty and light - might include a lovely Wexford strawberry salad with a peppered Blackwater cheese basket: a perfect summer first course. Local meats like rack of Wexford lamb often top the bill - in a terrific house speciality, roast rack with an Irish stew consommé, for example, which is a modern twist on a very traditional theme - and seafood dishes tend to the contemporary, as in Dublin Bay prawns with mead salsa. But this is a kitchen which likes to end meals on a high note - so, whatever you do, make sure you save a little space for a spectacular dessert... Catherine leads a well-trained and efficient dining room staff with the charm and panache that typifies all aspects of the hospitality at this exceptional country house. An informative wine list which leans towards the classics includes a nice selection of half bottles and wines by the glass. The early dinner menu and Sunday lunch offer particularly good value. [Kevin Dundon has recently written a lovely cookery book, 'Full On Irish', which features many of the dishes from the restaurant and cookery school at Dunbrody.] **Seats 80** (outdoor seating, 10). Reservations required. Toilets wheelchair accessible. D Mon-Sat 6.30-9.15. L Daily 1.30-2.30. Set L €35. Early D €35 (6.30-7.30); Set D €50/€60. House wines €21. SC discretionary. Not suitable for children after 8pm. Closed 18-27 Dec. Amex, Diners, MasterCard, Visa, Laser **Directions:** N11 to Wexford, R733 from Wexford to Arthurstown.

Arthurstown
€ ◉ B&B

Glendine Country House

Arthurstown New Ross Co Wexford
Tel: 051 389 500/258 Fax: 051 389677
Email: glendinehouse@eircom.net Web: www.glendinehouse.com

FARMHOUSE OF THE YEAR

Ann and Tom Crosbie's large nineteenth century farmhouse is approached up a driveway off the main road to Arthurstown, and has magnificent views across the estuary. It is a spacious house and makes a very comfortable and hospitable place to stay at a reasonable price; it would be ideal for a family holiday as there are sandy beaches nearby and there's a safe, enclosed playground for children beside the house - and they also enjoy the highland cows, Jacob sheep and horses which the Crosbies keep in paddocks around the house. A pleasant guest drawing room has plenty of comfortable seating and excellent views down to the harbour, and across the estuary, and the immaculately maintained bedrooms are very large, as are the en-suite bathrooms. Five new guest rooms have recently been completed and they are really lovely - large, bright and airy, they are individually decorated but the tone is quite contemporary and they have smart bathrooms; the original rooms are more traditional, with a cosy atmosphere, and all nine rooms have sea views. Service at Glendine House is a priority; the Crosbies take pride in giving their guests personal attention and lots of advice on local amenities - and sending everyone off well-fed for the day after a really good breakfast that offers home-baked breads, fresh and cooked fruits, organic porridge and a range of hot dishes include smoked salmon & scrambled eggs and French toast as well as the full Irish. Children welcome (cot available, baby sitting arranged; children's playground). Pets allowed by arrangement. Garden, walking. **Rooms 5** (2 suites, 3 superior, 4 shower only); room service (limited hours), turndown service offered; B&B about €50 pps, ss about €15. Room service (limited hours). Light meals (soup & home-baked bread, open sandwiches) available all day. *Off-season breaks offered. 2 self-catering cottages are also available - details on application. Closed at Christmas. Diners, MasterCard, Visa, Laser. **Directions:** From Wexford, turn right before Talbot Hotel, onto R733; 22 miles to Arthurstown; entrance on right before village.

Campile
€ CAFÉ

Dunbrody Abbey Tea Rooms

Dunbrody Visitor Centre Campile New Ross Co Wexford
Tel: 051 388933 Email: theneptune@eircom.net Web: www.cookingireland.com

The 12th century Dunbrody Abbey, and adjacent Dunbrody Castle and visitor centre make an interesting place to break a journey, or an excellent destination for a family outing - children will find plenty to enjoy here, including a full size yew hedge maze in the castle gardens (one of only two in Ireland), a small museum containing the Dunbrody Castle Doll's House and much else of historical interest, also pitch & putt for when it's time to let off steam (clubs can be hired in the craft shop). It is also home to good home cooking, in the Tea Rooms run by well-known chefs Pierce & Valerie McAuliffe, who run cookery courses all year round, at the adjoining Dunbrody Abbey Cookery Centre. In summer, they bake up a range of treats every day to make sure there's a fresh supply of simple good things to delight and refresh: usually a home-made soup of the day with Guinness & walnut brown soda bread, a selection of fresh filled rolls or sandwiches, home-made biscuits, muffins, tarts and cakes and a choice of teas, coffees and hot chocolate. There's also a range of Dunbrody Abbey food products on sale (mustard dressing, ginger marmalade, hot pepper relish). **Seats 35.** Open: 11-6 in high season (Jul/Aug); 12-5 shoulder seasons (May-Jun & 1st half Sep). Tea Rooms closed late Sep-end Apr. Cookery Centre open all year. Amex, MasterCard, Visa **Directions:** On main New Ross-Hook Peninsula road; 3 miles from John F Kennedy Memorial Park, 2 miles from Passage East car ferry.

Campile
 ◉ COUNTRY HOUSE/RESTAURANT

Kilmokea Country Manor

Great Island Campile Co Wexford
Tel: 051 388 109 Fax: 051 388 776
Email: kilmokea@eircom.net Web: www.kilmokea.com

Mark and Emma Hewlett's peaceful and relaxing late Georgian country house is set in 7 acres of Heritage Gardens, including formal walled gardens (open to the public, 9-5; refreshments, for guests and garden visitors, are served in The Pink Teacup Café in the Georgian conservatory). The house is elegantly and comfortably furnished, with a drawing room overlooking the Italian Loggia, an honesty library bar, and a restaurant in the dining room. The individually-designed and immaculately maintained bedrooms command lovely views over the gardens and towards the estuary beyond; they have no television to disturb the tranquillity (though there is one in the drawing room). In an adjoining coach house there are newer rooms and self-catering suites; they have a separate entrance and lighter, more contemporary atmosphere than the main house - as they are so different it is wise to discuss your preferences when booking. Mark and Emma have also continued their ongoing programme of improvements to the property - the latest additions are a tennis court and an indoor swimming pool, no less, plus a gym and aromatherapy treatment rooms (Emma is a trained aromatherapist). And work continues on a large organic vegetable garden, planted in the old potager design - it's great to see a revival of this charming fashion. Conferences/banqueting (60/60). Children welcome (under 3s free in parents' room, cots available without charge; baby sitting arranged). Pets allowed in some areas by arrangement. Gardens, fishing, tennis, walking; swimming pool, gym, spa, aromatherapy. **Rooms 6** (5 en-suite, 1 with private bathroom; 3 superior, 2 ground floor, 1 shower only, 1 disabled, all no smoking). B&B €85 pps; ss €30. Self-catering also available. Light meals in conservatory Pink Teacup Café, 10-5 daily when house and gardens are open; gift shop. Closed Dec & Jan. **Peacock Dining Room:** The dining room overlooks the lovely gardens at the back, and is a delightful place. Head chef Thomas FitzHerbert offers seasonal menus, based on local ingredients - especially seafood and, of course, fresh garden produce; a choice of six starters might offer one or two unusual dishes not often found on Irish menus, such as globe artichokes with garlic & herb butter, and a similar number of main courses will offer a well-balanced choice including favourites like crisp duck (roast half duckling, de-boned and served on a noodle nest, with beansprouts and orange brandy sauce) and local fish, such as lemon sole stuffed with chili cheese and served with tomatoes, baby courgette and a chive cream sauce. Vegetarian dishes are offered and change daily, and quite classical which might include some retro dishes like soufflé milanaise. But the big surprise for a small country house restaurant is the wine list, which is unexpectedly extensive - and offers some serious bottles. Somebody is having fun here. **Seats 20** (private room, 30). Reservations required (non-residents welcome). Children welcome. Toilets wheelchair accessible. D Wed-Sun, 7-9 (Sun to 10); (L available in Ping Teacup Café, 12-3). A la carte. House wines from €19.95. Amex, MasterCard, Visa, Laser, Switch. **Directions:** Take R733 south from New Ross to Ballyhack, signposted for Kilmokea Gardens.

Duncanon
N RESTAURANT WITH ROOMS

Aldridge Lodge

Duncannon New Ross Co Wexford
Tel: 051 389116 Fax: 051 389116
Email: info@aldridgelodge.com Web: www.aldridgelodge.com

NEWCOMER OF THE YEAR

Euro-Toques chef Billy Whitty's good cooking has attracted a following around the south-east in recent years, and now he and his partner Joanne Harding have opened their own restaurant and guesthouse. Their modern stone fronted dormer home, overlooking the picturesque fishing village of Duncannon, enjoys lovely views of the beach and mountains - and has quickly earned a reputation for excellence in fine modern Irish cooking. The restaurant is bright and airy, with patio doors out onto a deck area, tables smartly set up with white linen runners and comfortable high backed leather chairs. Billy's fine training shows through in the many delightful dishes on dinner menus which are changed daily and offer six or eight appealing dishes on each course, including steak, poultry and some imaginative vegetarian options, although the emphasis is on seafood. First class ingredients are cooked with skill - a moist, flavourful and deliciously crumbly Hook Head crab cake, for example, makes a wonderful starter, served with wilted spinach and crème fraîche, and lobster (which is offered at a very moderate €5 supplement on the dinner menu) is a treat of a main course, perfectly baked and served with lemon & saffron butter sauce, with the head re-filled with and delicious pomme duchesse potatoes. Soups, breads and side vegetables are all lovely, and a tasting plate of half a dozen desserts (followed by a well-made espresso) rounds off a meal here nicely. The wine list is sensibly limited and offers good value. **Seats 32** (+12 outdoors;private room, 22). Reservations required. Toilets wheelchair accessible. Children welcome but not after 7pm. D daily in summer, 6.45-9.30. L Wed-Fri & Sun, 1-2.30. Early D, €25 (6.45-7.15); Set D 35; à la carte d and Vegetarian Menu also available. Weekday lunch €18, Set Sun L €22.50. SC discretionary. Closed Mon, 24-30 Dec. **Accommodation:** Four well-appointed bedrooms (one with full bath and shower, the others with shower only) are quiet and comfortable, with a residents lounge area on the landing. After a relaxing sleep, guests can look forward to an excellent breakfast with treats like fresh Dover sole on the bone (if you are lucky!), or pancakes, as well as an excellent 'full Irish'. This could be a hard place to leave. **Rooms 4** (all en suite, 3 shower only, 1 junior suite). Turndown service. Pets allowed by arrangement. Garden. B&B €40, no ss. MasterCard, Visa, Laser. **Directions:** Overlooking beach on Fethard-on-Sea road.

Duncanon
B RESTAURANT

Sqigl Restaurant & Roches Bar

Quay Road Duncannon New Ross Co Wexford
Tel: 051 389188 / 389700 Fax: 051 389346
Email: sqiglrestaurant@eircom.net

Sqigl (pronounced Squiggle) is located in a converted barn behind Bob and Eileen Roche's family pub, and is run by their daughter Cindy Roche, supported by chef Denise Bradley who continues to produce outstanding dishes, especially using local seafood. Sqigl aims to make the most of local produce and does it well with a sensibly limited menu, particularly the white fish landed at the harbour round the corner, wild locally caught salmon and Wexford beef and lamb. Décor is light, bright and modern and the cooking style is modern too, except that portions are aimed at generous Wexford appetites: creamy seafood chowder, or timbale of fresh crab with celery, avocado, smoked paprika mayonnaise & garlic crab claw, for example, make fine substantial starters. With local seafood the star, a speciality to keep an eye open for is whole grilled black sole, which is always a great treat, but here they ring the changes a little and they serve it with prawns in garlic butter and mushrooms.

But meat lovers have plenty to look forward to - rack of Wexford spring lamb is a regular, or you might try pan-fried fillet of Irish pork with hoi sin & plum sauce, served with fragrant rice; there's always an interesting vegetarian option too - saffron cous cous and grilled vegetables with deep fried goats cheese, perhaps... Finish off with a rich dessert like hot chocolate fondant with marmalade ice cream, or a more refreshing refreshing tart tatin with granny smith sorbet. Cindy supervises a friendly front of house team, and Sqigl offers good value for money, especially on midweek 'Value' menus. A thoughtfully selected wine list offers some lovely wines, including a good choice of quarter bottles and half bottles. **Seats 34** (outside seating, 10). Reservations advised. D Tue-Sat, 7-10; house wines from €15.50. Closed D Sun & Mon (except bank hol Suns), 24-27 Dec, 6 weeks Jan-Feb. MasterCard, Visa, Laser. **Directions:** R733 from Wexford & New Ross. Centre of village.

Enniscorthy
👁 COUNTRY HOUSE

Ballinkeele House

Ballymurn Enniscorthy Co Wexford
Tel: 053 38105 Fax: 053 38468
Email: john@ballinkeele.com Web: www.ballinkeele.com

Set in 350 acres of parkland, game-filled woods and farmland, this historic house is a listed building; designed by Daniel Robertson, it has been in the Maher family home since it was built in 1840 and remains at the centre of their working farm. It is a grand house, with a lovely old cut stone stable yard at the back and some wonderful features, including a lofty columned hall with a big open fire in the colder months, and beautifully proportioned reception rooms with fine ceilings and furnishings which have changed very little since the house was built. Nevertheless, it is essentially a family house and has a refreshingly hospitable and down-to-earth atmosphere. Large bedrooms are furnished with antiques and have wonderful countryside views. Margaret, who is a keen cook and a member of Euro-Toques, enjoys preparing 4-course dinners for guests (nice little wine list to accompany too). There's croquet on the lawn, a long sandy beach nearby at Curracloe, and bicycles (and wellingtons!) are available for guests' use; horse riding, fishing and golf can be organised nearby - and a lake in the grounds has been restored and is to be stocked for coarse fishing. Garden. Not suitable for children under 3. No pets. **Rooms 5** (all en-suite, 3 shower only, all no smoking). B&B €85 pps; ss 20. Residents Set D €40 at 7.30 (book by noon); house wine from €16.50. Private parties up to 14. Closed 30 Nov-28 Feb. MasterCard, Visa, Laser. **Directions:** From Wexford N11, north to Oilgate Village, turn right at signpost.

Enniscorthy
🌿 ⓔ 👁 COUNTRY HOUSE

Salville House

Enniscorthy Co Wexford **Tel: 054 35252**
Email: info@salvillehouse.com Web: www.salvillehouse.com

Set high on a hillside outside Enniscorthy, Gordon and Jane Parker's large mid-19th century house has sweeping views over the Slaney River Valley but the main point of interest is indoors in the dining room, where Gordon Parker's delicious dinners are served to guests around a communal table, elegantly set up with candles and fresh flowers in the evening - and where splendid breakfasts are served next morning. Seasonal dinners have an emphasis on local seafood and organic produce from the garden - but there isn't a formal menu with choices, so it's wise to mention any allergies or dislikes when booking. Gordon's cooking is modern and he seeks out superb ingredients, notably ultra fresh fish; a typical dinner might offer a fish satay on lemongrass, with a Vietnamese dipping sauce, or Kilmore Quay scallops with rocket & pancetta salad, then sea bream with tomato coulis or salmoriglio dressing, with a classical pudding like Eton mess to finish. After dinner, guests can relax in front of the drawing room fire, or play a game of backgammon before heading up to one of the three large rooms in the main house, which have views over the Slaney and are comfortably furnished with some style, or one of two in a self-contained apartment at the back. (All have tea/coffee making facilities, but no TV). A really good breakfast sends everyone on their way in good heart - freshly squeezed juice, lovely fruit compôtes, freshly-baked bread warm from the oven and hot dishes cooked to order, like undyed smoked haddock with rösti and poached eggs, or local smoked salmon with scrambled egg. Laid back hospitality, great food and good value make this comfortable house a fine base for exploring the area, or somewhere to break a journey. Children welcome. Pets allowed by arrangement. Garden. Croquet, Tennis, Boule. **Rooms 5** (3 en-suite, 2 with private bathrooms, 1 shower only). B&B €48, ss €10. 3-course Set D €35, at 8pm (book a day ahead - residents only; no D on Sun). BYO wine.*1/2 day weekend house party packages available for groups of 6+ (exclusive use of house). Closed Christmas. **No Credit Cards. Directions:** Off N11, 2 miles from Enniscorthy on Wexford side (look out for the sign on river side of main road). Go up hill & turn left; house on left.

Ferrycarrig Bridge
🏛👁 HOTEL/RESTAURANT

Ferrycarrig Hotel
Ferrycarrig Bridge Co Wexford
Tel: 053 20999 Fax: 053 20982
Email: res.ferrycarrig@ferrycarrighotel.com Web: www.ferrycarrighotel.ie

téile bia This modern hotel is in a lovely location overlooking the Slaney estuary and has excellent amenities, including a superb health and fitness club. An appealing contemporary bar with a large outside seating area where you can relax and enjoy the view and, in addiiton to imaginative bar food, appealing dining options are offered in The Boathouse Bistro (informal) and Tides Restaurant (fine dining). All of the well-appointed bedrooms have splendid views across the water and some have balconies with wooden loungers. Staff are exceptionally welcoming and friendly, and special breaks are offered.: Conference/banqueting (400/350). Leisure centre, swimming pool, beauty salon. Garden. Children welcome (cots available, baby sitting arranged; playroom - limited hours). No pets. **Rooms 102** (4 suites, 5 junior suites, 2 for disabled, 76 no smoking). Lift. All day room service. B&B €120 pps; ss €35. Open all year. **Seats 160.** Air conditioning. D Mon Sun 6.00-9.45 pm (limited opening in winter). A la carte. House wines from €20.00. sc discretionary. Not suitable for children after 7.30. * Dry Dock Bar: Wonderful contemporay style and waterfront location offering an entensive bar menu with imaginative kids meals. Enjoy your cocktail on the beautiful riverside deck. Food is also available daily, 12.30-9.00 pm. Amex, Diners, MasterCard, Visa, Laser **Directions:** Located on N11, 2 miles north of Wexford Town.

Gorey
🏛🏛☆ 🍽 COUNTRY HOUSE/RESTAURANT

Marlfield House
Courtown Road Gorey Co Wexford
Tel: 053 942 1124 Fax: 053 942 1572
Email: info@marlfieldhouse.ie Web: www.marlfieldhouse.com

téile bia Often quoted as 'the luxury country house hotel par excellence', this impressive house was once the residence of the Earls of Courtown, and is now an elegant oasis of unashamed luxury offering outstanding hospitality and service, where guests are cosseted and pampered in sumptuous surroundings. It was first opened as an hotel in 1978 by Mary and Ray Bowe who have lavished care and attention on this fine property ever since - imposing gates, a wooded drive, antiques and glittering chandeliers all promise guests a very special experience - and, although Mary and Ray are still very much involved, their daughters Margaret and Laura Bowe now continue the family tradition of hospitality established by their parents. The interior is luxurious in the extreme, with accommodation including six very grand state rooms, but the gardens are also a special point of interest: there is a lake and wildfowl reserve, a formal garden, kitchen garden, and beautiful woodland with extensive woodland walks - and a number of gardens open to the public are within easy access, including Mount Usher, Powerscourt, Altamont and Kilmokea. Conference/banqueting (40/30). Secretarial services. Dogs and children are welcome by prior arrangement (cots available without charge, baby sitting arranged). Tennis, cycling, walking. Garden. **Rooms 20** (6 state rooms, 14 superior, 8 ground floor, all no smoking). B&B €137.50pps. Room service (limited hours). Closed mid Dec-1 Feb. **Restaurant:** Dining is always an exceptional experience in Marlfield's fine restaurant, where the graceful dining room and Turner style conservatory merge into one, allowing views out across the gardens, including a fine kitchen garden that is a delight to the eye and provides a wide range of fresh produce for the restaurant. The conservatory, with its hanging baskets, plants and fresh flowers (not to mention the odd stone statue), is one of the most romantic spots in the whole of Ireland, further enhanced at night by candlelight a wonderful setting in which to enjoy chef Micheál MacCurtain's accomplished cooking. His strongly seasonal menus are changed daily and outline the produce available in the kitchen garden (which is Ray Bowe's particular point of pride), and the origin of other ingredients used. Although contemporary in style and presentation, there is a strong classical background to the cooking, and it is all the better for that. Specialities that indicate the style include an elegant starter terrine of braised ham and foie gras with beetroot jelly and celeriac roulade, and a fish main course of baked Dunmore East hake with creamed orzo, baby pak choi and violet artichokes. Equally creative vegetarian choices are always offered, lovely puds reflect the best fruit in season at the time, and a cheese selection from Sheridans cheesemongers. Then it's off to the drawing room for coffee and petits fours to round off the feast. Very professional service is a match for this fine food and an informative wine list, long on burgundies and clarets, offers a wine of the month and a page of special recommendations. Not suitable for children under 8 at D. **Seats 65** (private room, 50; outdoor,14). Reservations advised. Air conditioning. Toilets wheelchair accessible. D daily, 7-9 (Sat to 10, Sun to 8); L Sun only 12.30-2. Early D €36 (Sun-Thu, 6-7), also à la carte; Set Sun L €36. House wine €24. SC discretionary. Light à la carte lunches are served daily in Library, 12.30-5. Amex, Diners, MasterCard, Visa, Laser **Directions:** 1 mile outside Gorey on Courtown Road (R742).

Rosslare Area
🏛 COUNTRY HOUSE

Churchtown House

Tagoat Rosslare Co Wexford **Tel: 053 32555**
Email: info@churchtownhouse.com Web: www.churchtownhouse.com

Patricia and Austin Cody's Georgian house is extremely handy for the Rosslare ferryport, about four miles away, but it is a really lovely place and deserves a longer stay - it would make a beautifully relaxing base for a few days exploring the area. It's set in about eight and a half acres of wooded gardens and dates back to 1703 but it has been completely renovated by the Codys, and elegantly furnished to make a comfortable country house retreat for discerning guests. Public areas are spacious, with plenty of seating in rooms of different character allowing a choice of mood for guests. Bedrooms are equally pleasing - large, and furnished to the highest standards in country house style, with generous beds, phones, TV and well-finished bathrooms. The Codys are renowned for their hospitality and, if you're lucky enough to arrive at this well-run house at around teatime, you'll be served delicious home-made cake and tea in the drawing room. Good food is an important feature here and a fine Irish breakfast is served in the bright dining room, where dinner is also served to residents (at separate tables), by arrangement. Garden. Children welcome. No pets. **Rooms 12** (1 junior suite, 5 shower only, all no smoking). B&B €65 pps; ss €15. Residents' D, 8pm; Set D €39, book by noon. House wines €20. Closed week ends Nov, all of Dec -Mar. MasterCard, Visa, Laser. **Directions:** On R736 half mile from N25, at Tagoat.

Rosslare Strand
👁 HOTEL/RESTAURANT

Kelly's Resort Hotel

Rosslare Co Wexford
Tel: 053 32114 Fax: 053 32222
Email: kellyhot@iol.ie Web: www.kellys.ie

FAMILY HOTEL OF THE YEAR

téile bia The history of this renowned family-run hotel spans three centuries - yet constant renovating, refurbishing and building work each winter keep raising standards ever higher. Quite simply, the hotel has everything, for both individuals and families, many of whom return year after year (the number of children is limited at any one time, to prevent creating an imbalance). The many public rooms range from a quiet reading room and the snooker room to a supervised crèche and gallery lounge: paintings (mostly modern) throughout the hotel form an outstanding art collection. Many of the bedrooms have sea views, some with balconies; all the expected amenities are there except tea/coffee making, which is available on request. Leisure facilities include two indoor swimming pools, a recently opened well-being centre 'SeaSpa' which has 11 treatment rooms, seawater vitality pool, steam room, rock sauna and much else besides, indoor tennis, and - a bit of fun for Francophiles - boules. Outside the summer holiday season (end June-early Sept), ask about special breaks (including special interest breaks - everything from wine appreciation to golf clinics), when rates are reduced. No conferences or functions are accepted. Fishing (sea). Snooker, pool table. Hair dressing. Children welcome (under 3 months free in parents' room, cot available without charge, baby sitting arranged). Supervised play-room & children's playground. Walking, cycling, pitch & putt. Garden. No pets. **Rooms 120** (2 suites, 2 junior suites, 2 superior, 20 ground floor, 2 disabled). Lift. Room service (limited hours). Turndown service offered. B&B €90, ss €10; SC10%. Hotel closed 11 Dec-mid Feb. **Beaches Restaurant:** This L shaped room, which has been run under the eagle eye of Pat Doyle since 1966, was completely redesigned in 2003 to retain a sense of traditional opulence yet with a fresh, almost gallery-esque approach - an ideal home for some favourites from the hotel's famous art collection. Executive Chef Jim Aherne has been pleasing guests with his classic cuisine for over thirty years now - and, although more exotic ingredients like ostrich also appear, his menus reflect the value placed on fresh local produce: Rosslare mackerel, Slaney salmon and locally sourced vegetables, for example, are used in daily-changing menus that ensure variety for residents who may be staying for some time. The hotel's renowned wine list is meticulously sourced, always changing, and excellent value. Highly informative (and a good read), most wines are directly imported and there are many treats in the collection, which includes organic and bio-dynamic wines, and an exceptional choice of half bottles. **Seats 250** (private room 40); air conditioning. L &D daily: L1-2.15, D 7.30-9; Set L €25; Set Sun L €26; Set D €42. House wine €21; SC discretionary. **La Marine:** This informal restaurant has its own separate entrance and offers a relaxed alternative to the dining experience in Beaches Restaurant. A zinc bar imported from France is the focal point of the rather pubby bar, where you can have an aperitif - although the turnover in La Marine is brisk and it is better to go directly to your table if it is ready. Comfort is not a top priority: fashionably sparse tables have fresh flowers, good quality cutlery and paper napkins, but space is at a premium so be prepared for a bit of a squeeze. Head chef Eugene Callaghan's ingredients are carefully sourced, using local seasonal produce as much as possible, and a finely judged balancing act between traditional and contemporary fare is achieved on menus offering plenty of choice: a starter of Caesar salad with crispy Thai crab wontons rubs shoulders with classic grilled Bannow Bay mussels with garlic & parsley butter, while main courses lead off traditionally with seared Hereford sirloin steak, with gratin dauphinois, but also offer a lively repertoire of colourful dishes - now tending to be less Asian and more European in style. Desserts are deliciously classic - dark chocolate mousse on a crispy praline wafer, perhaps, and there's always a selection of Irish cheese. Service is swift and friendly. The downside of the popularity of this bar and restaurant is that heavy usage can take its toll, especially towards the end of season, so it may lose the pristine appearance essential to the modern style. Sunday lunch, which is very good value, tends to be a little more traditional and may include upbeat versions of traditional roasts. As in the hotel, there is very good wine list. Booking strongly advised, especially at weekends. A light snack menu is also available every afternoon, 3-6pm. Wines reflecting the style of food, are fairly priced (selection off main list). **Seats 70.** L daily, 12.30-2.15; D 6.30-9.30. Amex, MasterCard, Visa, Laser. **Directions:** Take the signs for Wexford/Rosslare/Southeast. 20 km from Wexford Town alongside Rosslare Strand beach.

Wexford

€ CAFÉ/RESTAURANT

La Dolce Vita

6/7 Trimmers Lane Wexford Co Wexford
Tel: 053 70806 Fax: 053 20267

In an unexpected little oasis of calm just off North Main Street, one of Ireland's favourite Italian restaurateurs has a smashing daytime restaurant and deli that is so popular with the locals that lunchtime hopefuls must arrive early, or be prepared for a long wait. You'll spot the trademark stripy awning (and tables outside in summer) from either end of this unexpectedly spacious spot, then see through the big window a bright spacious eating area set up with smart lighted tables and chairs, surrounded by shelves stacked with Italian goodies. Good glasses and elegant tableware heighten the sense of anticipation - and so to Roberto Pons's seriously tempting menus, in Italian with English translations, arranged so that you can have as little or as much as you wish: just a bite, such as home-made Italian bread with oil (€1.95), fresh soup of the day (€3.95), or risotto of the day (€7.50), perhaps, or Tuscan salad (one of six super salads, all under €10), antipasto with roasted vegetables (for €8.75 you get a generous platter of top class authentic Italian salami and meats - enough for two to share as a starter), and a range of pasta dishes, all under €10. Then there are some more 'serious' dishes, like grilled seabass with salmoriglio dressing or Italian sausage with lentils. Don't leave without tasting at least one of Roberto's lovely desserts too - a perfect pannacotta, orange & lemon tart - and, of course, a classic tiramisu, with a really good coffee. But, anyway, there's still the shopping to do - all sorts of Italian treats, including wines (16 are offered by the glass) are imported directly by Roberto and, should you be lucky enough to live nearby (or staying in self-catering accommodation), there's even a short takeaway menu including delights like grilled chicken & courgette with creamy gorgonzola, and suckling pig with homemade chutney. Now that's style. **Seats 45;** Toilets Wheelchair Accesible; Open all day (12-4, no evening meals). L from 12 noon. Set L €10-12; House Wine from €13. Closed Sun, Mon, Bank Hols & 4 days Christmas. MasterCard, Visa, Laser. **Directions:** Off the northern end of the main street - look out for the big green, red & white canopy.

Wexford

☆ RESTAURANT

La Riva

2 Henrietta Street Crescent Quay Wexford Co Wexford
Tel: 053 24330 Fax: 053 24330 Email: warrengillen@dol.ie

féile bia Warren Gillen's first floor restaurant is approached up rather steep stairs, creating a wonderful contrast as you emerge into a bright room which overlooks the quay and twinkling lights along the shore - and is imbued with that indefinably warm atmosphere of happy people dining. And those with their backs to the harbour get compensation a-plenty: as the complementary view is of Warren and his team at work in the kitchen, creating delicious things for you to enjoy. Welcoming staff show arriving guest to smartly appointed tables, and the opening details - really delicious breads and a complimentary amuse-bouche - are very impressive. Warren's aim is 'to serve non-pretentious seasonal food, that allows the best local ingredients to shine' and this he does very well, as some of the finest food in the south-east is to be found here: menus are quietly impressive; without resorting to long or flowery descriptions, dishes like Kilmore crab risotto with chilli, ginger, mango & coriander, or fried Croghan Farm goats cheese, with salad of roast peppers & red onion, and home-dried tomatoes are extremely appealing - and they consistently follow through on the plate, in memorable dishes which are beautifully balanced in presentation, flavour and texture. Given the location, seafood is hard to resist but local meats are well represented too - medallions of Hereford beef, perhaps, with a white onion confit, parsley pesto mushroom and a truffle oil & marjoram consommé; vegetarian dishes are creative enough to have mainstream appeal, and you can finish off what is sure to be a memorable meal with a lovely dessert, such as a warm chocolate & pistachio brownie with Baileys custard & coffee granita: simply superb. Well-trained, attentive staff complement the creative cooking - the wonder is how they can produce such outstanding food in a kitchen of this size. A short wine list is expanded by nine or ten monthly specials and a page of bin ends; the two-course early dinner menu offers exceptional value. **Seats 50** Air conditioning. Not suitable for children after 8pm. D, daily in summer, 6-10 (open Sun of Bank Hols only). Early D €25 (6-7 Mon-Fri). Set D, 2/3 courses €32/37; 7-course tatsing Menu, €45; also à la carte. House wine from €19.70; sc discretionary. Closed Sun (except oon Bank Hol weekends), last week of Feb. MasterCard, Visa, Laser. **Directions:** Opposite Commodore Barry Statue.

Wexford

🍴 € B&B

McMenamin's Townhouse

3 Auburn Terrace Redmond Road Wexford Co Wexford
Tel: 053 46442 Fax: 053 46442
Email: mcmem@indigo.ie Web: www.wexford-bedandbreakfast.com

BEST B&B BREAKFAST

Seamus and Kay McMenamin's redbrick end-of-terrace Victorian house is within walking distance of the town centre and has been one of the most highly-regarded places to stay in this area for many years. It is useful for first or last night overnight stops for travellers on the Rosslare ferry (15 minutes), as a base for the Wexford Opera, or for a short break exploring this fascinating corner of Ireland. Flooding in late 2004 caused serious damage to the interior, requiring complete refurbishment and redecoration - that it now looks as if nothing had happened is a tribute to the TLC the McMenamins have since lavished on the house. The bedrooms, which have been individually redecorated, have neat shower rooms and some have four posters - but all have top quality beds and bedding, and everything that you need to be comfortable away from home, including TV and tea/coffee-making facilities. The McMenamins' extensive local knowledge is generously passed on to guests and this, together with a really good breakfast, gets you off to a good start and helps to make the most of every day. Quite extensive breakfast menus include a range of fruits and juices, home-made yoghurts, old-fashioned treats like kippers and also fresh local fish such as delicious fillets of plaice, lambs' kidneys in sherry sauce, omelettes or pancakes - all served with a choice of several freshly baked breads and home-made preserves, including an excellent marmalade and unusual jams such as loganberry. The breakfast room is attractively set up with linen tablecloths and fresh flowers, food is beautifully prepared and presented, and cooked dishes served piping hot: you will want to return as soon as possible! Hunting, shooting, fishing, walking, nearby. Also scenic drives, historic walks, racing, boating, swimming & tennis. Children welcome (under 2s free in parents' room, cots available without charge). No pets. **Rooms 6** (all shower only). B&B €45 pps; ss €10. Private parking. Closed 20-30 Dec. MasterCard, Visa. **Directions:** Central near bus/rail station opposite cineplex.

COUNTY WICKLOW

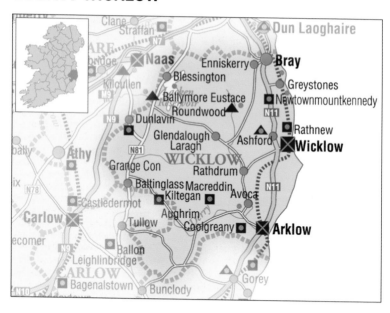

Ashford
🏵 FARMHOUSE

Ballyknocken House
Gleanealy Ashford Co Wicklow
Tel: 0404 44627 Fax: 0404 44696
Email: cfulvio@ballyknocken.com Web: www.ballyknocken.com

féile bia Perfectly placed for walking holidays in the Wicklow Hills, playing golf, or simply for touring the area, Catherine Fulvio's charming Victorian farmhouse provides comfort, cosiness, home-cooked food and hospitality. The farm has been in the Byrne family for three generations and they have welcomed guests for over thirty years - Catherine took over in 1999, she has since refurbished the house throughout in old country style. A gently Victorian theme prevails: bedrooms have been charmingly done up, with antique furniture and very good beds - and pretty bathrooms, five of which have Victorian baths. The dining room, parlour and sitting room are in a similar style and her energetic quest for perfection also extends to the garden, where new fruit tree, roses and herbs were planted, and her cookery school - which is in a renovated milking parlour in the grounds. Catherine cooks four course dinners for guests, based on local produce, including vegetables and herbs from the Ballyknocken farm (with wine list including some specially imported wines); the cooking style is modern and (influenced by her Italian husband Claudio) there's a Mediterranean flavour. All this, plus extensive breakfasts and a relaxing atmosphere ensure guests keep coming back for more. Short breaks are offered, also self-catering accommodation; details on these, and Ballyknocken Cookery School, on application. Ballyknocken was our Farmhouse of the Year in 2004. **Rooms 7** (all en-suite, 1 shower only, all no smoking). B&B €59 pps, ss €35. Residents D Tue-Sat, at 7.30. Set 4-course D €38; houses wines €19.95. No D on Sun or Mon. Non-resident group (8+) lunches catered for, by arrangement. Closed mid Dec- mid Jan. MasterCard, Visa. **Directions:** From Dublin turn right after Texaco Petrol Station in Ashford. Continue for 3 miles.House on right.

Blessington
€ CAFÉ

Grangecon Café

Kilbride Road Blessington Co Wicklow
Tel: 045 857 892 Email: grangeconcafe@eircom.net

Wholesome aromas will draw you into Jenny and Richard Street's smashing café, which retained its name when re-locating from the charming village of Grangecon to the bustle of Blessington Here they are in an old building that has been given new life by a lovely renovation job, with gentle modern decor and natural materials that should never date. But the fundamentals remain unchanged: the stated aim has always been "to provide you with a really good food stop", and this they continue to do brilliantly. Everything on the menu is made on the premises, including the breads, pastries and ice cream; the ham hocks for the quiche lorraine are cooked here, the pork meat used in the sausage rolls is organic, fruit and vegetables come from Castleruddery organic farm, and all other ingredients are of the very best quality, many of them also organic and/or free range. The menu is understandably fairly brief, but the cooking is good, and flavours superb: the quiche, fro example, is a little classic and comes with a scrumptious salad; similarly moist, freshly-baked brown bread arrives with home cooked ham, farmhouse cheese (Sheridan's) and homemade chutney, also garnished with salad: simple and excellent - not for the first time, we say: why aren't there more places like this? No wine at the time of going to press, but a wine licence is expected soon - meanwhile you can opt for delicious chilled Crinnaughton apple juice, which comes from Cappoquin, instead and B-Y-O wine is fine. Luscious Illy coffee to finish and maybe a slice of chocolate cake. This is not cheap food - how could it be when the ingredients are of such high quality - but there s nothing on the menu over €10 and it is extremely good value for money. **Seats 30.** Open all day Tue-Sat, 9am-5.30pm. Toilets wheelchair accessible; Baby Changing Facilities; Party Service; Closed Sun, Mon. Aug Bank Hol weekend & 25 Dec - 1 Jan. MasterCard, Visa, Laser. **Directions:** Centre of Blessington village, around the corner from Downshire House Hotel.

Dunlavin
COUNTRY HOUSE

Rathsallagh House, Golf & Country Club

Dunlavin Co Wicklow
Tel: 045 403 112 Fax: 045 403 343
Email: info@rathsallagh.com Web: www.rathsallagh.com

féile bia This large, rambling country house is just an hour from Dublin, but it could be in a different world. Although it's very professionally operated, the O'Flynn family insist it is not an hotel and - although there is an 18-hole golf course with clubhouse in the grounds - the gentle rhythms of life around the country house and gardens ensure that the atmosphere is kept decidedly low-key. Day rooms are elegantly furnished in classic country house style, with lots of comfortable seating areas and open fires. Bedrooms, as in all old houses do vary - some are spacious with lovely country views, while other smaller, simpler rooms in the stable yard have a special cottagey charm; and there are newer rooms, built discreetly behind the main courtyard, which very big and finished to a high standard, with luxurious bathrooms. Rathsallagh is renowned for its magnificent Edwardian breakfast buffet which was, for the second time, the overall national winner of our Irish Breakfast Awards in 2005. Breakfast at Rathsallagh offers every conceivable good thing, including silver chafing dishes, full of reminders of yesteryear. A large sideboard display offers such an array of temptations that it can be hard to decide where to start - fresh juices, fruits and home-bakes, local honey and home-made jams and chutneys...Irish farmhouse cheeses, Rathsallagh ham on the bone, salamis and smoked salmon...then there are the hot dishes, including the full Irish, and then some - less usual dishes like smoked salmon kedgeree, and Kay's devilled kidneys are specialities worth travelling for. And, for the faint-hearted, there's another whole menu devoted to the Healthy Option Breakfast. If golf is not your thing, there are plenty of other ways to work off this remarkable meal - the Wicklow Hills beckon walkers of all levels, for example, or you could at least fit in a gentle stroll around the charming walled gardens. Great food and service, warm hospitality, and surroundings that are quiet or romantic to suit the mood of the day - Rathsallagh has it all. *Ask about the relaxing bath menus. Conference/banqueting (120/120). Golf (18). Swimming pool. Gardens, tennis, cycling, walking. Pool table. Beauty salon. Pets allowed by arrangement. **Rooms 29** (1 suite, 9 ground floor, 1 for disabled, all no smoking). B&B €125pps, ss €50. *Short breaks (incl golf breaks) offered, details on application. Open all year. **Restaurant:** Have an aperitif in the old kitchen bar while considering daily-changing menus based on local and seasonal produce, much of it from Rathsallagh's own farm and gardens. Head Chef John Kosturk clearly relishes everything that is going on at Rathsallagh; his menus, which are interesting and change daily, are based on local and seasonal produce, much of it from Rathsallagh's own farm and walled garden. Menus are not over-complicated but offer a well-balanced range of about five dishes on each course, changed daily: a beautifully constructed terrine of Belvelly Cove smoked eel & cured Blackwater salmon with garden asparagus is a speciality, and makes an unusual and elegant starter, while and main courses will usually include Wicklow lamb from Doyle's butchers - a roast rack, perhaps, served in summer with warm potato salad and red wine jus. Choices made, settle down in the graciously furnished dining room overlooking the gardens and the golf course to enjoy a series of dishes that are well-conceived and visually tempting but especially memorable for flavour. Leave room for luscious desserts, often based on fruit from the garden and served from a traditional trolley, or Irish farmhouse cheeses, before relaxing with coffee and petits fours in the drawing room or bar. An informative wine list offers many interesting bottles, notably in the Rathsallagh Cellar Collection, and includes a good choice of recommended wines under €30. Helipad. **Seats 120** (private room, 45). Reservations essential. D daily, 7-9.30. Set 5-course D €60; route meal €19.50; SC discretionary. *Not suitable for children under 12. Lunch is available only for residents (12-3), but food is served at Rathsallagh Golf Club, 9-9 daily. Non-residents welcome for dinner, by reservation. Amex, Diners, MasterCard, Visa **Directions:** 15 miles south of Naas off Carlow Road, take Kilcullen Bypass (M9), turn left 2 miles south of Priory Inn, follow signposts.

Greystones
 RESTAURANT

The Hungry Monk

Church Road Greystones Co Wicklow
Tel: 01 287 5759 Fax: 01 287 7183
Email: info@thehungrymonk.ie Web: www.thehungrymonk.ie

féile bia Well-known wine buff Pat Keown has run this hospitable first floor restaurant on the main street since 1988. Pat is a great and enthusiastic host; his love of wine is infectious, the place is spick and span and the monk-related decor is a bit of fun. A combination of hospitality, great wines and interesting good quality food at affordable prices are at the heart of this restaurant's success and sheer generosity of spirit ensures value for money as well as a good meal. Seasonal menus offered include a well-priced all-day Sunday lunch and an evening à la carte menu, with fish the speciality in summer, and game in winter. Blackboard specials guaranteed to sharpen the appetite include the day's seafood dishes, any special wine offers - and, perhaps, a special treat like suckling pig (a superb dish with a prune and apricot stuffing, apple sauce, a delicious jus and colcannon or champ). Menus give a slight nod to current trends - in dishes like a tian of Castletownbere crab with fresh ginger, apple & coriander flavoured coconut milk, for example - but there is no pretence at cutting edge style and you will also find faithful renditions of old favourites not often seen at the moment, like lambs kidneys dijonnaise. Vegetarian dishes and healthy heart options are highlighted on the menu and there is emphasis on high quality ingredients, including Angus steaks, Wicklow lamb and ultra-fresh seafood from Greystones harbour; The famous wine list ('The Thirsty Monk') is clearly a labour of love and, in turn, gives great pleasure to customers, especially as prices are very fair. Affordable favourites include a whole page of house wines listed by category - house wine Chile, house wine France, house wines organic, house champagne.... and so on - and also, of course, offers many special bottles for connoisseurs, from every great wine region in the world including a number of magnums and jeraboams (double magnums), which make a dramatic centrepiece for a party and are great value for money. Two pages of half bottles too, and a couple of dozen pudding wines... Wine lovers should arrive early to allow the time to relish this list. Children welcome. Restaurant **Seats 40.** Reservations advised. Air conditioning. D Wed-Sat 6.30-11; L Sun only, 12.30-8. D à la carte; also Vegetarian Menu; Set Sun L €25. House wines from €18, SC 10%. Restaurant closed Mon & Tue. Closed 24-26 Dec. *Downstairs, The Hungry Monk Wine Bar offers an informal menu of bistro style dishes (Monk's famous burger, Dublin Bay prawn scampi & chips...) and a carefully selected short wine list. Wine Bar open daily, 5-11. Closed 25-26 Dec. Amex, MasterCard, Visa, Laser **Directions:** Centre of Greystones village beside DART.

Kilmacanogue
🍴 € CAFÉ

Avoca Handweavers
Kilmacanogue Co Wicklow
Tel: 01 286 7466 Fax: 01 286 2367
Email: simon@avoca.ie Web: www.avoca.ie

This large shop and restaurant, off the N11 south of Dublin, is the flagship premises of Ireland's most famous group of craft shops and, in recent years, they have become almost equally well known for the quality of their food - people come here from miles around to shop - and to tuck into wholesome home-cooked food, which is as healthy as it is delicious. The importance of sourcing only the very best ingredients has always been recognised at Avoca, where food is based as much as possible on local and artisan produce, and there is a commitment to using products from recognised Quality Assurance Schemes. (In recognition, Avoca Cafés were the 2003 recipients of the Féile Bia Award). The style at Avoca is eclectic and, although they are perhaps especially well-known for great baking and wholesome traditional dishes like beef and Guinness casserole, their salads and vegetables are also legendary - and their repertoire also includes a lot of dishes influenced by other cultures, notably Mediterranean and middle-eastern. There is also a wide range of excellent delicatessen fare for sale in the shop - and you can make many of their dishes at home too, using recipes given in the two handsome Avoca Café Cookbooks. *Also at: Avoca, Powerscourt, & Suffolk Street, Dublin 2 (see entries). Toilets Wheelchair Accessible; Children welcome. **Seats 160** (+Outdoor Dining, 120). Air conditioning. Open daily, 10-5. House wine about €12.50. No s.c. Closed 25-26 Dec. Amex, Diners, MasterCard, Visa, Laser. **Directions:** On N11 sign posted before Kilmacanogue Village.

Kiltegan
€ 👁 COUNTRY HOUSE

Barraderry Country House
Barraderry Kiltegan Co Wicklow
Tel: 059 647 3209 Fax: 059 647 3209
Email: jo.hobson@oceanfree.net Web: www.barraderrycountryhouse.com

Olive and John Hobson's delightful Georgian house is in a quiet rural area close to the Wicklow Mountains and, once their family had grown up, the whole house was extensively refurbished and altered for the comfort of guests. Big bedrooms with country views are beautifully furnished with old family furniture and have well-finished shower rooms - and there's a spacious sitting room for guests' use too. Barraderry would make a good base for touring the lovely counties of Wicklow, Kildare, Carlow and Wexford and there's plenty to do nearby, with six golf courses within a half hour drive, several hunts and equestrian centres within easy reach and also Punchestown, Curragh and Naas racecourses - and, of course, walking in the lovely Wicklow Mountains. Garden; walking. Children welcome (cot available). No pets. **Rooms 4** (all ensuite, shower only & no smoking). B&B €45 pps; ss €5. Closed 15 Dec-15 Jan. MasterCard, Visa. **Directions:** N81 Dublin-Baltinglass; R 747 to Kiltegan (7km).

Kiltegan
🏛 ♈ 👁 COUNTRY HOUSE

Humewood Castle

Kiltegan Co Wicklow
Tel: **059 64 73215** Fax: 059 64 73382
Email: humewood@iol.ie Web: www.humewood.com

A fairytale 19th-century Gothic Revival castle in private ownership set in beautiful parkland in the Wicklow Hills, Humewood has been extensively renovated and stunningly decorated. While the castle is very large by any standards, many of the rooms are of surprisingly human proportions - the main dining room, for example, provides a fine setting for some two dozen guests, and there are more intimate rooms suitable for smaller numbers (residents only). Similarly, the luxuriously appointed bedrooms and bathrooms, while indisputably grand, are also very comfortable. Country pursuits are an essential part of life at Humewood, which is mainly a sporting estate - horseriding, fishing, shooting, deer stalking, hunting and falconry can all be arranged - but even if you do nothing more energetic than just relaxing beside the fire, this is a really special place for a break. It's also a wonderfully romantic location for a wedding, and conferences, product launches and corporate entertaining packages can be tailored to meet specific requirement.*Self-catering accommodation is also offered, in two-bedroomed lodges on the grounds. Conference/banqueting (120/80). Snooker. Garden, tennis, walking, cycling. Children welcome. Pets by arrangement. **Rooms 13** (all en-suite, 8 suites, all no smoking, 1 equipped for disabled). Room rate with breakfast, from €350 high season (for two). Residents' D about €65; house wine about €23. Amex, MasterCard, Visa **Directions:** Dublin - N81- Baltinglass - R747 Hacketstown Road.

Macreddin
♈ 👁 HOTEL

The BrookLodge Hotel

Macreddin Village Co Wicklow
Tel: **0402 36444** Fax: 0402 36580
Email: brooklodge@macreddin.ie Web: www.brooklodge.com

Built on the site of a deserted village in a Wicklow valley, this extraordinary food, drink and leisure complex exists thanks to the vision of three brothers, Evan, Eoin and Bernard Doyle. The driving force is Evan, a pioneer of the new organic movement when he ran The Strawberry Tree restaurant in Killarney. Now their new hotel and restaurant has earned a national recognition for its strong position on organic food (BrookLodge won the Guide's Natural Food Award in association with Euro-Toques, in 2003), and their little "street" is thriving, with an olde-worlde pub (Actons), a café, a micro-brewery and gift shops selling home-made produce and related quality products. Organic food markets, held on the first Sunday of the month (first and third in summer) have also proved a great success. Spacious and welcoming, the hotel has elegant country house furnishings, open fires and plenty of places to sit quietly or meet for a sociable drink - and the accommodation choices are between the original rooms, which are furnished with quite traditional free standing furniture, and state-of-the-art mezzanine suites, which will please those who enjoy very modern high-tech surroundings. A luxurious new spa centre, The Wells, features an indoor-to-outdoor swimming pool, gym, juice bar and a wide variety of exclusive beauty and health treatments. Midweek, weekend and low season special offers are good value. Staff are friendly and helpful, although service can sometimes be a little patchy, letting down an otherwise pleasing hotel. Conference/banqueting (350/191). Secretarial services, video conferencing (by arrangement). Equestrian centre. Off road driving. Hot tub. Garden, walking. Snooker. Children welcome (under 4s free in parents' room, cot available without charge, baby sitting arranged). Pets allowed in some areas by arrangement. **Rooms 56** (13 suites, 3 junior suites, 3 superior rooms, 4 ground floor, 2 family, 4 disabled, 35 no smoking). Lift. B&B from €110 pps; ss €40. Open all year. **The Strawberry Tree:** This is an unusual room, with a mirrored ceiling - quite unlike the rest of the hotel - a little strange in the daytime (Sunday lunch is served here), but very romantic when candlelit at night. It is Ireland's only certified organic restaurant, reflecting the BrookLodge philosophy of sourcing only from producers using slow organic methods and harvesting in their correct season. Menus are not too long or too fussy:

dishes have strong, simple names and, except when underlined on the menu as wild, everything offered is organic. Typical dishes might include starters like home smoked beef, with figs and balsamic dressing or grilled wild pollock with roast red pepper, and main courses such as grilled lamb withconfit carrots, wild cep and garlic cream, or a vegetarian dish of wild mushroom and brie tart with wild garlic pesto. There's a great buzz associated with the commitment to organic production at BrookLodge, and it makes a natural venue for meetings of like-minded groups such as Euro-Toques and Slow Food, especially on market days. Dining at the Strawberry Tree is a unique experience - and good informal meals can be equally enjoyable at The Orchard Café and Actons pub (both open noon-9pm daily). Given the quality of ingredients used and the standard of cooking, meals at BrookLodge represent very good value. **Seats 145** (private room, 50). Air conditioning. Toilets wheelchair accessible. D Mon-Sun 7-9.30 (to 9 Sun), L Sun only 1-3.30. Set D €55, Set Sun L €35. House wines €21. SC discretionary. *William Actons Pub - Bar food daily, 12-9; The Orchard Café, light meals 12-9. Amex, Diners, MasterCard, Visa, Laser **Directions:** Signed from Aughrim.

Newtownmountkennedy

Marriott Druids Glen Hotel & Country Club

 HOTEL/RESTAURANT

Newtownmountkennedy Co Wicklow
Tel: 01 287 0800 Fax: 01 287 0801
Email: mhrs.dubgs.reservations@marriotthotels.com Web: www.marriott.com

féile bia Just 20 miles south of Dublin, in a stunning location between the sea and the mountains and adjacent to Druids Glen Golf Club, this luxurious hotel has a feeling of space throughout - beginning with the marbled foyer and its dramatic feature fireplace. Suites and guest rooms, many of them "double/doubles" (with two queen sized beds), are all generously-sized, with individual 'climate control' (heating and air conditioning), and all bathrooms have separate bath and walk-in shower. A wide range of recreational facilities on site includes the hotel's spa and health club, while those nearby include horse riding, archery, quad biking - and, of course, the gentler attractions of the Wicklow Mountains National Park are on the doorstep. When dining in, choose between Flynns' Steakhouse (see below) and the bigger Druids Restaurant (where breakfast, carvery lunch and dinner are served daily). Bar meals also available in 'The Thirteenth' bar or, in fine weather, on a sheltered deck outside the two restaurants. Druids Glen Marriott was our Business Hotel of the Year in 2003 - and this is a place to relax and unwind, as well as do business. Conference/banqueting 250/220; business centre, secretarial services. Golf (2x18); leisure centre, swimming pool; spa, beauty/treatment rooms, walking, garden. **Rooms 148** (11 suites, 137 executive, 6 disabled). Lift. Children welcome (under 12s free in parents' room, cots available without charge; baby sitting arranged). 24 hr. room service, turndown service, laundry/valet service. B&B €113, ss €25. **Flynn's Steakhouse:** Quite small and intimate, with an open log fire and candlelight, Flynn's has more atmosphere than the bigger daytime Druids Restaurant, and reservations are essential. American style steaks and grills are the speciality but, demonstrating a welcome commitment to using Irish produce, a supply of Certified Irish Angus is contracted for the hotel; just remember that American-style means big - 24oz porterhouse and ribeye, for example...Rack of Wicklow lamb is another speciality and there's a sprinkling of other dishes with an Irish flavour which might not be expected in an international hotel, like Dingle crab cakes, Guinness braised mussels - and an Irish cheese platter. **Seats 55** (private room 20). Reservations essential. Not suitable for children under 12. D Thu-Sun, 6-10.30. Sun Brunch € 32.50, Set D €45, also à la carte. House wine, from €22; SC discretionary. *The larger Druid's Restaurant serves breakfast, lunch & dinner daily; L carvery, Druids Irish D Menu à la carte. Bar meals also available in 'The Thirteenth' bar or, in fine weather, on a sheltered deck outside the two restaurants. Amex, Diners, MasterCard, Visa, Laser **Directions:** 20 miles south of Dublin on N11, at Newtownmountkennedy.

Rathnew
⊙ HOTEL/RESTAURANT

Hunter's Hotel

Newrath Bridge Rathnew Co Wicklow
Tel: 0404 40106 Fax: 0404 40338
Email: reception@hunters.ie Web: indigo.ie/~hunters

A rambling old coaching inn set in lovely gardens alongside the River Vartry, this much-loved hotel has a long and fascinating history - it's one of Ireland's oldest coaching inns, with records indicating that it was built around 1720. In the same family now for five generations, the colourful Mrs Maureen Gelletlie takes pride in running the place on traditional lines with her son Richard, who is the manager. This means old-fashioned comfort and food based on local and home-grown produce with the emphasis very much on 'old fashioned' which is where its charm and character lie. There's a proper little bar, with chintzy loose-covered furniture and an open fire, a traditional dining room with fresh flowers from the riverside garden where their famous afternoon tea is served in summer - and comfortable country bedrooms. There is nowhere else in Ireland like it. Conference (30). Garden. Parking. Children welcome. No pets. **Rooms 16** (1 junior suite, 1 shower only, 1 disabled). Wheelchair access. B&B from €95 pps, ss about €20. **Restaurant:** In tune with the spirit of the hotel, the style is traditional country house cooking: simple food with a real home-made feeling about it - no mean achievement in a restaurant and much to be applauded. Seasonal lunch and dinner menus change daily, but you can expect classics such as chicken liver pâté with melba toast, soups based on fish or garden produce, traditional roasts rib beef, with Yorkshire pudding or old-fashioned roast stuffed chicken with bacon and probably several fish dishes, possibly including poached salmon with hollandaise and chive sauce. Desserts are often based on what the garden has to offer, and baking is good, so fresh raspberries and cream or baked apple and rhubarb tart could be wise choices. **Seats 50.** Toilets wheelchair accessible. L daily, 1-3 (Sun 2 sittings: 12.45 & 2.30). D daily 7.30-9. Set D €40. Set L €22. No s.c. House wine about €16. Afternoon tea €7.50. Closed 3 days at Christmas. Amex, Diners, MasterCard, Visa **Directions:** Off N11 at Ashford or Rathnew.

Rathnew
🏛️🍷 HOTEL/RESTAURANT

Tinakilly Country House & Restaurant

Rathnew Co Wicklow **Tel: 0404 69274** Fax: 0404 67806
Email: reservations@tinakilly.ie Web: www.tinakilly.ie

Josephine and Raymond Power have been running this fine hotel since January 2000 and they have retained those things which Raymond's parents, William and Bee Power, achieved to earn its reputation, while also bringing a new energy and enthusiasm which has lightened the atmosphere. Since opening for guests in 1983, after a sensitive restoration programme, caring owner-management and steadily improving amenities have combined to make it a favourite destination for both business and leisure. It's a place of great local significance, having been built in the 1870s for Captain Robert Halpin, a local man who became Commander of The Great Eastern, which laid the first telegraph cable linking Europe and America. Tinakilly is one of the country's top business and corporate venues, but there is also a romantic side to its nature as bedrooms have views across a bird sanctuary to the sea, and there are also period rooms, some with four-posters. To all this, add personal supervision by caring owners, friendly, well-trained staff, lovely grounds and a fine kitchen, and the recipe for success is complete. Conference/banqueting (65/80). Secretarial services. Fitness suite. Garden, walking, tennis. Golf nearby (brochure available on request). Children welcome (under 12s free in parents' room, cots available without charge, baby sitting arranged). No pets. **Rooms 51** (6 suites, 33 junior suites, 12 executive, 13 ground floor, 1 suitable for disabled). Lift. B&B €134pps; ss €61. Closed 24-26 Dec. **Brunel Restaurant:** This panelled split level restaurant is in the west wing of the house, which catches the evening sunlight, and it has a relaxed, intimate atmosphere. Comfort is the byword here, and tables are beautifully set up with lovely linen, stylish flowers and elegant glasses and china. Head chef Ross Quinn, who joined the team in 2004, presents refreshingly straightforward à la carte menus which are not overlong - half a dozen dishes on each course - yet offer plenty of choice. The best of local and home-grown ingredients are used in dishes showcasing local seafood (lobster salad with raspberry vinaigrette), local meats (loin of Wicklow lamb with fondant potatoes, ratatouille & garden thyme) and venison (in season. In the Guide's experience, cooking is skilful and confident, with good attention to detail in, for example, the choice of freshly baked breads offered, and simple side vegetables, cooked al dente, which complement the main dishes well. An Irish cheese selection is offered, also some tempting desserts, usually including several based on seasonal fruits (local raspberries with lemon mascarpone, perhaps) or, if a short rest is in order before your dessert, try the dark chocolate fondant with poached pear and lemon ice cream, which takes 10 minutes to make. Finish with tea or coffee from a short menu. Caring and professional service, under the direction of restaurant manager Joanne Hamilton, match the high quality of food and cooking. **Seats 80** (private room, 30). Reservations required. Air conditioning. Toilets wheelchair accessible. D Brunel Restaurant Tue-Sat 7.30-9; 5-course D about €48, from à la carte menu. Sun & Mon shorter 'Tinakilly House' à la carte menu. L Sun and Mon from 1-8pm, otherwise light meals in bar. House wine from €21. SC discretionary. Closed 24-26 Dec. Amex, Diners, MasterCard, Visa, Laser. **Directions:** From N1(main Dublin - Wexford road) to Rathnew village; Tinakilly is 500 metres from village on R750 to Wicklow town.

Roundwood

 PUB/RESTAURANT

Roundwood Inn
Roundwood Co Wicklow
Tel: 01 281 8107

 Jurgen and Aine Schwalm have owned this 17th century inn in the highest village in the Wicklow Hills since 1980. There's a public bar at one end, with a snug and an open fire, and in the middle of the building the main bar food area, furnished in traditional style with wooden floors and big sturdy tables. The style that the Schwalms have developed over the years is their own unique blend of Irish and German influences: excellent bar food includes Hungarian goulash, fresh crab bisque, Galway oysters, smoked Wicklow trout, smoked salmon and hearty hot meals, notably the excellent house variation on Irish stew. The food at Roundwood has always had a special character, which together with the place itself and a consistently high standard of hospitality, has earned it an enviable reputation with hillwalkers, Dubliners out for the day and visitors alike. Bar meals 12-9.30 daily. Bar closed 25 Dec, Good Fri. **Restaurant:** The restaurant is in the same style and only slightly more formal than the main bar, with fires at each end of the room (converted to gas, alas), and is open by reservation. The menu choice leans towards more substantial dishes such as rack of Wicklow lamb, roast wild Wicklow venison, venison ragout, pheasant and other game in season. German influences are again evident in long-established specialities such as smoked Westphalian ham and wiener schnitzel, but there are also classic specialities which cross all the usual boundaries: roast stuffed goose often appears on winter menus, especially around Christmas time, for example - and the roast suckling pig is not to be missed. An interesting mainly European wine list favours France and Germany, with many special bottles from Germany unlikely to be found elsewhere. Not suitable for children after 6.30. **Seats 45** (private room, 25). D Fri & Sat, 7.30-9; à la carte. L Sun only, 1-2. (Children welcome for lunch). House wine from about €16; SC discretionary; reservations advised. No SC. Restaurant closed L Mon-Sat, D Sun-Thu. Amex, MasterCard, Visa, Laser. **Directions:** N11, follow sign for Glendalough.

BELFAST CITY

Belfast
🅔 RESTAURANT

Aldens Restaurant

229 Upper Newtownards Road Belfast BT4 3JF
Tel: 028 9065 0079 Fax: 028 9065 0032
Email: info@aldensrestaurant.com Web: www.aldensrestaurant.com

A neat canopy in aubergine-toned livery highlights the discreetly distinctive public face of Jonathan Davis's fine contemporary restaurant, an indication of the quality that lies within. Although the choice of location seemed unlikely at the time, Aldens was at the forefront of Belfast's first wave of chic, uncluttered modern restaurants when it opened in 1998, and it immediately became a destination address; head chef Cath Gradwell has been here since the restaurant opened (bringing cosmopolitan experience at Roux restaurants and others), and has since retained a fine reputation in the face of growing city centre competition. Aldens serves its area extremely well - it is convenient to Stormont, and there is a strong business following. A welcoming bar/reception area has comfortable seating and pleasing details - fresh flowers, choice of olives, newspapers and food guides to browse over a drink - while tables are smartly set up with quality linen, tapenade, olive oil and butter, along with several types of bread; opaque glass windows soften the light and give a sense of privacy, with strips of mirror adding reflections on painted walls. Lively international menus, changed daily, are admirably simple and use seasonal ingredients in cookincg that especially emphasises flavour combinations, fish and local produce - and dishes are generally executed with flair. While not overlong, menus offer plenty of choice (perhaps more middle of the road than formerly - luxurious dishes like seared foie gras are less in evidence, which is probably a sign of the times); updated classics, like chicken liver paté with hot toast & red onion marmalade and roast breast of duck with orange sauce sit happily alongside prime fish and meats (fillet of seabass, sirloin steak, rump of lamb), and humbler everyday foods like mushroom curry with braised rice or (one of several mainstream vegetarian choices, usually also including a tempting twice-baked spinach & parmesan soufflé), served with imaginative side dishes. Consistent cooking and professional service from smartly-uniformed staff make this one of Northern Ireland's finest restaurants and it offers very good value, notably the lunch specials and a short dinner menu. An interesting and informative wine list offers a great range of wines at very fair prices. **Seats 70.** Children welcome. No smoking area; air conditioning. L Mon-Fri,12-2.30; D Mon-Thu 6-10, Fri & Sat 6-11; Set D from £17.95 (Mon-Thu), à la carte. House wines from £11.95; sc discretionary. Closed L Sat, all Sun, public hols. Amex, Diners, MasterCard, Visa, Switch. **Directions:** On the Upper Newtownards Road at junction with Sandown Road.

Belfast
🅔 GUESTHOUSE

An Old Rectory

148 Malone Road Belfast BT9 5LH
Tel: 028 90 66 7882 Fax: 028 90 68 3759
Email: info@anoldrectory.co.uk Web: www.anoldrectory.co.uk

Conveniently located near the King's Hall, Public Records Office, Lisburn Road and Queen's University, Mary Callan's lovely late Victorian house is set well back from the road in mature trees, with private parking. A former Church of Ireland rectory, it had the benefit of being in the Malone conservation area and retains many original features, including stained glass windows. There's a lovely drawing room with books, sofas, comfortable armchairs with cosy rugs over the arms - and a very hospitable habit of serving hot whiskey in the drawing room at 9 o'clock each night. Accommodation is on two storeys, every room individually decorated (and named) and each has both a desk and a sofa, magazines to browse, also beverage trays with hot chocolate and soup sachets as well as the usual tea and coffee; better still there's a fridge on each landing with iced water and fresh milk, helpful advice on eating out locally is available (including menus) and, although they don't do evening meals, pride is taken in providing a good breakfast. A ground floor room suitable for disabled guests is planned for 2007. Children welcome (under 5 free in parents' room). Garden, walking. No pets. **Rooms 5** (3 en-suite, 2 with private bathrooms - 2 shower only, 3 with bath & shower, all no smoking). B&B £25-30 pps, ss £18. Closed Christmas & Easter. **No Credit Cards. Directions:** Between Balmoral Avenue and Stranmillis Road.

Belfast

☗ ATMOSPHERIC PUB

Crown Liquor Saloon

46 Great Victoria Street Belfast BT2 7 BA
Tel: 02890 279 901 Fax: 02890 279 902

Belfast's most famous pub, The Crown Liquor Saloon, was perhaps the greatest of all the Victorian gin palaces which once flourished in Britain's industrial cities. Remarkably, considering its central location close to the Europa Hotel, it survived The Troubles virtually unscathed. Although now owned by the National Trust (and run by Bass Leisure Retail) the Crown is far from being a museum piece and attracts a wide clientele of locals and visitors. A visit to one of its famous snugs for a pint and half a dozen oysters served on crushed ice, or a bowl of Irish Stew, is a must. The upstairs restaurant section, "Flannigans Eaterie & Bar", is built with original timbers from the SS Britannic, sister ship to the Titanic. Crown: bar food served Mon-Sat 12-3. Flannigans: 11-9. Closed 25-16 Dec. Diners, MasterCard, Visa. **Directions:** City centre, opposite Europa Hotel.

Belfast

☆ RESTAURANT

James Street South

21 James Street South Belfast BT2 7GA
Tel: 028 9043 4310 Fax: 028 9043 4310
Email: info@jamesstreetsouth.co.uk Web: www.jamesstreetsouth.co.uk

Just across the road from the Europa Hotel, Niall and Joanne McKenna's cool modern restaurant is well located and well-appointed in a beautifully understated style with white walls and crisp white linen, relieved by fresh flowers and effective lighting - no wonder it attracted immediate attention when it opened in 2004. And, thanks to the determination of a talented team to bring something fresh and exceptionally good to Belfast, this gem of a restaurant has thrived. Niall McKenna arrived at this address via Marco Pierre White's Canteen and two of Gary Rhodes' restaurants, Greenhouse and City Rhodes, and it shows in simple, evocative menus which are not long yet offer many a treat. There's a welcome European tone to menus that are classical / Mediterranean, with an emphasis on quality ingredients - and a merciful absence of fusion influences; menus are changed frequently and, although simply presented there are plenty of very tempting options - including lovely vegetarian dishes like wild mushroom papardelle with crème fraîche, luxurious starters like sautéed foie gras with glazed pears in sauternes, great seafood - as seen in a late summer dish of wild seabass with crab & prawn bouillabaisse - and utterly irresistible desserts including a delectable fondue (to share) and choice of combination plates - a Swedish plate offers variations on apples, a chocolate one includes imaginative white and dark chocolate creations... This is an exciting restaurant, and genuinely creative, beautifully judged cooking and excellent service by smartly-dressed and well trained staff should ensure a memorable meal here. Lunch and pre-theatre menus offer exceptional value. A disciplined, somewhat inscrutable, wine list is arranged mainly by grape variety and includes regional varieties; although mainly under £30, there is also a short selection of fine wines. Gourmet wine evenings are sometimes held. **Seats 70.** Reservations advised. No smoking area. Children welcome. L Mon-sat, 12.30-2.45; D daily, 5.45-10.30 (Sun 5.30-9). Pre theatre D Mon-Thu, also A la Carte. Closed 25-26 Dec, 12-13 July. Amex, MasterCard, Visa, Switch.. **Directions:** City centre.

Belfast

N 🏛

Malmaison Hotel

34-38 Victoria Street Belfast BT1 3GH **Tel: 028 9022 0200**
Email: belfast@malmaison.com Web: www.malmaison-belfast.com

Previously the McCausland Hotel, this beautiful building (especially striking when lit up at night) was recently taken over by the stylish UK group Malmaison who have introduced a wow factor, beginning with the reception area where everything is black and white, with opulent drapes and large church candles. Friendly, efficient staff at reception set arriving guests at their ease and guest accommodation - spacious, contemporary, luxurious, with all the technical gizmos you could possibly want - is given a human dimension with the offer of early morning delivery of a quarter pint of fresh milk. The Brasserie offers simple whole-some fare (steaks from The Duke of Baccleuch's Scottish Estate, for example), good breakfasts are smartly served, and the bar (extensive cocktail menu, flat screen television, huge leather sofas, flick-ering lights. loud music) is an in-place at night. Multi storey car park nearby. **Rooms 62.** Brasserie: L & D daily. Amex, MasterCard, Visa, Switch. **Directions:** Centre of Belfast.

Belfast
🏆 🍷 € GUESTHOUSE

Ravenhill House

690 Ravenhill Road Belfast BT6 0BZ
Tel: 028 9020 7444 Fax: 028 9028 2590
Email: info@ravenhillhouse.com Web: www.ravenhillhouse.com

Although it is beside a busy road, the Nicholson family home is a late Victorian redbrick house and has some sense of seclu-sion, with mature trees, private parking and a quiet tree-lined street alongside. A comfortable ground floor lounge has an open fireplace, a big sofa, lots of books and a PC for guests who want to use the Internet (at a modest charge). Bedrooms, which are a mixture of single, twin and double rooms, are comfortably furnished with style - beds and other furniture have been specially commissioned from an Islandmagee craftsman; all are en-suite, with tea/coffee making facilities and TV. After a good night's sleep, breakfast is sure to be the highlight of a visit here: served in a bay-windowed dining room with white-damasked tables, the breakfast buffet is displayed on the sideboard in a collection of Nicholas Mosse serving bowls - a feel for craft objects that is reflected elsewhere in the house. A printed breakfast menu shows a commitment to using local produce of quality and includes a vegetarian cooked breakfast; the Nicholsons buy most of the ingredients at the weekly St George's Farmers' Market, and support the concept behind it; eggs and meat are bought directly from known farms, and they make what they can on the premises, including marmalade and wheaten bread for breakfasts. All these good things, plus a particularly helpful attitude to guests, make this an excellent, reasonably priced base for a stay in Belfast. Children welcome (under 2s free in parents' room, cot available without charge). No pets. Garden. **Rooms 5** (all en-suite, 3 shower only, all no smoking). B&B £32.50. ss £12.50. Open all year. MasterCard, Visa, Switch. **Directions:** Follow signs for A24 to Newcastle. 2 miles from city centre, located on corner of Ravenhill Road and Rosetta Park, close to junction with Ormeau Road (A24).

Belfast
★★ 🍷 RESTAURANT

Restaurant Michael Deane

36-40 Howard Street Belfast BT1 6PF
Tel: 028 9033 1134 Fax: 028 9056 0001
Email: info@michaeldeane.co.uk Web: www.michaeldeane.co.uk

Michael Deane's reputation for offering meticulously prepared dishes, served with old world efficiency and charm in an elegant ambience remains unchallenged This is exceptional food, based on great classic cooking, and the difference is on the plate: it always has been, and remains, on a different level to anything else in Belfast, and equal to the best in Ireland. Perhaps the contrast is all the more striking as, to reach the oasis of the restaurant, diners walk through the bustling **Deane's Brasserie** on the ground floor, climb the broad staircase and are admitted to the inner sanctum. Here all is comfort; the fin de siècle sitting room, the elegant dining room, the smart, attentive and knowledgeable staff and that open kitchen with the ever-present Deane meticulously controlling the pace of events and timing food to perfection. A two- or three-course dinner menu is offered, with four choices on each course - typically including a starter of roast scallops with potato bread, Clonakilty black pudding, cauliflower & brown butter, and a main of local lamb with crushed scallion potato, artichoke & Irish wholegrain mustard - and is extremely good value (£35/£42); this will be a wonderful dining experience by any standards, allowing you to savour food cooked by the hand of the master. But to experience the sheer breadth and refinement of Michael Deane's cooking, the eight course Menu Prestige (£62) is the yardstick against which all serious cooking in Northern Ireland should be judged: all the little niceties will be observed, leading off with an amuse bouche while you consider a menu that reads like a shopping list: monkfish; squab; scallop; foie gras; salmon; venison; cheese; dessert; chocolate. Simple on the page - simply superb on the plate; this is understatement taken to its extreme limit. Michael Deane was one of the first chefs in Ireland to cook fusion food - something in which he succeeded brilliantly, although it has failed in so many other hands - and, although it is now for his classical skills that he is (rightly) receiving recognition, he also blends fusion themes into classic menus. The wine list is grand as befits the standards of the restaurant and its food, yet not overawing, and the discreet advice given to match wines with the meal is outstanding. There is still no chef in Ireland who can surpass Michael Deane, and this small restaurant offers an increasingly rare alternative to the current fashion for informality. The first floor restaurant is only open for dinner on four evenings a week (except by arrangement for private parties at other times), so it may be necessary to make a reservation several weeks in advance. ***Deanes Brasserie** on the ground floor is open for L&D Mon-Sat. **Seats 30.** Air conditioning D Wed-Sat 7-9.30; L Fri only, 12.15-2. D £33-£59; sc discretionary (10% added to bills of 6+). Closed Sun-Tue, Christmas, New Year, 1 week July. Amex, MasterCard, Visa, Switch. **Directions:** Tavelling towards M1 from rear of City Hall, about 150 m on left.

Belfast

N E RESTAURANT

Roscoff Brasserie

7-11 Linenhall Street Belfast BT2 8AA

Tel: 028 9031 1150 Fax: 028 9031 1151 Web: www.rankingroup.co.uk

In what has recently become something of a restaurant row - TENsq, Deane's and James Street South are all very close by - Belfast's original fine dining restaurant, the famous Roscoff, returned in a great new guise in 2004. And, to the delight of those who admire the Rankins' food but don't enjoy the ambience, fine dining food is now available once again, in a relaxed atmosphere. Avoiding sharp contemporary style, the decor is timelessly classic: with white linen-clad tables, soft neutral toned furnishings, effective lighting and sultry background jazz, the overall effect is attractively subdued and low key. You can slow down with a drink in the little reception bar, and smart well-trained staff are pleasant and hospitable, presenting menus that offer a wide choice of the more restrained, classical dishes that have been noticeable by their absence in many restaurants of late: starters like carpaccio of beef with artichoke, mustard cress and sauce 'cipriani', or smoked eel with roast beetroot & horseradish cream; and main courses like lemon sole with capers, and a comforting dish of beef short ribs with red wine, carrots & parsnip mash - or, perhaps, the supreme luxury dish, lobster thermidor, served with new potatoes and green beans. Head chef Conor McCann's cooking is accomplished, and well-conceived dishes both look and taste wonderful. There's a good ripened cheese plate and delicious desserts, which have always been a Roscoff tour de force, include good home-made ice creams and a dessert du jour - a boon for regular diners. Impressive, tasty cooking, soothing surroundings and excellent service add up to a winning combination. **Seats 86.** Toilets Wheelchair Accessible; children welcome. L 12-2.30; D 6-10.15 (to 11.15 Sun). 2/3 course Set L, £15.25/19.50; Set 2/3 course D, £21.50/27.00. Separate vegetarian à la carte menu available. C losed Jan 1, Jul 12, Dec 25/26. Amex, Diners, MasterCard, Visa **Directions:** Near the City Hall.

Belfast

E RESTAURANT

Shu

253 Lisburn Road Belfast BT9 7EN

Tel: 028 90 381655 Fax: 028 90 681632

Email: eat@shu-restaurant.com Web: www.shu-restaurant.com

A smartly painted Victorian frontage and traditional arched windows provide a vivid contrast to the stainless steel efficiency of the bar and de rigeur 'on view' kitchen of this fashionable restaurant. After a courteous welcome, guests are led into a large L shaped room which is light and airy, with shiny metal softened by terracotta pillars and discreet covers. This is a smoothly run operation, with many regulars of all age groups. Head chef Brian McCann presents admirably simple menus based on carefully sourced ingredients, and offering a combination of classical and brasserie fare that is complemented by restaurant manager Julian Henry's marshalling of a tip top waiting staff. An outstanding bread selection will ease you through the menu stage, and may well be a highlight of the meal. Menus - à la carte, and a set dinner menu that is good value at £17.50 - are well balanced, allowing equally for the adventurous and more conservative diner. The ubiquitous salt & chilli squid (surely Belfast's favourite starter) makes its mandatory appearance, for example, but is well cooked and presented (and makes a beautiful light lunch dish), while a deliciously well-flavoured vegetarian penne pasta with tomatoes, fennel & rocket is one of a number of dishes offered as starter or main course portions. Dry aged sirloin will be a treat for those who cannot envisage a meal without steak but, judging by the success of a perfectly cooked and flavoursome dish of hake with white bean purée, ragôut of beans and mushrooms and pea & truffle velouté, fish may be an equally good choice. Upbeat classical desserts to finish, or cheese (not necessarily Irish farmhouse) with classy crackers. Cooking, on a recent visit, seemed to be even better than previously - and, together with great atmosphere, efficient service and good value for money this adds up to a restaurant that is always busy. If cocktails and tapas are your thing, head for the basement. Not suitable for children after 8 pm. **Seats 80** (private room 24). L Mon-Sat, 12-2.30, D Mon-Sat 6-10. 2-course menu £17.50; otherwise à la carte (average main course £14), also Vegetarian Menu. House wines £13.50; s.c. discretionary (10% on parties of 6+). Closed Sun, 24-26 Dec. Amex, MasterCard, Visa, Switch. **Directions:** Half mile south on Lisburn Road.

Belfast
🏛️🍷 HOTEL/RESTAURANT

TENsq

10 Donegall Square South Belfast BT1 5JD
Tel: 028 9024 1001 Fax: 028 9024 3210
Email: reservations@tensq.co.uk Web: www.ten-sq.com

This delightful boutique hotel has established a special niche for discerning visitors to Belfast: it is situated in a particularly attractive listed Victorian building and the location - just opposite the City Hall, and within walking distance of the whole city centre area - is superb. The interior is refreshingly contemporary, and has been achieved with sensitivity to the original building: a striking feature, for example, is the lovely old stained glass in many of the original windows, which is now subtly echoed in the interior design. Accommodation - in generous high-windowed rooms, theatrically decorated in an uncompromisingly modern style - is simple yet very luxurious; even the most dyed-in-the-wool traditionalist would be won over by the sheer style of these rooms and they have wonderful bathrooms to match. Features include well-planned lighting, state-of-the-art entertainment systems and - going a stage further than the usual mini-bar (which, however, includes fresh milk for your freshly brewed tea or coffee) - a collection of drinks, nibbles and bits and pieces that would be worthy of a small corner shop, all neatly tucked away out of sight. Conference/banqueting 100/150. Not suitable for children. No pets. **Rooms 23** (1 suite, 21 superior, 2 for disabled). Lift. 24 hour room service. Turndown service. Air conditioning, safe, ISDN, TV/DVD/video channel, tea/coffee-making facilities, iron & trouser press. B&B room rate £160 (max 2 guests). Open all year. **Restaurant:** The dashingly informal Grill Room & Bar, which occupies the whole of the ground floor, has become one of Belfast's most popular restaurants and is always busy with non-residents, which gives the hotel a great buzz; the Grill Room is the perfect antidote to other fashionable restaurants in the city, as the focus is firmly on wholesome traditional all-day fare and very reasonable prices. The theme is colonial and, although there is actually quite a wide range offered on menus that smack of retro, red meat is king here (and very good meat it is too); char-grilled steaks and burgers are served with super chips and well-made classic sauces and other comforting dishes include finger-lickin' barbecued ribs. The timing was perfect for the return of this down to earth food - the Grill Room's instant success is the proof. Staff are warm, welcoming and generally efficient, with none of the stuffiness sometimes encountered in exclusive hotels. All round, this stylish and increasingly accomplished hotel is retaining its well-earned its reputation as the number one destination in Belfast for discerning travellers. **Seats 120** (private room, 30); Live music Wed & Sun. Food served daily 7am-10.30pm; L 12-3, D 6-10. A la carte. SC discretionary. Amex, MasterCard, Visa, Switch. **Directions:** Corner of Linenhall Street at rear of City Hall.

COUNTY ANTRIM

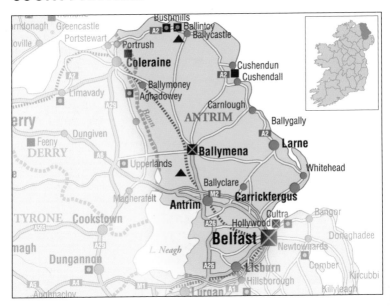

Ballintoy
€ ◉ COUNTRY HOUSE

Whitepark House

150 Whitepark Road Ballintoy Ballycastle
Co Antrim BT54 6NH **Tel: 028 207 31482**
Email: bob@whiteparkhouse.com Web: www.whiteparkhouse.com

A warm welcome from chatty and well-informed hosts Bob and Siobhán Isles awaits visitors to this pretty old house, which is set in well-maintained gardens and enjoys stunning views of Whitepark Bay, and has a path down to the beach straight across the road. The three bedrooms have only one bathroom between them but this is a house of great charm and character, and guests do not find it too difficult to forfeit a little convenience for the pleasure of being here. Bedrooms all have distinctive colour themes and lots of exotic touches to give each its special personality, and there is also a very comfortable and homely sitting room looking onto the garden, with couches, easy chairs and an open fire to relax beside - and, as elsewhere in the house, much of interest for the interested guest. Bob likes to see guests well prepared for the day ahead and, as a vegetarian, he's well placed to offer an alternative, in addition to the traditional Ulster Fry. Not suitable for children. No pets. Garden, walking. **Rooms 3** (one bathroom for all; all no smoking). B&B from £30 pps, ss £5. 5% surcharge on credit card payments. MasterCard, Visa. **Directions:** On Antrim coast road A2, between Giants Causeway and Ballntoy; on east side of Whitepark Bay.

Ballymena
🏛◉ HOTEL

Galgorm Manor Hotel

136 Fenaghy Road Ballymena Co Antrim BT42 1EA
Tel: 028 2588 1001 Fax: 028 2588 0080
Email: mail@galgorm.com Web: www.galgorm.com

This converted gentleman's residence is set amidst beautiful scenery, with the River Maine running through the grounds. Well-tended parkland, and an impressive reception area with antiques and a welcoming log fire create a good impression, and there's an elegant drawing room and a traditional bar, as well as the more casual Ghillies Bar in a characterful converted building at the back of the hotel (where informal meals are also served). Comfortably furnished guest rooms and suites include some with four-posters, and most have river views. Major developments under way at the time of going to press will add new bedrooms, and leisure facilities. Conference/banqueting (500); golf (9/18); fishing; horse-riding; walking; garden. Children welcome (under 4s free in parents room, cot £10, babysitting arranged). Wheelchair accessible. No pets. **Rooms 24** (3 suites, 2 disabled) B&B about £55 pps, ss about £40. L &D available daily. Open all year. Amex, Diners, MasterCard, Visa. **Directions:** From the Galgorm roundabout, take the third exit for Cullybackey (Feneghy road). About 2 miles, on the left.

Bushmills
🏨 HOTEL/RESTAURANT

Bushmills Inn

9 Dunluce Rd. Bushmills Co Antrim BT57 8QG
Tel: 028 2073 3000 Fax: 028 2073 2048
Email: mail@bushmillsinn.com Web: www.bushmillsinn.com

Originally a 19th-century coaching inn, recent developments have been undertaken with senstivity, improving amenities without loss of character. The tone is set by the turf fire and country seating in the hall and public rooms bars, the famous circular library, the restaurant, even the Pine Room conference room carry on the same theme. Bedrooms are individually furnished in a comfortable cottage style and even have "antiqued" bathrooms but it's all very well done and avoids a theme park feel. It's hard to think of a better base for a holiday playing the famous golf courses of the area (Royal Portrush is just four miles away) - or simply exploring this beautiful coastline and its hinterland; taking the Magilligan-Greencastle ferry, day trips can comfortably include a visit to the beautiful Inishowen peninsula in Co. Donegal. Garden. Fishing. Children welcome (cot available, £10). No pets. **Rooms 32:** 22 in Mill House, 10 in Coaching Inn; (6 superior, 7 shower only, all no smoking, 1 for disabled) B&B from £79 pps.*Short breaks offered. **Restaurant:** The inn is known for its wholesome food and makes a good place to plan a break when touring, as it offers both day and evening menus in cosy surroundings. Pride in Irish ingredients is seen in A Taste of Ulster menus that offer a range of traditional dishes with a modern twist: an unusual speciality, for example, is Dalriada cullen skink, a 'meal in a soup bowl' based on smoked haddock and topped with an (optional) poached egg; another is onion & Guinness soup, which is topped with a cheese croûton like the French soup that inspired it - and, of course 'Bushmills coffee', which is better than a dessert any day. Wheelchair accessible. **Seats 110** (private room, 40). Reservations advised. Not suitable for children after 7pm. D daily 6.30-9.30 (Sun 6-9); L daily, Day Menu 12-6.00; (Sun: carvery from 12.30-2.30pm and day menu to 6pm); bar food Sun only 12-4 (soup & sandwiches). House wines from £12; SC discretionary. Closed Dec 25. MasterCard, Visa, Switch. **Directions:** On the A2 Antrim coast road, in Bushmills village, as it crosses the river.

Dunadry
👁 HOTEL

Dunadry Hotel & Country Club

2 Islandreagh Drive Dunadry Co Antrim BT41 2HA
Tel: 028 9443 4343 Fax: 028 9443 3389
Email: info@dunadry.com Web: www.dunadry.com

This attractive riverside hotel is well-located, close to Belfast internation Airport and convenient to the city centre. It was formerly a mill and succeeds very well in combining the character of the old buildings with the comfort and effriciency of an international hotel. Surrounded by 10 acres of grounds, it makes a good business venue or a weekend retreat, with spacious public areas and stylish accommodation. The Mill Race Bistro makes the most of its romantic riverside location. Excellent facilities for business and leisure. *Sister hotel to Wellington Park Hotel (Belfast) and Armagh City Hotel. **Rooms 83** (all en-suite, 2 disabled). No Pets. B&B from £40 pps. Closed 24-26 Dec. Amex, Diners. MasterCard, Visa, Switch. **Directions:** Near Belfast airport. look for sgns to Antrim/Dunadry.

Maddybenny Farmhouse

Portrush
🏆 💶 B&B

Loguestown Road Portrush Coleraine Co Antrim BT52 2PT

Tel: 028 7082 3394 Email: beds@maddybenny.com Web: www.maddybenny.com

Just two miles from Portrush, Rosemary White's Plantation Period farmhouse was built before 1650. Since extended, and now modernised, it makes a very comfortable and exceptionally hospitable place to stay, with a family-run equestrian centre nearby (including stabling for guests' own horses). There is also snooker, a games' room and quiet sitting places, as well as a garden and an area for outdoor children's games. The accommodation is just as thoughtful. The bedrooms are all en-suite and there are all sorts of useful extras electric blankets, a comfortable armchair, hospitality tray complete with teacosy, a torch and alarm clock beside the bed, trouser press, hair dryer and, on the landing, an ironing board, fridge and pay phone for guest use. Across the yard there are also some self-catering cottages, open all year (one wheelchair friendly). No evening meals are offered, but Rosemary guides guests to the local eating places that will suit them best - and her breakfasts are legendary, so make sure you allow plenty of time to start the day with a feast the like of which you are unlikely to encounter again. Maddybenny was our Farmhouse of the Year in 2000. Golf, fishing, tennis and pitch & putt nearby. Equestrian, walking; snooker. Children welcome (cot available without charge). No pets. Garden. **Rooms 3** (all en-suite) B&B £27.50pps (children £10),no ss . Closed Christmas, New Year. MasterCard, Visa. **Directions:** Signposted off A29 Portrush/Coleraine road.

Ramore Wine Bar

Portrush
💶 RESTAURANT

6 The Harbour Road Portrush Co Antrim BT56 8BN

Tel: 02870 824 313 Fax: 02870 823 194

Email: clare@ramorerestaurants.co.uk Web: www.ramorerestaurants.co.uk

An upmarket fast food operation is at present all that remains of the wonderful Ramore Restaurant, which was once the leading light of cosmopolitan fine dining in Northern Ireland - however George and Jane McAlpin are planning to bring back the spirit of the old Ramore in 2006, with an 80-seater fine dining restaurant that will complement the three existing casual eating places* that they operate overlooking Portrush harbour and, while the atmosphere is to be relaxed, reservations will be accepted. Meanwhile, although it is noisy and not very comfortable, the Wine Bar offers a wide selection of contemporary dishes based on quality ingredients - chicken goujons with dips, lamb kebabs with choice of sauces, and home battered scampi with French style peas are typical - and prices are very moderate. *'Coast' pasta/pizza bar is directly under the Wine Bar, and The Harbour Bistro is at the nearby Harbour Bar, where there is also a live music venue, although the old front bar retains its original character. *The nearby Harbour Bar is in the same ownership; the old front retains its original characte (L&D served daily). Ramore Wine Bar **Seats 170.** L&D daily: L12.15-2.15, D 5-10 (Sun,12.30-3 & 5-9); Coast Italiano **Seats 90** (Mon-Sat 4-10.30, Sun 3-9.30). Toilets wheelchair accessible. Closed 25 Dec. MasterCard, Visa, Switch. **Directions:** At the harbour in Portrush.

COUNTY ARMAGH

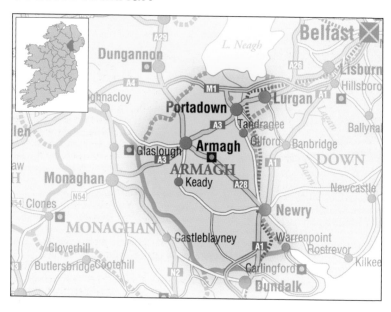

Lurgan
€ RESTAURANT

The Brindle Beam Tea Rooms

House of Brindle 20 Windsor Avenue Lurgan Co Armagh BT67 9BG
Tel: 028 3832 1721

This in-store self-service restaurant is a real one-off. Nothing is bought in and the kitchen team, puts the emphasis firmly on real home cooking. There are two freshly-made soups each day and hot dishes like beef stew, made with well trimmed fat-free chump steak - with no onions. None of the pies or casseroles contain onions as some customers don't like them, but they're still full of flavour. Their salad cart is a special attraction, with anything up to 30 different salads served each day, and several different hot dishes including baked or grilled chicken breasts, salmon and always some vegetarian dishes too. There's also a huge variety of tray bakes and desserts - and only real fresh cream is used. Scrupulously clean, with reasonable prices (not cheap, but good value for the quality) and real home cooking, this place is a gem. **Seats 110** (private room 50). No smoking restaurant, Open Mon-Sat, 10-5, L 12-2, Aft Tea 2-4.30 (Sat to 4.45). A la carte self-service except special set menus, e.g. Christmas. Unlicensed. Closed Sun, 25-26 Dec, Easter, 12-13 Jul. MasterCard, Visa. **Directions:** Town centre; located in The House of Brindle Store.

Portadown
€ RESTAURANT

Yellow Door Deli & Restaurant

Woodhouse Street Portadown Co Armagh BT62
Tel: 028 3853 3528

Previously well known for a restaurant of the same name in Gilford, Co Down, Simon Dougan opened the Yellow Door Deli in 1998 and it immediately became such a success that the restaurant was sold a couple of years later to allow time to focus on the new venture. It has an in-house bakery, producing some of the finest bread in Northern Ireland (an area renowned for its good home baking) and, as well as retailing a wide selection of the best speciality foods from Ireland and abroad, they also have a number of home-made specialities, including patés, terrines, chutneys, salads and ice cream, which are sold in the shop and served in the café - discerning customers from all over the north home in on this smashing shop, to top up with goodies and have a tasty bite of lunch. (Also at: 427 Lisburn Road, Belfast. Café **seats 80**. Breakfast from 9am, L 12-2.30, otherwise food from deli all day. MasterCard, Visa, Switch.

Slieve Gullion

 RESTAURANT WITH ROOMS

Annahaia

Slieve Gullion Courtyard 89 Drumintee Road
Killeavy Co Armagh BT35 8SW
Tel: 028 3084 8084 Fax: 028 3084 8028
Email: info@annahaia.com Web: www.annahaia.com

If you aren't familiar with the hilly area just west of Newry and Dundalk, you are in for a treat, especially if you enjoy walking. Slieve Gullion Courtyard is owned by the Forestry Commission and set in countless acres of woodland, with excellent walking along the miles of paths that criss-cross the area. Afterwards, the Guide recommends a little refreshment in a favourite pub, the **Slieve Gullion Inn** at Forkhill, which is only a few minutes' drive from Annahaia - a name which proprietors Michael Rath (chef) and Ardal O'Hanlon (manager), discovered on a map of the area. You enter through a glass door inside the courtyard, which leads directly into an unexpectedly stylish little modern bar decorated in subtle greys and putty tones, with gleaming tables, banquets and smart little stools in leather and quirky cowhide. Rural this may be, but rustic it is not. The same could be said of menus which offer plenty for the well-travelled palate: a house rendition of Caesar Salad comes with grilled peppers, chorizo & pecorino shavings, an intriguing soup of butternut squash and smoked haddock, salmon gravlax with cucumber & red onion pickles and grilled bruschetta, a risotto of goats cheese, with red onion and sautéed mushrooms and, for the more traditionally minded, perhaps, a chicken liver parfait (with apple & pear chutney, leaf salad & cranberry relish), or a special of penne with Clogherhead prawns and scallops. Main courses might include a tempting tagine of lamb, with spiced cous cous, a Thai chicken curry and a vegetarian dish. The restaurant is a long room with windows overlooking the courtyard and tables appealingly set up in the contemporary classic style (white napery, simple glasses, good heavy cutlery no gimmicks) with good home-made breads offered. Michael Rath;s cooking is accomplished and solicitous staff ease guests gently through a most enjoyable dining experience - do remember to leave a space for treats like pear tart tatin (an individual tartlet with lots of tender, juicy pear, clotted cream and honey) or a chocolate plate of excellent crisp-crusted chocolate fondant, a luscious piece of orange chocolate marquise and some white chocolate ice cream... Finish well with good coffee. Compact , interesting wine list. Slieve Gullion Courtyard also offers accommodation (details on application) and promises to become a great destination for short breaks. Conference/banqueting (120/80). Children welcome. **Seats 40** (private room, 6-80; outdoor seating, 10); Toilets wheelchair accessible. Reservations required. D Thu-Sat, 7-9, Sun L only 1-3. Set D £36, Set Sun L £15. House wine £11.95. Closed Mon-Wed, Christmas and Jan. Amex, MasterCard, Visa, Laser, Switch. **Directions:** 10 mins south of Newry - Forkhill road.

COUNTY DOWN

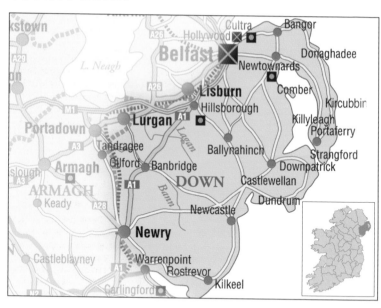

Crawfordsburn
HOTEL/RESTAURANT

The Old Inn

11-15 Main Street Crawfordsburn Co Down BT19 1JH
Tel: 028 9185 3255 Fax: 028 9185 2775
Email: info@theoldinn.com Web: www.theoldinn.com

The pretty village setting of this famous and hospitable 16th century inn the oldest in continuous use in all Ireland belies its convenient location close to Belfast and its City Airport, and the Ulster Folk & Transport Museum and the Royal Belfast Golf Club are also nearby. Oak beams, antiques and gas lighting emphasise the natural character of the building, an attractive venue for business people and private guests alike. A welcoming fire and friendly staff in the cosy reception area set the tone for the whole hotel, which is full of charm, very comfortable - and always smartly presented. Bedrooms are individually decorated and, due to the age of the building, vary in size and style - most have antiques, some have romantic four-posters and a few have private sitting rooms. There are several dining options in the hotel: '1614' is the fine dining restaurant, informal evening meals are served in the Churn Bistro, and food is also served in the bar during afternoon and early evening. **'1614' Restaurant:** After an aperitif in the bar or the large and comfortable residents' lounge, a meal in this characterful old-world dining room should be very enjoyable. Interesting menus offer plenty of choice and, in the Guide's recent experience, the standard of cooking is well above that normally expected of hotel dining rooms; service can be a little uneven but this is offset by the high quality of food and cooking, plus the pleasant surroundings. Typical dishes might include pan-fried foie gras with sweet & sour red onion or a retro starter of '1614' prawn cocktail, with cherry tomatoes, avocado, salad & homemade tomato ketchup, and perhaps an unusual and attractively presented main course of pork fillet with puy lentils. A nice dessert menu offers more refreshing fruit-based dishes than usual, and coffee is served in the lounge. Conference/banqueting (100/125) Ample parking. Garden, walking. Children welcome (under 12s free in parents' room; cot available, £10). No pets. **Rooms 32** (1 suite, 3 junior suites, 12 superior). 24 hr room service. Room rate £85. **'1614' Restaurant:** D Mon-Sat, 7-9, L Sun only 12.30-2; closed D Sun. Churn Bistro: D Mon-Sat, 7-9.30; closed Sun. Bar meals: 12 noon-7pm daily. *Short breaks offered. Closed 25 Dec. Amex, MasterCard, Visa, Switch. **Directions:** Off A2 Belfast-Bangor, 6 miles after Holywood (exit B20 for Crawfordsburn).

Donaghadee

ATMOSPHERIC PUB/RESTAURANT

Grace Neill's

33 High Street Dongahdee Co Down BT21 04H
Tel 028 9188 4595 Fax 028 9188 9631
Email: info@graceneills.com Web: www.graceneills.com

Dating back to 1611, Grace Neill's is one of the oldest inns in all Ireland; Grace Neill herself was born when the pub was more than two hundred years old, and died in 1916 at the age of 98. In recent ownerships, improvements have been completed with sensitivity to the age and character of the original front bar, which has been left simple and unspoilt, while the back of the building has been imaginatively developed, creating a bright, high-ceilinged contemporary restaurant - where accomplished modern cooking, efficient service and a lively atmosphere keep bringing people back. Children welcome before 8pm. No smoking restaurant. Live music (weekends). **Seats 104.** L & D daily (set D £20/30, also à la carte); sc discretionary. Closed 25 Dec, 12 Jul. Amex, Diners, MasterCard, Visa, Switch.

Hillsborough
 RESTAURANT/PUB

The Plough Inn

3 The Square Hillsborough Co Down BT26 6AG
Tel: 028 9268 2985 Fax: 028 9268 2472
Web: www.barretro.com

Established in 1752, this former coaching inn is owned by the Patterson family who have built up a national reputation for hospitality and good food, especially seafood. Somehow they manage to run three separate food operations each day, so pleasing customers looking for a casual daytime meal and more serious evening diners. The evening restaurant is in the old stables at the back of the pub, and renowned for seafood and fine steaks, booking is required. Recent developments and makeovers mercifully left the characterful old bar intact (fairly traditional bar food is still available there) and also the original Plough Restaurant, which has a separate entrance from the carpark. However the rest of the pub, including the adjacent building, is now stylishly contemporary and comprises the trendy Barretro Café & Bistro, which is open most of the day. The bistro is above the old bar and offers more substantial international dishes; bookings are taken there for business lunches, but not in the evening. Lots of cool leather seating, interesting lighting, incorporating existing features like the old mahogany bar into a design which is uncompromisingly modern, yet warm and welcoming, are just some of the attractions. While there is obvious youth appeal, people of all ages feel comfortable here and the staff, who are clearly very proud of it, are friendly and helpful. It is very extensive, so allow yourself time to have a good look around and get your bearings before settling down to eat. [The Plough Inn was our Pub of the Year in 2004]. *The Pheasant Inn at Annahilt. is a sister establishment. Children welcome in the café, but the bar is unsuitable for children. Sun terrace. Parking. **Seats 200** (private room, 20) No smoking area. Air conditioning. L daily, 12-2.30 (Sun to 5) D 5-9.30 daily. Closed 25 Dec (no food 26 Dec). Amex, Diners, MasterCard, Visa, Switch. **Directions:** Off the main Dublin-Belfast road, turn off at Hillsborough roundabout; in village square.

Holywood
HOTEL

Hastings Culloden Estate & Spa

Bangor Road Holywood Co Down BT18 0EX
Tel: 028 9042 1066 Fax: 028 9042 6777
Email: guest@cull.hastingshotels.com Web: www.hastingshotels.com

Formerly the official palace for the Bishops of Down, Hastings Hotels' flagship property is a fine example of 19th-century Scottish Baronial architecture with plasterwork ceilings, stained glass windows and an imposing staircase. It is set in beautifully maintained gardens and woodland overlooking Belfast Lough and the County Antrim coastline. Period furniture and fine paintings in spacious high ceilinged rooms give a soothing feeling of exclusivity, and comfortable drawing rooms overlook the lough. Spacious, lavishly decorated guest rooms include a large proportion of suites and a Presidential Suite, with the best view; a are lavishly furnished and decorated with splendid bathrooms and details such as bathrobes, welcoming bowl of fruit, and nice touches like ground coffee and a cafetière on the hospitality tray Wireless internet access is available in all areas, and there are video/DVD players in suites. The hote has an association with The Royal Belfast Golf Club, four minutes away by car (book the complimen tary hospitality limousine) also a fine health club; the 'Cultra Inn', a bar and informal restaurant in th grounds, offers an alternative to The Mitre Restaurant. The hotel is licensed to hold weddings on th premises. Conference/banqueting (1,000/600); business centre, secretarial services. Leisure centr (swimming pool; spa; beauty salon; hairdressing). Garden. Children welcome (under 3s free in parents room; cot available without charge, baby sitting arranged). No pets. **Rooms 79** (2 suites, 17 junic suites, 22 executive rooms, 2 disabled, 40 no-smoking). Lift. Air conditioning. 24 hr room servic B&B £100 pps, ss about £60.* Short breaks offered. Parking (500). Helipad. Open all year. **The Mitr Restaurant:** The fine dining restaurant is in a long room overlooking the lough, with a discreet an luxurious ambience - and, with well-padded and very comfortable upholstered chairs, conducive t lingering. Tables are beautifully appointed in classic style, and extensive menus live up to the promise: there may be a perfectly cooked starter crown of asparagus, for example, presented standin up with little jewels of tapenade around it, and a speciality main course, of tender saddle of veniso from nearby Clandeboye Estate, comes with crushed root vegetables and buttered greens. Classi cooking, lovely surroundings and correct, attentive service all make this a restaurant with a sense c occasion. Extensive wine list to match. **Seats 110** (private room, 50). Reservations required. N smoking restaurant. Children welcome. Toilets wheelchair accessible. Piano & Jazz Fri/Sat/Sun. daily, 7-9.30, Set D £32.50; L Sun only, 12.30-2.30. Set Sun L, £28. House wine £17. Amex Diners, MasterCard, Visa, Switch. **Directions:** 6 miles from Belfast city centre on A2 towards Bangor

Holywood Area
 B&B

Beech Hill Country House
23 Ballymoney Road Craigantlet Holywood Co Down BT23 4TC
Tel: 028 9042 5892 Fax: 028 9042 589;
Email: info@beech-hill.net Web: www.beech-hill.ne

Victoria Brann's attractive Georgian style house i set in the peaceful Holywood Hills. It has grea style - and the benefit of an exceptional hospitable hostess, who does everything possible t ensure that guests have everything they need Ground floor bedrooms have panoramic views ove the North Down countryside and are furnished wit antique furniture - and, believe it or not, the bed are made up with fine Irish linen; all also have en suite bathrooms with lots of special little extras Breakfast is a meal worth allowing time to enjoy and it is served in a spacious conservatory overlooking a croquet lawn. *Self catering accommodatior is also available inn The Colonel's Lodge, in Beech Hill garden (also available for B&B). **Rooms, 3** (al en-suite, 1 shower only, all no smoking.) B&B £35.00pps. ss £15.00. Open all year. *Self-caterin accommodation or B&B also offered in The Colonel's Lodge (£280-£380 per week self catering, £7C per night B&B). MasterCard, Visa, Switch. **Directions:** A2 from Belfast; bypass Holywood; 1.5 miles from bridges at Ulster Folk Museum, turn right up Ballymoney Road signed Craigantlet - 1.75 miles on left

Portaferry
👁 HOTEL

Portaferry Hotel
The Strand Portaferry Co Down BT22 1EF
Tel: 028 427 28231 Fax: 028 427 28999 Email: info@portaferryhotel.com

This 18th-century waterfront terrace presents a neat, traditional exterior overlooking the lough toward the attractive village of Strangford and the National Trust property, Castleward, home to an oper festival each June. The inn is now one of the most popular destinations in Northern Ireland - not leas for its reputation for good food, including lunchtime bar meals. Accommodation is comfortable and most of the individually decorated en-suite bedrooms have views of the water - those on the fron attract a small supplement. The hotel changed hands shortly before we went to press but the previou owners have stayed on during the changeover period, and reports continue to be favourable. **Rooms 14** B&B about £50pps, ss £10. Open all year except Christmas. Amex, Diners, MasterCard, Visa **Directions:** On Portaferry seafront.

COUNTY FERMANAGH

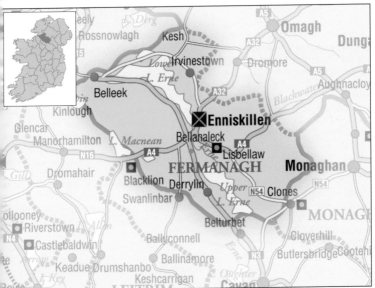

E ATMOSPHERIC PUB/RESTAURANT

Blakes of the Hollow

6 Church Street Enniskillen Co Fermanagh BT74 6JE
Tel: 028 6632 0918 Fax: 028 6632 0918

One of the great classic pubs of Ireland, Blakes has been in the same family since 1887 and, up to now, has always been one of the few places that could be relied upon to be unchanged. Not a food place, a pub. Maybe a sandwich, but mainly somewhere to have a pint and put the world to rights. Major changes have recently been taking place at this historic establishment. The original Victorian bar still remains untouched after 115 years, while several extra features have been developed on the rest of the site, including Café Merlot (serving informal, bistro-style food) on the lower ground floor, and The Atrium - a gothic style bar spread over two floors. **Number 6:** The combination of Gerry Russell's ambitious cooking, a relaxed fine dining atmosphere and caring service under the knowledgeable supervision of Johnny Donnelly add up to one of the most interesting dining experiences in the area. It's an attractive space right up at the top of the house with a comfortably furnished reception area where you can wind down and ponder the choices on a concise à la carte menu. The restaurant is elegantly appointed for fine dining. With all the little extras, that give guests that pampered feeling. Imaginatively updated classics may include charred dry aged fillet (beef), a deliciously modern take on the nation's favourite dish, and you may find a speciality of roast belly pork with langoustines, black pudding, creamed cabbage & puy lentils doing something similar for surf'n'turf. Fish cookery is very good and side dishes are taken unusually seriously. Wine is Johnny Donnelly's passion, and this is reflected in both an interesting list, and interested guidance and service. **Café Merlot** (casual dining), L daily 12-3.30; D daily 5-9.30; a la carte, also 2-course early D £11.95 (5.30-7.30). No 6: D Fri-Sat 6-10; A la carte; will open any day for parties 12+. Open all year. MasterCard, Visa, Laser, Switch. **Directions:** Town centre.

Enniskillen
🅔 RESTAURANT/COUNTRY HOUSE

Ferndale Country House & Restaurant

139 Irvinestown Road Enniskillen
Co Fermanagh BT74 4RN
Tel: 028 663 28374 Fax: 028 663 25706
Email: ferndalechandr@gmail.com Web: www.ferndalecountryhouseandrestaurant.com

Peter Mills' took over this restaurant (previously Le Chateau) in 2004, and the decor is quite restrained providing a good backdrop for striking modern paintings, and there are open fires in both the reception room and restaurant. Menus are simply written, confidently offering five or six choices on each course: starters are relatively straightforward - warm organic salmon with broad beans and rosemary, or risotto 'primavera' - but main courses promise real punch: cannon of lamb is a speciality, served with a sweetbread beignet and confit shoulder, for example. Everything on the plate lives up to the subtle promise of the menu, and desserts could include a speciality hot fondant which takes 15 minutes to prepare, meanwhile, the canny guest will have a little taste of Irish speciality cheeses. Service, mainly by friendly local staff, is willing and helpful. Peter Mills is a skilled and creative chef, and has gathered a fine team around him - Ferndale offers excellent food and a sense of occasion at realistic prices. **Seats 50** (private room, 30). No smoking restaurant. D Wed-Sun, D 7-9.30, L Sun only 12-2.30. Set 2/3 course Sun L £16.50/20.95; Set 2/3/6 course D £27/33/38. House wines from £10.95. SC discretionary. Vegetarian menu available. Closed Mon, Tue. ***Accommodation** is offered in six individually decorated rooms, and is in keeping with the country house feel: two of the bedrooms have four-posters and all are comfortably appointed. **Rooms 6** (all en-suite & no smoking). Children under 4s free in parents' room, cot available without charge, baby sitting arranged). B&B £27.50 pps, (£37.50 pps for deluxe room with 4 poster bed) ss £10. *Weekend / golfing breaks offered. A dinner bed & breakfast offers great value. MasterCard, Visa, Switch. **Directions:** Signed on main Enniskillen-Irvinestown road.

Lisbellaw
🏛️◉ COUNTRY HOUSE

Belle Isle Castle

Belle Isle Estate Lisbellaw Co Fermanagh BT94 5HG
Tel: 021 6638 7231 Fax: 028 6638 7261
Email: accommodation@belleisle-estate.com Web: www.belleislecastle.com

Belle Isle is owned by the Duke of Abercorn, and magically situated on one of eleven islands on Upper Lough Erne that are owned by the Estate; the original castle dates back to 1680 and has mid-19th century additions, including a courtyard and coach house which have been converted to make very appealing self-catering accommodation. The castle itself has a delightfully exclusive away-from-it-all country house atmosphere and is impressively furnished with antiques, striking paintings and dramatic colour schemes (the work of the internationally renowned interior designer, David Hicks); in addition to the eight romantic bedrooms, which all have their special character, guests have use of a magnificent drawing room and also the Grand Hall, complete with minstrels' gallery, where dinner is served. Under the eagle-eyed supervision of hosts Charles and Fiona Plunket, maintenance and housekeeping are immaculate throughout - and this romantic places could be the perfect choice for a small wedding: they are licensed to hold civil weddings. There are many wonderful things to do in this idyllically beautiful area - fishing is an obvious first choice but there are also golf courses nearby, field sports can be arranged and there are historic houses and gardens to visit. But, most tempting of all, perhaps, might be a course at the Belle Isle School of Cookery, which is very professionally operated and offers an extensive range of courses of varying lengths throughout the year. **Cookery School:** Tel 028 6638 7231; www.irishcookeryschool.com. Small weddings (30). Children welcome (under 3s free in parents' room, cot available without charge; playground). Pets allowed in some areas. Garden, walking, fishing, tennis **Rooms 8** (1 en-suite, 7 with private bathrooms, 1 shower only, all no smoking). B&B £70 pps, ss £15. No SC. Residents D daily, 8pm, £24; wines from £8. *Self-catering also offered in 10 apartments & 3 cottages, with 1-3 bedrooms; larger groups may use both castle & apartments. Open all year. MasterCard, Visa. **Directions:** From Belfast, take A4 to Lisbellaw - follow signs to Carrybridge.

COUNTY LONDONDERRY

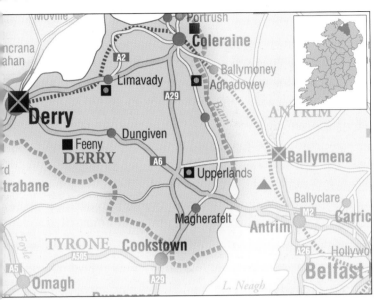

Aghadowey

🏆 € FARMHOUSE

Greenhill House

24 Greenhill Road Aghadowey Coleraine Co Londonderry BT51 4EU
Tel: 028 7086 8241 Fax: 028 7086 8365
Email: greenhill.house@btinternet.com Web: www.greenhill.house.btinternet.co.uk

Framed by trees with lovely country views, the Hegarty family's Georgian farmhouse is at the centre of a large working farm. In true Northern tradition, Elizabeth Hegarty is a great baker and greets guests in the drawing room with an afternoon tea which includes a vast array of home-made teabreads, cakes and biscuits - and home baking is also a highlight of wonderful breakfasts that are based on tasty local produce like bacon, sausages, mushrooms, free range eggs, smoked salmon, strawberries and preserves. There are two large family rooms and, although not luxurious, the thoughtfulness that has gone into furnishing bedrooms makes them exceptionally comfortable everything is in just the right place to be convenient - and Elizabeth is constantly maintaining and improving the decor and facilities. Bedrooms now have direct dial telephones, and little touches - like fresh flowers, a fruit basket, After Eights, tea & coffee making facilities, hair dryer, bathrobe, good quality clothes hangers and even a torch -
are way above the standard expected of farmhouse accommodation. There's also internet access, a safe, fax machine, iron and trouser press available for guests' use on request. Guests have been welcomed to Greenhill House since 1980 and, wonderfully comforting and hospitable as it is, Elizabeth constantly seeks ways of improvement, big and small: this lovely house and the way it is run demonstrate rural Irish hospitality at its best. [Greenhill House was our Farmhouse of the Year Award for 2003.] *There are plans to convert some of the outhouses, for self-catering accommodation. Children welcome, cot available. No pets. Garden. **Rooms 6** (all en-suite, 2 shower only, 2 bath only, all no smoking). B&B £27.50 pps, ss £7.50. Closed Nov-Feb. Amex, MasterCard, Visa, Switch.
Directions: On B66 Greenhill Road off A29, 7 miles south of Coleraine, 3 miles north of Garvagh.

Aghadowey

B HOTEL/RESTAURANT

The Brown Trout Golf & Country Inn

209 Agivey Road Aghadowey Co Londonderry BT51 4AD
Tel: 028 7086 8209 Fax: 028 7086 8878
Email: jane@browntroutinn.com Web: www.browntroutinn.com

Golf is one of the major attractions at this lively family-run country inn, both on-site and in the locality, but it's a pleasant and hospitable place for anyone to stay and golfers and non-golfers alike will soon find friends in the convivial bar, where food is served from noon to 10 pm every day - and outside in a pleasant barbecue too, in fine weather. Accommodation is not especially luxurious, but very comfortable, in good-sized en-suite rooms which are all on the ground floor, arranged around the main courtyard, and have plenty of space for golfing gear. New cottage suites overlooking the golf course (just 100 yards from the main building) are the first of this standard to be completed in Northern Ireland. As well as bar food, there's an evening restaurant up a steep staircase (with chair lift for the less able), overlooking the garden end of the golf course. A dedicated kitchen team aims to produce good home cooking with local fresh ingredients for daytime food (soups, freshly made sandwiches and open sandwiches, baked potatoes, pasta) and evening meals like hot garlic Aghadowey mushrooms or ribeye steak with a Bushmills whiskey sauce. Small conference/private parties (50/40). Tennis, horse-riding, golf (9), fishing. Gym. Children welcome (under 4s free in parents' room; cots available without charge, baby sitting arranged). Pets permitted. Garden, walking. Traditional music in bar (Sat). **Rooms 15** (all en-suite; 1 for disabled & most wheelchair friendly). B&B £45pps, ss £15. Stair lift. Toilets wheelchair accessible. No smoking restaurant. Bar meals, 12-9 daily (to 10 in summer). Restaurant D only, from 5 pm. A la carte; house wine £8.95; sc discretionary. Bar meals: 12-9.30. Open all year. Amex, Diners, MasterCard, Visa, Switch. **Directions:** Intersection of A54/B66,7 miles south of Coleraine.

Feeny

€ **◉** COUNTRY HOUSE

Drumcovitt House

704 Feeny Road Feeny Co Londonderry BT47 4SU
Tel: 028 7778 1224 Fax: 028 7778 1224
Email: drumcovitt.feeny@btinternet.com Web: www.drumcovitt.com

Drumcovitt is an intriguing house with an impressive Georgian front dating from 1796 - and, behind it a much older farmhouse, built about 1680. It is a listed building and many of the windows and wonderful interior features have been retained but, however interesting its history, today's creature comforts are very much in evidence - central heating extends throughout the house and an adjacent converted barn, and there are big log fires to relax beside while enjoying a fine collection of books, or making a jigsaw. Outdoor pursuits aplenty too: this unspoilt area is perfect for walking, bird-watching, visiting archaeological sites in the Sperrins and much else besides - horse riding, golf and angling are all available nearby and the Giants Causeway, beaches, Bushmills, Derry city and much of Donegal are within easy striking distance. The three guest rooms in the house are the two main front bedrooms (both with a double/ king-size bed and single) and a twin in the older part; in true country house fashion bathrooms are not en-suite, but two good modern showers (one over bath) are shared by the three rooms and there are plans to improve the bathrooms; all the rooms are spacious and comfortably furnished with tea/coffee-making, television and phone. The Sloan family are solicitous but relaxed hosts, who enjoy sharing their unique home and the area around it with guests; Chris Sloan and his partner Sarah Wallis took over day to day running of the house in 2005, but Chris's mother, Florence, is still involved and cooks for guests. This is a delightful place, but not one to rush through so allow more than one night if you can. Fax, safe and ironing facilities available for guests' use. Family celebrations/reunions for up to about 20 can be catered for in house and three barn cottages, which are available for self-catering. **Rooms 3** (with ISDN, phone, tv). Children welcome (cot available without charge; games room). B&B £29, no ss. Closed Christmas. Amex, Diners, MasterCard, Visa, Switch. **Directions:** Half a mile east of Feeny Village on B74 off A6.

Limavady
🅔 RESTAURANT

Lime Tree Restaurant

60 Catherine Street Limavady Co Londonderry BT49 9DB
Tel: 028 7776 4300
Email: info@limetreerest.com Web: www.limetreerest.com

Loyal customers come from far and wide for the pleasure of dining at Stanley and Maria Matthews' restaurant on the handsome, wide main street of this attractive town. And no wonder, as it is always a pleasant place to be, Stanley is a fine chef and Maria a welcoming and solicitous hostess. Ingredients are carefully sourced, many of them local; menus are generous, with a classical base that Stanley works on to give popular dishes a new twist. Specialities include their own home-made wheaten bread, which is the perfect accompaniment for a chowder of Atlantic fish & local potatoes, or Irish smoked salmon (supplied by Donegal prime Fish), with cucumber salad, while main course favourites include Sperrin lamb (with honey & rosemary) fillet or sirloin steak (from the award-winning local butcher, Hunters) and seafood thermidor (Stanley's selection of fresh fish with a mild cheese & brandy sauce. Menus are not over-extensive, but change frequently to suit different occasions - there's an attractive early dinner menu which is exceptional value, followed by a dressier set dinner for the main evening menu, which also has an accompanying (and more adventurous) à la carte. Stanley's cooking is refreshingly down-to-earth - new dishes are often introduced, but if it's on the menu it's because it works: there are no gimmicks. Good cooking and good value go hand in hand with warm hospitality here and it is always a pleasure to visit The Lime Tree - indeed, many discerning guests enjoy it so much that they plan journeys around a meal here. Children welcome. A concise, interesting wine list also offers predictably good value. **Seats 30.** Reservations advised. Children welcome. Toilets wheelchair accessible. D Tue-Sat, 6-9 (Fri/Sat 9.30). Early D £10.50 (6-7pm only, excl Sat). Set D £17.50/19.95 2/3 course; also à la carte; house wine £10.95; sc discretionary. Closed Sun & Mon, 25-26 Dec. Amex, MasterCard, Visa, Switch. **Directions:** On the outskirts of town, main Derry-Limavady road.

Limavady
🏛️👁️ HOTEL

Radisson SAS Roe Park Resort

Roe Park Limavady Co Londonderry BT49 9LB
Tel: 028 7772 2222 Fax: 028 7772 2313
Email: reservations@radissonroepark.com Web: www.radissonroepark.com

Built on rising ground in lovely rolling countryside, this imposing hotel dates back to the eighteenth century when a Captain Richard Babington built the original house from which today's extensive hotel has grown. There is a pleasant air of relaxed luxury - the tone is set in an impressive foyer, with columns and a curved gallery overlooking a seating area smartly set up with comfortable sofas and armchairs in strong contemporary colours. conferences play a major part in present-day business - and the surrounding greensward provides relaxation for delegates, along with many others who come here specifically to enjoy the excellent leisure facilities. Spacious bedrooms, in more restful shades, are designed in the modern classic mode with double and single beds and all the features expected of this type of hotel (all have desk areas, some with computers) and well-finished bathrooms - and all look out over the golf course or a courtyard garden. Dining options allow for different moods: formal dining in Greens Restaurant (dinner daily and lunch on Sunday) or a more relaxed style in The Coach House Brasserie. Separate vegetarian menu offered. Conferences (450). Leisure centre (indoor swimming pool, spa). Golf (18 hole), fishing. Children welcome (under 5 free in parents' room; cot available, baby sitting arranged, playroom). No pets. Garden, walking, cycling. Pool table. **Rooms 118** (5 suites, 3 junior suites, 110 executive, 1 disabled). Lift. 24 hr room service. B&B about £100 pps. *Wide range of special breaks offered. Open all year. Amex, Diners, MasterCard, Visa, Laser, Switch. **Directions:** On the A2 L'Derry-Limavady road, 1 miles from Limavady (Derry City 16 miles).

Limavady

🏛️⚫ COUNTRY HOUSE

Streeve Hill

25 Dowland Road Limavady Co Londonderry BT49 6HP
Tel: 028 7776 6563 Fax: 028 7776 8285
Email: pandjwelsh@yahoo.co.uk

Peter and June Welsh have welcomed guests to their lovely 18th century home since they moved here in 1996. It is a very charming house, with a Palladian facade of rose brick and fine views over parkland towards the Sperrin Mountains but there is also beauty closer to home, in and around the house itself and in the nearby gardens of their former home, Drenagh. The stylish country house accommodation at Streeve Hill is extremely comfortable and the food and hospitality exceptional. Although the maximum number they can accommodate is six, they are happy for guests to bring friends to dine (but dinner is only provided by arrangement and 24 hours notice is required). Breakfast is another high point and, in the event of fine summer weather, it can be even more enjoyable if served on the terrace outside the drawing room. Horse-riding, fishing, golf, garden visits nearby. Children welcome (under 4s free in parents' room; cots available without charge). No Pets. garden, walking. **Rooms 3** (all en-suite & no-smoking,1 shower only). B&B £45pps, ss £10; sc discretionary. Closed Christmas/New Year. Amex, MasterCard, Visa. **Directions:** B021 for Castlerock, follow Estate wall on right. 200 yards past lodge turn right at end of wall.

Londonderry

🏛️ HOTEL/RESTAURANT

Beech Hill Country House Hotel

32 Ardmore Road Londonderry Co Londonderry BT47 3QP
Tel: 028 7134 9279 Fax: 028 7134 5366
Email: info@beech-hill.com Web: www.beech-hill.com

Just south of Londonderry, surrounded by peaceful woodland, waterfalls and gardens, this house dates from 1729 and retains many of its original details; it will be of special interest to American guests as the US Marines had their headquarters here in World War II and there is an informative small museum of the US Marine Friendship Association in the hotel. Proprietor Patsy O'Kane is an hospitable and caring hostess and her ever-growing collection of antiques adds character to guest accommodation and public areas alike, including a traditional bar, a fine dining restaurant, which is in the former snooker room, now extended into a conservatory overlooking the gardens. Aside from golf, there is plenty to do, with a fitness suite, extensive grounds and tennis on site, fishing and equestrian nearby and, of course, Derry city to explore. Conference/banqueting (100/90); secretarial services. Fitness centre, beauty salon. Tennis. Golf, fishing, equestrian nearby. Children welcome (under 3s free in parents' room cot available without charge, babysitting arranged). Pets allowed by arrangement; garden, walking. **Rooms 27** (2 suites, 3 junior suites, 10 executive rooms,). B&B about £60pps, ss about £10. SC discretionary. Lift. *Special interest breaks are good value. Open all year except Christmas. **The Ardmore Restaurant:** The restaurant has always been an attractive feature of Beech Hill: it is elegantly appointed in traditional style and well-positioned overlooking gardens (which is particularly pleasant at breakfast time) - and, although there are sometimes changes in the kitchen, there is a tradition of using local ingredients to advantage in updated classical French cuisine, and the combination of high standards of cooking and caring service has earned a loyal local following. Various combinations of menus are offered, sometimes including luxurious ingredients as in a starter of salad of warm lobster tossed in truffle butter, with oven dried tomatoes and a main course of spring lamb with celeriac dauphinoise, rosemary & black olive jus indicating the style - and there's a separate vegetarian listing of five or six interesting dishes which can be served as a starter or main course. The wine list offers good value - and a number of famous New World wines with Northern Ireland connections. Reservations required. No smoking restaurant. **Seats 100.** Reservations accepted. No smoking restaurant. Children welcome. Toilets wheelchair accessible. L daily, 12-2; D daily 6.30-9. Set L £17.95, Set Sun L £17.95. Set 2/3 course D, £21.95/£27.95. A la carte and vegetarian menu also available. House wines (6), £12.95. SC discretionary. Amex, MasterCard, Visa, Switch. **Directions:** Main Londonderry road A6.

Londonderry
🅔 RESTAURANT

Browns Restaurant, Bar & Brasserie

1-2 Bonds Hill Londonderry Co Londonderry BT47 6DW
Tel: 028 7134 5180 Fax: 028 7134 5180
Email: eat@brownsrestaurant.com Web: www.brownsrestaurant.com

The city's leading contemporary restaurant has a devoted local following. Always immaculate, inside and out, it's a relaxed space with subtle blends of natural colours, textures and finishes - proprietor-chef Ivan Taylor's cool cooking keeps them coming back for more; his approach to food never stands still, and the cooking is consistently creative. Wide-ranging menus offer a range of fresh-flavoured dishes, including delicious starters like spiced crumbled beef served in a light vegetable broth with pecorino, and a perfectly judged main dish of char-grilled rare-breed sirloin steak on a fine balsamic onion gravy with a horesradish Yorkshire pudding & pea puree and braised root vegetables - one of several examples of classics that have been modernised without forgetting the basics. Desserts also ring some changes with the classics - or espresso, vin santo & home-made biscotti might make a pleasing alternative. All round, there's imagination, a certain amount of style, dedication and consistency - not bad after more than 20 years in business. *At the time of going to press, a new Browns2Go service is planned, for boardroom lunches and corporate entertaining. L Tue-Fri, 12-2.15; D Tue-Sat, 5.30-Late. Early Set D Tue-Fri, £10.95 (5.30-7.15). House wine £11.95. Closed Sun & Mon, 1st 2 weeks Aug. Amex, MasterCard, Visa, Laser, Switch. **Directions:** In a cul-de-sac pposite the old Waterside railway station: Belfast-Derry road (A6), turn left at Melrose Terrace & branch right at sign. (Or park at station and walk across).

Upperlands
🏛 COUNTRY HOUSE

Ardtara Country House

8 Gorteade Road Upperlands Maghera
Co Londonderry BT46 5SA
Tel: 028 7964 4490 Fax: 028 7964 5080
Email: valerie_ferson@ardtara.com Web: www.ardtara.com

Former home to the Clark linen milling family, Ardtara is now an attractive, elegantly decorated Victorian country house with a genuinely hospitable atmosphere. Well-proportioned rooms have antique furnishings and fresh flowers, and all the large, luxuriously furnished bedrooms enjoy views of the garden and surrounding countryside and have king size beds, original fireplaces and LCD TV and DVDs, while bathrooms combine practicality with period details, some including free-standing baths and fireplaces. Breakfast should be a high point, so allow time to enjoy it. Ardtara would make an excellent base for exploring this beautiful and unspoilt area. Tennis, golf practice tee. Pets allowed by arrangement. Garden, woodland walk. Conferences/Banqueting (50). **Rooms 8** (3 suites) B&B £75pps, ss £10. *Short breaks offered. **Restaurant:** The dining room was previously a snooker room and still has the full Victorian skylight and original hunting frieze, making an unusual setting for fine dining. A new head chef, Olivier Boudon, joined the team here in 2005, bringing experience from countries as diverse as China and Poland, so you may expect some unusual influences in the cooking and presentation (including a number of 'gala servings' such as serving caviar on ice), although the main influence is classical French. Olivier presents daily-changed menus offering three or four choices on each course - smoked salmon & fish terrine with salmon roe & fresh cream; pan-fried fillet of local beef (from McKees' butchers) with gratin dauphinoise, ratatouille and morel & armagnac sauce; and passion fruit parfait with blackcurrant sauce are typical - and you may finish with Irish cheeses & the famous locally-made Ditty's biscuits. However, there is also an extensive and much more ambitious à la carte menue offered, which is quite unlike anything you are likely to find in the neighbourhood. **Seats 65** (private room,30). Reservations required. No smoking restaurant. Children welcome. Toilets wheelchair accessible. L Daily 12-2.30, Sun L 12-4. Set L £24, Set Sun L £20. D daily 6.30-9.30 (to 9 Sun). Set 2/3 course D £24/30. House wines from £11.65. Amex, MasterCard, Visa, Switch. **Directions:** M2 from from Belfast to A6. A29 to Maghera. B75 to Kilrea.

COUNTY TYRONE

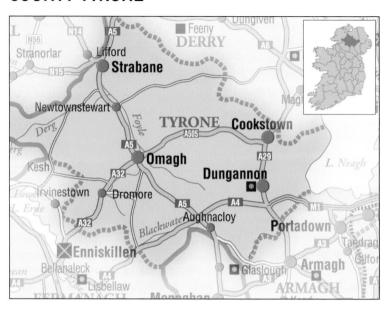

Dungannon
🏛️ 🍴 COUNTRY HOUSE

Grange Lodge

7 Grange Road Dungannon Co Tyrone BT71 7EJ
Tel: 028 8778 4212 Fax: 028 8778 4313
Email: stay@grangelodgecountryhouse.com Web: www.grangelodgecountryhouse.com

Norah and Ralph Brown's renowned Georgian retreat offers comfort, true family hospitality and extremely good food. The house is on an elevated site just outside Dungannon, with about 20 acres of grounds; mature woodland and gardens (producing food for the table and flowers for the house) with views over lush countryside. Improvements over the years have been made with great sensitivity and the feeling is of gentle organic growth, culminating in the present warm and welcoming atmosphere. Grange Lodge is furnished unselfconsciously, with antiques and family pieces throughout. Bedrooms (and bathrooms) are exceptionally comfortable and thoughtful in detail. Norah's home cooking is superb and they will cater for groups of 10-30. Grange Lodge is fully licensed and dinner menus change daily (in consultation with guests). Resident dinner (from £26) must be pre-booked, especially if you want to dine on the day of arrival. Breakfasts are also outstanding, so allow time to indulge: a sumptuous buffet beautifully set out on a polished dining table might typically include a large selection of juices, fruit and cereals and porridge is a speciality, served with a tot of Bushmills whiskey, brown sugar and cream - and that's before you've even reached the cooked breakfast menu, served with lovely fresh breads and toast and home-made preserves. * "Cook with Norah" cookery classes have been running since 2002, and are now very successful; details on application. Conferences/banqueting (20/30). Garden, walking, snooker. Not suitable for children under 12. Pets allowed in some areas. **Rooms 5** (3 shower only, all no smoking).Room service (limited hours). Turndown service. B&B £39 pps, ss £16. D Mon-Sat, 7.30-8.30pm, by arrangement; Set D £26. Non-residents welcome by reservation. Closed 20 Dec-1 Feb. MasterCard, Visa, Switch. **Directions:** 1 mile from M1 junction 15. On A29 to Armagh, follow "Grange Lodge" signs.

Starred Restaurants & Pubs

★★ 2 STAR

Dublin, Restaurant Patrick Guilbaud
Dublin, Thornton's

★ 1 STAR

Dublin, Chapter One
Dublin, L'Ecrivain
Dublin, One Pico Restaurant
Co Cavan, MacNean Bistro, Blacklion
Co Clare, Dromoland Castle
Co Cork, Ballymaloe House, Shanagarry
Co Kerry, Park Hotel, Kenmare
Co Kerry, Sheen Falls Lodge, Kenmare
Co Kildare, Kildare Hotel, Straffan
Co Sligo, Cromleach Lodge, Castlebaldwin
Co Waterford, The Tannery, Dungarvan

☆ DEMI STAR

Dublin, Bang Café
Dublin, Clarence Hotel, The Tea Room
Dublin, Mermaid Café
Dublin, Merrion Hotel, Cellar Restaurant
Dublin, Mint
Dublin, Pearl Brasserie
Dublin, Roly's Bistro
Co Dublin, King Sitric, Howth
Co Dublin, Bon Appetit, Malahide
Co Dublin, Portmarnock Hotel, Osborne
  Restaurant
Co Cavan, Olde Post Inn, Cloverhill
Co Clare, Cherry Tree, Killaloe
Co Clare, Sheedy's, Lisdoonvarna
Cork city, Café Paradiso
Cork city, Fleming's
Cork city, Isaacs
Cork city, Jacob's on the Mall
Cork city, Jacques
Cork city, Lovett's
Co Cork, Otto's, Butlerstown
Co Cork, Blairs Cove House, Durrus
Co Cork, Good Things, Durrus
Co Cork, Casino House, Kilbrittain
Co Cork, Longueville House, Mallow
Co Cork, Toddies, Kinsale
Co Galway, St Clerans, Craughwell
Co Kerry, Chart House, Dingle
Co Kerry, Mulcahy's, Kenmare
Co Kerry, Packie's, Kenmare
Co Kerry, Killarney Park Hotel, Killarney
Co Kerry, Restaurant David Norris, Tralee

Co Limerick, Mustard Seed at Echo Lodge,
  Ballingarry
Co Mayo, Ashford Castle, Cong
Co Monaghan, Nuremore Hotel,
  Carrickmacross
Co Tipperary, Gannons Above the Bell, Cahir
Co Tipperary, Cliffords, Clonmel
Co Westmeath, Left Bank Bistro, Athlone
Co Westmeath, Wineport Lodge, Glasson
Co Wexford, Dunbrody House, Arthurstown
Co Wexford, Marlfield House, Gorey
Co Wexford, La Riva, Wexford

🍺 PUB STARS (for good food & atmosphere)

Dublin, Clarendon Café Bar
Dublin, The Porterhouse
Co Dublin, Purty Kitchen, Dun Laoghaire
Co Carlow, Lennons Café Bar, Carlow
Co Cork, The Bosun, Monkstown
Co Cork, Bushe's, Baltimore
Co Cork, Mary Ann's, Castletownshend
Co Cork, Hayes Bar, Glandore
Co Clare, Vaughans Anchor Inn, Liscannor
Co Galway, Moran's Oyster Cottage, Kilcolgan
Co Kildare, The Ballymore Inn, Ballymore
  Eustace
Co Kilkenny, Marble City Bar, Kilkenny
Co Leitrim, The Oarsman, Carrick-on-Shannon
Co Offaly, The Thatch, Crinkle
Co Offaly, The Wolftrap, Tullamore
Co Roscommon, Keenans, Tarmonbarry
Co Waterford, Buggy's Glencairn Inn, nr
  Lismore
Co Wicklow, Roundwood Inn, Roundwood

NORTHERN IRELAND:

★★ 2 STAR

Belfast, Restaurant Michael Deane

☆ DEMI STAR:

Belfast, James Street South

🍺 PUB STARS (for good food & atmosphere)

Belfast, Crown Liquor Salon
Co Down, The Plough, Hillsborough

Establishment Index

INDEX

INDEX

INDEX

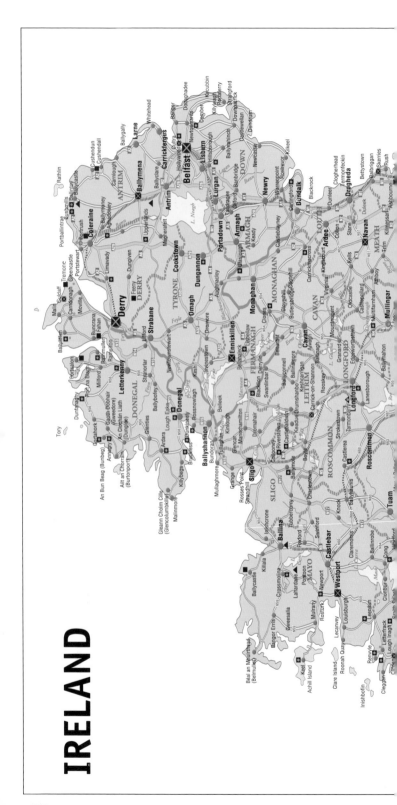

IRELAND

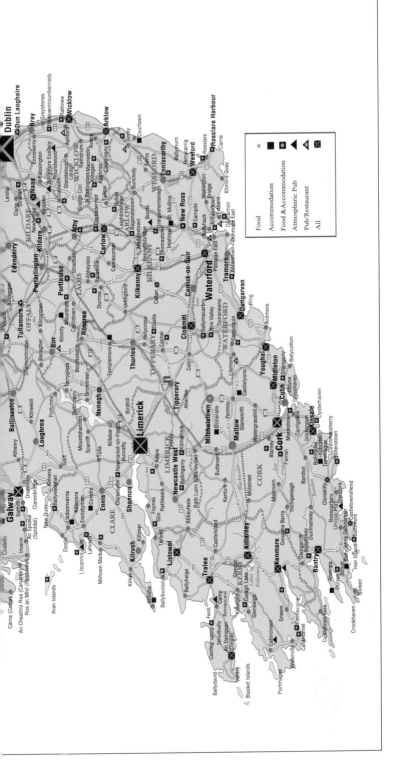

Georgina Campbell's Ireland...

...the Guide

For great food and gorgeous places to stay throughout Ireland - simply indispensable!

"Ireland's premier guide" The London Guardian

"encyclopaedic" Tom Doorley, The Irish Times

"This is the business" Cara Magazine

"By far the most reliable" Food & Wine Magazine

...the Dublin Guide

The essential guide to the best places to eat, drink and stay in Dublin city and county.

...for Gourmet Golfers
co-authored by Dermot Gilleece

Discover Ireland's finest golf courses and the very best places to eat and stay while playing them. The essential guide to planning your golfing trip in Ireland

Coming Soon:

All publications available from good bookshops, or on-line from

www.ireland-guide.com

where you will also find many more great places to eat, drink and stay!